HAS GOD
SPOKEN?

Other Books by Hank Hanegraaff

HAS GOD SPOKEN?

Memorable Proofs of the Bible's Divine Inspiration

HANK HANEGRAAFF

THOMAS NELSON
Since 1798

NASHVILLE   DALLAS   MEXICO CITY   RIO DE JANEIRO

Published in Nashville, Tennessee, by Thomas Nelson. Thomas Nelson is a registered trademark of Thomas Nelson, Inc.

Thomas Nelson, Inc. titles may be purchased in bulk for educational, business, fund-raising, or sales promotional use. For information, please e-mail SpecialMarkets@ThomasNelson.com.

Unless otherwise noted, Scripture quotations are taken from the Holy Bible, New International Version®, NIV®. © 1973, 1978, 1984, 2011 by Biblica Inc.™ Used by permission of Zondervan. All rights reserved worldwide. www.zondervan.com. Italics added to NIV quotations indicate the author's emphasis.

Scripture quotations marked NASB are taken from the New American Standard Bible®. © The Lockman Foundation 1960, 1962, 1963, 1968, 1971, 1972 1973, 1975, 1977. Used by permission.

Scripture quotations marked NKJV are taken from the New King James Version®. © 1982 by Thomas Nelson, Inc. Used by permission. All rights reserved.

Scripture quotations marked KJV are taken from the Holy Bible, King James Version.

Scripture quotations marked ESV are taken from the English Standard Version. © 2001 by Crossway Bibles, a division of Good News Publishers.

Unless otherwise noted, quotations from the Apocrypha are taken from the New Revised Standard Version Bible, © 1989, by the Division of Christian Education of the National Council of the Churches of Christ in the United States of America.

ISBN 978-0-8499-4891-6 (IE)

Library of Congress Cataloging-in-Publication Data

Hanegraaff, Hank.
  Has God spoken? : memorable proofs of the Bible's divine inspiration / Hank Hanegraaff.
    p. cm.
  Includes bibliographical references (pp. 347–361) and indexes.
  ISBN 978-0-8499-1970-1 (hardcover)
  1. Bible--Inspiration. I. Title.
  BS480.H26 2011
  220.1'3--dc23

2011021034

Printed in the United States of America

11 12 13 14 15 QG 6 5 4 3 2 1

To Hank—
my son in flesh and faith,
a talented golfer and apologist in the making.

Contents

Contents

Acknowledgments

First, I am deeply grateful to God for giving me health and strength to complete a life goal—that of providing seekers and saints with a memorable means by which to internalize answers to the three great apologetic issues of this or any other generation. My prayer is that our heavenly Father will use this book, along with my books on *origins* and *resurrection*, for his glory and for the extension of his kingdom—not by might, nor by power, but by his Spirit.

Furthermore, kudos to Kathy and the kids—without a solid and secure foundation at home, I'd be impotent in mission and ministry. I am also deeply grateful for the staff and support of the Christian Research Institute and the *Bible Answer Man* broadcast, particularly for their prayer and practical input. I am particularly beholden to my friend and coworker Stephen Ross, who has faithfully worked alongside me now for two decades, also to Warren Nozaki, researcher *par excellence*.

Finally, I would like to express my appreciation to Matt Baugher and the Thomas Nelson team. From editing to encouragement you have provided joy for the journey.

Introduction

The Bible is a rock of diamonds, a chain of pearls, the sword
of the Spirit; a chain by which the Christian sails to eternity;
the map by which he daily walks; the sundial by which he
sets his life; the balance in which he weighs his actions.

—THOMAS WATSON

Has God spoken? If there is a more significant question, I am wholly unaware
of what it might be. Muslims answer by pointing to the Qur'an as God's *only*
credible uncorrupted revelation. From the Muslim perspective, God spoke
through the archangel Gabriel, who dictated the Qur'an to Muhammad
over a period of twenty-three years.[1] Mormons likewise are certain that God
has spoken through a revelation called the Book of Mormon, which their
prophet Joseph Smith called "the most correct of any book on earth and the
keystone of our religion."[2] Joseph Fielding Smith, the sixth president of the
Mormon Church, went so far as to say that not only were the words correct
but "every letter was given to [Smith] by the gift and power of God."[3]

But has God *really* spoken through the Qur'an or the Book of Mormon?
The answer is emphatically—*no!* The Qur'an is a hopelessly flawed document full of faulty ethics and factual errors. In Sura 4:3, for example,
Muhammad allegedly received a revelation from God allowing men to
"marry women of your choice, two, three, or four." And in Sura 33:50 he
received a divine sanction to marry "any believing woman who dedicates

her soul to the Prophet if the Prophet wishes to wed her." While other men were permitted to marry up to *only* four wives, Allah provided Muhammad with a divine exception for his marriage to at least twelve women—including Aishah, whom he married at the tender age of eleven.[4] Also troubling is the fact that the Qur'an allows men to "beat" their wives in order that the women might "return to obedience" (Sura 4:34).

Factual errors are similarly problematic. A classic case in point involves the Qur'anic denial of Christ's crucifixion. The denial is explicit and emphatic: "They killed him not, nor crucified him, but so it was made to appear to them" (4:157). As will be established, truth points in the opposite direction. The fatal suffering of Jesus Christ as recounted in the New Testament is one of the most well-established realities of ancient history. In today's modern age of scientific enlightenment, there is virtual consensus among credible scholars, both conservative and liberal, that Jesus did in fact die on a Roman cross.[5]

The Book of Mormon fares no better. While Mormons claim that their prophet, Joseph Smith, found golden plates containing the "fullness of the everlasting gospel" written in "reformed Egyptian hieroglyphics," the facts say otherwise. Not only is there no archaeological evidence for a language such as "reformed Egyptian hieroglyphics"; there is no archaeological support for lands such as the "land of Moron" (Ether 7). Nor is there any archaeological evidence to buttress the notion that the Jaredites, Nephites, and Lamanites migrated from Israel to the Americas. On the contrary, both archaeology and anthropology demonstrate conclusively that the people, places, and particulars chronicled in the Book of Mormon are little more than the products of a fertile and faulty imagination.[6]

According to critics, the notion that God has spoken—that the Bible is a credible repository of what he has said—likewise does not stand up to the light of cold, hard facts. President Barack Obama is the quintessential example. In his "Call to Renewal" keynote address to religious leaders, he asked, "Which passages of Scripture should guide our public policy? Should we go with Leviticus, which suggests slavery is okay and that eating shellfish is an abomination? Or we could go with Deuteronomy, which suggests stoning your child if he strays from the faith."[7] While I applaud the president's injection of religious dialogue into public policy debates, the manner in which he mischaracterizes and marginalizes Scripture is appalling. Nowhere does the Bible suggest that slavery is okay. Nor does the Bible suggest stoning your child should he stray from the faith. While I will address such mischaracterizations within this volume, it is worth noting now that Obama's words are eerily similar to those voiced by President Bartlet in the once wildly popular television series *The West Wing*.[8] Not only so, but his sentiments are comparable to those of a new breed of antitheists who make similar charges, albeit in far more strident and expanded fashion.

Christopher Hitchens, contributing editor to *Vanity Fair*, is noteworthy. In *God Is Not Great: How Religion Poisons Everything*, Hitchens suggests that "the Bible contains a warrant for trafficking in humans, for ethnic cleansing, for slavery, for bride-price and for indiscriminate massacre."[9] Like Hitchens, Oxford professor Richard Dawkins does not consider the Bible a trustworthy standard for life and living. In his *New York Times* bestselling book *The God Delusion*, he describes the God of the Bible as "the most unpleasant character in all of fiction: jealous and proud of it; a petty, unjust, unforgiving control-freak; a vindictive, bloodthirsty ethnic cleanser; a misogynistic, homophobic, racist, infanticidal, genocidal, filicidal, pestilential, megalomaniacal, sadomasochistic, capriciously malevolent bully."[10] He vacuously asserts that "a designer God cannot be used to explain organized complexity because any God capable of designing anything would have to be complex enough to demand the same kind of explanation in his own right. God presents an infinite regress from which he cannot help us to escape."[11] Thus, says Dawkins, "The whole argument turns on the familiar question, 'Who made God?'"[12]

Bart Ehrman, chair of the Religious Studies Department at the University of North Carolina at Chapel Hill, makes a plethora of accusations against the Bible and biblical authors as well. Of one thing he is certain: God has *not* spoken! While still a student at Princeton Theological Seminary, he submitted a paper that attempted to resolve a supposed difficulty in Mark 2. The gospel writer records Jesus saying that David ate the shewbread "in the days of *Abiathar* the high priest" (Mark 2:26), although the

Old Testament account indicates David ate the shewbread when *Abiathar's father, Ahimelech*, served as high priest (1 Samuel 21:1–16). While reading Ehrman's paper, his professor scribbled a simple comment in the margin: *"Maybe Mark just made a mistake."* After contemplation, Ehrman came to the realization that his solution was indeed "a stretch" and concluded "maybe Mark *did* make a mistake."[13] This epiphany opened the floodgates. Says Ehrman, "Maybe, when Jesus says later in Mark 4 that the mustard seed is the 'smallest of all seeds on the earth,' maybe I don't need to come up with a fancy explanation for how the mustard seed is the smallest of all seeds when I know full well it isn't. And maybe these 'mistakes' apply to bigger issues"[14]—issues such as the false prophecies of an alleged Messiah.[15]

Ehrman deems the very manuscripts preserving the New Testament to be flawed, reasoning that we do not have the original autographs but possess only copies of copies centuries removed from the originals, which contain errors in "thousands of places," such that "there are more differences among our manuscripts than there are words in the New Testament."[16] Thus, "just as human scribes had copied, and changed, the texts of Scripture, so too had human authors originally *written* the texts of Scripture. *This was a human book from beginning to the end.*"[17] The copyists, he contends, were animated by virulent anti-Semitic hatred and were copying *forged* manuscripts—the contention of his latest offering: *Forged: Writing in the Name of God—Why the Bible's Authors Are Not Who We Think They Are*. In short, Ehrman seeks to convince his ever-growing cadre of devotees that the Bible is a dishonest book littered with deceptions, errors, and outright lies. "Eventually I came to realize that the Bible not only contains untruths or accidental mistakes. It also contains what almost anyone today would call lies," intones the professor.[18] "The use of deception to promote the truth may well be considered one of the most unsettling ironies of the early Christian tradition."[19]

The battle against the Bible is not relegated to politicians, publishers, or professors. Punmeister Bill Maher gets in on the act by effectively characterizing people who hold that God has spoken and that the Bible contains an accurate record of what he has said as obscurantists who for all intents and purposes have lost their brains somewhere in the narthex of a church. "I believed all this stuff when I was young," says Maher. "I believed there was a virgin birth, I believed a man lived inside of a whale, and I believed that the Earth was five thousand years old. But then something very important happened to me—I graduated sixth grade."[20] A major reason that biblical Christianity is so dangerous, according to Maher, is that "it stops people from thinking."[21] Displaying a breathtaking form of idiosyncratic fundamentalism from the left, Maher asserts that the Bible "was not meant to be history. It was not meant to be literal. They were parables. People read it back then and read into it something that was not literal. We're the dummies who read it literally."[22]

Maher, of course, is dead wrong. Even a cursory reading of the Bible is sufficient to recognize that the Bible is a treasury replete with a wide variety of literary styles, ranging from poetry and psalms to historical narratives, didactic epistles, and apocalyptic revelations. To dogmatically assert that the Bible was written in parables and that those who read it literally must be "idiots" is a serious misunderstanding of the literal principle of biblical interpretation. The Bible does contain parables, but it is not entirely parabolic. The virgin birth account, referred to by Maher, is clearly presented by Scripture as a historical narrative. Had Maher read the Bible with an open mind—paying attention to such basics as genre, grammar, syntax, semantics, and context—he would have readily recognized that his faith was placed in a dogmatic assertion rather than a defensible argument. Moreover, as apologetics is a discipline through which the validity of the virgin birth can be historically established, so literary analysis is the method by which the virgin birth account is discerned to be an historical narrative.

Media magnets such as Barack, Bart, and Bill are merely the tip of the proverbial iceberg. Through media, manuscripts, and movies—and now most notably through the Internet—a procession of political pundits, professors, and public personalities is raising doubts in the minds of multiplied millions regarding the notion that God has spoken and the Bible is a reliable repository of what he has said.

This book counters such contentions and crafts a cumulative case for the absolute authority of the Bible. It answers the question, *Has God spoken?* in the affirmative and demonstrates beyond a reasonable doubt that the Bible is divine rather than merely human in origin. Without such assurance, Christianity would not have any more authority for faith and practice than does Islam, Mormonism, or a host of other misguided movements. In countering objections to the Bible's trustworthiness, I focus primarily on personalities such as Barack, Bart, and Bill in that they represent a cadre of likeminded critics who in most cases do not have as great a market penetration.

On a personal note, *Has God Spoken?* is the culmination of my life goal to provide seekers, skeptics, and saints alike with a memorable means by which to internalize answers to the three great apologetic issues of this or any other generation. These answers are ultimately foundational to life and living and to living after life.

The first in the trilogy is a book dealing with the issue of origins. My contention here is that how you view your origins will ultimately determine how you live your life. If you believe you are a function of random mutations, you will live your life by a different standard than if you know you are created in the image of God and thus accountable to him. In this book, *The Face That Demonstrates the Farce of Evolution,*[23] I develop the acronym F-A-C-E to make it easy for anyone to remember how to substantiate the farce of evolution.

The second is *Resurrection.*[24] Here I use the memorable acronym F-E-A-T (as in the greatest *feat* in the annals of recorded history) to demonstrate that Christ had the power to lay down his life and to take it up again, thus demonstrating that he is God in human flesh. Without this assurance—as Paul, Apostle to the Gentiles, explains to the Corinthians—"our preaching is useless and so is your faith" (1 Corinthians 15:14).

And now the capstone in the trilogy: *Has God Spoken?* Here I use the acronym M-A-P-S to place in your mind the four-part line of reasoning by which you can demonstrate that the Bible is divine as opposed to merely human in origin:

*M*anuscript Copies
*A*rchaeologist's Spade
*P*rophetic Stars
*S*criptural Lights

Since most Bibles contain maps revealing that its words are rooted in history and evidence, this should prove a meaningful and memorable association. But that's not all. Each of the four parts is further made memorable by means of easy-to-remember subacronyms.

Part 1 employs the subacronym C-O-P-I-E-S, which by God's grace turns out to be a perfect way of remembering the sequential line of reasoning that demonstrates that extant manuscript *copies* faithfully preserve the words of the original text. When you finish the chapters in part 1, you will be equipped to communicate the certainty that no essential of the biblical message has been compromised, and nonessential copyist errors have been resolved through manuscript comparisons, consideration of context, and plain old common sense.

Part 2 utilizes the subacronym S-P-A-D-E. The archaeologist's spade documents time and time again, that in direct contrast to pagan mythology from Mormonism to Mithras, the people, places, and particulars found in sacred Scripture have their roots in history and evidence. As such, what was concealed in the soil corresponds to what is revealed in the Scriptures. From steles and stones to the Epic of Gilgamesh, archaeological artifacts cry forth from antiquity: God has spoken—"Scripture cannot be broken" (John 10:35 NASB).

Part 3 employs the subacronym S-T-A-R-S. Prophetic *stars* in the constellation of biblical prophecy—like manuscript C-O-P-I-E-S and the archaeologist's S-P-A-D-E—are powerful proofs that God has spoken, that the Bible is divine rather than merely human in origin. In the words of the Almighty, "I told you these things long ago; before they happened I announced them to you so that you could not say, 'My idols did them; my wooden image and metal god ordained them'" (Isaiah 48:5). Or as Jesus put it, "I have told you now before it happens, so that when it does happen you will believe" (John 14:29). Counterfeit prophecy stars have one thing in common: they are consistently wrong. In illumined contrast, genuine prophecy stars are infallibly correct. And unlike the pretenders, their prophetic prowess cannot be pawned off to good luck, good guessing, or deliberate deceit.

Finally, in part 4, I use the subacronym L-I-G-H-T-S. At this point you will be sufficiently equipped to answer the question, *Has God spoken?* in

M·A·P·S

M ANUSCRIPT C-O-P-I-E-S

A RCHAEOLOGIST'S S-P-A-D-E

P ROPHETIC S-T-A-R-S

S CRIPTURAL L-I-G-H-T-S

Manuscript Copies	Archaeologist's Spade	Prophetic Stars	Scriptural Lights
Copyist Practices	Steles and Stones	Succession of Nations	Literal Principle
Oral Culture	Pools and Fools	Typological Prophecy	Illumination Principle
Papyrus and Parchment	Assyrian Archaeology	Abomination of Desolation	Grammatical Principle
Internal Evidence	Dead Sea Scrolls	Resurrection Prophecies	Historical Principle
External Evidence	Epic of Gilgamesh	Superstar ABCs	Typology Principle
Science of Textual Criticism			Synergy Principle

MANUSCRIPT C-O-P-I-E-S **A**RCHAEOLOGIST'S S-P-A-D-E **P**ROPHETIC S-T-A-R-S **S**CRIPTURAL L-I-G-H-T-S

Copyist Practices	Steles and Stones	Succession of Nations	Literal Principle
Oral Culture	Pools and Fools	Typological Prophecy	Illumination Principle
Papyrus and Parchment	Assyrian Archaeology	Abomination of Desolation	Grammatical Principle
Internal Evidence	Dead Sea Scrolls	Resurrection Prophecies	Historical Principle
External Evidence	Epic of Gilgamesh	Superstar ABCs	Typology Principle
Science of Textual Criticism			Synergy Principle

the affirmative. As such, you will know that you know the Bible is divine rather than merely human in origin. There is an attendant question, however. *If God has spoken, what has God said?* Answering this question is crucial in that a great many people worldwide discount the Bible as the infallible rule for faith and practice because they misunderstand its meaning. Thus, the goal in part 4 is to internalize the rules in the art and science of biblical interpretation. Our objective is to remember *what* each of the rules represents and *how* to apply them in mining the Bible for all its worth.

So let's dig in!

Manuscript
C-O-P-I-E-S

The tooth of time gnaws all books but the Bible . . . Nineteen centuries of experience have tested it. It has passed through critical fires no other volume has suffered, and its spiritual truths have endured the flames and come out without so much as the smell of burning.

—W. E. SANGSTER

Talk about insurmountable problems! Not only do we not have original biblical manuscripts, but the copies we do have are centuries removed from the events they chronicle and clearly contaminated. Indeed, there are more mistakes in the copies than there are words in the New Testament. In the end, all we have are copies of copies of copies with fresh errors introduced during each stage of the copying process.

Worse yet, the biblical manuscripts are chock-full of cleverly invented stories—tales that have no real basis in reality. Take, for example, the central event upon which all of Christianity either rises or falls. If ever there was a time to get the story straight this is it. Instead, *Matthew* says that the discoverers of the empty tomb were Mary Magdalene and another Mary (28:1–7); *Mark* says they were Mary Magdalene, Mary the mother of James, and Salome (16:1–8); *Luke*, Mary Magdalene, Joanna, Mary the mother of James, and others (24:1–12); and *John*, Mary Magdalene (20:1–18).

The straw breaking the proverbial camel's back, however, is the fact that manuscripts ultimately making their way into the biblical text were clearly codified by corrupt collaborators—historical winners bent on propagating their own peculiar prejudices. Thus, anti-Semitic manuscripts such as the gospel of John made it into the Bible, while credible manuscripts such as the gospel of Judas simply lost out. In short, the Bible was "forged," making it a very dishonest book. To put it bluntly— the Bible was conspired by men rather than inspired by God.

The contention that the Bible is human as opposed to divine in origin— the product of contaminated copies, cleverly invented stories, and corrupt collaborators—is nothing new. It has been the stock and trade of bastions of higher learning for centuries. Not so today. What was once the province of private academia is now being popularized in the public arena.

While hundreds of examples are available, one stands out above the rest. It involves the spiritual terrorism of Bart Ehrman, distinguished professor of religious studies at the prestigious University of North Carolina at Chapel Hill, who appears peculiarly proud of causing the faith of many of his students to waver. "Some students," says Ehrman, "resist for a long time, secure in their knowledge that God would not allow any falsehoods into his sacred book. But before long, as students see more and more of the evidence, many of them find that their faith in the inerrancy and absolute historical truthfulness of the Bible begins to waver."[1]

As this professor gone wild is managing to shake the faith of multitudes in the classroom, he is likewise succeeding in shaking the faith of multitudes in the culture. Through popular books such as *Forged: Writing in the Name of God—Why the Bible's Authors Are Not Who We Think They Are* being featured in *Time* magazine and appearances on NBC's *Dateline*, *The Daily Show with Jon Stewart*, CNN, The History Channel, major NPR shows, and other top media outlets,[2] Ehrman has systematically forwarded the notion that the Bible is not only hopelessly contradictory but a dangerous book to believe.

With a straight face Ehrman tells his ever-burgeoning audience that "there are more differences among our manuscripts than there are words in the New Testament";[3] that copyists were motivated by anti-Semitism; and the autographs themselves were, well, forged. In his view, "many of our cherished biblical stories and widely held beliefs concerning the divinity of Jesus, the Trinity, and the divine origins of the Bible itself stem from both intentional and accidental alterations by scribes."[4] Further, Ehrman seduces audiences with the notion that the Gospels are rife with cleverly invented stories—Luke going as far as to modify the words of Christ in order to absolve him of false prophecies.[5]

And he is not alone. According to a vast majority of scholars chronicled in newspapers such as *USA Today* and consulted on television broadcasts such as *National Geographic*, the greatest story ever "told" might well be the greatest story ever "sold." Says Michael White, director of the Institute for the Study of Antiquity and Christian Origins at the University of Texas at Austin, "Scripture, like history, was codified by the winners, by those who emerged with the greatest numbers at the end of three centuries of Christianity."[6] As such, he is persuaded that manuscripts like the "long-lost gospel of Judas" did not make it into the Bible because they were not in line with the direction "winners" wanted to take their newly minted religious notions—the result being that dozens of credible gospels simply lost out.

Princeton University religious scholar Elaine Pagels is similarly persuaded. She dubbed the gospel of Judas "an astonishing discovery that along with dozens of similar texts in recent years have transformed our understanding of early Christianity."[7] For his part, the aforementioned Ehrman is so enamored with the gospel of Judas that from his esteemed perspective, had we embraced the gospel of Judas instead of the gospel of John, we might well have avoided the Holocaust.[8]

In short, a new generation of popular communicators is disseminating the notion that the copy of a copy of a copy we now hold in our hands is merely the product of historical winners who preferred the dark anti-Semitic overtones of manuscripts such as the gospel of John over racially sensitive gospels such as the gospel of Judas.

Such predilections are likewise being disseminated through authors such as Dan Brown (*The Da Vinci Code*), Michael Baigent (*Holy Blood, Holy Grail*), and William Klassen (*Judas: Betrayer or Friend of Jesus?*).[9] Dan Brown, for example, lends credence to the notion that more than eighty gospels were considered for the New Testament canon, but only four were chosen. Matthew, Mark, Luke, and John edged out the others because history is codified by triumphal winners rather than trustworthy witnesses.[10] Michael Baigent dismisses the canonical gospels as legendary and characterizes Christ's crucifixion as an elaborate hoax.[11] And Klassen pulls the race card by suggesting that John wanted "to vilify Judas"; thus, his gospel gets "caught up in anti-Jewish propaganda."[12]

Robert Funk, founder of the popular Jesus Seminar, took it one step further when he suggested not only that the Gospels are legendary but that

4

concocters of the legend may have even invented Judas as an anti-Semitic slur. According to Funk, the story of Judas's betrayal of Jesus was "probably a fiction because Judas looks to many of us like the representation of Judaism or the Jews as responsible for [Jesus'] death. If it is a fiction it was one of the most cruel fictions that was ever invented."[13]

Before giving an answer—the reason for the hope that lies within us (1 Peter 3:15)—a word about the critics is in order. Most, if not all, might aptly be described as fundamentalists from the left. As such, they are prone to pressing the biblical text into a woodenly literal labyrinth. Professor Bart Ehrman comes immediately to mind. One of the reasons he cites for transitioning from fundamentalist on the right to fundamentalist on the left is a biblical reference to a mustard seed as the smallest of all seeds (Mark 4:31). As he opines in his bestseller *Misquoting Jesus*, "Maybe, when Jesus says later in Mark 4 that the mustard seed is 'the smallest of all seeds on the earth,' maybe I don't need to come up with a fancy explanation for how the mustard seed is the smallest of all seeds when I know full well it isn't. And maybe these 'mistakes' apply to bigger issues."[14]

The problem with Ehrman's misinterpretation is that, like fellow fundamentalists (here Bill Maher comes to mind), he attempts to make the language of Scripture "walk on all fours." The kingdom of God is obviously not like a mustard seed in every way. A kingdom does not look like a mustard seed, nor is a mustard seed the smallest seed in the kingdom. Rather the kingdom of God is like a mustard seed in the sense that it begins small and becomes large. Jesus' parable was not intended to provide a lesson on plant development and growth. Nor did Jesus mistakenly think that a black mustard seed was smaller than an orchid seed. Instead he was using the smallest of seeds *familiar to Palestinian farmers* to illustrate that, while the kingdom of God began in obscurity, in the end it would fill the earth and "endure forever" (Daniel 2:35, 44).

Moreover, Ehrman seems bent on turning biblical writers into mechanical dictation machines who channeled God's words with nary a variation. As such, he posits an all-too-convenient cock-crowing conundrum in his blockbuster *Jesus, Interrupted*: "In Mark's Gospel, Jesus tells Peter that he will deny him three times 'before the cock crows twice.' In

Matthew's Gospel he tells him that it will be 'before the cock crows.' Well, which is it—before the cock crows once or twice?"[15]

A more idiosyncratic fundamentalism from the left is hard to imagine. As his more attentive students know full well, Matthew does not indicate how many times the rooster crowed—he simply tells us *that* the rooster crowed (Matthew 26:74). In recounting past events or telling stories, we obviously don't all highlight the same details. In the case at hand, Mark simply provides a bit more detail than does Matthew (Mark 14:72). In point of fact, Ehrman has set up a rigged game in which it is impossible to lose. Since Matthew and Mark do not provide identical testimonies, he cries, "Contradiction!" Conversely, if they had, he could conveniently charge them with collusion.

In sharp contrast, credible scholarship always seeks a reliable core set of facts in order to validate an historical account. Far from seeking word-for-word uniformity, they expect the biblical authors to provide complementary perspectives. Divine inspiration never supposes biblical authors are automatons devoid of personality or individual style but rather men who "spoke from God as they were carried along by the Holy Spirit" (2 Peter 1:21).[16]

Solomon—no doubt the wisest man who ever lived—proverbed, "The first to present his case seems right, till another comes forward and questions him" (Proverbs 18:17). His words have relevance to the matter at hand. One who contends that biblical manuscripts are hopelessly riddled by error, cherished biblical stories are legendary rather than legitimate, the crucifixion of Christ and his subsequent resurrection is a cruel hoax rather than credible history, and history was codified by triumphant "winners"—those who preferred the dark anti-Semitic overtones of manuscripts such as the gospel of John over more racially sensitive texts such as the gospel of Judas—"seems right, till another comes forward and questions him."

Cross-examination demonstrates beyond the peradventure of a doubt that the skin of the truth has been stuffed with a significant lie. When reason prevails over rhetoric, a completely different perspective emerges. Far from a liability, extant manuscript copies bear eloquent testimony to the reality that the Bible is divine rather than merely human in origin. This is not merely a dogmatic assertion; it is an eminently defensible argument.

In evidence, we now take a closer look at extant manuscript copies. In doing so, the acronym C-O-P-I-E-S will serve as a useful guide. We begin with the *C*, which will remind you of *copyists* commissioned to the solemn task of preserving the sacred text. In carrying out their copyist commission, these biblical scribes were keenly aware that tampering with the sacred text was tantamount to playing with fire. With quill in hand they were ever mindful of Nadab and Abihu, the priestly sons of Aaron who violated the holiness of God through the offering of unauthorized fire and were thus summarily consumed (Leviticus 10). Constrained by the command "Do not add to it or take away from it" (Deuteronomy 12:32; cf. Deuteronomy 4:2; Proverbs 30:6; Revelation 22:18–19), biblical scribes fulfilled their task with meticulous zeal.

1

Copyist Practices

The Bible is the chief moral cause of all that is good, and the best corrective of all that is evil, in human society; the best Book for regulating the temporal concerns of men, and the only Book that can serve as an infallible guide . . . the principles of genuine liberty, and of wise laws and administrations, are to be drawn from the Bible and sustained by its authority. The man therefore, who weakens or destroys the Divine authority of that Book may be accessory to all the public disorders which society is doomed to suffer.

—NOAH WEBSTER

Writing a book is an arduous process. In the early years all I had at my disposal were a yellow pad and a Pentel with an eraser invariably worn down to the nub. Thankfully, those days were short-lived. Greg Laurie, one of the best evangelists on the planet, dropped by my office and sold me on "the gospel according to Mac." I instantly converted, enrolled in typing classes at a community college, found my way to the nearest Apple store, purchased a computer, and never looked back. Today, more than two decades later, I can't even imagine going back to writing a manuscript with a pen and a yellow pad.

Yet for thousands of years a Pentel and a piece of paper would have been considered a luxury. Throughout history people etched their words on materials ranging from stone and silver to papyrus and parchment. Paul references his etchings on parchment when he implores Timothy to bring "the cloak that I left with Carpus at Troas, and my scrolls, especially the parchments" (2 Timothy 4:13), and John mentions the use of "paper and ink" in his second epistle (2 John 1:12). Someone writing some seven centuries before Christ etched the priestly benediction found in Numbers 6 on silver amulets uncovered in a burial chamber outside the Old City of Jerusalem at Ketef Hinnom—these tiny, rolled-up silver sheets representing the oldest of all extant Hebrew manuscript fragments.[1] And Joshua, son of Nun, one of two legendary figures who survived the wilderness wanderings to lead the Israelites into the promised land, "copied on stones the law of Moses, which he had written" (Joshua 8:32).

Those who copied the autographs of biblical writers likewise faced an arduous task. Imagine being an Old Testament copyist engaged in the practice of hand-copying biblical manuscripts prior to the invention of computers. Perhaps you were one of the exiles who had just exited Babylon and reentered the land of promise. Your hero might well have been Ezra— the Michael Jordan of scribes. Thrilled to be back in the homeland, you coupled yourself to a community of copyists committed to the preservation of the sacred text. In your wildest imagination you could not have conjured up the image of movable type—much less a Mac computer or a mechanized copier.

Each day, you engaged in the tedious process of hand-copying an Old Testament missive—letter by letter by letter. No letter could be inscribed without looking back at it and verbalizing the text. As a Sopher (literally, a counter), you had to tally the words and letters to make certain that nothing was amiss. You must ever remain aware of the middle letter of the middle word of the manuscript so as to have an enduring reference point by which to make certain that not a jot was found missing. You must even allow for a prescribed number of letters and words in each column of the painstaking practice. Should the most exalted dignitary address you during your labors, you must ignore him, for you are a copyist in the employ of the King of kings and Lord of lords. And you must not so much as hazard to write the sacred name YHWH with a freshly dipped reed lest it blotch and desecrate the name of your God. Indeed, as part of the Jewish Sopherim, you would have had such an exalted view of the Old Testament text that you would perceive the missing of a mere tittle—a microscopic appendage at the end of a Hebrew letter—to be an affront to the holiness of your Creator. In short, you would make certain that your copy was as good as the copy that preceded it.

In time the Jewish Masoretes would succeed you. And they would be ever as vigilant. As underscored by professor of Old Testament Dr. Kenneth Barker, the Masoretes developed a system of checks and balances to ensure that every copy produced was as perfect as humanly attainable.

> To make certain they had not added or left out even a single letter, they counted the number of times each letter of the alphabet occurred in each book. They noted and recorded the middle letter of the entire Old Testament. They recorded the middle letter on each page and the number of letters and words in each column. They examined every copy of the Old Testament and withdrew from circulation all copies in which any error was discovered. These carefully copied Hebrew texts have remained virtually unchanged since about 600 to 700 AD. In 1947 the discovery of the Dead Sea Scrolls yielded copies from all the major sections of the Old Testament, except Ruth, dating back more than a century before Christ. When compared to these ancient copies, the Masoretic texts were found to be virtually identical.[2]

The point here should not be missed. The Dead Sea Scrolls predated the earliest extant text—Masoretic—by more than a millennium.[3] Yet when compared to one another, differences in style and spelling were noted but no significant difference in substance. The Great Isaiah Scroll (c. 100 BC), discovered in the first of the Qumran caves, is an apt illustration. When compared to the text of the Masorites (c. AD 1000), it was found to be virtually identical—despite the passage of eleven hundred years. The famous fifty-third chapter contained only seventeen variants from the Masoretic text. Ten were a matter of spelling, four a matter of style, and three accounted for by the Hebrew letters in the word *light*. None substantially alters the meaning of the text.[4]

Even where copyist errors exist in the text, they are generally relegated to mere matters of mistaken names or numbers. A classic case in point is 2 Chronicles 22:2—riveted in our minds due to a memorable address as well as the political intrigue involved. Some translations of 2 Chronicles, such as the King James Version and New King James Version, identify Ahaziah—youngest son of Jehoram (fifth king of the Southern Kingdom)—as forty-two years of age. The parallel passage (2 Kings 8:26) has him exactly twenty years younger when he mounted the throne. Thus, the problem. Was Ahaziah twenty-two or forty-two when he became king? As with other copyist errors, this question is easily resolved by a cursory look at context. Two verses prior to the error, we read that Ahaziah's father, Jehoram—whose death, like that of Judas, includes a description of spilled-out bowels—was *forty years old* when he died (2 Chronicles 21:20). Thus, the "aha" moment. Ahaziah would, obviously, not have been older than his father!

In sum, Old Testament scribal luminaries ranging from Ezra to the Masorites set an unimaginable standard of excellence in their copyist practices—a standard that should provide us with complete confidence in the Old Testament canon. Says Barker, "Bible students of today can be confident that the text available to us is not significantly different from the texts which Jesus and his disciples read twenty centuries ago."[5]

In contrast to Old Testament copyists, New Testament counterparts were not constrained by the same systematized copyist practices. Instead they were rather like you and me. They likely loved the Lord and thus willingly sacrificed themselves to the tedious practice of copying the sacred text. And considering the hardships involved, copying the text was more than a career; it was a considerable calling.

Some stood at writing desks, and others worked in unbearable cold. One New Testament copyist describes the physiological effects in daunting terms: "Writing bows one's back, thrusts the ribs into one's stomach, and fosters a general debility of the body."[6] Another adds a marginal warning akin to that found in the Apocalypse of John: "If anyone adds anything [words] to them, God will add to him the plagues described in this book.

And if anyone takes words away from this book of prophecy, God will take away from him his share in the tree of life and in the holy city, which are described in this book" (Revelation 22:18–19). Guided by the admonition "Do not add to it or take away from it" (Deuteronomy 12:32), New Testament copyists engaged their copyist practices with reverential awe akin to their Old Testament predecessors.

Did they make mistakes? Of course! While they engaged their craft with care, they were far from infallible. Unlike preprogrammed automatons, they were subject to all the frailties that are part and parcel of the human condition. The beauty from a biblical perspective, however, is the wealth of manuscripts by which textual critics can sort out their errors even apart from context and common sense.

While fundamentalists on the left[7] obsess over their many errors, textual critics render them trite, trivial, and easy to resolve. What is more difficult to resolve is public sentiment to the contrary. People en masse are being deluded by books such as *Misquoting Jesus: The Story Behind Who Changed the Bible and Why*, in which Bart Ehrman alleges "mistakes and changes that ancient scribes made to the New Testament and shows the great impact they had upon the Bible we use today."[8] Says Ehrman, "The more I studied the manuscript tradition of the New Testament, the more I realized just how radically the text had been altered over the years at the hands of scribes, who were not only conserving scripture but also changing it."[9] Worse yet, according to Ehrman, were the dark and sinister motives of the copyists. According to Ehrman, "the anti-Jewish sentiment of early Christian scribes made an impact on the texts they were copying."[10] For in text after text, "it was anti-Jewish sentiment that prompted the scribal alteration."[11] In evidence he offers the following copyist variant from Matthew 27:26:

Pilate is said to have flogged Jesus and then "handed him over to be crucified." Anyone reading the text would naturally assume that he handed Jesus over to his own (Roman) soldiers for crucifixion. That makes it all the more striking that in some early witnesses—including one of the scribal corrections in Codex Sinaiticus—the text is changed to heighten even further the Jewish culpability in Jesus' death. According to these manuscripts, Pilate "handed him over *to them* [i.e., to the Jews] in order that *they* might crucify him." Now the Jewish responsibility for Jesus' execution is absolute, a change motivated by anti-Jewish sentiment among the early Christians.[12]

If anything, Ehrman succeeds only in demonstrating his own anti-Christian bias. Had copyists genuinely been motivated by anti-Jewish sentiments, the very next words (Matthew 27:27) would attribute the stripping, mocking, and crucifying of Jesus to Jews, not Romans. Moreover, it is instructive to note that the variants in question occur only in two manuscripts and are at best ambiguous.[13]

While the public has taken a significant bite out of this poison apple, textual critics are well aware of the fact that Ehrman has presented the skin of the truth stuffed with a lie. Even if Ehrman has rightly judged copyists as anti-Semitic, the notion that their sinister motives lie undetected in modern Bibles would be laughable if it were not so tragic. The sheer volume of extant manuscripts is more than sufficient to retrieve the original message of New Testament authors.

This, however, has not deterred the sophists. A new generation of scholars is now disseminating the notion that not just copyists, but the gospel writers themselves were singularly anti-Semitic. As noted, William Klassen (*Judas: Betrayer or Friend of Jesus?*), like Ehrman, suggests that John wanted "to vilify Judas," thus his gospel gets "caught up in anti-Jewish propaganda."[14] Robert Funk, founder of the Jesus Seminar, took it one step further by suggesting that Judas might well have been invented as an anti-Semitic slur. As we have seen, Funk claims the story of Judas's betrayal of Jesus was "probably a fiction because Judas looks to many of us like the representation of Judaism or the Jews as responsible for His death. If it is fiction it was one of the most cruel fictions that was ever invented."[15]

The problem here, of course, is not anti-Semitism but ahistorical sophistry and vindictive prejudice. New Testament writers and their copyists clearly proclaimed that salvation through the Jewish Messiah was given first to the Jewish people and then to the rest of the world (Matthew 15:24; Romans 1:16). Additionally, Peter's vision followed by Cornelius's receiving the Holy Spirit (Acts 10) and the subsequent Jerusalem council (Acts 15) clearly demonstrate both the inclusive nature of the church as well as the initial Jewish Christian resistance to Gentile inclusion (Galatians 2:11–14).

Far from being anti-Semitic, New Testament manuscripts simply record the outworking of redemptive history as foretold by the Jewish prophets who foresaw that one of Christ's companions would betray him (Psalm 41:9; John 13:18). There is nothing subtle about the crucifixion narrative. The Jewish gospel writers explicitly state that it was their leaders who condemned Christ of blasphemy (Matthew 26:57–68; Luke 22:60–71; John 19:1–15). There would be no motive to fabricate a fictional Judas to represent the quintessential Jew.

As is obvious to any unbiased person from scholar to schoolchild, the New Testament is anything but anti-Semitic. Jesus, the twelve apostles, and the apostle Paul were all Jewish! In fact, Christians proudly refer to their heritage as the Judeo-Christian tradition. In the book of Hebrews, Christians are reminded of Jews from David to Daniel who are members of the faith hall of fame. Indeed, Christian children grow up with Jews as their heroes! From their mothers' knees to Sunday school classes, they are treated to Old Testament stories of great Jewish men and women of faith from Moses to Mary and from Ezekiel to Esther.

The Bible goes to great lengths to underscore the fact that when it comes to faith in Christ there is no distinction between Jew and Gentile (Galatians 3:28) and that Jewish people throughout the generations are no more responsible for Christ's death than anyone else. As Ezekiel put it, "The son will not share the guilt of the father, nor will the father share the guilt of the son" (Ezekiel 18:20). The "cruel fiction" referred to by Funk is not Judas but the notion that Christian copyists were anti-Semitic. Truly, such scholars owe the world an apology for an idiosyncratic brand of fundamentalism from the left that foments bigotry and hatred by entertaining the absurd notion that the biblical accounts of Judas were fabricated because "'Judas' meant 'Jew.'"[16]

While biblical authors and their copyists were clearly not anti-Semitic, they were, as previously acknowledged, far from perfect. Thus Ehrman's contention that "there are more differences among our manuscripts than there are words in the New Testament"[17] is factually defensible. The notion that these copyist changes "dramatically affected" everything from the "divinity of Jesus" to the "divine origins of the Bible" is not.[18] While such assertions make for great rhetoric, they are clearly ridiculous. Most copyist variants are mere matters of spelling and style and as such are easily discernable. Where the text was altered by copyists, no essential teaching of the faith was compromised.[19] Moreover, as I will demonstrate shortly, the quality and quantity of manuscripts is sufficient to ferret out copyist slips and supplements.

In short, the contention that careless, capricious copyists created cartloads of clearly contaminated copies simply does not correspond to reality.

2

Oral Culture

I know of no other single practice in the Christian life more rewarding, practically speaking, than memorizing Scripture. That's right. No other single discipline is more useful and rewarding than this. No other single exercise pays greater spiritual dividends! Your prayer life will be strengthened. Your witnessing will be sharper and much more effective. Your counseling will be in demand. Your attitudes and outlook will begin to change. Your mind will become alert and observant. Your confidence and assurance will be enhanced. Your faith will be solidified.

—CHARLES SWINDOLL

"Imagine playing 'telephone,'" writes Professor Bart Ehrman, "not in a solitary living room with ten kids on a sunny afternoon in July, but over the expanse of the Roman Empire (some 2,500 miles across!), with thousands of participants, from different backgrounds, with different concerns, and in different contexts, some of whom have to translate the stories into different languages all over the course of decades. What would happen to the stories?"[1]

Ehrman does not leave us guessing. Biblical stories would be "modified, amplified, and embellished"—even concocted with "reckless abandon."[2]

Thus, they are no more reliable than ten kids in a circle whispering stories to one another on a sunny July afternoon. In other words, Jesus is not "a liar, a lunatic, or the Lord."[3] The one word that fits him best is *legend*.

While I confess that neither I nor my kids have spent much time playing "telephone," we have spent more than one sunny afternoon seeing who could spot fallacies in the latest Ehrman talk or text. In the case at hand, he commits the anachronistic fallacy. As such, he judges people in the past by values and standards in the present. In sharp contrast to the present, past generations chose oral transmission as a principal means by which to pass along historical truths. As Plato proffered, written history is a mere accommodation for the forgetfulness that comes with old age.[4]

Post-Gutenberg we are primarily people of the printed page. As the offspring of Johannes Gutenberg, and more recently Steve Jobs and Bill Gates, we associate sound education with the capacity for reading and writing rather than memorizing and reciting. Not so with the ancients. In a predominately oral culture, people practiced the principles of memory. Indeed, learning was virtually synonymous with memorization. This, of course, does not imply that the ancients did not employ written records. Instead, it is to put the emphasis on the right syllable. Manuscript repositories augmented mental recall, not vice versa.

If there is one thing preserved in the text of Scripture, it is the injunction to record God's words upon the tablet of your heart. Think back for a moment to the early stages of Scripture. In what may well be among the most memorable of all biblical texts, Moses exhorts the people of God to impress the words of the Almighty upon the tablet of their consciousness. "Impress them on your children. Talk about them when you sit at home and when you walk along the road, when you lie down and when you get up. Tie them as symbols on your hands and bind them on your foreheads. Write them on the doorframes of your houses and on your gates" (Deuteronomy 6:7–9). Above all, exhorts Moses, "do not forget" (6:12).

And Moses is not alone. Solomon, who prayed for a wise and discerning heart, implored his hearers to bind the Word of God around their fingers and their necks and to write it on the tablet of their hearts (Proverbs 3:1–4). More poignantly yet, the Word made flesh entreated hearers, "Let these words sink into your ears" (Luke 9:44 NASB). Joshua, the "Jesus" of the Old Testament, likewise beseeched the people of the promise, "Do not let this Book of the Law depart from your mouth; meditate on it day and night, so that you may be careful to do everything written in it. Then you will be prosperous and successful" (Joshua 1:8). It was not enough to record the sayings of understanding on a common tablet; it was to be inscribed upon the tablet of one's consciousness.

Not only were saints in an oral culture required to discipline and dedicate themselves to recall the sayings of understanding, but sages were predisposed to present their sayings in an inherently memorable fashion. Jesus, heir to the linguistic treasure trove of the old covenant tutors and a greater wisdom teacher than them all, was a Master of mnemonics. Employing repetition, rhythm, and rhyme, he forged the inherently memorable Sermon on the Mount.

In *Jesus & the Rise of Early Christianity*, Paul Barnett, Anglican bishop of North Sydney, Australia, underscores the reality that Jesus expressed his teachings "in a form that could be memorized in the parallelism of Hebrew poetry"—parallelisms that may well have "represented the greater part of his teaching."[5] The brilliant German New Testament scholar Rainer Riesner—a veritable academic superstar and author of the essay "Jesus as Preacher and Teacher"—determined that approximately "eighty percent of the separate saying units" spoken by Christ "are formulated in some kind of *parallelismus membrorum* [parallelism of members, i.e., lines of poetry.] To this one has to add other poetical techniques such as alliteration, assonance, rhythm, and rhyme."[6] Far from being merely pleasing to the ear, such mnemonic devices were purposefully powerful. "The poetical structure of the words of Jesus made them, like the meshalim [figurative language] of the Old Testament prophets, easily memorizable and could preserve them intact. Even the form of the sayings of Jesus included in itself an imperative to remember them. It seems that the use of mnemonic devices is very seldom studied from the point of view of the psychology of the memory, but our own experience demonstrates how easy it is to learn and even to reconstruct large bodies of material, if they are in a poetical form."[7]

Riesner goes on to note that scholars who reconstruct the original wording of Jesus' sayings recognize "a cultivated oral tradition."[8] In contrast to today's theological students who drown in a "sea of opinions" and fear formulating concepts in concise, clear, and memorable prose, "Jesus condensed the main points of his theological and ethical teaching in summaries, the aphoristic meshalim" (e.g., parables or extended metaphors). "If Jesus created a deliberate formulation and a poetical form of a teaching, then it was done not to make his hearers forget but to make them memorize. This would have been possible through the highly poetic form of most of the sayings and supported by some rote learning, either encouraged by Jesus himself or spontaneously done."[9]

Suffice it to say, the disciples recognized the intended summaries of their Master because of the poetic form in which he communicated them, the stress he placed on them, and the manner in which he repeated them in his longer speeches. "These narrative meshalim were consciously premeditated and intended for further meditation. This meditation would have been impossible without having the mashal as an identifiable, fixed, 'oral text.' Only such a text could ensure that one meditated not one's own thoughts but 'the mystery of the kingdom.'"[10]

All of this, of course, is completely lost on Ehrman. Ever the fundamentalist, he not only misses the majesty of the Master's memorable meshalim but demands that his words be repeated by the disciples with every jot and tittle intact. In other words, it is not enough for the disciples to *capture the essential voice of Jesus*; he demands they necessarily *capture the exact verbiage of Jesus*. As such, Ehrman makes a federal case out of the words of Christ before Caiaphas—which must surely have his students muttering under their collective breath. When Caiaphas asks Jesus if he is the "Messiah, the Son of the Blessed One," Mark has Jesus responding with the following words: "I am. And you will see the Son of Man seated at the right hand of Power and coming with the clouds of heaven" (Mark 14:61–62). Conversely, Luke has Jesus saying: "I am, and from now on the Son of Man will be seated at the right hand of the power of God" (Luke 22:69).[11] Thus, from Ehrman's perspective there is a serious contradiction between Mark and Luke.

Needless to say—at least it ought to be needless to say—both Mark and Luke capture the essential voice of Jesus here. What Ehrman seems blithely unaware of is that his literalistic interpretation of the Jewish clouds metaphor is precisely what Luke sought to preclude. Christ was not telling Caiaphas that he would see him riding on a cloud-chariot of sorts, but that with the destruction of Jerusalem and the temple, the court that was condemning him would understand that he had indeed ascended to the right hand of power as the Judge of heaven and earth.

Unfortunately, error begets error. Thus Ehrman's error with respect to the clouds metaphor leads to the further error that Luke (who in his view was writing after the death of Caiaphas and the destruction of the temple in AD 70) modifies the words of Christ to absolve him of a false prophecy.[12] Had Ehrman taken seriously the historical meaning of the metaphor, he would have recognized that Luke was simply communicating the phrase "coming on clouds" in the common vernacular of his day.[13]

The point that should be underscored here is that the disciples, moved by the Holy Spirit, codified *the essential wisdom of Jesus*—not *the exact words of Jesus*. Put another way, they left us a memorable oral tradition rather than the words of their Master on tape.[14] Indeed, like their Teacher, the disciples employed vibrant associations, vivid imagery, and visual/emotive stimuli, so that we might not only read but remember. With the background music of the Law and the Prophets coursing through their minds,[15] they wrote of their Master, the antitype who fulfilled all the types and shadows of the old covenant constructs. When the beloved disciple spoke of two witnesses, for example, he employed a language system already deeply embedded in the minds of those familiar with the literature of the Old Testament (Revelation 11:3ff; see Deuteronomy 19:15; cf. John 8:17).

In Zechariah's day the two witnesses were Zerubbabel, the governor of Judah who returned to Jerusalem to lay the foundation of a second temple, and Joshua, the high priest commissioned to preside over its altar (Zechariah 3–4; cf. Ezra 3; 5–6; Haggai 1–2). In John's apocalypse this imagery is invested in two witnesses who, as literary characters in an oral tradition, represent the entire line of Hebrew prophets in testifying against apostate Israel. Like Moses, the witnesses have power to turn water into blood and to strike the earth with plagues (Revelation 11:6; cf. Exodus 7ff.). Like Elijah, they have power to call down fire from heaven to consume their enemies and to shut up the sky so that it will not rain for three and a half years (Revelation 11:6; cf. 1 Kings 17:1). Like Jesus they become sacrificial lambs before the fury of a beast. Their corpses unceremoniously litter the streets of the very city in which their Lord was crucified. The city is figuratively called Sodom in that it epitomized human wickedness and heavenly wrath, and Egypt in that it is emblematic of the slavery from which only Jesus can emancipate. Their resurrection after three and a half days parallels the resurrection of Christ in much the same way that their three and a half years of ministry mirrors that of Messiah (Revelation 11:7–12).

In sum, the witnesses form a composite portrait of the Law and the Prophets, memorably culminating in the life, death, resurrection, and ascension of a Prophet and Priest who is the earnest of all who are his witnesses and who will reign with him in a New Jerusalem wherein dwells righteousness.

The vibrant associations, vivid imagery, and visual/emotive stimuli employed by John hardly mirror Ehrman's sophomoric parlor game. Nor were writers of sacred Scripture, such as the apostle John, equivalents of "illiterate" schoolboys as Ehrman opines.[16] Indeed, in context, the "unlearned" apostles astonished Jewish teachers with their knowledge and wisdom in much the same way as Jesus himself had (Mark 1:22)—though he, too, was without the prerequisite rabbinic training demanded by Ehrman. An entire adult lifetime devoted to study and the ministry of the Word of God (Acts 6:2) can easily account for the literary expertise with which Christ's disciples transmitted oral history in the context of an oral culture.

In the early verses of 1 Corinthians 15, the Apostle to the Gentiles employs technical Jewish terminology to transmit oral history through the use of such words as "delivered" and "received" (15:3 ESV). Scholars view this as evidence that Paul is passing along information (in this case a creed) that he received from another source. The eminent scholar Joachim Jeremias points to non-Pauline phrases such as "for our sins" (15:3), "according to the Scriptures" (15:3, 4), "he was raised" (15:4), "third day" (15:4), "he appeared" (15:5, 6, 7, 8), and "the Twelve" (15:5) to demonstrate that Paul is passing along accurately codified and well-defined oral history. Not only so, but "the creed is organized in a stylized, parallel form" that reflects oral history.[17]

Oxford scholar and philosopher Dr. Terry Miethe concurs. Says Miethe, "Most New Testament scholars point out that one of the ways we know [15:3–8] is a creedal statement is that it appears to have been in a more primitive Aramaic, and it's also in hymnic form. This means it was stylized Greek, non-Pauline words, and so on, which indicates that it predated Paul and was widely used, probably even used and recited in worship experiences as a form of worship or a song or a hymn or a creedal statement, and was therefore universally acknowledged."[18]

The short time span between Christ's crucifixion and the composition of this early Christian creed precludes the possibility of legendary corruption.[19] Legends draw from folklore, not from people and places that are demonstrably rooted in history. It is mind-boggling to realize that Christianity can confidently point to a creed that some of the greatest scholars, theologians, philosophers, and historians have traced to within just three to eight years of Christ's crucifixion.[20]

Peter, Paul, and the rest of the apostles claimed that Christ appeared to hundreds of people who were still alive and available for cross-examination (15:6).[21] Paul claims that Christ "appeared to more than five hundred of the brothers at the same time, most of whom are still living, though some have fallen asleep" (15:6). It would have been one thing to attribute such oral history to people who had already died. It was quite another to attribute it to multitudes who were still alive. As the New Testament scholar of Cambridge University C. H. Dodd points out, "There can hardly be any purpose in mentioning the fact that most of the 500 are still alive, unless Paul is saying, in effect, 'The witnesses are there to be questioned.'"[22] If Paul were merely playing telephone, his assertions regarding the eyewitnesses who had seen the resurrected Christ could have easily been refuted.

And think about the consequences of passing along "modified," "embellished" stories with "reckless abandon."[23] Paul gave up his position as an esteemed Jewish leader, a rabbi, and a Pharisee who had studied under the famed teacher Gamaliel (Acts 22:3). He gave up the mission to stamp out every vestige of what he considered an insidious Christian heresy (22:4). Yet the historical reality of Christ and the resurrection transformed his allegiance from Gamaliel to the gospel. As such, he traded in his position as a Pharisee for poverty, prison, and persecution (Acts 9:1–19; 22:6–21; 26:1–32; 2 Corinthians 11:16–33).

James the half brother of Jesus was likewise willing to die for the transmission of truth. One is left to wonder what could possibly impel one to risk life and limb for the notion that a half brother knit him together in his mother's womb.[24] The only reasonable explanation is that it was the unadulterated, unembellished transmission of truth emblazoned upon the tablet of his consciousness. Such is hardly the stuff of legends. It is the substance of oral history corroborated in papyrus and parchment.[25]

3

Papyrus and Parchment

Do not think that I have come to abolish the Law or the Prophets; I have not come to abolish them but to fulfill them. I tell you the truth, until heaven and earth disappear, not the smallest letter, not the least stroke of a pen, will by any means disappear from the Law until everything is accomplished.

—JESUS CHRIST

"It's a bit hard to know what the words of the Bible mean," says Professor Ehrman, "if we don't even know what the words are!" If God did not bother to miraculously save the original writings (autographs), there seems to be "no reason to think that he performed the earlier miracle of inspiring those words."[1] Thus, the elephant in the room: all we have are copies of copies of copies with fresh errors cropping up in each stage of the copying process but no original writings!

While God could obviously have preserved the autographs, the attendant problems would have been significant. First, given the proclivities of humanity, we would no doubt have made idols out of them. In evidence, one need look no further than the Muslim veneration of Adam's white stone—enshrined within the Great Mosque of Mecca—that is now allegedly black through the absorption of the sins of multiplied millions of pilgrims.[2]

Furthermore, how would we determine the originals to be the originals? Think Shroud of Turin. Even in an age of highly advanced technology, there is no certainty that this is the original burial cloth that shrouded the face of Christ.[3] Moreover, who would control the originals—Jesuits, rabbis, imams? Would they be under glass in the Vatican or enshrined on Temple Mount in the Muslim Dome of the Rock? Perhaps parchment would take precedence over practice, form over faith.

Finally, as aptly noted by Dr. James White, the wisdom of God is evident through the way he "protected the text from the one thing we, centuries and millenia later, could never detect: wholesale change of doctrine or theology by one particular man or group who had full control over the text at any one point in its history." Instead, "because the New Testament books were written at various times and were quickly copied and distributed as soon as they were written, there was never a time when anyone or any group could gather up all the manuscripts and make extensive changes in the text itself, such as cutting out the deity of Christ or inserting some foreign doctrine or concept." In other words, says White, no one could "gather up the texts and try to make them all say the same thing by 'harmonizing' them." Instead we have absolute assurance that this did not happen! "By the time anyone did obtain great ecclesiastical power in the name of Christianity, texts like P66 or P75 already were long buried in the sands of Egypt, out of the reach of any attempted alteration."[4]

In brief, if we had an identifiable autograph, the material paper and ink would likely replace God as the object of our worship, the rancor of control would be unimaginable, and we would have no assurance that the text was indeed the text. Had God acquiesced to Ehrman's conditions, we may well have an autograph enshrined in Rome, but we would lack the epistemic certainty of its authenticity. Instead, the autographs are forever immortalized within a supernaturally preserved corpus of manuscripts. Instead of having less than the autographs, we have far more—a treasure trove of manuscripts! In excess of 5,660 manuscripts of the New Testament have now been uncovered.[5] Some made of papyrus, others of parchment.

By far the earliest extant manuscript fragments were inscribed upon papyrus—a plant that proliferated in the marshlands of the Nile. At present, almost one hundred papyrus manuscript fragments have come to light, the most famous of which is the John Rylands manuscript (P52). Most scholars hold that this excerpt from the gospel of John is separated from its original writing by mere decades.[6]

In addition to papyrus manuscripts, there are approximately twenty-four hundred extant lectionaries or church readings inscribed on a parchment (vellum) material derived from animal skins saturated in lime. Such manuscripts—dating as far back as the seventh century AD—employ a sequence of church readings that continues in Orthodox churches to this very day. Variants found in lectionaries frequently involve the substitution of nouns for purposes of clarification. As such, proper nouns like *Jesus* or *Lord* are substituted for pronouns like *he* or *him*.

The oldest parchment manuscripts—uncials—were written in a script comparable to capital letters. By far the most recognized of the three hundred–plus manuscripts in this category are Codex Sinaiticus and Codex Vaticanus, dating all the way back to the middle of the fourth century AD. Codex Sinaiticus is so named because it was discovered at the foot of Mount Sinai and represents the oldest complete New Testament manuscript discovered to date.

The remaining parchment manuscripts, some twenty-eight hundred, were dubbed minuscules in that they employed a running cursive as opposed to the more bulky caps. Minuscule manuscripts, dating back to the ninth century, quickly became the parchment of choice throughout the Greek-speaking world. Because the smaller cursive lettering facilitated more words per page, minuscules proved easier to handle and less costly to replicate.

Cumulatively, the sheer volume of papyrus and parchment undergirding sacred Scripture dwarf that of any other work in classical history. Consider, for example, Homer's *Iliad*, Bible to the ancient Greeks. While its manuscript numbers are singularly impressive—650 copies—this pales by comparison to the almost 6,000 Greek manuscript fragments undergirding the New Testament.

This is ever more impressive when compared to other celebrated works of antiquity. *The Jewish War* by Jewish historian Flavius Josephus is buttressed but by nine Greek manuscripts; Plato's *Dialogues* commended by seven; and the *Annals of Imperial Rome* by Roman historian Cornelius Tacitus, supported by two.

Even six thousand Greek manuscripts, however, do not tell the full story. There are an additional ten thousand in Latin, and a sea of other translations in the Slavic, Ethiopian, and Armenian dialects adding an additional eight thousand to the treasury. In the words of distinguished Greek scholar F. F. Bruce, "There is no body of ancient literature in the world that enjoys such a wealth of textual attestation as the New Testament."[7]

Additionally, it should be noted that the relatively short time interval between the earliest extant copies and their autographs precludes the possibility of legendary contamination.[8] Incredible but true, scholars now piece together most of the New Testament using fragments dated within just two centuries of the death of Christ.[9] And the famed Chester Beatty Papyrus II (P46), which contains a majority of Paul's writings, is credibly dated to within a century of its autograph.[10] This reality is ever more salient when compared to the aforementioned works of antiquity. Homer's *Iliad*, written eight centuries before Christ, is separated from its autograph by a full millennium. Thirteen hundred years separate Plato's *Dialogues* (fifth century BC) from their earliest extant copies, and the two existing manuscripts that support the *Annals* are dated to the ninth and eleventh centuries.[11]

Lastly, a word about proximity between the original writings and the events they chronicle. If an autograph is written hundreds of years after the events it records, it is likely to be far less reliable than if it is written early. Thus it would stand to reason that the gospel of Judas, carbon-dated to around AD 280,[12] is less reliable than a gospel such as John, which was most certainly written prior to the Jerusalem holocaust of AD 70.[13]

What can be said with respect to the dating of John can likewise be said of Matthew, Mark, and Luke. Dr. Luke, who recorded the Acts of the Apostles as well as his gospel narrative, concluded his two-part series with the apostle Paul still under house arrest in Rome. Since Paul was martyred under Nero in the early to mid-60s AD,[14] the Acts of the Apostles must have been written prior to that.[15] Since Acts is the second book in Luke's two-part account (Acts 1:1), it stands to reason that the gospel of Luke is dated even earlier. A majority of New Testament scholars hold that Luke and Matthew each rely in part on Mark, thus the gospel of Mark is dated earlier still.[16] But it gets even better. A consensus of both liberal and conservative scholars date the apostle Paul's first letter to the Corinthian Christians to the AD 50s, no more than twenty-five years after Jesus' death.[17]

While some fundamentalists on both left and right dogmatically dispute such realities, liberal scholars like John A. T. Robinson, author of *Redating the New Testament*, have been compelled by evidence to rethink late-dating paradigms. Indeed, Robinson's research led him to contend that all of sacred Scripture was completed prior to the fall of Jerusalem. Says Robinson, "One of the oddest facts about the New Testament is that what on any showing would appear to be the single most datable and climactic event of the period—the fall of Jerusalem in AD 70, and with it the collapse of institutional Judaism based on the temple—is never once mentioned as a past fact."[18]

Robinson's redating is not just a dogmatic assertion, but it is a defensible argument. If vast portions of the New Testament are late-dated, as per fundamentalists, it seems incredible that there would be no mention of the most apocalyptic event in Jewish history—the demolition of Jerusalem and the destruction of the temple at the hands of Titus. Imagine writing a history of New York today and making no mention of the destruction of the Twin Towers of the World Trade Center at the hands of terrorists on September 11, 2001. Or, more directly, imagine writing a thesis on the future of terrorism in America and failing to mention the Manhattan Massacre.[19]

Consider another parallel. Imagine you are reading a history concerning Jewish struggles in Nazi Germany and find no mention whatsoever of the Holocaust. Would it be reasonable to suppose this history was written prior to the outbreak of World War II? The answer is self-evident. Just as it stretches credulity to suggest that a history on the Jews in Germany would be written in the aftermath of World War II and yet make no mention of the Holocaust, so, too, it is unreasonable to think that sacred Scripture was written in the aftermath of the destruction of Jerusalem and yet makes no mention of the most apocalyptic event in Jewish history. This by itself should be enough to cause a fundamentalist to temper dogmatism.

Those who hold dogmatically to late-dating schemes face an even more formidable obstacle. Consider one of the most amazing prophecies in all of Scripture. Jesus is leaving the temple when his disciples call his attention to its buildings. As they gaze upon the temple's massive stones and magnificent buildings, Jesus utters the unthinkable: "I tell you the truth, not one stone here will be left on another; every one will be thrown down" (Matthew 24:2; see also Mark 13:2 and Luke 21:6). One generation later this prophecy, no doubt still emblazoned upon the tablet of their consciousness, became a vivid and horrifying reality.

As incredible as Christ's prophecy and its fulfillment one generation later are, it is equally incredible to suppose that authors of the New Testament would make no mention of its fulfillment. As the student of Scripture well knows, New Testament writers were quick to highlight fulfilled prophecy. Phrases such as, "This was to fulfill what was spoken of by the prophet," permeate the pages of the New Testament. Thus, it is inconceivable that Jesus would make an apocalyptic prophecy concerning the destruction of Jerusalem and the Jewish temple and that John would fail to mention that the prophecy was fulfilled one generation later just as Jesus had predicted.[20]

The reality is this: there is a relatively short time interval between the earliest papyrus and parchment copies of the New Testament and the original autographs and less than a generation between the autographs and the events they chronicle. Indeed, upon consideration of Robinson's thesis that the whole of the New Testament should be redated prior to AD 70, the esteemed New Testament scholar C. H. Dodd responded in a letter to Robinson with legendary wit:

You are certainly justified in questioning the whole structure of the accepted "critical" chronology of the New Testament writings, which avoids putting anything earlier than 70, so that none of them are available for anything like first-generation testimony. I should agree with you that much of this late dating is quite arbitrary, even wanton, the offspring not of any argument that can be presented, but rather of the critic's prejudice that if he appears to assent to the traditional position of the early church he will be thought no better than a stick-in-the-mud. The whole business is due for radical re-examination, which demands *argument* to show, e.g., that Mark *must* be post-70—or *must* be so because anything earlier than that could present such a plain, straightforward story: that would be to neglect the findings of the fashionable *Redaktionsgeschichte*. It is surely significant that when historians of the ancient world treat the gospels, they are quite unaffected by the sophistications of *Redaktionsgeschichte*, and handle the documents as if they were what they professed to be (Sherwin-White, with all his limitations, is the latest instance). But if one approaches them in that way, does not the case for late dating collapse?[21]

As Robinson's treatise demonstrates, the answer is most certainly—yes. Thankfully, Robinson was less concerned with being thought a stick-in-the-mud than being stuck in muddled thinking—an obscurantist obsessively bent on late-dating the autographs.[22]

In sum, what we have learned thus far is this: The Old Testament canon was meticulously cared for by a cadre of copyists commissioned to the solemn task of preserving the text. The Dead Sea Scrolls remain an enduring testimony to the reverential awe with which they engaged their sacred task. No less an authority than Jesus Christ himself placed an eternal stamp on its authenticity. "Your word is truth," he said, "Scripture cannot be broken" (John 17:17; 10:35).

In like fashion, we can be absolutely certain that the New Testament is the infallible repository of redemptive revelation, supernaturally preserved by the hand and purposes of God. The veritable mountain of manuscripts from which the autograph emerges is proof positive that God has preserved his Word over time, that there is a relatively short time interval between the manuscripts and the original writing, and that less than a generation passed between the original writings and the truths they chronicle. The promise of Jesus to his disciples stands sure: "The Counselor, the Holy Spirit, whom the Father will send in my name, will teach you all things and will remind you of everything I have said to you" (John 14:26).

4

*I*nternal Evidence

I will put down all apparent inconsistencies in the Bible to my own ignorance.

—JOHN NEWTON

So far we have come face-to-face with the prejudicial caricature of copyists as inept anti-Semites. We tackled the anachronistic fallacy posited by sophists bent on marginalizing the significance of oral culture. We highlighted the quantity and quality of papyrus and parchment manuscripts, which assure us that the message and intent of the original autographs have been passed on to the present generation without compromise. Shortly, we will encounter the science of textual analysis by which "the tenacity of the text" reveals the original writings. Here, we explore the *internal evidence* that undergirds the absolute reliability of the biblical text.

EYEWITNESS TESTIMONY

First and foremost is *eyewitness testimony*. Moses, for example, participated in and was an eyewitness to the remarkable events of the Egyptian captivity, the Exodus, the forty-year sojourn in the wilderness, and final encampment before entering the promised land—all of which are chronicled accurately in the text of the Old Testament Torah.[1] He correctly identifies Egyptian names, words, customs, and even geography. As I document in part 2, the archaeologist's spade has done much to bury the bravado of modern-day Exodus deniers. It is as unlikely that Jews falsified the Exodus as it is that they fabricated the Holocaust. Archaeology provides a wholly plausible framework for Jewish contentions regarding their enslavement and emancipation. While archaeology has thoroughly discredited the Book of Mormon,[2] internal evidence provides credence to the people, places, and particulars found in the biblical text. Jesus placed the stamp of authenticity squarely on Mosaic authorship when he said, "If you believed Moses, you would believe me, for he wrote about me. But since you do not believe what he wrote, how are you going to believe what I say?" (John 5:46–47).

As with the Old, the New Testament is replete with eyewitness testimony. Luke says that he gathered eyewitness testimony and "carefully investigated everything" (Luke 1:1–4). Once bent on disproving the historical reliability of Dr. Luke, acclaimed archaeologist Sir William Ramsay was thoroughly converted as one after the other the historical allusions in Luke's writings proved accurate.[3] Like Luke, John testifies to his firsthand experience with the resurrected Christ. Says John, "That which was from the beginning, which we have heard, which we have seen with our eyes, which we have looked at and our hands have touched—this we proclaim concerning the Word of life" (1 John 1:1). John's gospel provides ample internal evidence that it was written by an author who was intimately acquainted with locations and events he recorded, not someone writing under an alias hundreds of years later. As such, he references a Pool of Bethesda surrounded by five covered colonnades (John 5:2) as well as a Pool of Siloam used by those who were infirm (John 9:7). Archaeology has verified the descriptions and locations of both of these pools.[4] John also correctly notes changes in elevation between Cana in Galilee, Capernaum, and Jerusalem (John 2:11–13). Other examples include the two Bethanys—one less than two miles from Jerusalem on the road to Jericho where Mary, Martha, and Lazarus lived (John 11:18); the other beyond the Jordan River, which only a first-century Palestinian could have identified (John 1:28).[5] In the case of Gnostic gospels, such as Thomas and Judas, there is no evidence they were written by anyone familiar with the geographical setting that existed in Palestine prior to the holocaust of AD 70.[6]

The words of Peter are instructive: "We did not follow cleverly invented stories when we told you about the power and coming of our Lord Jesus Christ, but we were eyewitnesses of his majesty" (2 Peter 1:16). If internal evidence points to anything, it is to the reality that far from inventors of internally inconsistent stories, such gospel writers were inspired to faithfully narrate a core set of facts by which they had been radically transformed. While it is conceivable that they would have faced torture, vilification, and even cruel deaths for what they fervently believed to be true, it is inconceivable that they would have been willing to die for cleverly invented stories they knew to be lies.

No one drove this point home more eloquently than did Dr. Simon Greenleaf, Harvard's Royall Professor of Law. Greenleaf, undoubtedly the greatest American authority on common law evidence of the nineteenth century, authored the tour de force, titled *A Treatise on the Law of Evidence*. His words, poignant and profound, demand our utmost attention:

> The great truths which the apostles declared were that Christ had risen from the dead, and that only through repentance from sin, and faith in Him, could men hope for salvation. This doctrine they asserted with one voice, everywhere, not only under the greatest discouragements, but in the face of the most appalling terrors that can be presented to the mind of man.
>
> Their master had recently perished as a malefactor, by the sentence of a public tribunal. His religion sought to overthrow the religions of the whole world. The laws of every country were against the teachings of His disciples. The interests and passions of all the rulers and great men in the world were against them. The fashion of the world was against them.
>
> Propagating this new faith, even in the most inoffensive and peaceful manner, they could expect nothing but contempt, opposition, revilings, bitter persecutions, stripes, imprisonments, torments, and cruel deaths.

Yet this faith they zealously did propagate; and all these miseries they endured undismayed, nay, rejoicing.

As one after another was put to a miserable death, the survivors only prosecuted their work with increased vigor and resolution. The annals of military warfare afford scarcely an example of the like heroic constancy, patience, and unblenching courage. They had every possible motive to review carefully the grounds of their faith, and the evidences of the great facts and truths which they asserted and these motives were pressed upon their attention with the most melancholy and terrific frequency. It was therefore impossible that they could have persisted in affirming the truths they have narrated, had not Jesus actually risen from the dead, and had they not known this fact as certainly as they knew any other fact.

If it were morally possible for them to have been deceived in this matter, every human motive operated to lead them to discover and avow their error. To have persisted in so gross a falsehood, after it was known to them, was not only to encounter, for life, all the evils which man could inflict from without, but to endure also the pangs of inward and conscious guilt; with no hope of future peace, no testimony of a good conscience, no expectation of honor or esteem among men, no hope of happiness in this life, or in the world to come.

Such conduct in the apostles would moreover have been utterly irreconcilable with the fact that they possessed the ordinary constitution of our common nature. Yet their lives do show them to have been men like all others of our race; swayed by the same motives, animated by the same hopes, affected by the same joys, subdued by the same sorrows, agitated by the same fears, and subject to the same passions, temptations, and infirmities as ourselves. And their writings show them to have been men of vigorous understandings.

If then their testimony was not true, there was no possible motive for this fabrication.[7]

As Greenleaf masterfully communicated, the Twelve[8] were thoroughly transformed by truth. Peter, once afraid of being exposed as a follower of Christ, was transformed into a valiant defender of the faith.[9] Paul, likewise, was transformed. In the end, he paid the ultimate price for the truth he promulgated. The stone inscription beneath the high altar at St. Paul's Basilica in Rome simply reads, "To Paul, Apostle and Martyr."[10] And they were not alone. Within weeks of the resurrection, thousands of Jews willingly divorced themselves from sociological and spiritual traditions that had forged their personal and national identities.[11] To suggest they turned an empire upside down on the basis of cleverly invented stories is an insult to their collective memories.

ERRONEOUS TESTIMONY

Furthermore, we should note that the *eyewitness testimony* of those who willingly died for the truths they presented stands in stark contrast to the *erroneous testimony* purveyed by those seeking to discredit them. An ever-growing error tribunal is focused on discrediting the eyewitness testimonies of Matthew, Mark, Luke, and John, with respect to the central historical event upon which all of Christianity either rises or falls. As noted, if ever there is a crucial internal test, this is it. *Matthew* says that the discoverers of the empty tomb were Mary Magdalene and another Mary (28:1–7); *Mark* says they were Mary Magdalene, Mary the mother of James, and Salome (16:1–8); *Luke*, Mary Magdalene, Joanna, Mary the mother of James, and others (24:1–12); and *John*, Mary Magdalene (20:1–18).

Despite false testimony to the contrary, the evidence overwhelmingly turns in favor of the biblical text. If John had stipulated that Mary Magdalene was the *only* female to discover the empty tomb while the other gospels claimed that more than one woman was involved, we would be faced with an obvious contradiction. Instead, the complementary details provided by the four gospel writers simply serve to flesh out the rest of the story. As such, credible scholars look for a reliable *core* in order to validate historical accounts. In this case, liberal and conservative scholars alike agree that the body of Jesus was buried in the tomb of Joseph of Arimathea. (As a member of the Jewish court that convicted Jesus, Joseph is unlikely to be Christian fiction.)[12] Additionally, as philosopher and apologist William

Lane Craig points out, "when you understand the role of women in first-century Jewish society, what's really extraordinary is that this empty tomb story should feature women as the discoverers of the empty tomb in the first place." And Craig concludes, "The fact that women are the first witnesses to the empty tomb is most plausibly explained by the reality that—like it or not—they *were* the discoverers of the empty tomb! This shows that the gospel writers faithfully recorded what happened, even if it was embarrassing. This bespeaks the historicity of this tradition rather than its legendary status."[13] If each of the gospel writers presented secondary details in exactly the same manner, critics might well dismiss their accounts on the basis of *collusion*. Instead, the Gospels provide unique yet mutually consistent testimonies that are internally consistent one with the other.

Yet another erroneous testimony designed to discredit the biblical manuscripts on the basis of internal inconsistencies involves angels at the tomb of Christ. After reading the Synoptic Gospels, Professor Ehrman claims he was unable to figure out whether the women saw "a man, as Mark says, or two men (Luke), or an angel (Matthew)."[14] One is left to wonder why one of Professor Ehrman's students didn't expose his erroneous testimony by pausing to unpack the mystery for him. As Sherlock Holmes would say, "Elementary, my dear Watson." Wherever there are two angels, there is always one! Always, always, always, without exception!

The fact that Mark only references the angel who addressed the women shouldn't be problematic even for someone who has made a virtual art form out of exploiting "discrepancies" in secondary details of the Gospels. Moreover, even though Luke does not specifically refer to the two men as angels, the fact that he describes these beings as "men in clothes that gleamed like lightning" should have been a dead giveaway (Luke 24:4). As a historian addressing a predominantly Gentile audience, Luke no doubt measured his words carefully so as to not give unnecessary rise to pagan superstitions.

As with Mark, the fact that Matthew only references one angel does not preclude that two angels were present. Indeed, after reading the accounts of Matthew, Mark, and Luke (or John, for that matter), there is ample data by which a historian can determine that the "man" described by Mark was an angel; that the "men in clothes that gleamed like lighting" were angelic;

and that though Matthew only mentions an angel, he clearly does not preclude the possibility that another was present.

One final example of an alleged error posited by Ehrman, and then we move on. This time it involves his erroneous testimony against the internal coherence of Matthew and Mark. It is dubbed by Ehrman "one of my favorite examples," and involves an alleged discrepancy between Matthew 12:30 and Mark 9:40. "In Matthew, Jesus declares, '*Whoever is not with me is against me.*' In Mark, he says, '*Whoever is not against us is for us.*'" Ehrman's conundrum—"How can both be true at once?"[15] In the process of responding, the admonition of Solomon immediately springs to mind:

> *Do not answer a fool according to his folly,*
> *or you will be like him yourself.*
> *Answer a fool according to his folly,*
> *or he will be wise in his own eyes.*

(PROVERBS 26:4–5)

"How can both be true at once?" At first blush the words of Solomon, like those of the Savior, may appear to be in conflict, but on closer examination their wisdom is revealed. At times a fool posits more questions than a veritable army of wise men can answer, so answering would only contribute to their misguided sense of self-significance. At other times, an apt answer may prod the fool toward a true valuation of things so that they may be poured out in new and better fashion. In any case, the truly wise know when—and when not—to answer a fool.

As with Solomon, truisms abound in the teachings of the Savior. In the case at hand, context is critical. In Matthew, the enemies of Christ have just accused him of casting out demons by the power of Beelzebub. Thus, when Jesus says, "He who is not with me is against me" (12:30), he is warning his followers of following in the footsteps of his antagonists. In Mark the situation is reversed. A friend of Christ is casting out demons in his name. Thus, in saying, "Whoever is not against us is for us" (9:40), Jesus is warning his disciples not to make an unjust judgment. One might well imagine that Jesus, heir to the linguistic riches of the Old Testament prophets, uses truisms that require thoughtful reflection and resist knee-jerk rejection. Conscientious consideration has turned many an enemy of Christ into an eyewitness willing to testify to the point of shedding his or her own blood.

Elegant Tapestry

Finally, we should carefully note the *elegant tapestry* that serves as an internal evidence for the divine authorship of the biblical text. The tapestry of Scripture is a divine composite of surpassing brilliance and beauty. It is simply incredible that this exquisite masterpiece is fashioned from sixty-six books, written by forty different human authors in three different languages (Hebrew, Aramaic, and Greek), over a period of fifteen hundred years, on thousands of different subjects, and yet is unified and consistent throughout. How is that possible? The individual writers had no idea that their message would eventually be assembled into one Book, yet each work fits perfectly into place with a unique purpose as a synergistic component of an elegant masterpiece.

The synergistic harmony of the Bible is a powerful testimony and an enduring reminder that God has spoken—that these are his very words. Clearly, the elegant tapestry of the text added to the eyewitness testimony of its authors is surpassingly powerful internal evidence to its absolute and irrevocable trustworthiness.

5

$\mathcal{E}$xternal Evidence

The truly wise man is he who always believes the
Bible against the opinion of any man.
—R. A. TORREY

Internal evidence is sufficient to establish the biblical manuscripts as authentic, reliable, and complementary. *External* evidence, however, provides remarkable corroborating attestation. Details and descriptions found in the sacred text are attested to by external evidence provided, in many instances, by foes of Christ, not just by the friends of Christ. Indeed, from such external witnesses it is possible to piece together highlights of the life and death of Christ wholly apart from the Bible.[1]

FLAVIUS JOSEPHUS

Apart from biblical manuscripts themselves, the writings of Jewish historian Flavius Josephus provide the most authoritative ancient corroboration for the people, places, and particulars that populate the text of Scripture.

In *The Jewish War* and *Jewish Antiquities*, he provides a vivid recapitulation of Jewish history from Genesis to Jerusalem's fall in AD 70. As noted by Dr. Paul Maier, professor of ancient history at Western Michigan University and author of *Josephus: The Essential Works*, "Many people use Josephus without even knowing it. What, for example, was the name of Herodias's daughter whose dancing led to the beheading of John the Baptist? Salome, of course, and yet the girl is not named in the Gospels but by Josephus, who also furnishes additional details about John the Baptist as well as James, the half-brother of Jesus."[2]

Josephus was born in AD 37 and as such was an eyewitness to many of the details and descriptions found in the New Testament. In *Antiquities* 20, he refers to James as "the brother of Jesus who was called the Christos" as well as describing the manner of his death by stoning. As underscored by Dr. Maier, *Antiquities* 20:200 "shows no tampering whatever and is present in all Josephus manuscripts."[3] The most noteworthy reference to Jesus appears in *Antiquities* 18:63, where Josephus comments on his character, crucifixion, and resurrection:

> At this time there was a wise man called Jesus, and his conduct was good, and he was known to be virtuous. Many people among the Jews and the other nations became his disciples. Pilate condemned him to be crucified and to die. But those who had become his disciples did not abandon his discipleship. They reported that he had appeared to them three days after his crucifixion and that he was alive. Accordingly, he was perhaps the Messiah, concerning whom the prophets have reported wonders, and the tribe of the Christians, so named after him, has not disappeared to this day.[4]

While the translation of this passage by church historian Eusebius may well have contained Christian interpolations,[5] a majority of scholars view the translation above as historically reliable and authentic—particularly in view of a newly discovered text by Melkite historian Agapius, which bears no indication of tampering. As Maier makes clear, "Josephus must have mentioned Jesus in authentic core material at 18:63 since this passage is present in all Greek manuscripts of Josephus, and the Agapian version accords well with his vocabulary and grammar elsewhere."[6]

CORNELIUS TACITUS

Born twelve or so years after the death of Christ and a contemporary of Flavius Josephus, Cornelius Tacitus is widely deemed the greatest first-century historian of the ancient Roman Empire. His *Annals* span the time frame from the death of Augustus to the death of Nero, and his *Histories* proceed through the death of Domitian toward the end of the first century. In *Annals*, Tacitus amplifies the nefarious nature of Nero Caesar, who falsely accused Christians of causing the great fire of Rome and subjected his followers to "the most exquisite tortures." He had them "covered with the skins of beasts," "torn by dogs," "nailed to crosses," and "burned to serve as a nightly illumination."[7]

More significantly, Tacitus chronicles the death of the "Christus," who "suffered the extreme penalty during the reign of Tiberius at the hands of one of our procurators, Pontius Pilatus." Of particular note is the phrase that immediately follows: "*and a most mischievous superstition*, thus checked for the moment, again broke out not only in Judaea, the first source of the evil, but even in Rome, where all things hideous and shameful from every part of the world find their centre and become popular."[8]

Consider that Tacitus not only provides corroborating testimony to the biblical account of Christ's crucifixion at the hands of Pontius Pilate during the reign of Tiberius Caesar, but draws attention to a Christian movement that had spread from Judaea to Rome. While some have sought to negate the impact of his words, their import is singularly significant. The "Christus" had recently been slaughtered in hideous and humiliating fashion. Yet his followers celebrate his crucifixion with exuberance and joy. Only the resurrection, demeaned by Tacitus as "a most mischievous superstition," can account for that. Imagine devotees of Martin Luther King Jr. getting together to celebrate his assassination at the hands of James Earl Ray. They may well celebrate his contributions to civil rights or his captivating charisma, but never his brutal killing.

GAIUS SUETONIUS TRANQUILLUS

Suetonius, contemporary of Tacitus, was chief secretary to Emperor Hadrian, dubbed "the Greekling."[9] Best known for *The Twelve Caesars*, Suetonius covered Roman history from Jupiter Julius, father of the Roman Empire; through the death of the nefarious Nero and the resurrection of the empire under Vespasian; to Domitian, whose death marked the end of the Flavian dynasty. Suetonius is well known for gathering historical data from eyewitnesses as well as citing conflicting accounts without prejudice or partiality.[10]

Like Tacitus, Suetonius makes reference to the "mischievous religious belief" of Jewish devotees willing to suffer ignominious punishments for the sake of "Chrestus."[11] They had been taught from the time of Abraham that they were to sacrifice animals as the symbol of atonement of sin. After the resurrection, however, they suddenly stopped sacrificing. They finally understood that Chrestus was the substance that fulfilled the symbol of animal sacrifices. That he was the sacrificial "Lamb of God, who takes away the sin of the world" (John 1:29).

Equally telling is a citation by Suetonius that bears remarkable similarity to Acts 18:2, where the biblical historian Luke notes that a Jew named Aquila, a native of Pontus, had recently left Italy with his wife, Priscilla, "because Claudius had ordered all the Jews to leave Rome." Says Suetonius, Claudius "expelled the Jews from Rome, on account of the riots in which they were constantly indulging, at the instigation of Chrestus."[12]

PLINIUS THE YOUNGER

Contemporary and employer of Suetonius and friend of Tacitus, Plinius was a highly skilled rhetorician well known for letters rightly dubbed literary classics. Tragically, he is equally notorious for the interrogation, torture, and murder of Christians. By his own account he extracted information from two church deaconesses by means of torture. His manner was to ask three times whether the person was a follower of Christ. If the answer was yes, says Plinius, "I order them to be taken away for execution;

whatever they have admitted to, I am sure that their stubbornness and inflexible obstinacy ought to be punished."[13]

If a person responded by denying the faith, Plinius had them repeat an invocation to the gods, offer rites with wine and incense before the statue of Trajan, and "utter imprecations at the same time against the name of Christ."[14] For Plinius the end game was the reclamation of multitudes from the worship of Christ to the worship of Caesar. While to modern ears the manner and methods of Plinius were monstrous, to Roman Caesars and citizens, the spiritual supremacy of the state was inviolate. One need only remember the jeers of the Jews in Jerusalem when Pilate presented Jesus as "King of the Jews." In one voice they shouted, "Anyone who claims to be a king opposes Caesar." Again when Pilate asked, "Shall I crucify your king?" they roared back, "We have no king but Caesar" (John 19:12, 15). As such, they worshipped Caesar as both Savior and Lord.

If Plinius illustrates anything, it is that even the wrath of man shall please God. His tenth book stands as a credible external witness to the details and descriptions inherent in the biblical manuscripts.[15] His ninety-sixth letter reads as though it emanated from the very hand of Luke himself:

> The Christians were in the habit of meeting on a certain fixed day before it was light, when they sang in alternate verses a hymn to Christ, as to a god, and bound themselves by a solemn oath, not to any wicked deeds, but never to commit any fraud, theft or adultery, never to falsify their word, nor deny a trust when they should be called upon to deliver it up; after which it was their custom to separate, and then reassemble to partake of food—but food of an ordinary and innocent kind.[16]

Plinius goes on to assert that Christianity had permeated every echelon of society, impacting male and female alike, the young as well as the old, those in the city and those in the country. Yet he confidently asserted that through intimidation and threat of death the tide of Christianity could be stemmed. In the end, he was wrong. From catastrophe and carnage would sprout the greatest civilization the world has ever known—a civilization based on the DNA of a biblical worldview.

Unreliable Sources

"Caution, you are entering the no-spin zone." Bill O'Reilly, host of *The O'Reilly Factor* on Fox News, is well known for claiming that he presents facts without spin from either the left or the right. Whether the broadcast lives up to its own standard, I leave for you to decide. One thing is certain: when engaging the case for and against external evidence buttressing biblical realities, one has definitely not entered the no-spin zone.

Fundamentalists on the left spin facts so that the gospel of Judas appears to be more credible than the gospel of John. This despite the fact that its thirteen papyrus pages are carbon-dated to the late third century.[17] Likewise, fundamentalists on the right spin reality by presenting second- and third-century documents as credible external evidence. As such, it is not uncommon to see unreliable sources like Lucian of Samosata, Toledot Yeshu, or the Babylonian Talmud listed as extrabiblical attestation for the veracity of Christ and Christianity.

Lucian of Samosata

While reading *The Passing of Peregrinus* by Lucian—the satirical story-teller of Samosata in Syria—Bill Maher flashed through my mind. Like Maher, Lucian of Samosata not only displayed utter contempt for Christ and Christianity but reveals remarkable ignorance respecting primary sources. As such, the second-century satirist contemptuously characterizes Christ as a "crucified sophist" and Christians as ignorant and easily led.[18] Born long after the Jerusalem holocaust, Lucian shows no evidence of being familiar with primary sources and is hardly a credible witness. At best he is an example of what a pagan punmeister writing long after the fact might have heard about Christ and Christianity from contemporary sources.

Toledot Yeshu

The medieval Jewish polemic Toledot Yeshu is equally suspect. In this fifth-century version of the Passover plot hypothesis, a gardener named Juda discovers the disciples' devious plan to steal the body of Jesus. Beating them to the punch, he robs Jesus' body from the tomb of Joseph and disposes of it in a freshly dug grave. He then tells the foes of Christ what he has done and offers them the body of the Savior for thirty pieces of silver. The Jewish leaders buy the cadaver and subsequently drag it through the streets of the city in evidence that Christ has not risen from the dead as he said he would. While Toledot Yeshu lends credence to the empty tomb, it is a late, fanciful story devoid of historical merit.[19]

Talmud

Like Lucian's *The Passing of Peregrinus* and the Jewish polemic Toledot Yeshu, the Mishnah and its commentary (Gemara), which together comprise the Talmud, completed by Rabbi Judah around AD 200, shows no evidence of presenting early, independent eyewitness testimony to the orations of Christ or the orthodoxy and orthopraxy of New Testament Christianity. Creative storytelling in the Talmud runs the gamut from Mary's extramarital lover to Jesus' extra-long Jewish trial. The most telling indication that the Talmud was not derived from independent eyewitness testimony is its failure to place the death of Christ in the right century.[20]

In sum, from early external evidences provided by credible historians—such as the Jewish Josephus and the Romans Tacitus, Suetonius, and Plinius—it is possible to piece together highlights of Christ and Christianity wholly apart from the internal evidences themselves. The contrast between such credible first-century external evidences and later, less-credible sources could not be starker. Tacitus is rightly regarded as the greatest first-century historian of the ancient Roman Empire, while the Talmud rarely mentions historical details surrounding second temple Judaism and, where it does, consistently muddles them.

It is simply incredible to think that Tacitus, widely considered to be the greatest first-century historian of the ancient Roman Empire, would provide credible external evidence for the biblical account of Christ's crucifixion at the hands of the Roman governor Pontius Pilate. Or that the Jewish Josephus, writing to please the Romans, would provide ancient authoritative attestation to the authenticity of the sacred text. But such is precisely the case.

The words of the hymn writer ring loud: "How firm a foundation, ye saints of the Lord, is laid for your faith in his excellent Word."[21]

6

Science of Textual Criticism

*"Like a Rock of Gibraltar embedded in a sea of manuscript copies,
the Bible is yet and forever will be an immovable bulwark fueling
our faith and shattering the waves of skepticism and doubt."*

Imagine writing a monograph on neo-terrorism and then asking five of
your closest friends to produce handwritten copies of it. Suppose each of
your friends asked five of their closest friends to produce copies of the copies. Of one thing you can be sure: your friends will make mistakes, and
so will *their* friends! Indeed, by the fifth generation, four thousand flawed
manuscript copies of *Neo-Terrorism* would exist somewhere on the planet.
Moreover, imagine that during the copying process your original monograph was discarded due to wear and tear or even destroyed.

If you informed Professor Ehrman of your problem, he would give you
no hope. He would no doubt wax eloquent concerning the conundrum
of contaminated copies due to "poor copying practices." He might even
woefully communicate that there are more mistakes in the copies than
there are words in the original *Neo-Terrorism* monograph. In the end, you
would have to resign yourself to the reality that no one would ever be able

to understand your timely message regarding terrorism in the twenty-first century.

Upon reflection, however, the clouds of doubt and despair would begin to dissipate. It would dawn on you that your five copyist friends all made mistakes, but it is unlikely that they all made the same mistakes. The same would be true of their friends and their friends' friends. Not only so, but most of the mistakes would be obvious—such as misspelled words or missed conjunctions. As such, no essential aspect of your treatise on terrorism would be tainted and even nonessential copyist errors could be resolved through the science of textual criticism.

What is true of your beloved monograph is true of the biblical manuscripts. While original writings are no longer available, we can be certain that the copies accurately reflect the intent of the original writers. The original autographs were not copied perfectly, but they were hardly copied in cavalier fashion. Thus, no essential of the biblical message is compromised, and nonessential copyist errors are easily resolved through manuscript comparisons, consideration of context, and in many cases, plain old common sense.

Indeed, that is what the science of textual criticism is all about. Textual critics compare "all known manuscripts of a given work in an effort to trace the history of variations within the text so as to discover its original form."[1] The beauty from a biblical perspective is that the wealth of biblical manuscripts empowers textual critics to credibly ferret out copyist errors and allow the autographs to emerge. This is precisely what scholars mean when they speak of the tenacity of the text. As Dr. James White explains, "Once a variant reading appears in a manuscript, *it doesn't simply go away*. It gets copied and ends up in other manuscripts."[2] This is transcendently significant in that variant readings of the text never disappear from the textual record. Therefore, though the autograph is not encased in the Basilica of St. Peter or under glass in the University of North Carolina, Chapel Hill, it is forever memorialized within a veritable mountain of manuscripts. Says Dr. White, "The tenacity of the New Testament text, while forcing us to deal with textual variants, also provides the assurance that our work is not in vain. One of those variant readings is indeed the original. We are called to invest our energies in discovering which one it is."[3]

The fact that no two handwritten copies of the biblical text are identical is hardly the problem. Indeed, if we found a hundred manuscripts that were actually identical, we would know that something was seriously amiss! The real problem involves unwarranted assumptions. Fundamentalists on the right suppose that, like the autographs, the King James Version is wholly infallible and inerrant. Dr. Peter Ruckman of the Pensacola Bible Institute considers the King James Version itself to be the quintessential autograph. From his perspective, even the "mistakes in the A.V. 1611 are advanced revelation."[4]

The assumptions of fundamentalists on the left are equally benighted. As noted, Dr. Bart Ehrman assumes inerrancy involves presenting even secondary details of the biblical narratives with word-for-word exactness—it is not enough for gospel writers to capture *the essential voice of Jesus*; he demands they necessarily capture *the exact verbiage of Jesus*. This, of course, is wrongheaded thinking. The King James Version is not an "advanced" infallible revelation, nor were the gospel writers preprogrammed automatons. Moved by the Spirit, they codified *the essential wisdom of Jesus*, not always the *exact words of Jesus*.

Incredibly, even when fundamentalists are right they are wrong. They are right to reveal that "there are more differences among our manuscripts than there are words in the New Testament."[5] But wrong to conceal that the vast majority of such differences are insignificant. *Not one is a game-changer.* Even the most unwarranted of variants do not adversely affect essential Christian doctrine. As Dr. Philip Schaff has well said, of the 1 percent of variants that matter, not one affects "an article of faith or a precept of duty which is not abundantly sustained by other and undoubted passages."[6] Similarly, Dr. A. T. Robertson notes that variants of concern are but a "thousandth part of the entire text."[7] Perhaps Dr. White said it best: "The reality is that the amount of variation between the two most extremely different New Testament manuscripts would not fundamentally alter the message of the Scriptures!"[8]

That, of course, is not to undermine the significance of the science of textual criticism. In the process of textual analysis, noteworthy alterations have come to light. Foremost among them is the Comma Johanneum, which adds the following italicized words to 1 John 5:7–8: "For there are three that bear record *in heaven: the Father, the Word, and the Holy Spirit; and these three are one. And there are three that bear witness on earth*: the Spirit, the water, and the blood; and these three agree as one" (KJV).

Though *manifestly orthodox*, the Comma (clause) is clearly not part of John's original epistle. It occurs in the margins of a half dozen or so manuscripts, all of which are late. In the words of the venerable Greek scholar Bruce Metzger: "The passage is quoted by none of the Greek Fathers, who, had they known it would most certainly have employed it in the Trinitarian controversies (Sabellian and Arian). Its first appearance in Greek is in a Greek version of the (Latin) Acts of the Lateran Council in 1215."[9] As documented by textual critics, this gloss (interpolation) was first inserted in the margins of several Latin manuscripts and finally incorporated into the text by a copyist.

The story of how the Comma Johanneum (aka the "three witnesses") was imported into the biblical text is as interesting as it is instructive. In 1516, Desiderius Erasmus of Rotterdam, the most influential humanist of the Northern Renaissance, published the very first printed edition of the Greek New Testament. His translation, which became the primary source for the King James Bible, challenged Saint Jerome's Vulgate—a translation that had stood the test of time for a thousand years. The Vulgate included the Comma. Erasmus did not. Why? "I find only this about the threefold testimony," said Erasmus, "Spirit, water, and blood."[10]

Under extreme pressure, however, Erasmus relented. Thus, in the third edition he added the "three witnesses" to the text "so as not to give anyone an occasion for slander."[11] While the Comma continues on in King James tradition, most modern translations appropriately omit it.

Another significant variant brought to light through the science of textual criticism involves the final line of the most majestic of all prayers. In its King James rendering, it is as spectacular as it is symmetrical:

> Our Father which art in heaven,
> Hallowed be thy name.
> Thy kingdom come,

> Thy will be done in earth, as it is in heaven.
> Give us this day our daily bread.
> And forgive us our debts, as we forgive our debtors.
> And lead us not into temptation, but deliver us from evil:
> *For thine is the kingdom, and the power, and the glory, for ever. Amen.*
> (Matthew 6:9–13 KJV, italics added)

Problem is, while the ascription (in italics) adds symmetry, it is textually unsustainable. As the science of textual criticism makes clear, the concluding line was added by a copyist somewhere between the late first century and early second century. Dr. Bruce Metzger explains: "The absence of any ascription in early and important representatives of the Alexandrian, the Western, and the pre-Caesarean types of text, as well as early patristic commentaries on the Lord's Prayer (those of Tertullian, Origen, Cyprian), suggests that an ascription, usually in the threefold form, was composed (perhaps on the basis of 1 Chronicles 29:1–13) in order to adapt the Prayer for liturgical use in the early church."[12]

As with the Comma Johanneum, the King James Version rendering of the Lord's Prayer is thoroughly biblical but textually bogus. Early on in Christian history, a variation of 1 Chronicles 29:11 was added to recitations of the model prayer. Over time this liturgical variation was ingrained through recitation and quite naturally incorporated by a copyist as part and parcel of the prayer. While skeptics such as Ehrman beat their fundamentalist chests over such ascriptions, neither the deity of Jesus nor the divine origins of the Bible are affected by their inclusion.

One final example of a significant textual variant uncovered through the science of textual criticism should suffice. It involves the riveting story of a woman caught in the act of adultery:

But Jesus went to the Mount of Olives. At dawn he appeared again in the temple courts, where all the people gathered around him, and he sat down to teach them. The teachers of the law and the Pharisees brought in a woman caught in adultery. They made her stand before the group and said to Jesus, "Teacher, this woman was caught in the act of adultery. In the Law Moses commanded us to stone such women. Now what do you say?" They were using this question as a trap, in order to have a basis for accusing him.

But Jesus bent down and started to write on the ground with his finger. When they kept on questioning him, he straightened up and said to them, "If any one of you is without sin, let him be the first to throw a stone at her." Again he stooped down and wrote on the ground.

At this, those who heard began to go away one at a time, the older ones first, until only Jesus was left, with the woman still standing there. Jesus straightened up and asked her, "Woman, where are they? Has no one condemned you?"

"No one, sir," she said.

"Then neither do I condemn you," Jesus declared. "Go now and leave your life of sin." (John 8:1–11)

As with previous examples, this passage is not found in the oldest and most reliable manuscripts as is clearly noted in virtually all modern translations of the Bible. Nonetheless, Ehrman characterizes this insertion as both an "enormous" textual problem and an "enormous" theological problem. Says Ehrman, did Jesus "really think that the Law of God given by Moses was no longer in force and should not be obeyed: Did he think sins should not be punished at all?"[13]

Of course, in context, Jesus hardly abrogates the law of Moses. Instead, he says, "If any one of you is without sin, let him be the first to throw a stone at her" (John 8:7). Nor does he think that sin should go unpunished. Indeed, the central message of Scripture is that Jesus both forgives and bears the punishment of sin.

As the story of the woman caught in adultery is theologically defensible, so, too, it is historically defensible. Biblical scholar Merrill Tenney aptly notes, "Its coherence and spirit show that it was preserved from a very early time, and it accords well with the known character of Jesus."[14] Dr. Craig Blomberg is equally emphatic: "Whereas the story of the woman caught in adultery is not at all likely to have been in the original Gospel of John, a good case can be made that it preserves an account of something Jesus actually did. It fits Jesus' nature, teaching, and ministry, and may well have been handed down by word of mouth until some scribe copying the gospel decided it was too good to leave out."[15]

In the end, we can be deeply grateful for the practices of *copyists* who fulfilled their task with meticulous zeal and reverential awe; for an *oral culture in* which saints disciplined and dedicated themselves to recall the sayings of understanding, and in which sages were predisposed to present their sayings in inherently memorable fashion; for the sheer volume of *papyri and parchments* dwarfing those of any other work in classical history; for the eyewitness testimony of those willing to shed their blood for the great truths they communicated; for the elegant tapestry that serves as enduring *internal evidence* for the divine authorship of the biblical text; for ancient authoritative *external evidences* that testify to the authenticity of the Bible; and for the *science of textual criticism* by which the autographs emerge from the mountain of manuscript evidence. Like a Rock of Gibraltar embedded in a sea of manuscript copies, the Bible is yet and forever will be an immovable bulwark fueling our faith and shattering the waves of skepticism and doubt. As the acronym C-O-P-I-E-S reminds us, God has spoken and the Bible is the infallible repository of what he has said.

Memorable Snapshots

*C*opyist Practices

In demonstrating that extant manuscript copies faithfully preserve the words of the autographs, we first looked at *copyists*, who, constrained by the command "Do not add to it or take away from it" (Deuteronomy 12:32), fulfilled their task with meticulous zeal. Unlike preprogrammed automatons, however, they were subject to all the frailties that are part and parcel of the human condition. As such, the copies they produced were good but hardly perfect. Indeed, it is outrageous to suppose that any fallible human being, no matter how disciplined and dedicated, could avoid minor mistakes such as misspelling names or misstating numbers.

Oral Culture

We are primarily people of the printed page. Not so the ancients. In a predominately oral society, learning was virtually synonymous with memorization. Not only were saints required to discipline and dedicate themselves to recall the sayings of understanding, but sages were predisposed to present their sayings in an inherently memorable fashion. Jesus' sermons and sayings are presented with repetition, rhythm, and rhyme. In like fashion, his disciples employed vibrant associations, vivid imagery, and visual/emotive stimuli, so that their hearers might not only hear but remember.

Papyrus and Parchment

The sheer volume of papyrus and parchment undergirding sacred Scripture dwarf that of any other work in classical history. In excess of 5,660 manuscripts of the New Testament have now been uncovered. Not only is there a relatively short time interval between the earliest papyrus and parchment copies of the New Testament and their autographs, but there is less than a generation between the autographs and the events they chronicle. The quantity and quality of papyrus and parchment manuscripts assure us that the message and intent of the original autographs has been passed on to the present generation without compromise.

Internal Evidence

Peter reminds hearers, "We did *not* follow cleverly invented stories when we told you about the power and coming of our Lord Jesus Christ, but we were eyewitnesses of his majesty" (2 Peter 1:16). Luke says he gathered eyewitness testimony and "carefully investigated everything" (Luke 1:1–4). If internal evidence points to anything, it is to the reality that the gospel writers were inspired to faithfully narrate a core set of facts by which they had been radically transformed. While it is conceivable that they would have faced torture, vilification, and even cruel deaths for what they fervently believed to be true, it is inconceivable that they would have been willing to die for cleverly invented stories they knew to be lies.

External Evidence

Internal evidence is sufficient to establish the biblical manuscripts as authentic, reliable, and complementary. *External* evidence, however, provides remarkable corroborating attestation. From early external evidence provided by credible historians such as the Jewish Josephus and the Roman Tacitus, Suetonius, and Plinius, it is possible to piece together highlights of Christ and New Testament Christianity wholly apart from the internal evidence itself. Josephus, for example, was born in AD 37 and as such was an eyewitness to many of the details and descriptions found in the New Testament. The most noteworthy reference to Jesus appears in *Antiquities* 18:63, where Josephus comments on Jesus' character, crucifixion, and resurrection.

Science of Textual Criticism

Not only are the details and descriptions encountered in our journey through the biblical text buttressed by credible external evidences, but by way of a science known as *textual criticism*, we can be absolutely certain that the biblical text authentically recapitulates the words of the original writers. Indeed, that is precisely what textual critics do. They compare known manuscripts in an effort to trace the history of variations so as to discover the authentic wording of the autographs. The beauty from a biblical perspective is that the wealth of biblical manuscripts empowers textual critics to credibly sort out copyist errors so that the autograph can emerge. As demonstrated, we can be certain that no essential of the biblical message has been compromised, and nonessential copyist errors are resolved through manuscript comparisons, consideration of context, and plain old common sense.

Archaeologist's
S-P-A-D-E

Steles and Stones

Pools and Fools

Assyrian Archaeology

Dead Sea Scrolls

Epic of Gilgamesh

If we abide by the principles taught in the Bible, our country will go
on prospering and to prosper; but if we and our posterity neglect its
instructions and authority, no man can tell how sudden a catastrophe
may overwhelm us and bury all our glory in profound obscurity.

—DANIEL WEBSTER

Open the Book of Mormon, and the first words you will encounter are these: "The Book of Mormon is a volume of holy scripture comparable to the Bible. It is a record of God's dealings with the ancient inhabitants of the Americas and contains, as does the Bible, the fullness of the everlasting gospel."[1]

The Book of Mormon is the record of two great civilizations. The first, Jaredites, left the Tower of Babel and immigrated to the Americas twenty-two hundred years before Christ. The second migrated from Jerusalem around 600 BC and divided into two great nations: Nephites and Lamanites. The Lamanites were "white, and exceedingly fair and delightsome." However, due to sin, "the Lord God did cause a skin of blackness to come upon them" (2 Nephi 5:21). They became "the principal ancestors of the American Indians."[2]

The lone Nephite survivor in the final battle (AD 421) with their Lamanite enemies was a mighty military commander named Moroni. Along with his father, Mormon, Moroni inscribed the "most correct of any book on earth"[3] in reformed Egyptian hieroglyphics and buried it in the hill Cumorah. After being resurrected as an angel, Moroni "appeared to the Prophet Joseph Smith [1823] and instructed him relative to the ancient record and its destined translation into the English language."[4] In due course, Smith found golden plates along with a pair of magical eyeglasses that he used to translate the Egyptian into English. The result was a new revelation called the Book of Mormon, which chronicles "the personal ministry of the Lord Jesus Christ among the Nephites soon after His resurrection. It puts forth the doctrines of the gospel, outlines the plan of salvation, and tells men what they must do to gain peace in this life and eternal salvation in the life to come."[5]

But there's a problem: No archaeological evidence for a language such as "reformed Egyptian" hieroglyphics.[6] No archaeological evidence for the great civilizations chronicled in the Book of Mormon. No archaeological evidence for such lands as the "land of Moron" described in Ether 7:6. No anthropological evidence that the Nephites and Lamanites migrated from Jerusalem to Mesoamerica. Indeed, both archaeology and anthropology militate against the people, places, and particulars that are part and parcel of the Book of Mormon and demonstrate conclusively that the book is little more than the product of a fertile and enterprising imagination.

Like the Book of Mormon, the Bible has been roundly denounced as a cleverly invented story. Unlike the Book of Mormon, however, the Bible is buttressed by history and evidence. While the archaeologist's spade continues to mount up evidence against the Book of Mormon, it has piled up proof upon proof for the people, places, and particulars inscribed on the parchment and papyrus of biblical manuscripts.

Case in point: Like Nephites, the Hittites—from whom Abraham purchased a burial plot for his wife, Sarah—have long been rendered the stuff of myths and fables. "In 1906, however, archaeologists digging east of Ankara, Turkey, discovered the ruins of Hattusas, the ancient Hittite capital at what is today called Boghazkoy, as well as its vast collection of Hittite historical records, which showed an empire flourishing in the mid-second millennium BC."[7]

Time and time again, comprehensive archaeological fieldwork has affirmed the reliability of the Bible. It is telling when secular scholars must revise their biblical criticism in light of solid archaeological evidence. As noted, one of the most well-known New Testament examples concerns the books of Luke and Acts. Sir William Ramsay, a biblical skeptic trained as an archaeologist, set out to disprove the historical reliability of this portion of the New Testament. But through his painstaking Mediterranean archaeological trips, he became converted as, one after another, the historical allusions of Luke were proved accurate.[8]

Recently, archaeologists discovered a reservoir of archaeological nuggets that provide a powerful counter to objections raised by scholars against the biblical account of Christ's crucifixion and burial. In *U.S. News and World Report*, Jeffrey Sheler highlights the significance of the recent discovery of the remains of a man crucified during the first century—a discovery that calls into question the scholarship of liberals who contend Jesus was tied rather than nailed to the cross and that his corpse was likely thrown into a shallow grave and eaten by wild dogs that roamed the execution grounds:

> Explorers found the skeletal remains of a crucified man in a burial cave at Giva'at ha-Mitvar, near the Nablus road outside of Jerusalem. It was a momentous discovery: While the Romans were known to have crucified thousands of alleged traitors, rebels, robbers, and deserters in the two centuries straddling the turn of the era, never before had the remains of a crucifixion victim been recovered. An initial analysis of the remains found that their condition dramatically corroborated the Bible's description of the Roman method of execution.
>
> The bones were preserved in a stone burial box called an ossuary and appeared to be those of a man about 5 feet, 5 inches tall and 24 to 28 years old. His open arms had been nailed to the crossbar, in the manner similar to that shown in crucifixion paintings. The knees had been doubled up and turned sideways, and a single large iron nail had been driven through both heels. The nail—still lodged in the heel bone of one foot, though the executioners had removed the body from the cross after death—was found bent, apparently having hit a knot in the wood. The shin bones seem to have been broken, corroborating what the Gospel of John suggests was normal practice in Roman crucifixions.[9]

Recent finds have also corroborated biblical details surrounding the trial that led to the fatal torment of Jesus Christ—including the burial grounds of Caiaphas, the high priest who presided over the religious trials of Christ. In 1990 a burial chamber dating back to the first century was discovered two miles south of Temple Mount. "Inside the chamber, archaeologists found twelve limestone ossuaries. One of the boxes, elaborately decorated with six-petaled rosettes, contained the bones of a sixty-year-old man and bore the inscription *Yehosef bar Qayafa*—'Joseph, son of Caiaphas.'"[10]

The archaeologist's S-P-A-D-E continues to accumulate evidence for the trustworthiness of Scripture and is an apt acronym for remembering that what is discovered in the soil corresponds to what is detailed in the Scriptures. We begin with the *S*, which will remind you of *steles and stones* that cry out.

7

Steles and Stones

God writes with a pen that never blots, speaks with a tongue
that never slips, acts with a hand that never fails.

—CHARLES HADDON SPURGEON

It was the most important week in history. As Jesus rode into Jerusalem, the crowds cried out, "Blessed is the king who comes in the name of the Lord!" (Luke 19:38). But Jesus knew their cries to be empty. In a few days' time, they would cry out again. This time, "Crucify him! Crucify him! We have no king but Caesar" (Matthew 27:22–23; cf. John 19:15). The Pharisees demanded that Jesus rebuke the crowds. But Jesus replied, "If they keep quiet, the stones will cry out" (Luke 19:40).

Jesus knew full well what was coming. "The days will come upon you when your enemies will build an embankment against you and encircle you and hem you in on every side," he said. "They will dash you to the ground, you and the children within your walls. They will not leave one stone on another, because you did not recognize the time of God's coming to you" (19:43–44).

Two thousand years hence, with our own eyes, we can still see the horrifying fulfillment of those words. A temple that had given the Jews their theological and sociological significance, destroyed, never to be rebuilt again. "Not one stone here," Jesus had cried out, "will be left on another; every one will be thrown down" (Matthew 24:2).

As stones of the ancient temple cry out, so, too, the steles and stones of ancient times. The Merneptah and Dan Steles immediately come to mind. As do the Moabite and Pilate Stones. Together, the inscriptions of these ancient monuments cry forth the words: *"God has spoken!"*

THE MERNEPTAH STELE

The most virulent attacks on the historicity of the Bible are often reserved for the Exodus. In 2005 the Exodus was singled out by a gathering of biblical minimalists in Rome and summarily dismissed with three words: "It never happened."[1] In *A History of Ancient Israel and Judah*, J. Maxwell Miller and John H. Hayes render the Exodus "an artificial and theologically influenced literary construct."[2] In lockstep, Thomas L. Thompson (*The Mythic Past: Biblical Archaeology and the Myth of Israel*) judges Israel and the Exodus "a theological and literary creation."[3] University of Sheffield's Philip Davies is of the same mind. "Most Biblical scholars accept that there was no historical counterpart to this epoch and most intelligent biblical archaeologists accept this too."[4]

Brilliant Jewish Old Testament expert Professor Nahum Sarna is of a completely different mind. In his esteemed judgment, "no nation would be likely to invent for itself, and faithfully transmit century after century and millennium after millennium, such an inglorious and inconvenient tradition unless it had an authentic historical core."[5] Sir Alan Gardiner, no doubt the greatest Egyptologist of the twentieth century, was similarly persuaded: "That Israel was in Egypt under one form or another no historian could possibly doubt; a legend of such tenacity representing the early fortunes of a peoples under so unfavorable an aspect could not have arisen save as a reflexion, however much distorted, of real occurrences."[6]

It is as unlikely that Jews invented the Exodus as it is that they invented the Holocaust. Indeed, as it turns out, archaeology provides a wholly plausible framework for Jewish contentions regarding their slavery and emancipation. First is the Exodus account of Egyptian slave masters using the children of Israel as forced labor in producing "mud bricks." Archaeologists have uncovered a tomb schematic showing Semitic slaves making mud bricks at the Egyptian city of Thebes on the Nile.[7] Likewise, a well-known inscription at the private tomb of Rekhmire, the highest-ranking official under pharaohs Tuthmosis III and Amenophis II, depicts slaves making mud bricks during the construction of the Karnak Temple Complex.[8] Egyptian-born professor of Old Testament and Ancient Near Eastern history and archaeology James Hoffmeier aptly points out that "the practice of using forced labor for building projects is only documented for the period 1450 to 1200, the very time most biblical historians place the Israelites in Egypt."[9]

Furthermore, the "mixed multitude" described being liberated from Egypt in Exodus 12 accords well with the archaeological record. A line in an Egyptian document dubbed Leiden Papyrus 348 contains a directive that food be distributed to "the Apiru" dragging materials to a great pylon.[10] Dr. Frank Moore Cross, professor of Hebrew and other Oriental languages at Harvard, points out that *"Apiru* is the origin of the term Hebrew."[11] As such, Papyrus 348 seems to provide contextual evidence for a mixed multitude of Semitic people who are described as being liberated from bondage in Exodus 12:38.

Finally, the very name *Moses* provides corroborating evidence for the biblical account of the Exodus. Etymologically, the name *Moses* is rooted in Egyptian tradition and fits well with the Exodus era. As journalist Jeffrey Sheler explains, "The name is derived from the Egyptian *mose* ('is born'), a term that often was combined—sometimes in modified form—with the name of a deity, as in the names of the pharaohs Thut*mose* ('Thoth is born') and Ra*meses* ('Ra is born'). Some scholars theorize that in the earliest traditions, Moses' name also may have been linked with a deity. Or it simply may have stood alone in its original form as if to signify the one who gave birth to Israel as a covenant nation."[12]

While the *mud bricks*, *mixed multitude*, and name *Moses* provide a wholly plausible framework for the Exodus, an archaeological discovery known as the *Merneptah Stele* presents a positively formidable challenge to Exodus deniers. The stele—a seven-and-one-half-foot-tall black granite stone slab inscribed in Egyptian hieroglyphics—boasts of the military conquests of Pharaoh Merneptah, son of Rameses II. He is hailed "The victorious ruler!" "Exalted!" "King among the gods!" "Merneptah has subdued all," says the stele—"Ashkelon . . . Gezer . . . Yanoam." The penultimate line boasts: "Israel is wasted, bare of seed"—a metaphor implying that Israel's store of grain was destroyed and they no longer posed a military threat. The significance of this archaeological discovery is dramatic.

First, the Merneptah Stele (variously known as the Israelite Stele) is the earliest reference to Israel in extrabiblical sources and quite literally explodes the "myth of Israel" contention of doubting Thomases such as the aforementioned Thompson.[13] In light of modern archaeological discoveries, there is no longer warrant—apart from extreme prejudice—for suggesting that the people of Israel, including her proud patriarchs, prophets, and potentates, are the mere stuff of myths and fables. Extant evidence shouts to the contrary. And, no doubt, the archaeologist's spade will again break a momentary silence.

Furthermore, the Merneptah Stele qualifies *Israel* with an Egyptian hieroglyphic determinative. While *Ashkelon*, *Gezer*, and *Yanoam* are contextually qualified with hieroglyphic determinatives that recognize them as established city-states (a throw stick plus three mountains), *Israel* is qualified with the hieroglyphic determinative for a less politically established people group (a throw stick plus a man and a woman over three vertical lines).[14] This, of course, comports perfectly with the biblical text. Pharaoh Merneptah's northern military campaigns (1237–1227 BC) took place during the time of the Jewish judges.[15] "In those days," says Samuel, "there was no king in Israel; every man did what was right in his own eyes" (Judges 17:6 NASB).

Finally, the Merneptah Stele, inscribed shortly before 1200 BC, demonstrates that as of 1230 BC Israel was already in the land of promise as a significant socioethnic entity meriting the attention of the mighty Merneptah.[16] Professor Sir William Matthew Flinders Petrie, an English Egyptologist who held the first chair of Egyptology in the United Kingdom, knew full well the archaeological significance of the Merneptah Stele. "This stele," he said, "will be better known in the world than anything else I have found."[17]

TEL DAN STELE

Unearthing of the Merneptah Stele was to the late nineteenth century what unearthing the Tel Dan Stele was to the late twentieth century: a demonstration in spades that what is found in the soil corresponds to that which is found in Scripture. In recent years, skeptics have bloviated to the contrary. Not only was there no Exodus, they say, but David, the archetypal king of Israel, was either an imaginative falsehood or an inept freebooter whose reach scarcely extended beyond his own nose. Journalist Daniel Lazare asserts as much in a *Harper's* article titled "False Testament: Archaeology Refutes the Bible's Claim to History":

> Archaeologists believe that David was not a mighty potentate whose power was felt from the Nile to the Euphrates but rather a freebooter who carved out what was at most a small duchy in the southern highlands around Jerusalem and Hebron. Indeed, the chief disagreement among scholars nowadays is between those who hold that David was a petty hilltop chieftain whose writ extended no more than a few miles in any direction and a small but vociferous band of "biblical minimalists" who maintain that he never existed at all.[18]

For Thomas Thompson, professor of theology at the University of Copenhagen, there is little room for debate. The biblical accounts of King David, he pontificates, "are no more factual than the tales of King Arthur."[19] The problem with such dogmatism is that it is largely founded on an argument from silence. The archaeological record had not as yet spoken; therefore, it was presumed that King David did not exist. Problems with such fanaticism abound. First, as Egyptologist Kenneth Kitchens has well said, absence of evidence is not evidence of absence.[20] Furthermore, the divine Christ, a far greater authority than Professor Thompson, referred to David as a significant historical figure (Matthew 12:1–8; 22:41–46). And, above all, the archaeological record is anything but silent.

Indeed, in 1993, the stones cried out from the past. The headline of the August 6 *New York Times* flashed: "News of House of David." The first sentence summed up the essence of a scintillating story. "An Israeli archaeologist has discovered a fragment of a stone monument with inscriptions bearing the first known reference outside the Bible to King David and the ruling dynasty he founded, the House of David."[21] Dr. Avraham Biram, head of the Institute for Archaeology at Hebrew Union College in Jerusalem, knew immediately that he and his archaeological team had unearthed an extraordinarily significant historical artifact. In the previous three decades he had discovered a host of significant treasures—including discovery of an inscription identifying the site of his archaeological labors as the biblical city Dan—but nothing to compare with this.[22]

As *Time* magazine rightly observed, "The skeptics' claim that King David never existed is now hard to defend."[23] Biram's discovery—identified as part of a shattered stele commemorating a military victory by Ben-Hadad, king of Damascus, over the king of Israel and House of David—was a bolt from the blue, devastating the "Pope-like confidence" of biblical nihilists who had long rendered David and his dynasty the stuff of myths and fables.[24]

In addition to shattering the sensationalism of David deniers, the Dan Stele devastated the sophistry of biblical minimalists who had relegated the quintessential king of Israel a "petty hilltop chieftain" of a "small duchy in the southern highlands of Jerusalem." As revealed by Dr. Biram, "Periods separate each word in the text, except for the two words for House of David. It was as if to emphasize the special status of the expression and thus to indicate the prominence of the dynasty in the political affairs of the day."[25]

Jeffery Sheler, author of *Is the Bible True?*, notes a variety of arguments biblical skeptics continue to raise respecting the veracity of the Dan Stele. One prominent skeptic argued that the stele "referred not to David or his dynasty but to the house of dod—probably a Canaanite god, although no one had ever heard of one by that name. Or perhaps it was intended to signify a place rather than a person or a dynasty—a place that was inscrutably named house of beloved, or house of uncle, or even house of kettle. A few even suggested, without offering a shred of evidence, that the inscriptions were modern forgeries that had been planted at the Dan site."[26]

Such sophistry has done little to tarnish the significance of the Dan Stele. In 1994 two more chunks of black basalt stone were excavated. Together with the original Dan Stele they add testimony to the house and lineage of David. In the past, the spade underscored the painstaking accuracy of Luke's historical allusions in his gospel and the Acts of the Apostles—allusions that led to the conversion of no less an ardent skeptic than Sir William Ramsay.[27] In the present, the spade adds credence to Dr. Luke's assertion that Jesus "was of the house and lineage of David" (Luke 2:4 KJV).

And still the stones cry out . . .

THE MOABITE STONE

Our Lord, Dr. Luke, and the 1993 discovery of the Dan Stele are not alone in testifying to the house and lineage of David. Shortly after the Dan Stele was discovered, the stones cried out again. In 1994, French scholar André Lemaire reported the results of an exhaustive seven-year study of the Moabite Stone housed in the Louvre museum in Paris. In line 31 he identified a previously indiscernible letter as the D in the moniker "House of David." As noted by Lemaire, "The missing part of the inscription described how Mesha also threw off the yoke of Judah and conquered the territory southeast of the Dead Sea controlled by the House of David."[28] Thus, a year after the Dan Stele was unearthed; a second ninth-century reference to the Davidic dynasty was unveiled.

Discovered August 19, 1868, in Dhiban, Jordan, twenty miles east of the Dead Sea, the Moabite Stone is one of the most significant archaeological discoveries in the sands of the Middle East. The Moabite victory monument consisting of thirty-four lines memorializes repression of the Moabites under "Omri King of Israel" and revolt under Mesha King of Moab.[29] The significance of Mesha's memorial, inscribed on a stone slab three feet high and two feet wide, would be difficult to overstate. In addition to its stunning reference to the House of David, the Moabite Stone corroborates details and descriptions encapsulated in the sacred text of Scripture.

To begin with, in concert with Scripture, the Moabite Stone makes mention of King Omri, one of the most significant kings of the Northern Kingdom. Omri is best known for purchasing the hill of Samaria, building a city on the site, and making it capital of the Northern Kingdom (1 Kings 16:24). Omri was infamous not only for the worship of worthless idols but for fathering the wicked Ahab, who "did more evil in the eyes of the Lord than any of those before him" (1 Kings 16:30). In concert with Scripture, lines 4 and 5 of the Moabite Stone recognize Omri's kingship and reference its chief god: "As for King Omri of Israel, he humbled Moab many years, for Chemosh was angry at his land."[30]

Furthermore, in line 14, Mesha boasts that Chemosh—chief god of the Moabites, in whose honor the Moabite Stone was erected—directed him to attack the town of Nebo originally captured by the tribe of Reuben (Numbers 32:3). This Moabite reference validates one of the most significant sites in all of sacred Scripture. Mount Nebo was not only the site from which the Lord showed Moses "the land I promised on oath to Abraham, Isaac and Jacob" (Deuteronomy 34:4) but the very place in Moab where Moses died and was buried (34:5–6).

Finally, lines 17 and 18 chronicle the earliest known extrabiblical reference to Yahweh, God of Israel.[31] Included in the spoils of Mesha's capture of Nebo were *the altar-hearths of Yahweh*. As such, Mesha boasts, "I took the vessels of YHWH and I dragged them before Chemosh." This, the earliest known extrabiblical reference to Yahweh, also makes mention of the pagan deity Chemosh. Apart from this archaeological discovery, obscurantists might well have continued in their contention that Chemosh is the stuff of biblical myths and fables. The Moabite Stone, however, has left no doubt of the Bible's correctness in chronicling Yahweh the "Creator of heaven and earth" (Genesis 14:19) and "Chemosh the vile god of Moab" (2 Kings 23:13).

Prior to discovery of the Moabite Stone, the reality of kings such as Omri and Mesha and places such as Nebo and Moab might yet be distained as fictional. The stones, however, cry fact!

THE PILATE STONE

Archaeology confirms not only the people and the places of the Bible, but even its particulars. Such is the case with the Pilate Stone. Excavations at the ruins of an ancient Herodian theater at Caesarea—the Roman capital of Judea—uncovered a first-century inscription confirming Pilate as the Roman governor during the epoch in which Jesus Christ was tried and crucified.

Italian archaeologists excavating the theater at Maritima uncovered a two-by-three-foot limestone block bearing the Latin inscription *Tiberieum . . . [Pon]tius Pilatus . . . [praef]ectus Juda[ea]e.* Dr. Paul Maier, eminent professor of ancient history at Western Michigan University, renders the complete inscription as follows: *"Pontius Pilatus, Prefect of Judea, has presented the Tiberieum to the Caesareans."*[32] The archaeological discovery of the Pilate Stone is a momentous confirmation of biblical particulars for at least three reasons.

First, the Pilate Stone corroborates the biblical assertion that Pilate was the Roman authority in Judea at the time that Christ was crucified. Thus, the gospel writer Mark is proved right in asserting that the chief priests, with the elders, the teachers of the law and the whole Sanhedrin "bound Jesus, led him away and handed him over to Pilate" (Mark 15:1). Likewise, the apostle John is correct in stating that "the Jews led Jesus from Caiaphas to the palace of [Pilate] the Roman governor" (John 18:28).

Furthermore, the Pilate Stone confirms the minute accuracy of Dr. Luke in asserting that Pilate ruled Judea during the reign of Tiberius Caesar when Herod was tetrarch of Galilee and Caiaphas followed Annas as high priest in Jerusalem: "In the fifteenth year of the reign of Tiberius Caesar— when Pontius Pilate was governor of Judea, Herod tetrarch of Galilee, his brother Philip tetrarch of Iturea and Traconitis, and Lysanias tetrarch of Abilene—during the high priesthood of Annas and Caiaphas, the word of God came to John son of Zechariah in the desert" (Luke 3:1–2). Moreover, as previously noted, the 1990 discovery of a burial chamber dating back to the first century validates the biblical assertion that Caiaphas was the high priest who presided over the religious trials of Christ.

Finally, the Pilate Stone confirms the particular that Pilate was *prefect* of Judea. As such, the Greek word rendered *governor* (Luke 3:1) is an accurate facsimile of the Latin word rendered *prefect*.[33] As aptly noted by Sheler, "Discovery of the so-called Pilate Stone has been widely acclaimed as a truly significant affirmation of biblical history. Although the writings of Josephus and Philo late in the first century have also attested to the existence of Pilate as procurator of Judea between 26 and 36 C.E.,[34] this is the first contemporary witness, and the only lithic inscription that bears his name and title." Sheler goes on to say, "It is now confirmed by non-biblical evidence that the man depicted in the gospels as Judea's Roman governor had precisely the responsibilities and authority that the gospel writers ascribed to him." Thus, concludes Sheler, "The evidence suggests that the gospel writers were thoroughly familiar with the form and function of the governmental structure in place at the time of the events they described."[35]

8

$\mathcal{P}$ools and Fools

There is a time for everything,
and a season for every activity under heaven: . . .
a time to be silent and a time to speak,
a time to love and a time to hate,
a time for war and a time for peace.

—Solomon

When I read the title of Bart Ehrman's latest offering, the words of Solomon flashed through my mind in neon. "There is a time for everything, and a season for every activity under heaven" (Ecclesiastes 3:1). "A time to be silent and a time to speak" (3:7). "A time for war and a time for peace" (3:8). A time "to answer a fool according to his folly" and a time to refrain from doing so (Proverbs 26:4–5).

The "shock doc" was at it again. This time the decibel level raised to new heights. The cover quite literally shrieks forth the word *Forged*. The contents, too, shout loudly. "I came to realize," writes Bart Ehrman, "that the Bible not only contains untruths or accidental mistakes. It also contains what almost anyone today would call lies. That is what this book is about."[1] And Ehrman has just begun sharpening his rhetoric. "The apostles," he intones, "could not have left an authoritative writing if their souls depended on it."[2]

Instead, their gospels were "forged" by "highly educated, Greek-speaking Christians who probably lived outside Palestine."[3] Worse yet, according to Ehrman, is that whoever "forged" the gospel of John was virulently "anti-Jewish."[4] And should that prove insufficient to gain attention, he piles on with the accusation that the "forgeries" were written long after the time of Christ. "By the time John was written, probably from 90 to 95 CE, that earlier generation had died out and most if not all the disciples were already dead."[5]

Reason and evidence prove precisely the opposite. The gospel of John was hardly written pseudonymously. Virtually all ancient, external evidences point to John, son of Zebedee, as the author of the fourth gospel.[6] Nor was John an illiterate. Following the resurrection of the Master Teacher, there is every indication that he devoted himself to the study and ministry of the Word of God (Acts 6:2). If Paul admonished Timothy to study to show himself approved, "a workman who does not need to be ashamed and who correctly handles the word of truth" (2 Timothy 2:15), how much more would an original apostle have devoted himself to that very thing?[7]

At the risk of precipitously answering a fool according to his folly, let me hasten to reiterate that John was hardly anti-Jewish. Contra Ehrman, the gospel of John explicitly tells us that the Romans crucified Christ.[8] Nor were the Gospels written late. As argued previously, eminent New Testament scholars, including the liberal John A. T. Robinson, author of *Redating the New Testament*, have been compelled by reason and evidence to rethink late-dating paradigms.[9]

Truth is, the gospels were not "forged." As proven through archaeology, the gospel of John provides ample internal evidence that it was written by an author who was intimately acquainted with the locations and events he recorded, not someone writing under a pseudonym hundreds of years later. As I have previously pointed out, John correctly describes changes in elevation between Cana in Galilee, Capernaum, and Jerusalem (2:11–13). He accurately depicts two Bethanys—one less than two miles from Jerusalem on the road to Jericho where Mary, Martha, and Lazarus lived (John 11:18); the other beyond the Jordan River, which only an ancient Palestinian could have identified (John 1:28). And he correctly portrays the Pool of Bethesda surrounded by five covered colonnades (John 5:2), as well as a Pool of Siloam used by those who were infirm (John 9:7).[10]

Until modern times, skeptics viewed the existence of such pools as little more than a religious conceit. A subjective, gullible, naive, superstitious ignorance—a mental predilection on the part of Christians to believe what they think is true *is* true, solely because they *think* it's true. Outside of the gospel of John there simply was no evidence that such pools existed. While they may have had metaphorical ramifications, they were not rooted in historical reality. "Scholars have said that there wasn't a Pool of Siloam," confides James H. Charlesworth, the George L. Collard Professor of New Testament Language and Literature at Princeton, "and that John was using a religious conceit to illustrate a point."[11] Only fools believe in John's pools.

POOL OF SILOAM

All of that changed in June 2004 when workers in the Old City of Jerusalem unearthed the very place that Jesus cured the man born blind. It was there, says John, that Jesus "spat on the ground and made clay with the saliva; and He anointed the eyes of the blind man with the clay. And He said to him, 'Go, wash in the pool of Siloam' (which is translated, Sent). So he went and washed, and came back seeing" (John 9:6–7 NKJV). "Now," says Professor Charlesworth, "we have the Pool of Siloam" and a narrative widely considered "pure theology is now shown to be grounded in history."[12]

The story of how the Pool of Siloam was unearthed is as interesting as it is instructive.[13] During construction to repair a large water pipe south of Jerusalem's Temple Mount, archaeologists identified two ancient stone steps in an area adjacent to the King's Garden. Further excavation demonstrated these to be steps into the very pool described in John's gospel. Professor Ronny Reich, chief archaeologist of Jerusalem, was first to authenticate the steps as belonging to the Pool of Siloam. Today there is no doubt. Archaeologists have excavated three sets of stairs, each containing five steps, and unearthed a pool the shape of a trapezoid 225 feet wide overlooking the Kidron Valley. Encased in the plaster were four coins of Alexander Jannaeus, king and high priest of Judea (103 to 76 BC), strongly suggesting that the Pool of Siloam was constructed during the reign of the Hasmonean kings.

This, however, is but the tip of an archaeological iceberg. In the layered history of Jerusalem, the Pool of Siloam harks back to the time of another Judahite king who reigned from Jerusalem in the eighth century BC; not just any king—the most celebrated king of the divided kingdom—a king of whom the Bible says, "There was no one like him among all the kings of Judah, either before him or after him. He held fast to the LORD and did not cease to follow him; he kept the commands the LORD had given Moses. And the LORD was with him; he was successful in whatever he undertook" (2 Kings 18:5–7).

Notwithstanding his significance as a Judahite king, Hezekiah was still a vassal of the mighty Assyrian Empire, which had exiled the Northern Kingdom the year Shalmaneser V died and Sargon II succeeded him (722 BC). In the face of the decimation of the Northern Kingdom, Hezekiah had the nerve to rebel against Sennacherib, son and successor to Sargon, and did not serve him. "When Hezekiah saw that Sennacherib had come and that he intended to make war on Jerusalem, he consulted with his officials and military staff about blocking off the water from the springs outside the city" (2 Chronicles 32:2–3). He buttressed the walls of Jerusalem and secured its water supply by building a tunnel from the Gihon Spring in the Kidron Valley to the Pool of Siloam near the King's Garden (2 Kings 20; 2 Chronicles 32; Isaiah 37).

As expected, two decades after Sargon's decimation of Samaria, Sennacherib defeated Hezekiah's allies, conquered the fortified cities of Judah, and besieged the walls of Jerusalem. Sennacherib also "wrote letters insulting the LORD, the God of Israel, and saying this against him: 'Just as the gods of the peoples of the other lands did not rescue their people from my hand, so the god of Hezekiah will not rescue his people from my hand'" (2 Chronicles 32:17).

When Hezekiah received the letter of Sennacherib, he spread it out before the Lord and prayed, "O LORD our God, deliver us from his hand, so that all kingdoms on earth may know that you alone, O LORD, are God'" (Isaiah 37:20). "And the LORD sent an angel, who annihilated all the fighting men and the leaders and officials in the camp of the Assyrian king. So he withdrew to his own land in disgrace. And when he went into the temple of his god, some of his sons cut him down with the sword" (2 Chronicles 32:21).

Until the nineteenth century, the very tunnel that channeled the precious waters of the Gihon spring into the Pool of Siloam—like Shalmaneser, Sargon, and Sennacherib—was largely considered to be the stuff of biblical mythology. In 1838, however, theologian Edward Robinson, frequently dubbed "the father of biblical archaeology," discovered the Siloam tunnel. Moreover, in 1880, the "Siloam inscription," a 701 BC commemoration in ancient Hebrew of the completion of the Siloam tunnel through 1,750 feet of limestone bedrock, was discovered. To this day, this inscription, originally cut twenty feet inside the pool end of the tunnel, sits enshrined in the Istanbul Archaeological Museum—an enduring testimony to one of the great engineering feats of ancient times. And that's not all. The Assyrian Annals of Sennacherib, including his siege of forty-six of Hezekiah's strong cities, his imprisonment of Hezekiah "like a bird in a cage," and his unsuccessful siege of Jerusalem, add eloquent testimony to the historical viability of the biblical account.[14]

POOL OF BETHESDA

In my book *The Prayer of Jesus: Secrets to Real Intimacy with God*,[15] I recount a story involving the Pool of Bethesda—a story Joni Eareckson Tada, a hero in the faith, personally shared with me. In 1967 she became a quadriplegic as the result of a diving accident. Stuck in the geriatric ward of a state institution in Maryland, she would listen for hours as her friends read her stories from the Scriptures. One of her favorites was the story of a man who had been an invalid for thirty-eight years. Jesus encountered him lying by the Pool of Bethesda and healed him.

As a result of the story, Joni began picturing herself lying on a straw mat by the Pool of Bethesda. For hours on end she pleaded with God for a miraculous healing. It seemed in those days that God did not reward her prayer with a response. Thirty years later, however, she received a revelation of sorts during a trip to Jerusalem with her husband, Ken. He pushed her wheelchair down the steps of the Via Dolorosa, made a left turn at the Sheep's Gate, walked by St. Anne's Church, and ran straight into the Pool of Bethesda. While resting her arms on the guard rail overlooking those now dry, dusty ruins, Joni's mind flashed back to thirty years earlier when she had pictured herself lying on a mat at this very place.

As if struck by a bolt of lightning, she suddenly realized that God had not given her the response she was looking for. He had given her a far better one. Overwhelmed with emotion, she began to thank him for *not* healing her. God had miraculously turned her wheelchair into a crown.

That day Joni might well have cried out, "O wheelchair, I bless thee!" For it was in the prison of her wheelchair that she learned the secret of intimacy with God. Unable to run here and there with perfectly formed limbs, she spent hours practicing the principles of devotion. And as her life grew ever richer and deeper, she was enabled to bless multitudes out of the overflow of a life spent with Jesus. It was in her wheelchair that she discovered that there were more important things than walking. And as she grew in intimacy with her Creator, she learned to bless the cross that crafted her character.

The Pool of Bethesda Joni encountered a decade or so ago would not have reemerged save for the miracle of archaeology. The story behind the story is extraordinary. Jesus chose the most infirm of men and healed him on the Sabbath (John 5). In doing so, he openly opposed the onerous legalistic traditions that had entwined themselves like barnacles around the Law. The immediate context cries forth that not just one but two mighty miracles took place—one physical, the other spiritual. And in those miracles the Master of the Sabbath was revealed for who he is—"not only was he breaking the Sabbath, but he was even calling God his own Father, making himself equal with God" (John 5:18).

But what about the history? The gloss contained in John 5:3–4 has been ably identified through the science of textual criticism. Not as readily identifiable were historical details surrounding the account. When John says, "Now there is in Jerusalem near the Sheep Gate a pool, which in Aramaic is called Bethesda and which is surrounded by five covered colonnades" (5:2), the critic cries, "Fantasy!" "Fabrication!" "Forged!" The modernist French critic Alfred Loisy set the standard in dismissing the five covered colonnades as a literary myth designed to correspond with the five books of the Law fulfilled by Jesus.[16]

Once again, however, archaeology undresses the critics. As noted by Drs. Timothy and Lydia McGrew, "Excavations of the pool of Bethesda in 1956 revealed that it was located where John said it was, bounded on the sides with four colonnades and spanned across the middle by a fifth."[17] Israeli archaeologist Shimon Gibson, who himself has been investigating the archaeological remains at Bethesda since 1995, likewise points out that the Johannine details fit well with the archaeological remains of the pool as they exist in the present:

> First, the pool had a twin basin, which explains why there were five columned porticoes: one portico on each of the four sides and one additional portico on the barrier wall in the middle separating the two basins. Second, the lame man was waiting for someone to take his bed down to the water of the pool, which suggests that one of the basins must have had broad steps with landings at intervals, otherwise invalids would have had difficulty in gaining access. Third, the man wanted to be put in the pool so that he could benefit from the waters that on occasion became "stirred up," indicating that some curative value was placed at that time on this phenomenon.[18]

Archaeological discoveries surrounding the pools of Bethesda and Siloam have proved a devastating blow to the sophistry of skeptics. Just as the Merneptah and Dan Steles present a one-two punch to the collective chins of Exodus deniers and to those pontificating that the biblical account of King David is no more factual than tales of King Arthur, so, too, discovery of the pools exposes the notion that only fools hold the gospel of John to be early, accurate, and ultimately rooted in eyewitness testimony.

Amazing but true, today in the city of David you can step into the very Pool of Siloam in which the blind man "washed, and came back seeing" (John 9:7 NKJV). You can traverse the Siloam tunnel that almost three thousand years ago provided the precious commodity of water to the inhabitants of Jerusalem during the siege of Sennacherib. You can see the Siloam inscription in the Istanbul Archaeological Museum commemorating one of the greatest engineering feats of ancient history. You can rest your arms on the guard rail overlooking the excavated ruins of the Pool of Bethesda, where Jesus cared for the physical and spiritual needs of a man who had suffered the ravages of sin for thirty-eight years. And you can be amazed at the grace that what was once secreted in soil accurately reflects that which is sealed in Scripture.

Solomon was right. Sometimes answering foolish objections can foster in the foolish a misguided sense of self-significance. At other times, however, a timely response to a foolish contention prods one toward a true valuation of things. Consequently, as the writings of Solomon make clear, true wisdom is found in knowing when—and when not—to respond to the cries of those shouting, "Forged!"

While archaeological evidences in and of themselves may not transform a single biblical skeptic, they serve admirably to temper biblical skepticism.

9

Assyrian Archaeology

*The faith will totter if the authority of the Holy Scriptures loses
its hold on men. We must surrender ourselves to the authority of
Holy Scripture, for it can neither mislead nor be misled.*

—Augustine

The biblical account of Israel's history from the fall of Adam to the rise of the
Assyrian Empire is as poignant as it is profound. Abram's call (Genesis 12:14–
17)—the divine antidote to Adam's fall (Genesis 3)—was but a preliminary
step in a progressive plan through which he and his heirs would inherit a land
of promise. The plan came into sharp focus when Moses led Abram's descendants out of a four-hundred-year bondage in Egypt (Exodus 12).

God's plan became a tangible reality when Joshua led the children of
Israel into the promised land (Joshua 6). The wanderings of Adam, Abram,
and Moses gave way to "rest on every side" (Joshua 21:44). But as Adam
had fallen in Paradise, Abram's descendants would fall in Palestine. Thus
Joshua's words in his final farewell take on an ominous reality. "If you violate the covenant of the LORD your God, which he commanded you . . . you
will quickly perish from the good land he has given you" (Joshua 23:16).

Though the land promises reached their zenith under Solomon—whose rule encompassed all of the land from the River Euphrates in the north to the River of Egypt in the south (1 Kings 4:20–21; cf. Genesis 15:18)—the land vomited out the children of the promise just as it had vomited out the Canaanites before them.[1] Solomon's zeal for God waned in his latter years as pagan wives turned his heart from God (1 Kings 11:1–8). In the end, the divided heart of the king birthed a divided kingdom indifferent to the precepts of God (2 Kings 11:9–40; 12:1–14:31).

The biblical record presents the tragic history of two nations on a collision course with captivity. In Israel's First Great War, Shalmaneser king of Assyria invaded the Northern Kingdom, "captured Samaria and deported the Israelites to Assyria" (2 Kings 17:6). Two decades after the destruction of the Northern Kingdom, Sennacherib, son of Sargon, destroyed forty-six walled cities in the Southern Kingdom, deported two hundred thousand inhabitants, and blockaded Jerusalem's walls. He "exacted from Hezekiah king of Judah three hundred talents of silver and thirty talents of gold" (2 Kings 18:14).

Hezekiah trusted in the Lord, and God spared the city. Sennacherib, however, was not spared. He withdrew from his siege to the chief city of Nineveh and met a bloody fate. "One day, while he was worshiping in the temple of his god Nisroch, his sons Adrammelech and Sharezer cut him down with the sword, and they escaped to the land of Ararat. And Esarhaddon his son succeeded him as king" (2 Kings 19:37).

Sennacherib had mocked Hezekiah as "a caged bird."[2] God, however, unlocked the cage and set the bird free. The Southern Kingdom would continue on for another 135 years until it experienced exile in a Second Great War. God used the Assyrian Empire as the ax of his judgment against the wickedness of the Northern Kingdom. But Assyria, too, experienced the ax of judgment (Isaiah 7:1–25; 10:1–19). By the time of Christ, there was no evidence that Assyria and its capital city had even existed. Said the second-century satirist Lucian of Samosata in Syria: "Nineveh has perished; no trace of it remains; no one can say where once it existed."[3]

From six hundred years before Christ until eighteen hundred years after him, Assyria and its chief city, Nineveh, lay entombed in the dustbin of history. But then the stones cried out once more. In 1845, Henry Austen Layard—an Indiana Jones if ever there was one—began digging along the Tigris River and unearthed Nineveh, diamond of Assyria, embedded in the golden arc of the Fertile Crescent midway between the Mediterranean and Caspian seas. In one of the most significant of all archaeological treasure troves, he uncovered Ashurbanipal's palace to the north, Sennacherib's palace to the south, and Ishtar's cultic temple in between.

SENNACHERIB'S PRISM

From a biblical perspective, one of the most illuminating archaeological gems discovered in the ruins of Nineveh is Sennacherib's Prism. Included in the eight military campaigns inscribed on this hexagonal clay prism is Sennacherib's assault on the Southern Kingdom of Judah. Like other archaeological discoveries, Sennacherib's Prism is a stunning corroboration of the historical core presented by the biblical text.[4]

To begin with, the prism squares with the biblical account of 2 Kings respecting Sennacherib's siege, capture, and despoiling of Judah's fortified cities. "As to Hezekiah, the Jew, he did not submit to my yoke, I laid siege to forty-six of his strong cities, walled forts, and the countless small villages in their vicinity," said Sennacherib. "I conquered them by means of well-stamped earthramps and battering rams brought near to the walls, combined with the attack by foot soldiers, using mines, breeches, as well as sapper work. I drove out of them 200,150 people, young and old, male and female, horses, mules, donkeys, camels, big and small cattle beyond counting, and considered them booty."[5]

Furthermore, as the Bible says, "The king of Assyria exacted from Hezekiah king of Judah three hundred talents of silver and thirty talents of gold" (2 Kings 18:14), so the prism claims Sennacherib exacted thirty talents of gold and eight hundred talents of silver—the discrepancy in silver explained as either an exaggerated rant or exchange rate differential. In any case, both accounts provide consistent cores in keeping with the criteria of credible historians.

Finally, in concert with Isaiah's prophetic word—"The king of Assyria: 'He will not enter this city or shoot an arrow here. He will not come before it with shield or build a siege ramp against it. By the way that he came he will return; he will not enter this city, declares the LORD'" (2 Kings 19:32–33)—Sennacherib boasts of shutting up Hezekiah "like a caged bird within Jerusalem" but makes no boast of capturing and despoiling the city.[6] Why? Various explanations have been forwarded. The Greek historian Herodotus writes, "During the night [Sennacherib's men] were overrun by a horde of field mice that gnawed quivers and bows and the handles of shields, with the result that many were killed fleeing unarmed the next day."[7] The Chaldean historian Berosus indicates that "God sent a pestilential distemper upon [Sennacherib's] army; and on the very night of the siege, a hundred four-score and five thousand, with their captains and generals, were destroyed."[8] In like fashion, the Bible says, "the angel of the LORD went out and put to death a hundred and eighty-five thousand men in the Assyrian camp." Thus, "Sennacherib king of Assyria broke camp and withdrew" (19:35–36).

It should also be noted that the account of Sennacherib's murder at the hands of his sons has been corroborated by the archaeological discovery of a clay tablet inscribed with the cuneiform rendering of the following words: "On 20th Tebet, Sennacherib king of Assyria—his son killed him in a revolt."[9] In keeping with Scripture, the inscription goes on to note that "Esarhaddon his son sat on the throne of Assyria."[10] The clay tablet now enshrined in the British Museum is the final mention of Sennacherib, whose very name came to embody extravagant ruthlessness.[11]

SHALMANESER'S BLACK OBELISK

Another stunning corroboration of biblical history was discovered south of Nineveh in 1946. Sir Henry Layard unearthed a seven-foot, four-sided, black alabaster obelisk etched with 190 lines of cuneiform script and replete with myriad images.[12] Three thousand years ago the Assyrian king Shalmaneser III erected the black obelisk as a testament to his victories. Today it looms large as a testimony to the veracity of the Old Testament.

To begin with, it represents the oldest ancient depiction of an Israelite in the celebrated history of biblical archaeology. Engraved in the obelisk is an image of King Jehu kneeling at the feet of the great Shalmaneser. Etched in cuneiform below the engraved pictorial is the Assyrian facsimile of the following words: "The tribute of Jehu, son of Omri. I received from him silver, gold—a golden bowl, a golden vase, golden tumblers, golden buckets—tin, staff and spears."[13]

This is the very king of Israel who fulfilled one of the most graphic and ominous prophecies in the storied history of the Old Testament. As prophesied by Elijah, "On the plot of ground at Jezreel dogs will devour Jezebel's flesh. Jezebel's body will be like refuse on the ground in the plot at Jezreel, so that no one will be able to say, 'This is Jezebel'" (2 Kings 9:36–37). Jehu commanded that the eunuchs throw Jezebel down from a window. "So they threw her down, and some of her blood spattered the wall and the horses as they trampled her underfoot" (9:33). Jehu commanded that Jezebel be buried, for she was a king's daughter. "But when they went out to bury her, they found nothing except her skull, her feet and her hands" (9:35). Thus Jehu fulfilled the words of Israel's quintessential prophet.

Jehu was also the king who destroyed Baal worship in Israel. He deceptively summoned all the prophets, priests, and ministers of Baal to a great sacrifice. When they went in to make sacrifices and burnt offerings to their god, Jehu ordered the guards to go in and kill them. "So they cut them down with the sword. The guards and officers threw the bodies out and then entered the inner shrine of the temple of Baal. They brought the sacred stone out of the temple of Baal and burned it. They demolished the sacred stone of Baal and tore down the temple of Baal, and people have used it for a latrine to this day. So Jehu destroyed Baal worship in Israel" (2 Kings 10:25–28). The text goes on to say that Jehu did not turn "the worship of the golden calves at Bethel and Dan" (10:29). Thus he himself remained the vassal of the pagan Shalmaneser.

Furthermore, Shalmaneser's Black Obelisk validates King Hazael of Syria (Aram), who like Jehu figures prominently in the text of Scripture. It was Hazael who was a thorn in the side of Israel during the reigns of Jehoram, Jehu, and Jehoahaz. During the reign of Jehoram, Hazael murdered

Ben-Hadad and fulfilled Elisha's prophetic word regarding torment of the Israelites: "You will set fire to their fortified places, kill their young men with the sword, dash their little children to the ground, and rip open their pregnant women" (2 Kings 8:12). During the days of Jehu, the Lord used Hazael to reduce the size and significance of Israel. As such, "Hazael overpowered the Israelites throughout their territory east of the Jordan in all the land of Gilead (the region of Gad, Reuben and Manasseh), from Aroer by the Arnon Gorge through Gilead to Bashan" (2 Kings 10:32–33). During the reign of Jehoahaz, Hazael continued his merciless assault on the Israelites. As chronicled in 2 Kings, only the mercy of God prevented Hazael from obliterating Israel a hundred years prior to the time when they would ultimately fall in 722 BC.

Finally, while the Bible does not overtly mention the subjugation of Jehu by Shalmaneser III, as does the Black Obelisk, it does overtly name Shalmaneser V, under whom Israel experienced ultimate assimilation and exile. In 2 Kings 17 we learn that Shalmaneser imprisoned Hoshea, the final king of Israel, as a traitor. And in 2 Kings 18 we become privy to grim details of the exile. "Shalmaneser king of Assyria marched against Samaria and laid siege to it. At the end of three years the Assyrians took it. So Samaria was captured in Hezekiah's sixth year, which was the ninth year of Hoshea king of Israel. The king of Assyria deported Israel to Assyria and settled them in Halah, in Gozan on the Habor River and in towns of the Medes. This happened because they had not obeyed the LORD their God, but had violated his covenant—all that Moses the servant of the LORD commanded. They neither listened to the commands nor carried them out" (18:9–12).

SARGON'S PALACE

During the siege of Samaria—a campaign that lasted three years—Shalmaneser V died and Sargon II succeeded him as king of Assyria. Thus, in Sargon, the words of Joshua took on ominous reality: "If you violate the covenant of the LORD your God, which he commanded you, and go and serve other gods and bow down to them, the LORD's anger will burn against you, and you will quickly perish from the good land he has given you" (Joshua 23:16). Though the land of the promise that God made to Abraham had reached a zenith under Solomon, the land vomited out the children of the promise just as it had the Canaanites before them. Scarcely two hundred years after establishment as a nation, the Northern Kingdom of Israel was taken into exile by Sargon and was no more.

But what if the great Assyrian king was but a fabled myth? Prior to the middle of the nineteenth century, the only reference to Sargon was found in the Old Testament book of Isaiah. Thus skeptics roundly denied his existence. In the words of Dr. James Orr, Scottish professor of apologetics and history at the University of Glasgow, "Ancient writers knew nothing of [Sargon]. He was a mystery: some did not hesitate to deny that he ever existed." Says Orr, "Sargon, after being forgotten for twenty-five centuries, is now again one of the best known kings of Assyria."[14]

Why? Because in 1843 the stones cried out again. Paul Emile Botta, French consul at Mosul, while working alongside Austen Layard, discovered archaeological evidence confirming the existence of Sargon precisely as referenced in Isaiah 20:1—"Sargon king of Assyria." Botta "struck into the mounds of Khorsabad, a little to the north of Nineveh, and soon, to his own surprise, was standing in the midst of an immense palace, which proved to be that of Sargon, the conqueror of Samaria."[15] Etched in the palace walls were exquisite reliefs that bore eloquent testimony to the stature and significance of the mighty Assyrian monarch.

Isaiah not only makes mention of Sargon as "king of Assyria" but writes that Sargon "came to Ashdod and attacked and captured it" (Isaiah 20:1). As noted by Bible commentators Keil and Delitzsch, Isaiah's words find archaeological confirmation "in the grand inscription found in the halls of the palace at Khorsabad."[16] There Sargon boasts that he marched with his army against Ashdod, and when the king fled from him into Egypt, he besieged Ashdod, and took it. Likewise, as documented by Isaiah, and confirmed through the unearthing of Sargon's palace, "The conquest of Samaria and Ashdod was followed by subjugation of the Egypto-Ethiopian kingdom."[17]

Furthermore, Sargon's words embedded in stone confirmed the biblical assertion that God used the Assyrians as the ax of his judgment upon

Samaria. Among the cuneiform contentions of Sargon's reliefs is the following ominous inscription: "I besieged and conquered Samaria. I took as booty 27,290 people who lived there."[18] According to the text of Scripture, "All this took place because the Israelites had sinned against the LORD their God, who had brought them up out of Egypt from under the power of Pharaoh king of Egypt. They worshipped other gods and followed the practices of the nations the LORD had driven out before them, as well as the practices that the kings of Israel had introduced" (2 Kings 17:7–8).

Finally, in harmony with the biblical text, a Sargonic boast echoes back from the cavernous walls of the palace at Khorsabad: "The town I rebuilt better than it was before and settled therein people from the countries which I myself had conquered."[19] As such, archaeology has verified what is etched in the sacred text of Scripture: "The king of Assyria brought people from Babylon, Cuthah, Avva, Hamath and Sepharvaim and settled them in the towns of Samaria to replace the Israelites. They took over Samaria and lived in its towns" (17:24). These are the Samaritans spoken of in the New Testament (Luke 10:25–37; John 4; cf. 8:48). The foreigners imported by Sargon intermarried with the remnant he had left in the land. Those who remained were relegated to a cultic corruption of Judaism mixed with pagan idolatry. At the time of Christ, these were the very Samaritans unrighteously demeaned as dogs.

Dr. A. T. Olmstead, author of *Western Asia in the Days of Sargon of Assyria 722–705 BC*, said it best. When Paul Emile Botta "left his consulate at Baghdad to excavate in the huge shapeless mound of Khorsabad, a new world came into being. A new people and a new language, new customs and a new art surprised the world; and Sargon thus far known only by a single reference in the Bible, suddenly took his place by the side of Cyrus or Croesus as one of the great monarchs of the ancient Orient."[20] Together Sennacherib's Prism, Shalmaneser's Black Obelisk, and the ruins of Sargon's palace cry out from the ruins of antiquity: *God has spoken*—"Scripture cannot be broken" (John 10:35).

10

*D*ead Sea Scrolls

I believe in the spade. It has fed the tribes of mankind. It has furnished
them water, coal, iron, and gold. And now it is giving them truth—
historic truth, the mines of which have never been opened till our time.

—OLIVER WENDELL HOLMES

Within a year of Nero's suicide, June 9, AD 68, the Roman Empire suffered
a near-fatal wound. In the twinkling of an eye, a dynasty that had resided
in the Julio-Claudian line of Roman Caesars for a century disappeared
from the face of the earth. Nero's death brought not only an end to the
Julio-Claudian dynasty but near extinction of imperial Rome. Civil war
raged in the territories as four Caesars, beginning with Nero, were felled
by the sword. Galba, who reigned but a little while (seven months), was
decapitated, impaled, and paraded around in grotesque and grisly fashion. Otho, rumored to have been one of Nero's lovers, stabbed himself to
death. And Vitellius, engorged and inebriated, was butchered and dragged
by hook into the Tiber.

The very symbols of Roman invincibility—shrines and sacred

sites—disintegrated in evidence of the empire's near extinction.[1] The imminent collapse of Rome seemed so certain that Vespasian and his son Titus lost all will to advance on Jerusalem. As all seemed lost, an empire tottering on the edge of extinction arose from its funeral dirge with renewed malevolence. General Vespasian was proclaimed emperor and succeeded in resurrecting Roman sovereignty, rehabilitating the Roman senate, and ushering in the Flavian dynasty, which would rule Rome until AD 96.

With the resurrection of the Roman beast, Vespasian and his son Titus once again set their sights on Jerusalem. By spring AD 70, Titus had besieged the city. By summertime he had surrounded it with a wall, relegating the Jews within to either starvation or surrender. By August the altar of the temple was littered with heaps of rotting corpses, and rivers of blood defiled the steps of the sanctuary. On August 30 the inconceivable occurred: "The very day on which the former temple had been destroyed by the king of Babylon,"[2] the second temple was set ablaze. By September 26 all Jerusalem was in flames.[3]

Three years later—AD 73—the Roman army advanced on the Zealots who had taken over the Herodian fortress atop Masada. Knowing that Roman soldiers would soon be marching through their sacred compound on the northwest shore of the Dead Sea, the Essenes wrapped their beloved texts in linen, placed them in jars of clay, and hid them in the caves one mile north of the Qumran community. After the Roman threat passed, they would surely retrieve the scrolls and resume the treasured task of copying their sacred texts. Tragically, the Essene community did not survive. Their scrolls, however, continued to live on in the cool, dry air of caves looming high above the lowest spot on earth.

Almost nineteen hundred years would come and go before the Qumran caves yielded their secreted treasures.[4] In 1947 the shattering of parchment-preserving pottery would pierce the silence of nearly two millennia. The hurling of a stone by a bedouin nicknamed "the Wolf" produced a seismic shock sequence that reverberates through bastions of higher learning to this very day. The sound of splintered pottery led to what famed archaeologist Dr. William Albright immediately recognized as "the greatest manuscript discovery of modern times!"[5] A discovery that would "revolutionize intertestamental studies."[6] Within a decade a veritable library of one hundred thousand fragments constituting nine hundred–plus documents have emerged from eleven caves at Wadi Qumran.[7]

It would be difficult to overestimate the importance of the scrolls from the purview of the Judeo-Christian tradition. Prior to discovery of the Dead Sea Scrolls, the oldest extant copies of the Old Testament in Greek were codices Sinaiticus (c. AD 350) and Vaticanus (c. AD 325) and in Hebrew, codices Leningrad (c. AD 1000) and Aleppo (c. AD 900). While the Nash Papyrus (c. 100 BC), now in the Cambridge University Library, is old and hugely significant, it contains little more than the Ten Commandments. With the discovery of the Dead Sea Scrolls, however, we have a virtual first-century Hebrew Old Testament library available at the click of a twenty-first-century mouse. Not only so, but the Dead Sea Scrolls predate the earliest extant Hebrew text—Masoretic—by a full millennium. As such, everyone from scholar to schoolchild can determine whether the Old Testament Scriptures have been corrupted by men or miraculously preserved by God. S-I-G-N-S of their miraculous preservation can be found in the *Samuel Scroll, Isaiah Text, Goliath Stature, "N" Verse*, and *Suffering Messiah passage*.[8]

SAMUEL SCROLL

The Samuel Scroll discovered in Cave 4 in September 1952 is a grand example of God's preservation of sacred Scripture. To begin with, this scroll demonstrates that the text of Samuel has been faithfully preserved over the span of a thousand years. Furthermore, the Samuel Scroll explains where Josephus found his color commentary regarding the Ammonite king Nahash's eye-gouging practice—in the Old Testament he used to inform the *Antiquities*. Finally, while adding this information to the end of 1 Samuel 10 would provide further specificity, the ruthlessness of Nahash is adequately accounted for in 1 Samuel 11.

ISAIAH SCROLL (1QIsaᴬ)

I can personally attest to a feeling of awe when I first encountered the Great Isaiah Scroll in Jerusalem's Shrine of the Book. This two-thousand-year-old scroll found in 1947 in Cave 1 contained virtually the entire text of Isaiah. Like the Samuel Scroll, the Great Isaiah Scroll demonstrates that God miraculously preserved his Word over time. When the text of this Dead Sea Scroll (c. 100 BC) was compared to the text of the Masorites (c. AD 1000) it was found effectively identical—this despite the passage of eleven hundred years. Although there are differences in style and spelling, no difference in substance appears. Consider the brightest star in the constellation of Isaiah prophecies—Isaiah 53. As noted, when compared to the Masoretic text there are seventeen differences. While at first blush that might sound significant, ten were differences in spelling, four a matter of style, and three involved the Hebrew letters for *light*. None alters the substance of the text whatsoever.⁹

GOLIATH STATURE

Even in a biblically illiterate culture, virtually everyone is familiar with the epic story of David and Goliath. In most modern translations, following the extant Hebrew text, Goliath is said to be "over nine feet tall" (1 Samuel 17:4). As noted by Dr. Craig Evans, however, "The Greek translation [Septuagint] of 1 Samuel says something different about Goliath's height. It says he was 'four cubits and a span,' or about six feet six inches tall. That is still very tall for antiquity, but it is at least within the conceivable anatomical range of humans." So how tall was Goliath? First, it should be noted that while the length of a cubit is not precisely known, there is general consensus that a cubit is measured from the elbow to the tip of the middle finger. Thus, a cubit is somewhere around eighteen inches—plus or minus 10 percent. And a span is approximately nine inches (half the length of a cubit). Furthermore, says Evans, "It turns out that the Samuel Scroll from Qumran, which is in Hebrew, reads the same as the Greek version (6'6")." This implies that the Hebrew from which the Greek translator was working also said that Goliath was "six feet six inches rather than nearly ten feet tall." Thus, Goliath would have been approximately the size of NBA big man Shaquille O'Neil.[10] Finally, since the Dead Sea Scrolls confirm both the Greek Septuagint and Josephus's *Antiquities*, the corruption resides in the extant Hebrew. As Evans concludes, "The findings at Qumran suggest that the seemingly impossible height of Goliath resulted from a corruption of the original version of 1 Samuel."[11]

"N" VERSE

Discovery of the Dead Sea Scrolls unravels a mystery that has long puzzled translators. Psalm 145, laid out in the fashion of an alphabetical Hebrew acrostic poem, is missing a verse supplied in the Greek version of the Old Testament text. In the Hebrew, all the letters in the acrostic are sequentially accounted for, save the letter *N*. To wit, the mystery—what happened to the "N" Verse in the Hebrew acrostic? This conundrum was resolved when the Psalms scroll was discovered February 1956 in Cave 11. The Psalms scroll abounds with words like "*Faithful* is God in all his words, and gracious in all his deeds." The word rendered "faithful" is the Hebrew *ne'eman*. As such, the Psalms scroll supplies the "N" Verse otherwise missing from the Hebrew acrostic. Says Evans, "Most modern English translations supply the missing verse now that it has been confirmed in Hebrew. Translators of the King James Version (1611) could not have known about the manuscript evidence that would be found centuries later at Qumran, so naturally they did not include it in their translation."[12]

SUFFERING MESSIAH

Read a standard list of prophecies made in the Old Testament and fulfilled in the New and you will inevitably see the crucifixion of Christ listed as a fulfillment of Psalm 22:16: "They have pierced my hands and my feet." A note in modern translations, however, has stumbled seekers and solidified skeptics in opposition to the biblical text: The note indicates that a majority reading of the Masoretic text renders Psalm 22:16, "Like the lion, my hands and my feet." As such, the word *pierced* has been rendered by skeptics "a not-too-ingenious Christian interpolation that was created by deliberately mistranslating the Hebrew word *ka'ari* as 'pierced.'"[13] This, however, is far from compelling. First, the difference between the Hebrew words *ka'aru* ("pierced") and *ka'ari* ("like a lion") is akin to the difference between a jot (the smallest letter in the Hebrew alphabet) and a tittle (a microscopic appendage at the end of a Hebrew letter). Furthermore, the phrase "like a lion" makes no sense in the immediate or broader context of the passage. Finally, and most significantly, is the discovery of a manuscript fragment at Nahal Hever in the region of the Dead Sea. This fragment, a millennium older than the Masoretic text, ended in the longer *vav* ("pierced") not *yod* ("like a lion")—a mere millimeter of ink making all the difference in the world. Moreover, as noted by Jewish scholar Dr. Michael L. Brown, "The Septuagint, the oldest existing Jewish translation of the Tanakh, was the first to translate the Hebrew as 'they pierced my hands and feet' . . . followed by the Syriac Peshitta version two or three centuries later." Brown continues, "Not only so, but the oldest Hebrew copy of the Psalms we possess (from the Dead Sea Scrolls, dating to the century before Yeshua) reads the verb in this verse as *ka'aru* (not *ka'ari*, 'like a lion'), a reading also found in about a dozen medieval Masoretic manuscripts."[14] Thus, the verdict: Psalm 22:16 in all of its prophetic significance stands.

As demonstrated thus far, the Dead Sea Scrolls powerfully underscore the miraculous reality that God has preserved his Word over time. Furthermore, as evidenced by the S-I-G-N-S acronym, the Dead Sea Scrolls provide significant insight into the text of the Old Testament. Finally, as we will now see, the Dead Sea Scrolls have added considerable clarity to the text of the New Testament as well.

Melchizedek is a classic case in point. Questions concerning him abound. Is he human? Is he an angel? Divine? A type of Christ? A Christophany? Such queries are precipitated in large part because mention of him is sparse in the biblical text. In Genesis, he is described as the priest and king of peace who blesses the patriarch Abraham and receives from him the tithe due the divine priesthood (Genesis 14:20). In the Psalms, the Lord Jesus Christ himself is designated "a priest forever in the order of Melchizedek" (Psalm 110:4). And in Hebrews, Melchizedek is depicted as "'king of peace.' Without father or mother, without genealogy, without beginning of days or end of life, like the Son of God he remains a priest forever" (Hebrews 7:2–3).

So who is Melchizedek? From antiquity there have been a wide variety of answers. Origen (AD 185–254) thought Melchizedek to be an angel.[15] Martin Luther (AD 1483–1546) thought him to be Shem, son of Noah.[16] In modern times the answers are equally divergent. Mormon apologist Bruce R. McConkie held that in "June, 1829, by divine appointment, Peter, James, and John came to Joseph Smith and Oliver Cowdery and conferred upon them the Melchizedek Priesthood."[17] In sharp contrast, Christian apologist Norman Geisler contends Melchizedek was a historical human who served as a type of Christ. Says Geisler, "There is no reason, archaeological or otherwise, to question the historical character of Melchizedek."[18]

In the midst of such confusion, Dr. Craig Evans contends that "the Melchizedek Scroll from Cave 11 helps us understand the larger context." Says Evans, "The DSS [Dead Sea Scrolls] may show that there is more to this argument than we previously realized. The author of Hebrews has taken pains to underscore Jesus' superiority to Moses, the angels, the prophets, and even the Levitical priesthood. To achieve the latter he links Jesus to the mysterious figure of Melchizedek. He says Melchizedek is 'without father, mother, or genealogy, having neither beginning of days nor end of life, but resembling the Son of God' (Hebrews 7:3)." Evans goes on to note that "this latter part was poorly understood until scholars discovered the DSS."[19]

To begin with, in Psalm 7 the Melchizedek Scroll depicts Melchizedek ruling from on high as the judge of the peoples. Furthermore, in Psalm 82 Melchizedek presides in the great assembly and makes judgment as the Almighty. Finally, the Melchizedek Scroll renders Isaiah 61:2, "the year of Melchizedek's favor," as opposed to "the year of the LORD's favor," again equating Melchizedek with the Almighty. "What the Melchizedek Scroll claims," says Evans, "is simply astounding: Melchizedek is God himself!"[20]

While the Dead Sea Scrolls are not the final word, the clarity of their revelation motivates us to look more closely at the biblical text. The epistle

to the Hebrews depicts professing believers losing confidence amid growing persecution. Some were distancing themselves from their Christian
communities and reverting back to Jewish practices superseded by the
atoning sacrifice of Christ. As such, the epistle to the Hebrews definitively
demonstrates that Christ is superior to the prophets (Hebrews 1), the
angels (Hebrews 2), Moses (Hebrews 3), the Sabbath rest (Hebrews 4), and
the priesthood itself (Hebrews 5). Indeed, according to Hebrews 5, Christ
"did not take upon himself the glory of becoming a high priest. But God
said to him, 'You are my Son; today I have become your Father.' And he
says in another place, 'You are a priest forever in the order of Melchizedek'"
(5:5–6). Hebrews 6 reemphasizes Jesus as "a high priest forever in the order
of Melchizedek" (6:20). Hebrews 7 renders Melchizedek as "king of righteousness" and "king of Salem," meaning "king of peace," and then goes on
to say, "without father or mother, without genealogy, without beginning of
days or end of life, like the Son of God he remains a priest forever" (7:2–3).

First, at face value it seems hollow to argue that when the text of Scripture
says that Melchizedek is "without father or mother, without genealogy, without beginning of days or end of life," that "is not to say that Melchizedek
had no father or mother."[21] In point of fact, that is precisely what the text
says—"without [had no] father or mother." Not only so, Melchizedek is said
to be "without genealogy." Had Melchizedek been an earthly king of such
surpassing substance and significance that the biblical text calls him the
"greater" and father Abraham "the lesser" (7:7), one would suppose sacred
Scripture to have ample supply of references to his genealogy.

Furthermore, from an earthly perspective, Abraham was king of Salem
(Jerusalem)—the very region where God gave him victory in the battle of
the kings (Genesis 14) and the very realm in which God called him to establish a righteous nation of kings and priests. From the perspective of heaven,
it is Melchizedek who is the "King of Salem" and "remains a priest forever."
As such, Melchizedek appears as a human king and priest yet is "without
beginning of days or end of life." A priest who offers bread and wine from
the Jerusalem that is above, is free, and is our mother (Galatians 4:21–31).

Finally, we should note that Scripture not only designates Melchizedek
"king of righteousness" and "king of peace" and overtly tells us that he is

"without father or mother, without genealogy, without beginning of days or end of life" but that "like the Son of God he remains a priest forever" (Hebrews 7:3). Though he "did not trace his descent from Levi, yet he collected a tenth from Abraham and blessed him who had the promises. And without doubt the lesser person is blessed by the greater. In the one case, the tenth is collected by men who die; but in the other case, by him who is declared to be the living" (7:6–8). Note that in contrast to men who die, Melchizedek "is declared to be the living."

Despite all the evidence, one word has caused me to question Melchizedek as a Christophany or preincarnate appearance of Christ. That word is the Greek *aphomoiôô*, pronounced aff-uh-moi-AH-ō and translated *like*—"*like* the Son of God he remains a priest forever" (7:3). *Like*, however, is hardly a game-changer. This particular Greek word is used only once in the entirety of the New Testament. Thus, dogmatism may be unwise.

Moreover, even if *aphomoiôô* is properly translated *like*, it does not negate the notion of Melchizedek as a Christophany. Consider the words of Daniel: "In my vision at night I looked, and there before me was one *like* a son of man, coming with the clouds of heaven. He approached the Ancient of Days and was led into his presence" (Daniel 7:13; cf. 3:25). Then contemplate the reality that despite the word *like*, Jesus combined this very passage with Psalm 110 in evidence of his deity (Mark 14:61–62).

Apart from the archaeological discovery of the Melchizedek Scroll, I may never have reexamined the case for Melchizedek as Christ.

11

Epic of Gilgamesh

In the divine Scriptures, there are shallows and there are deeps; shallows where the lamb may wade, and deeps where the elephant may swim.

—JOHN OWEN

From the perspective of a biblical worldview, the primordial deluge depicted in Genesis is the most catastrophic event in the history of humanity. From the perspective of fundamentalists from the left, it is also the most comical. A fundamentalist spoof currently circulating on the Internet makes plain that to believe the biblical flood account is just plain silly.[1] Flood caricatures all seem to have a common thread: a propensity for forcing the biblical text to "walk on all fours," a close-mindedness that permits natural but precludes supernatural explanations for an event such as the primordial deluge, and a failure to recognize that God speaks through both the Bible and the book of nature.

Bart Ehrman is the prime exemplar of the first of these flaws. Under the heading "Problems with the Bible," Ehrman asks, "When Noah takes the animals on the ark, does he take seven pairs of all the 'clean' animals, as Genesis 7:2 states, or just two pairs, as Genesis 7:9–10 indicates?"[2] In truth, the text says nothing of the sort. What it does say is that Noah is to take *pairs* of animals, male and female. In the case of clean animals and birds, seven pair, male and female; and in the case of unclean animals, one pair, male and female. Nowhere does the Bible suggest that Noah is to take "just two pairs," as Ehrman obsesses. Indeed, only an extreme literalist bent on undermining Scripture would attempt to make this passage stumble around ignominiously on all fours.

Furthermore, with respect to close-mindedness, it is instructive to note that miracles are not only possible but necessary in order to make sense of the universe in which we live. According to modern science, the universe not only had a beginning but is unfathomably fine-tuned to support life. Not only so, but the origin of life, information in the genetic code, irreducible complexity in biological systems, and the phenomenon of the human mind pose intractable difficulties for merely natural explanations. Thus, reason forces us to look beyond the natural world to a supernatural Designer who not only sustains the world but intervenes in the affairs of his created handiwork. If we are willing to believe that God created the heavens and the earth—as opposed to the untenable notion that nothing created everything—there is little difficulty respecting the Flood account.

Finally, the notion that God has two books seems completely lost on spoofers. "If the Flood covered the mountains," they sneer, "it would put the sea level at 29,055 ft, where everything on the Ark would have frozen to death and not had enough oxygen to breathe."[3] In reality the biblical text is not designed to communicate whether the Flood was global with respect to the earth or universal with respect to humanity. That debate is ultimately settled by a proper "reading" of the book of nature. Since civilization was largely confined to the Fertile Crescent, one need not automatically presume that the floodwaters covered the globe. When Scripture tells us that "the whole world sought audience with Solomon to hear the wisdom God had put in his heart" (1 Kings 10:24), only the most ardent fundamentalist supposes this to include aborigines from Australia and indigenous peoples of the Americas. As with spiritualized interpretations that empty the Scriptures of all objective meaning, so literalistic proclivities wreak havoc on the biblical text.

Of one thing we can be absolutely certain. The text of Scripture, both

Old and New, communicate the reality of a primordial deluge in which "only a few people, eight in all, were saved" (1 Peter 3:20). Until the late nineteenth century, the masses presumed that the great primordial deluge was relegated to the text of Scripture. All that changed, however, in December 1853 when Hormuzd Rassam, who a year earlier had replaced the great Assyriologist Henry Layard in the excavations at Nineveh, discovered the palace of Assurbanipal. There among the treasures of the great library of Assyria's last king, he uncovered twelve clay tablets.[4]

Rassam shipped the twelve tablets to London, where they were once again buried in the basement of the British Museum amid myriad archaeological artifacts. As if by accident, George Smith stumbled upon tablet 11 in November 1872. To the astonishment of the West, he translated the account "of a flood, a ship caught on a mountain, and a bird sent out in search of dry land—the first independent confirmation of a vast flood in ancient Mesopotamia, complete with a Noah-like figure and an ark."[5] On December 3, 1872, no less a dignitary than William Gladstone, prime minister of England, was present when Smith presented "The Chaldean Account of the Deluge" to the Society of Biblical Archaeology. Columbia University professor David Damrosch rightly referred to the Epic of Gilgamesh as "one of the most sensational finds in the history of archaeology."[6]

Yet this was only the beginning. Smith's newfound fame caused funds to materialize as if by magic. As such, he was empowered to pursue a previously unthinkable dream: the opportunity to personally explore the vast riches of Nineveh's archaeological treasure chest. In May 1873, "lightning struck again." In the library of Assurbanipal's northern palace, Smith uncovered seventeen lines of the Epic of Atrahasis, an even earlier version of the Flood story. In sum, Smith had uncovered not one but two cuneiform confirmations demonstrating that the Flood account had a currency outside the biblical text. While other flood accounts—some even older, such as Eridu Genesis—have continued to surface, the Epic of Gilgamesh remains the best known of the extrabiblical Mesopotamian Flood stories.[7]

Though the Epic of Gilgamesh has roots in an actual Sumerian ruler— Gilgamesh, fifth king of the first dynasty of the Sumerian city-state Uruk in Southeast Mesopotamia (c. 2700 BC)—it is rife with all the trappings of ancient mythology. The essence of the epic is a quest for immortality. Gilgamesh, terrified by the prospect of his own death, seeks out Utnapishtim, a Noah-like personage who survived the Great Deluge and became the singular mortal granted eternal life by the gods.[8]

The Epic of Gilgamesh portrays Gilgamesh as a physically stunning ruler, two-thirds god. His heart, however, is ruthless and wicked. As such, he victimizes men and robs women of their virginity. In response to the pleas of the people, the mother goddess Aruru creates Enkidu, a rival of equal strength and vigor. Enkidu blocks access to a marital chamber where Gilgamesh, as is his custom, seeks to ravish a bride on the night of her wedding. After a ferocious battle, the two become fast friends and embark together on a quest to claim cedar from a great forest where gods and goddesses make their secret abode. With the help of the sun god Shamash, they conquer the Humbaba—the terrible, demonic guardian of the cedars. As Gilgamesh cleanses himself from the heat of the battle and dons his royal robes, Ishtar, overwhelmed by the majesty of his form, asks that he become her lover. Knowing the fate of her other lovers, including Ishullanu, whom she had magically transformed into a dwarf, Gilgamesh spurns her advances. As a goddess scorned, she sends Taurus, the bull of heaven, to wreak havoc on Gilgamesh and the kingdom of Uruk. After a devastating rampage, Enkidu seizes the tail of the bull and instructs Gilgamesh to slay it. After its desecration, Enkidu has a dream in which he discovers that the gods have decided that he must die for destroying Taurus. The painful death of Enkidu puts Gilgamesh in touch with his own mortality. Thus, he sets out to find Utnapishtim and to discover the secret to eternal life.

After a dangerous journey through the Waters of Death, he encounters Utnapishtim on a distant shore. There he asks Utnapishtim to unveil the secret to immortality. Utnapishtim explains that death is inevitable, that "all men will be snapped off like a reed."[9] Yet, says Utnapishtim, I will reveal to you a hidden matter. He speaks of how Enlil son of An, the god of heaven and earth, had purposed to destroy all life with a great Flood and how the god Ea had warned him to forsake worldly goods, tear down his house, and build an ark. He was instructed concerning the dimensions of the ark, how it was to be built in the shape of a cube and sealed by pitch within and without. As the storm clouds approached, he boarded the ark with his family and "the seed of all living things." He battened up the entrance as the south storm blew, "submerging the mountains, overtaking the people like a battle." The Flood was so ferocious that even the gods were "frightened by the deluge, and, shrinking back, they ascended to the heaven of Anu."

> *Six days and six nights*
> *blows the flood wind, as the south storm sweeps the land.*
> *When the seventh day arrived,*
> *the flood-carrying south storm subsided in the battle,*
> *which it had fought like an army.*
> *The sea grew quiet, the tempest was still, the flood ceased.*
> *I looked at the weather; stillness had set in,*
> *and all of humanity had returned to clay.*
> *The landscape was as level as a flat roof.*
> *I opened a hatch, and light fell upon my face.*
> *Bowing low, I sat and wept,*
> *tears running down on my face . . .*
> *On Mount Nisir the ship came to a halt.*
> *Mount Nisir held the ship fast,*
> *allowing no motion . . .*
> *When the seventh day arrived,*
> *I sent forth and set free a dove.*
> *The dove went forth, but came back;*
> *since no resting place for it was visible, she turned round.*
> *Then I sent forth and set free a swallow.*
> *The swallow went forth, but came back;*
> *since no resting place for it was visible, she turned round.*
> *Then I sent forth and set free a raven.*
> *The raven went forth and, seeing that the water had diminished,*
> *he eats, circles, caws, and turns not round.*
> *Then I let out all to the four winds*
> *and offered a sacrifice.*
> *I poured out a libation on the top of the mountain.*

Seven and seven cult vessels I set up,
upon their potstands I heaped cane, cedarwood and myrtle.
The gods smelled the savor,
the gods smelled the sweet savor,
the gods crowded like flies about the sacrificer . . .
but let not Enlil come to the offering,
for he, unreasoning, brought on the deluge.

In time Enlil arrived at the gathering of the gods. He was filled with wrath. Has some living soul escaped? he asked. "No man was to survive the destruction!" When his wrath subsided, the capricious Enlil purposed to grant Utnapishtim the gift of immortality. The Flood story complete, Utnapishtim offers Gilgamesh a pretext to eternal life. If Gilgamesh can stay awake six days and seven nights, he, too, may achieve immortality. When Gilgamesh fails the test, Utnapishtim salves Gilgamesh's wounds by telling him of a plant "like a boxthorn, whose thorns will prick your hand like a rose. If your hands reach that plant you will become a young man again."[10] Gilgamesh, however, is outwitted by an ancient serpent, who steals the sea plant, sheds its skin, and slithers off in youthful bliss.

One thing should be obvious from my overview of the Epic of Gilgamesh. To transform such mythology into an account rooted in history and evidence would be formidable. And yet with all its pagan trappings, there are significant parallels between Gilgamesh and Genesis.[11] A cursory accounting reveals the following twelve:

1. There is divine judgment against humanity.
2. The hero is instructed to build a ship.
3. The dimension of the ship is specified.
4. The deluge is universal with respect to humanity.
5. The hero is saved along with his family.
6. The seed of all living things survives.
7. All humanity is destroyed.
8. The mountains are submerged.
9. The duration of the deluge is reported.

10. The ship comes to rest atop a mountain.

11. Birds are released in search of dry land.

12. Sacrifices of thanksgiving are offered.

Dissimilarities between Gilgamesh and Genesis are equally striking. In Genesis, a monotheistic God brings judgment because "the earth was corrupt in God's sight and was full of violence" (Genesis 6:11–12). In the polytheistic Gilgamesh account, the gods are capricious and random— the god Ea going so far as to accuse the god Enlil of the foolhardiness of bringing judgment by way of a flood. In Genesis the ark was not only large enough to fit the need (more than a million and a half cubic feet) but, according to modern engineering standards, ideally suited for floating and stability, as opposed to speed and navigation, and could withstand waves in excess of a hundred feet. In Gilgamesh, the case is precisely opposite. Not only is the ship insufficient in size but it is hardly seaworthy. Indeed, its cubed shape would render the ship unstable and likely to capsize and spin. In Genesis, "all the springs of the great deep burst forth, and the floodgates of the heavens were opened. And rain fell on the earth forty days and forty nights" (Genesis 7:11–12). In Gilgamesh it rains an insufficient "six days and six nights." And "when the seventh day arrived, the flood-carrying south storm subsided."

In Genesis, Noah first sent out a raven to "see if the water had receded from the surface of the ground." Then he sent out a dove. "But the dove could find no place to set its feet because there was water over all the surface of the earth; so it returned to Noah in the ark" (Genesis 8:8–9). After "seven more days [he] again sent out the dove from the ark. When the dove returned to him in the evening, there in its beak was a freshly plucked olive leaf! Then Noah knew that the water had receded from the earth. He waited seven more days and sent the dove out again, but this time it did not return to him" (8:10–12). In Gilgamesh, Utnapishtim first sets free a dove, then a swallow, and last of all a raven. The order makes little sense. Since ravens are highly adaptable, it would be prudent to send one out first as in Genesis but hardly last as in Gilgamesh. If a raven comes back, no further test is needed. The verdict is in—the environment is patently inhospitable. The sequence in Genesis is not only logical but directly related to the nature of birds. A raven would not think twice about dining on rotting carcasses, whereas a dove will settle only for that which is dry and sanitary.

This brings up the larger point. Historical details are conspicuous by their absence in Gilgamesh. Not so in Genesis. Here the details are congruent and fleshed out. When the first dove returned, it was crystal clear that the floodwaters had not sufficiently abated. Seven days later, however, the second dove returned with a freshly plucked olive leaf. At first blush, this biblical detail may not sound significant. Upon further consideration, however, its horticultural and historical value becomes clear. The olive is the heartiest of trees; it can grow in high lime content, on barren hillsides, and in water; and only months need lapse between the implantation of a cutting and the production of leaves. When the dove (think homing pigeon) did not return seven days later, Noah knew that "the water had dried up from the earth." Thus, a year after Noah and his family had entered the ark, they disembarked. For, as the text explains: "By the twenty-seventh day of the second month the earth was completely dry" (8:14).

With all its failings, the Epic of Gilgamesh is yet a significant archaeological treasure. Why? First, because it is wholly plausible to presume that the significant similarities between Genesis and Gilgamesh are best explained by a "common inheritance." As professor of archaeology Alfred J. Hoerth explains, "Both accounts derive from the same source—the actual event. There was a flood, and both the Bible and the Epic record it. As the descendants of Noah drifted apart and away from God, there must have been a long parade of human corruptions and polytheistic encrustations on the original and actual event."[12]

Furthermore, it is crucial to note that the existence of corrupted Flood accounts such as the Epic of Gilgamesh and the aforementioned Epic of Atrahasis and the even older Eridu Genesis serve to underscore the existence of a real McCoy. And that is precisely what the Genesis Flood account affords. It is written as history and corresponds to reality. No capricious gods clutter the text, and details that can be tested in an age of scientific enlightenment are wholly plausible. As model testing demonstrates, the ark is ideally suited to survive a primordial deluge; horticulture makes sense of the freshly plucked olive leaf; and ornithology underscores the logic behind Noah's use of birds.

Finally, the Epic of Gilgamesh reminds us that the reality of the Flood is impregnated on the collective consciousness of virtually every major civilization from the Sumerian epoch to the present age. In Hindu lore, the god Vishnu warned the Noah-like Manu of a great deluge that would destroy the earth in seven days. Manu saved himself in a boat that Vishnu in the form of a fish tows to a great mountaintop. When the waters recede, Manu repopulates and rules the world. In Greek mythology, Zeus, angered by human hubris, destroys the world with a flood. Deucalion and his wife, Pyrrha, are saved in an ark that comes to rest after nine days on the slopes of Mount Parnassus. Deucalion and Pyrrha make sacrifices to Zeus, who commands that they repopulate the world by throwing stones that are magically transformed into men and women. Hundreds of similar flood stories can be recounted from ancient Chinese legends to Mayan mythologies in the Americas. They all have one thing in common: in contrast to a Genesis account rooted in history and evidence, they see the waters of the Flood through the opaque lens of paganism.

And that is precisely the point. The S-P-A-D-E of the archaeologist demonstrates time and time again that in direct contrast to pagan mythology from Mormonism to Mithras, the people, places, and particulars found in sacred Scripture have their roots in history and evidence. As such, what was concealed in the soil corresponds to what is revealed in the Scriptures.

Memorable Snapshots

Steles and Stones

In demonstrating what was concealed in the soil corresponds to what is revealed in the Scriptures, the Merneptah and Dan Steles come immediately to mind. As do the Moabite and Pilate Stones. The Merneptah Stele presents as formidable a challenge to Exodus deniers as the Dan Stele does to those pontificating that the biblical account of King David is no more factual than tales of King Arthur. As *Time* magazine rightly observed, the skeptics' claim that King David never existed is now hard to defend.[13] In light of the Moabite Stone, it is also difficult to contend that biblical kings such as Omri and Mesha, and places such as Nebo and Moab, are the stuff of myth. Likewise, the Pilate Stone demonstrates in spades that Pilate was the Roman authority in Judea at the time Christ was crucified.

Pools and Fools

Until quite recently, skeptics viewed the existence of the pools depicted in John's gospel to be little more than *a religious conceit*. A predilection on the part of Christians to believe that what they think is true *is* true, solely because they *think* it's true. Only fools believed in John's pools. All of that changed in June 2004 when workers in the Old City of Jerusalem unearthed the place where Jesus cured the man born blind. Today, you can step into the very Pool of Siloam in which the blind man "washed and came back seeing." Likewise, you can rest your arms on the guard rail overlooking the excavated ruins of the Pool of Bethesda, where Jesus cared for the physical and spiritual needs of a man who suffered the ravages of sin for thirty-eight years. And you can stand amazed that what was once secreted in soil accurately reflects that which is sealed in Scripture.

Assyrian Archaeology

From six hundred years before Christ until eighteen hundred years after him, Assyria and its chief city, Nineveh, lay entombed in the dustbin of history. Then the stones cried out again. In 1845 Henry Austen Layard began digging along the Tigris River and unearthed Nineveh, diamond of Assyria. Among the stunning archaeological gems discovered there were Sennacherib's Prism, which provides a stunning corroboration of the biblical text with respect to Sennacherib's assault on the Southern Kingdom of Judah; Shalmaneser's Black Obelisk, representing the oldest ancient depiction of an Israelite in the celebrated history of biblical archaeology; and the palace of Sargon, previously known only by a single reference in Sacred Scripture. Together, Sennacherib's Prism, Shalmaneser's Black Obelisk, and the ruins of Sargon's Palace provide weighty testimony to the reliability of the biblical record.

Dead Sea Scrolls

The 1947 sound of splintered pottery led to what archaeologist Dr. William Albright recognized as one of the greatest archaeological discoveries of modern times. Incredibly, we now have access to virtually an entire first-century Old Testament Library at the click of a twenty-first-century mouse. Not only so, but the Dead Sea Scrolls predate the earliest extant Hebrew text—Masoretic—by a full millennium and demonstrate conclusively that the Old Testament Scriptures have been miraculously preserved by God over time. S-I-G-N-S of their miraculous preservation can be found in the Samuel Scroll, Isaiah Text, Goliath Stature, "N" Verse, and Suffering Messiah passage. Additionally, the Dead Sea Scrolls provide significant insight into the text of the Old Testament and add considerable clarity to the text of the New Testament as well.

Epic of Gilgamesh

Until the late nineteenth century, the masses presumed the great primordial deluge to be relegated to the text of Scripture. All that began to change in 1853 when Hormuzd Rassam discovered the palace of Assurbanipal. There among the treasures of Assyria's last king, he uncovered clay tablets that provide independent confirmation of a vast flood in ancient Mesopotamia, complete with a Noah-like figure and an ark. While the Epic views the waters of the flood through the opaque lens of paganism, it lends significant credence to an actual event. It is likewise a reminder that the reality of a great deluge is impregnated on the collective consciousness of virtually every major civilization from the Sumerian epoch to the present age.

Prophetic
S–T–A–R–S

Succession of Nations

Typological Prophecy

Abomination of Desolation

Resurrection Prophecies

Superstar ABCs

"Present your case," says the LORD. *"Set forth your arguments," says Jacob's King. "Bring in your idols to tell us what is going to happen. Tell us what the former things were, so that we may consider them and know their final outcome. Or declare to us the things to come, tell us what the future holds, so we may know that you are gods."*

—ISAIAH, SON OF AMOZ

"Astrology is a language," opined astrologer Dane Rudhyar. "If you understand this language, the sky speaks to you."[1] Multiplied millions regard Rudhyar as right. Thus, they employ prophetic stars to learn the lore and language of the astrological heavens. Nancy Reagan was among them. Fearing the safety of the president, following a failed assassination attempt on March 30, 1981, she turned to San Francisco astrologer Joan Quigley for advice on "virtually every major move or decision the Reagans made"[2]—thus holding the president's calendar hostage to the mythology of the stars.

Babylonian king Nebuchadnezzar was slightly more skeptical. In the second year of his reign, he was troubled by a dream. Thus, he summoned the royal astrologers to explain the dream and its meaning. "The astrologers answered the king in Aramaic, 'O king, live forever! Tell your servants the dream, and we will interpret it'" (Daniel 2:4). Nebuchadnezzar would have none of it. "If you do not tell me the dream, I will know that you have conspired to mislead me," he said. "However, if you can tell me the dream, I will know that you can rightly interpret it" (2:5–9; author's paraphrase). The astrologers knew the gig was up. They could no more tell the king his dream than they could tell him what his dream portended for the future. "Only the gods can do that," they muttered. "And the gods do not live among men" (2:10–11; author's paraphrase). Knowing the mythology of astrology, the prophet Daniel turned to the God of heaven "so that he and his friends might not be executed with the rest of the wise men of Babylon. During the night the mystery was revealed to Daniel in a vision" (2:18–19). Thus, he was empowered to reveal the dream and what would "take place in the future" (2:45).

The story of Daniel underscores the reality that the future known exhaustively by the Almighty is hidden to astrologers. Only God can reveal what passes through the mind of a human and what it portends for the future. Nevertheless, from Nebuchadnezzar to now, prophetic stars continue to exact their unhealthy influence. Augustine, the greatest of medieval theologians, "denounced belief in the influence of the stars as inconsistent with the Christian view of God and man."[3] Nonetheless, Philip Melanchthon, "famous disciple of Luther, occupied the chair of Astrology in Wittenberg,"[4] and self-styled Roman Catholic astrologer Michel de Nostredame (Nostradamus) became infamous for pretenses ranging from the rise of Hitler to the fall of the Twin Towers.[5]

Lamentably, *The Prophecies of Nostradamus* (aka *The Centuries*) are as prominent today as when first published in 1555. Lines from his quatrains flood the Internet in purported evidence of prophetic prowess. "Beasts ferocious from hunger will swim across the rivers: The greater part of the region will be against the Hister" is hailed as an amazing prediction concerning the rise of Hitler and the German army—although "Hister" was more likely known to Nostradamus as a region bordering the Danube.[6] "In the City of York there will be a great collapse; two twin brothers torn apart by chaos" portends to be a sixteenth-century prediction respecting the September 11, 2001, Manhattan Massacre—though in reality it is "an entirely non-Nostradamian fabrication."[7]

While the humanistic idealism of the eighteenth-century Enlightenment temporarily retarded astrological speculation, the Darwinian revolution of the nineteenth century brought foretelling back to the fore. The fatalism of a world in which everything is determined by brain chemistry and genetics made futuristic fever ever more fashionable—this time round biblicists as noteworthy as the progeny of Babylonians. On the cultic fringe, Mormon founder Joseph Smith propagated the notion that his generation was living in the very shadow of Christ's return. Smith claimed that God himself told him the return of Christ would take place before he was eighty-five years of age.[8] In more mainstream circles, gifted Baptist orator William Miller prophesied that Christ's return was scheduled for 1843.[9] Sensing that the fate of the planet was sealed, millions turned to Hal Lindsey's *The Late Great Planet Earth*[10] for dates and details. Professor of systematic theology William Dyrness observes that "it is no coincidence that the publication of Hal Lindsey's first book on prophecy coincided with the greatest revival of astrology in three hundred years," and "interesting to note how often his book appears in bookstores alongside astrology manuals. Man can escape as easily into prophecy as astrology. In either case, he is a pawn and thus relieved of moral responsibility."[11]

Predictably, gory end-time details would soon be as hip as glorified end-time date-setting. Prophetic luminary Dr. John Walvoord forwarded the gruesome prophetic presupposition that Jews returning to Palestine were "placing themselves within a vortex of this future whirlwind which will destroy the *majority* of those living in the land of Palestine."[12] In keeping with Walvoord's ominous prophecy, Hal Lindsey prophesied that "a numberless multitude" of Jews would be slaughtered in a bloodbath that would exceed the horrors of the Holocaust. He went on to predict a future beast who would make Nazi butchers "look like Girl Scouts weaving a daisy chain."[13] For his part, Tim LaHaye used biblical monikers such as "The Day of Israel's Calamity" to codify what he eerily described as Antichrist's "final solution" to the "Jewish problem."[14] Like Lindsey, he saw a future time of national suffering for Jews "far worse than the Spanish Inquisition of the sixteenth century or even the Holocaust of Adolph Hitler in the twentieth century."[15] According to LaHaye, the soon-coming time of Jewish Tribulation will be a nightmarish reality beyond imagination: "Take the horror of every war since time began, throw in every natural disaster in recorded history, and cast off all restraints so that the unspeakable cruelty and hatred and injustice of man toward his fellow men can fully mature, and compress all that into a period of seven years. Even if you could imagine such a horror, it wouldn't approach the mind-boggling terror and turmoil of the Tribulation."[16]

For newly minted prophetic stars, midnight, May 14, 1948, was the watershed moment. The return of Jews to Palestine not only vindicated prophetic charts but provided a basis for determining the exact timing of the return of Christ. As Lindsey explains in *The Late Great Planet Earth*, "When the Jewish people, after nearly 2,000 years of exile, under relentless persecution, became a nation again on 14 May 1948 the 'fig tree' put forth its leaves. Jesus said that this would indicate that He was 'at the door,' ready to return. Then He said, 'Truly I say to you, *this generation* will not pass away until all these things take place.'" Lindsey concluded that "this generation" referred to "the generation that would see the signs—chief among them the rebirth of Israel. A generation in the Bible is something like forty years. If this is a correct deduction, then within forty years or so of 1948, all these things could take place."[17] Thus, Christ's return was projected to take place in 1981 $(1948 + 40 - 7 = 1981)$.[18]

As the time frame for the manifestation of Jesus and the massacre of Jews came and went, the red-letter day in 1948 in which the secular state of Israel had been founded began to lose luster. As historian Timothy Weber observed, "The new nation that had been declared in May 1948 looked nothing like the maps of ancient Israel found in the back of their Bibles or hanging on the walls of their Sunday school rooms."[19] Even more perplexing was the fact that Jews did not control the Holy City and had not been able to reinstitute the types and shadows of Old Testament sacrifice in a rebuilt temple on the site where the Muslim Dome of the Rock yet stood.

Outlooks changed when June 10, 1967, replaced May 14, 1948, as the quintessential day in end-time speculations. The state of Israel launched preemptive attacks on Egypt, Syria, Iraq, and Jordan, and within six days occupied the Golan Heights, Gaza, the Sinai, the West Bank, and, most important, Jerusalem. This go-round the math was downright magical. Add 40 to 1967, subtract 7, and 2000 emerged as the new date portending the coming of Jesus and the carnage of Jews. However, once again, the stars failed to align. Prophetic superstar Jack Van Impe, ever the innovator, held false prophecy charges at bay by recalibrating "a generation" at 50 years— 51.2 to be exact. If you divide "77 generations into 4000 years from Adam to Christ, that comes out to 51.2, and if you add the extra six months, because the Six-Day War took place in June, you're almost at 52 years," says Van Impe. Add 52 to 1967 "and you come out pretty close to 2018, 2019. Subtract 7 years from that and we're talking about 2012."[20] Ironically, he found confirmation in Mayan astrology. "The Mayan calendar ends December 21, 2012. It's all here, ladies and gentlemen," exuded Van Impe.[21]

Of one thing we can be certain: December 21, 2012, will come and go as one more in a long litany of failed prophecies. Indeed, prophetic stars are as impotent in date-setting as astrologers in Nebuchadnezzar's court were in dream-telling. They pervert the natural use of Scripture ordained by God for a superstitious use disdained by God. Scripture is not intended to tell us *when* Christ will return—but *that* he will return. And, when he does, he will "put all things to right." He will fully and finally resolve the problem of sin and Satan. He will separate and judge the wheat and the tares (Matthew 13:24–30). He will resurrect the dead and re-create the universe without the stain of disease, destruction, decay, and death (Romans 8:21).

The point, quite simply, is this: biblical prophecy is not designed to help us pin the tail on the Antichrist or pinpoint a future tribulation. Prophetic S-T-A-R-S in the constellation of biblical prophecy—like manuscript C-O-P-I-E-S and the archaeologist's S-P-A-D-E—are powerful proofs that God has spoken, that the Bible is divine rather than merely human in origin. In the words of the Almighty, "I told you these things long ago; before they happened I announced them to you so that you could not say, 'My idols did them; my wooden image and metal god ordained them'" (Isaiah 48:5). Or in the words of Jesus, "I have told you now before it happens, so that when it does happen you will believe" (John 14:29).

As noted, counterfeit prophecy stars have one thing in common: they are consistently wrong. In illumined contrast, genuine prophecy stars are infallibly correct. And unlike the pretenders, their prophetic prowess cannot be pawned off to good luck, good guessing, or deliberate deceit.

12

Succession of Nations

It is not possible to rightly govern the world without God and the Bible.

—GEORGE WASHINGTON

The initial *S* in S-T-A-R-S will serve to remind us of the Bible's prophetic prowess in accurately predicting a succession of nations from the first Adam to the last. It begins with Adam's fall and Paradise lost. The very chapter that references the Fall, however, also prophetically records the divine plan for restoration (Genesis 3:15). The plan took on definition with God's promise to make Abram a great nation through which "all peoples on earth will be blessed" (Genesis 12:3). The promise came into sharper focus when Moses led Abram's descendants out of their four-hundred-year bondage in Egypt. For forty years of wilderness wandering, God tabernacled with his people and prepared them for a land of promise. Like Abram, however, Moses only saw the promise from afar. It wasn't until Joshua led Israel into the promised land that God's promises would be finally and fully fulfilled (Joshua 21:43–45; 23:14).

David was Israel's national hero and quintessential king, but his son Solomon brought Israel to the apex of its glory. "All the kings of the earth sought audience with Solomon to hear the wisdom God had put in his heart" (2 Chronicles 9:23). "When the queen of Sheba heard of Solomon's fame, she came to Jerusalem" and said to Solomon, "The report I heard in my own country about your achievements and your wisdom is true. But I did not believe what they said until I came and saw with my own eyes. Indeed, not even half the greatness of your wisdom was told me" (9:1, 5–6). Solomon's zeal for the God of his father, however, waned in later years as foreign women turned his heart toward idols (1 Kings 11:1–8). In the end, a divided heart produced a divided homeland (2 Kings 11:9–40; 12:1–14:31).

During the ensuing century, a divided nation—Israel to the north and Judah to the south—grew indifferent to God's prophets and precepts. Intended to be a light to the nations, they became a mere microcosm of pagan culture. The kings of Israel made unholy alliances with pagan nations from Egypt to Babylon. They adopted the religions of foreign lands and built altars and shrines to pagan gods. Thus, as God had forewarned them (Deuteronomy 28–30; Joshua 23:15–16; 1 Kings 9:6–9; 2 Chronicles 7:19–22), the land vomited out the Israelites as it had the Canaanites before them. The Northern Kingdom was exiled in Assyria (722 BC), and the Southern Kingdom was exiled in Babylon (606 BC).

God, however, was far from finished with his covenant people. Through Daniel, he revealed his present and eternal purposes for the world. As such, six centuries before the advent of Christ, Daniel was empowered by the Almighty to do what no soothsayer or astrologer could do. With breathtaking precision, he predicted a succession of nations from Babylon to the coming of the Babe of Bethlehem—a king who would usher in a kingdom that will never be vanquished or destroyed.

The detail and dynamics of Daniel's prophetic prowess are such that antisupernatural scholars have dogmatically declared Daniel to be written pseudonymously by a second-century author. Their argument is simple: a Jewish exile writing six centuries before Christ could not possibly have known what would happen to Jews living four centuries later during the tyrannical reign of the second-century Greco-Syrian despot Antiochus IV Epiphanes.

Such antisupernatural bias is hardly warranted, however. Jewish historian Josephus correctly chronicled Daniel as a contemporary of Nebuchadnezzar.[1] Furthermore, Jews roundly regard the writings of Daniel as authentic and include them in the Jewish canon.[2] Finally, the Jewish Jesus not only accepted Daniel as a genuine prophet but viewed his writings as genuinely prophetic. Indeed, Jesus looked back at "'the abomination that causes desolation' spoken of through the prophet Daniel" as the basis for prophesying that the temple that had been desecrated by the forces of Antiochus would ultimately be destroyed by the forces of Antichrist (Matthew 24:15; see Daniel 9:27; 11:31; 12:11).[3]

FROM BABYLON TO THE MEDES

Daniel begins his prophetic foretelling of the succession of nations by predicting that Babylon—who had broken down the wall of Jerusalem and carried off her treasures, had burned the temple and destroyed the royal palaces, and had carried the remnant of Israel into exile and servitude—would itself fall from its lofty perch as golden head of the nations. Nebuchadnezzar had expunged the glories of the Assyrian Empire and made Babylon supreme in splendor and strength. "You, O king," says Daniel, "have become great and strong; your greatness has grown until it reaches the sky, and your dominance extends to the distant parts of the earth" (Daniel 4:22). During a reign of over forty years, Nebuchadnezzar was without equal in all the earth. His insufferable arrogance is seen not only in the height and breadth of the most prodigious walls ever built around an ancient city (4:30),[4] but in the golden statue he erected to himself on the plain of Dura in the province of Babylon (Daniel 3:1).

However, following Nebuchadnezzar (605–562 BC) the glories of Babylon faded with mind-boggling rapidity. Evil-Merodach, who succeeded Nebuchadnezzar, ruled but two years before being assassinated, and Neriglissar, his brother-in-law, but three. Neriglissar's youngest son was murdered in June 556 BC after only two months as monarch of the rapidly declining empire. Nabonidus—who may well have suffered the same maladies that drove his father-in-law, Nebuchadnezzar, to a seven-year stint of mental madness—served as coregent with the insufferable Belshazzar, who on that fateful night in October 539 BC gave orders to bring in the gold and silver goblets that Nebuchadnezzar had taken from the temple of God in Jerusalem so that he and his nobles, his wives, and his concubines might drink from them as they praised the gods of gold and silver, of bronze, iron, wood, and stone (Daniel 5:2). "That very night Belshazzar, king of the Babylonians, was slain, and Darius the Mede took over the kingdom, at the age of sixty-two" (5:30–31).

From Nebuchadnezzar's death to Belshazzar's demise, Babylon was in disarray. As such, the most improbable of Daniel's prophecies became reality. Media—as inferior as silver is to gold—became dominant in the ancient world.[5] And with the ascendancy of the Medes, the prophetic words of Daniel, like those of the prophets before him, began to take on ominous and foreboding reality: "The LORD has stirred up the kings of the Medes, because his purpose is to destroy Babylon" (Jeremiah 51:11; cf. vv. 28–29; Isaiah 13:17–18; 21:2, 9; see Daniel 2:36–39; 7:4–5).[6]

FROM THE MEDES TO THE MEDO-PERSIANS

The Median star would light the eastern sky for but the briefest of times. Following the death of Nebuchadnezzar, Media—envisioned by Daniel as a beast that looked like a bear raised up on one of its sides, with three ribs in its mouth (Ararat, Minni, and Ashkenaz [Jeremiah 51:27–29])[7]—was instructed, "Get up and eat your fill of flesh!" (Daniel 7:5). Media's military expansion into such Babylonian territories as the city of Susa in the province of Elam, however, was short-lived. Twelve years after the ascendancy of the Median Empire, the mighty Astyages (whose sister Amytis was the queen for whom Nebuchadnezzar constructed Babylon's famed hanging gardens) was deposed by Cyrus the Great, who succeeded in uniting the Median and Persian Empires under a ramrod shield of bronze. Thus, while the Median Empire would have its "fill of flesh," in the end Babylon would fall not to the Medes but to unified Medo-Persian forces.

If Cyrus was anything, he was pragmatic. Through marrying the daughter of Astyages, he moved into a position of power in Persia as vassal of the mighty Medians and within a decade became their monarch. Upon unifying the Medes and the Persians, he moved swiftly against Lydia's decadent Croesus and then fixed his gaze on the ultimate prize. As Belshazzar drank wine from Jerusalem's gold and silver goblets, Cyrus diverted the Euphrates and stole into Babylon. Belshazzar was slain and citizens of a golden empire now in disarray embraced him as liberator. Thus, two decades after becoming king of Persia, Cyrus had not only conquered the Medes, Lydians, and Babylonians but led the Medo-Persians to dominance in the ancient world.

From the standpoint of fulfilled prophecy, Cyrus is a veritable superstar. To begin with, he was the embodiment of a kingdom of bronze that would "rule over the whole earth" (Daniel 2:39). In biblical vernacular bronze was symbolic of strength and beauty. Even as I write I am reminded of Zechariah, who portrayed the immovable dwelling place of God as "mountains of bronze" (Zechariah 6:1); Micah, who prophesied that the daughters of Zion would be given "hoofs of bronze" with which to break to pieces many nations (Micah 4:13); Ezekiel, who envisioned an angel "whose appearance was like bronze" (Ezekiel 40:3); and Jesus, whose feet are like burnished bronze (Revelation 2:18).

The strength of Medo-Persia was surpassed only by its size. After unifying the Median and Persian Empires, Cyrus conquered the Lydian Empire along with Sardes, "the richest city of Asia after Babylon."[8] His "defeat of Babylon and the Babylonian empire, along with his previous conquests, brought the whole of the Near East within the Persian Empire with the exception of Egypt."[9] Though immodest, the Cyrus Cylinder aptly sums up the extent of his rule: "I am Cyrus, king of the world, great king, powerful king, king of Babylon, king of the country of Sumer and Akkad, king of the four corners of the earth."[10]

Though Cyrus died a scant nine years after overwhelming the glory of the Chaldeans, three successors would significantly add to the size and scope of Persian power. Cambyses extended the empire through annexation of Egypt. Darius I added northern India, Thrace, Macedon, and northeastern Greece. And Xerxes ruled the earth in legendary opulence. Thus the prophecy of Daniel was fulfilled: "Three more kings will appear in Persia, and then a fourth, who will be richer than all the others" (Daniel 11:2; cf. 7:6). In all, they would succeed in creating the largest empire the world had ever known (Daniel 2:39)—an empire that would not be surpassed until Rome had reached its zenith.[11]

Furthermore, though he created an empire that would "rule over the whole earth," the ultimate prophetic significance of Cyrus was realized in his liberation of the Jews from exile in Babylon. As such, the words of the Lord to Jeremiah the prophet apply equally to Cyrus: "Before I formed you in the womb I knew you, before you were born I set you apart" (Jeremiah 1:5). Indeed, generations before he appeared on the stage of history, the prophet Isaiah did what prophetic imitators could not—he prophetically named Cyrus before he was born. Prophesying eight centuries before Christ, Isaiah predicted the following concerning the coming of Cyrus in the sixth century:

> This is what the LORD says—your Redeemer, who formed you in the womb:

> *I am the LORD,*
> *who has made all things,*
> *who alone stretched out the heavens,*
> *who spread out the earth by myself,*
> *who foils the signs of false prophets*
> *and makes fools of diviners,*
> *who overthrows the learning of the wise*
> *and turns it into nonsense,*
> *who carries out the words of his servants*
> *and fulfills the predictions of his messengers,*
> *who says of Jerusalem, "It shall be inhabited,"*
> *of the towns of Judah, "They shall be built,"*
> *and of their ruins, "I will restore them,"*
> *who says to the watery deep, 'Be dry,*
> *and I will dry up your streams,'*
> *who says of Cyrus, 'He is my shepherd*

and will accomplish all that I please;
he will say of Jerusalem, "Let it be rebuilt,"
and of the temple, "Let its foundations be laid."
This is what the LORD says to his anointed,
to Cyrus, whose right hand I take hold of
to subdue nations before him
and to strip kings of their armor,
to open doors before him
so that gates will not be shut.

(ISAIAH 44:24–45:1)

Cyrus, like Nebuchadnezzar before him, was deeply impacted by the reality that the Most High God knew precisely what would happen in future times. Upon the realization that he had been called by name long before he was formed in his mother's womb and commissioned to be the agent by which the Holy Temple would be reestablished in Jerusalem, Cyrus made the following proclamation throughout all of Asia: "Since the Most High God has appointed me king of the habitable world, I am convinced that He is the God whom the Israelites worship. He foretold my name through the prophets, and that I was to build his temple in Jerusalem.'"[12] As elucidated by Josephus, "Cyrus knew this from reading Isaiah's prophecies given 210 years earlier. He marveled at the divine power, and he was controlled by desire to fulfill what was written. Gathering the most distinguished Jews in Babylon, Cyrus told them that he would permit them to return to their native land and rebuild Jerusalem and their temple. He would be their ally and would write his satraps and governors near Judea to contribute gold and silver for the building of the temple."[13]

Finally, we should note that it was the edict of Cyrus that fulfilled the prophetic words of Jeremiah: "When seventy years are completed for Babylon, I will come to you and fulfill my gracious promise to bring you back to this place" (Jeremiah 29:10). Thus, it was that "Daniel, understood from the Scriptures, according to the word of the LORD given to Jeremiah the prophet, that the desolation of Jerusalem would last seventy years" (Daniel 9:2). Again the words of eminent historian Josephus are enlightening: "In the first year of Cyrus' reign, which was the seventieth year since the Jewish migration to Babylon, God took pity on the captive people. Jeremiah the prophet had predicted that after they had been held in bondage 70 years they would again be restored to the land of their fathers and rebuild the temple."[14]

Particularly noteworthy about Jeremiah's prophecy is the time meted out for Babylonian rule. *"When seventy years are completed for Babylon,"* says Jeremiah, "I will come to you and fulfill my gracious promise to bring you back to this place" (Jeremiah 29:10). The particular precision of the prophet here is awe inspiring. Had Belshazzar been paying attention he might have thought twice about his defiance of the living God by drinking wine from the gold and silver goblets that Nebuchadnezzar had taken from the temple in Jerusalem. For that very night—seventy years after Babylon had conquered Assyria (609 BC)[15]—Belshazzar was slain and Cyrus turned over rule of Babylon to Darius the Mede (539 BC; Daniel 5:30).

As with prophecies concerning Cyrus, the precision of Daniel's prophetic and historical renderings should not be passed over lightly. First, it should be noted that in contrast to the Median Empire, which is characterized as "inferior," the Medo-Persian Empire is rightly referred to as a vast empire that would "rule over the whole earth" (Daniel 2:39). Furthermore, prior to unification, Media and Persia are identified separately—the former as a bear, the latter as a leopard (Daniel 7). However, "in the third year of King Belshazzar" (8:1), the symbolism is aptly altered in order to depict the unified Medo-Persian Empire as a singularity. As such, Daniel sees one "ram with two horns, standing before the canal, and the horns were long. One of the horns was longer than the other but grew up later" (Daniel 8:3). Gabriel identifies the horns as Media and Persia: the former as an independent Median Empire and the latter—which grew up later and longer—as the dominant Persian Empire. Finally, it is instructive to note that in seeing the vision of the ram, Daniel was transported to "the citadel of Susa in the province of Elam" (8:2) so that "here in the future royal citadel of the Persian kingdom he might witness the destruction of this world power, as Ezekiel was removed to Jerusalem that he might there see the judgment of its destruction."[16]

FROM THE MEDO-PERSIANS TO THE GREEKS

From the citadel of Susa in the province of Elam—the very birthplace of Cyrus the Great—God showed Daniel what would happen three centuries hence as the Medo-Persian Empire was shattered by Grecian hordes. "Suddenly," writes Daniel, "a goat with a prominent horn between his eyes came from the west, crossing the whole earth without touching the ground. He came toward the two-horned ram I had seen standing beside the canal and charged at him in great rage. I saw him attack the ram furiously, striking the ram and shattering his two horns. The ram was powerless to stand against him; the goat knocked him to the ground and trampled on him, and none could rescue the ram from his power" (8:5–7). Lest we mistake the meaning of the vision, the angel Gabriel provides Daniel with 20/20 clarity. "The two-horned ram that you saw," says Gabriel, "represents the kings of Media and Persia. The shaggy goat is the kingdom of Greece, and the large horn between his eyes is the first king" (8:20–21).

This king, of course, is none other than Alexander the Great, son of Philip II of Macedon and the Epirote princess Olympias.[17] Philip, infamous for spurning Olympias for the younger Cleopatra, exacted vengeance on the Persians for burning Greek temples during the reign of Xerxes, but it was his son Alexander who would ultimately conquer the prodigious Persian Empire.[18] Astride the mighty black Bucephalus, its massive brow adorned by a glistening white star, Alexander sent tremors of terror down the spines of the Medo-Persian military. Following the assassination of his father and against all odds, Alexander defeated the mighty Persian armies at Granicus in May 334 BC. A year later he changed the course of Western civilization at the battle of Issus. Outnumbered six to one, he set his sights on conquering a kingdom as large as his ambition. Leading from the front, the military genius overwhelmed the Persians at Issus (333 BC). When Darius III offered him the entirety of the Persian Empire west of the Euphrates in return for peace, he merely responded in bloody pursuit. Alexander defeated Darius at Gaugamela and there, in concert with the prophecies of Daniel, became supreme monarch of the ancient world (331 BC; see Daniel 2:40; 7:7; 8:5–7; 11:3).

Furthermore, "the shaggy goat" with "the large horn between his eyes" fulfilled one of the most amazing prophecies in the whole of Scripture. Following the battle of Issus, Alexander continued down the Mediterranean coast, capturing Persian seaports along the way. Upon reaching Tyre, he demanded access to the temple of Hercules so as to make oblations. Supposing security in an island fortress surrounded by pounding waves, the Tyrians refused. Undaunted, Alexander devised one of the most extraordinary feats in the annals of military warfare and, in doing so, fulfilled a prophecy made by Ezekiel more than two and a half centuries earlier.[19] To better understand the scope of Alexander's feat, let's look first at Ezekiel's prophecy.

Following Judah's deportation to Babylon (586 BC), Ezekiel prophesied that Tyre, who viewed the fall of Jerusalem as the pathway to further prosperity, would ultimately be destroyed. God would bring a succession of nations against Tyre "as the ocean brings up its waves." The first of these nations would be Babylon, who would besiege the mainland, break down the walls of Tyre, and butcher its citizens. Moreover, according to the prophet, Tyre would be scraped bare as a rock and its rubble thrown into the midst of the sea (Ezekiel 26:3–5).

What happened is a matter of history. A year after the destruction of Jerusalem, Nebuchadnezzar set his sights on destroying mighty Tyre—a gaudy and glittering oasis of luxury and wealth, queen of the seas as Babylon was king of the land. After a prolonged siege he succeeded in breaching the walls, destroying Tyre's strong towers and reducing the mainland to ruin and rubble. His efforts, however, went largely unrewarded. Recognizing the inevitability of the siege, the Tyrians transferred the bulk of their wealth to such colonies as Carthage or to their island citadel a kilometer off the mainland in the aqua blue waters of the Aegean Sea.

In time Babylon would fall to the allied forces of Media and Persia, but the island citadel of Tyre would continue its dance with prosperity. From the unassailable fortifications of their island fortress, the Tyrians could still see the broken walls of a once prosperous satellite city yet standing in mute testimony to broken and unfulfilled prophecy. Destroy Tyre? Throw the dust and debris of its mainland into the midst of the Aegean Sea? Impossible—or so it seemed!

Time continued its inexorable march into the future, and yet another empire would crumble into the dustbin of history. This time the kingdom forged by Cyrus the Great would succumb to the iron fist of Alexander the Great. After soundly defeating Sidon, the Macedonian continued his relentless march toward Tyre. His emissaries enjoined the Tyrians to embrace peace. They responded in haughtiness and haste, throwing the dead bodies of Alexander's ambassadors into the raging waters that surrounded their unbreachable citadel.

This time, however, the Tyrians had met their match. As I mentioned, Alexander purposed to do the unthinkable. He commissioned Diades of Pella to engineer a resplendent causeway from the ruined city on the seashore to the regal citadel in the sea. Thus was fulfilled the most improbable of prophecies. In keeping with Ezekiel's epic words, the mainland was scraped bare as a rock and its stones, timber, and rubble thrown into the sea. With the causeway finally complete and battering rams in position, the island fortress was mercilessly crushed. Thirty thousand Tyrians were sold into slavery, two thousand more morbidly crucified. And still Alexander was not done. To ensure that Tyre would never regain its lofty status as the center of world commerce, Alexander purposed to make his namesake—Alexandria—the commercial capital of the world.

And still the prophecy was not complete. "I will bring many nations against you," Ezekiel had prophesied, "like the sea casting up its waves." Babylon, Greece, Egypt, and Rome would all have their way with the once peerless Phoenician capital. After the Arab conquest in AD 638, deterioration devolved toward destruction. In 1291 Muslim hordes swept what little remained into the ash bin of history. In 1838, Edward Robinson, widely regarded as "the father of biblical geography," penned the following sobering thoughts:

> I continued my walk along the whole western and northern shore of the peninsula, musing upon the pomp and glory, the pride and fall of ancient Tyre. Here was the little isle, once covered by her palaces and surrounded by her fleets; where the builders perfected her beauty in the midst of the seas; where her merchants were princes, and her traffickers the honourable

of the earth; but alas! "Thy riches and thy fairs, thy merchandise, thy mariners, and thy pilots, thy calkers, and the occupiers of thy merchandise, and all thy men of war, that were in thee and in all thy company,"—where are they? Tyre has indeed become like "the top of a rock, a place to spread nets upon!" The sole remaining tokens of her more ancient splendour, lie strewed beneath the waves in the midst of the sea; and the hovels which now nestle upon a portion of her site, present no contradiction of the dread decree, "Thou shalt be built no more!"[20]

The king of Tyre said of Jerusalem, "Aha! The gate to the nations is broken, and its doors have swung open to me; now that she lies in ruins I will prosper" (Ezekiel 26:2). The King of kings said of Tyre, "Because you think you are wise, as wise as a god, I am going to bring foreigners against you, the most ruthless of nations; they will draw their swords against your beauty and wisdom and pierce your shining splendor. They will bring you down to the pit, and you will die a violent death in the heart of the seas" (Ezekiel 28:6–8). Aerial photography provides a graphic pictorial of the precision with which Ezekiel's prophecies have been fulfilled. Tyre's once resplendent island citadel—complete with herculean temples, extravagant palaces, and opulent housing—is but a shipwreck; Tyre's satellite city on the shore is abysmally bedecked by blacktop and block housing; and Diades's ingenious causeway has become an impoverished peninsula, pointing as a finger toward the once legendary city now largely submerged in the heart of the seas.[21]

Finally, we should note that even in death Alexander set the stage for the fulfillment of prophecy. After laying siege to Tyre, Alexander turned his attention to the Jewish state. He demanded that the high priest forsake his allegiance to Darius the Great. The high priest refused. Thus, following the fall of Tyre and his conquest of Gaza, Alexander set his sights on Jerusalem. "When Jaddua, the high priest, heard that Alexander was coming, he was terrified, and ordered his people to join him in sacrifice and prayer to God. Appearing to him in a dream, God told him to take courage and decorate the city with wreaths. The people were to clothe themselves in white and the priests with the robes of their order. Then they were to march out of the gates to meet the Macedonians, for they would not be harmed."[22]

When Alexander saw the priestly procession advancing toward him, he did the unthinkable. He prostrated himself before Jaddua. "His officers wondered if he had suddenly become insane. One of them, Parmenio, went up to Alexander and asked him to explain. He replied, 'When I was at Dium in Macedonia, considering how I could become master of Asia, I saw this very person in my sleep, dressed as he is now. He urged me not to delay, but to cross over confidently and take dominion over the Persians.'"[23]

Much to the delight of the Jews, Alexander proceeded into Jerusalem and offered up sacrifices in the Jewish temple. "And when the book of Daniel was shown to him, which predicted that one of the Greeks would destroy the Persian Empire, he thought himself to be the one so designated. When he offered the Jews whatever they desired, the high priest asked that they might observe their own laws and be exempt from the tribute every seventh year. Alexander granted these requests. They further asked that the Jews in Babylon and Media be allowed their own laws, and he also agreed."[24] So it was that a brittle relationship was forged between the empire of Greece and the elect of God. On one hand, the Hebrew Bible would be translated into Greek. On the other, Hellenism would be embraced by Jewish elite. In the end, however, Hellenism did not mingle any better with Judaism than iron mingles with clay.

Scarcely a decade after entering Jerusalem, Alexander was dead—a month short of his thirty-third birthday. In keeping with Daniel's prophecy, "At the height of his power his large horn was broken off, and in its place four prominent horns grew up toward the four winds of heaven" (Daniel 8:8). In a moment, in the twinkling of an eye, an empire was "broken up and parceled out toward the four winds of heaven." The massive empire did not go to Alexander's posterity but was "uprooted and given to others" (Daniel 11:4). As prophesied the four horns that emerged—"but not with the same power"—symbolized four generals who gained control of the Grecian Empire following the battle of Ipsus—Cassander, the western portion of the empire; Seleucus, the eastern; Lysimachus, the northern; and Ptolemy, the southern.[25] The four fractured domains summarily morphed into two dominant empires—the Ptolemys of Egypt (kings of the south) and the Seleucids of Syria (kings of the north). The border state of Israel sandwiched between north and south was initially controlled by the Ptolemys. Following the battle of Panias (198 BC), however, the "ten-horned" Seleucid Empire (Daniel 7:7) controlled Israel and became the worst of Jewish nightmares—for out of the ten horns would arise a "horn that looked more imposing than the others and that had eyes and a mouth that spoke boastfully" (7:20).[26]

This "little horn" with "eyes like the eyes of a man and a mouth that spoke boastfully" (7:8) was envisioned to be a "stern-faced king, a master of intrigue" (Daniel 8:23), and "a contemptible person who has not been given the honor of royalty" (Daniel 11:21). He would grow in power, "speak against the Most High and oppress his saints and try to change the set times and the laws. The saints will be handed over to him for a time, times and half a time" (Daniel 7:25). He would vent his fury against covenant keepers but "show favor to those who forsake the holy covenant. His armed forces will rise up to desecrate the temple fortress and will abolish the daily sacrifice. Then they will set up the abomination that causes desolation. With flattery he will corrupt those who have violated the covenant, but the people who know their God will firmly resist him" (Daniel 11:30–32).

As "the large horn" prophesied by Daniel was Alexander the Great, "the little horn" that "grew until it reached the host of the heavens" was Antiochus IV, last of the Seleucid monarchs, king of the north, son of Antiochus the Great, and chief villain of the Greco-Syrian Empire (Daniel 8:10). Daniel describes Antiochus as a beast that would trample its foes underfoot; as a little horn that would grow in power and become the greatest of four kings; and as a master of intrigue who would ruthlessly oppress the saints for a time, times, and a division of time. In superhuman arrogance Antiochus declared himself the incarnation of Zeus, father of the gods. Though he recklessly deemed himself *Epiphanes*—"the divine majesty"—detractors rightly dubbed him *Epimanes*—"the deluded madman."[27]

In keeping with the words of Daniel, Antiochus IV Epiphanes, opposer of the purposes of God, was "destroyed, but not by human power" (8:25). The death of Antiochus marked the manifest power of God over the kingdoms of humankind and signaled the soon coming of "a kingdom that will never be destroyed, nor will it be left to another people. It will crush all those kingdoms and bring them to an end, but it will itself endure forever"

(Daniel 2:44). This is the "rock cut out of the mountain but not by human hands—a rock that broke the iron, the bronze, the clay, the silver and the gold to pieces" (2:45).

In sum, one of the most significant demonstrations that the Bible is divine rather than merely human in origin is the undeniable reality that Daniel, writing six centuries before the advent of Christ, was empowered by the almighty God to do what no soothsayer or astrologer could. With awe-inspiring precision, he predicted a succession of nations from Babylon through the Median and Persian Empires, to the persecution and suffering of the Jews under the second-century Greco-Syrian beast Antiochus IV Epiphanes, including the despot's desecration of the Jerusalem temple, his untimely death, and freedom for the Jews under Judas Maccabaeus (for more on Antiochus, see chapter 14).[28]

Moreover, as Daniel looked down the corridor of time, he got a glimpse of the first-century coming of Messiah. As prophesied by Jeremiah, Jerusalem would experience a partial restoration "when seventy years are completed for Babylon" (Jeremiah 29:10); however, as revealed to Daniel through the angel Gabriel, the return from exile was merely a type of the antitypical freedom that would be experienced through Judas Maccabaeus, which itself was typological of ultimate restoration through the messianic Jesus. As such, Daniel's "seventy sevens" (Daniel 9:24–27) encompassed ten Jubilee eras[29] and represent the extended exile of the Jews that would end in the fullness of time—the quintessential Jubilee—when the people of God would experience ultimate redemption and restoration, not in a holy city but in the holy Christ, who inaugurated a kingdom that "will itself endure forever" (Daniel 2:44).

Truly, the succession of nations immortalized by the book of Daniel is a surpassingly spectacular star in the constellation of biblical prophecy.

13

$\mathcal{T}$ypological Prophecy

God's word of itself is pure, clean, bright, and clear.

—MARTIN LUTHER

Matt was a new Christian, zealous for the things of God. As such, he found a book on "evidences" and began memorizing a list of prophecies made in the Old Testament, fulfilled in the New. His favorite was the "virgin birth" prophecy of Isaiah 7:14—"Therefore the Lord himself will give you a sign: The virgin will be with child and will give birth to a son, and will call him Immanuel."

If ever there was a clear-cut case of fulfilled prophecy, this was it. The very first chapter of the very first book of the New Testament chronicles the birth of Jesus, seven and a half centuries later, as the glorious fulfillment of what the Lord had said through the prophet Isaiah—"'The virgin will be with child and will give birth to a son, and they will call him Immanuel'—which means, 'God with us'" (Matthew 1:23).

Overflowing with exuberance, Matt shared the prophecy and its fulfillment with Izzy, his Jewish coworker. Things immediately became difficult. Izzy, an articulate Jewish apologist fluent in Hebrew, had heard it all before. He quickly disabused Matt of the notion that Isaiah had a virgin birth in view.

"The Hebrew word *almah* has nothing to do with virginity," he retorted dismissively. "It simply designates a young woman of marriageable age. If Isaiah had had virginity in mind, he would have used the word *betulah*."

Izzy had just caught his stride. "Context, context, context," he repeated indignantly. "If only people would pay attention to context! Isaiah was *not* prophesying a virgin birth. He was prophesying that the birth of his son Maher-Shalal-Hash-Baz would be a sign guaranteeing God's temporal salvation of Judah, in danger of being destroyed by two superpowers to the north. Read it for yourself! The fulfillment of Isaiah 7:14 is found in Isaiah chapter 8."

Matt was stunned. "I'll research and return," he stammered weakly.

"I'll be waiting," Izzy retorted triumphantly.

A week later, they happened upon each other at the local Starbucks. This time Matt was prepared. He had enlisted more "evidences" and read Isaiah 7 and 8 more times than he could remember. Over coffee and bagels he reported what his research had revealed. "Isaiah's prophecy was fulfilled twice: once in the eighth century BC and a second time at the dawn of the Christian epic in the first."

Izzy could not help but roll his eyes. "A whole week and the best you can come up with is double fulfillment?" he sputtered sarcastically. "Think! Do you really want to say that Isaiah's wife was a virgin when she gave birth? Or that Judah was saved from two superpowers when Jesus was born?"

Izzy left Starbucks solidified in unbelief. As far as he was concerned, single-fulfillment was all there was or ever would be. Isaiah's prophecy was fulfilled in his own generation, and that was the end of its significance. The Christian notion that Isaiah's "virgin birth" prophecy was fulfilled in Jesus Christ was sheer nonsense.

Matt followed moments later, badly shaken in his faith. His attempts to answer Izzy's objections were born out of sheer desperation. He now realized that Isaiah 7:14 was fulfilled in Isaiah 8. And it didn't take a budding theologian to know that double-fulfillment brought with it a host of unintended consequences.

Tragically, Matt and Izzy were completely unaware of the explanatory power inherent in what is known as *typological fulfillment*. Thus, their communication was short-circuited. Had Matt understood the difference between typological and predictive fulfillment, he may well have been able to reach Izzy. Had Izzy understood the difference, he may not have dismissed Messiah on the pretext of a mere literalistic Old Testament interpretation.

THE SPLENDOR OF TYPOLOGICAL PROPHECY

Predictive prophecy is fairly straightforward. Micah 5:2 immediately comes to mind. When Herod asked the chief priests and the teachers of the law where Christ was to be born, they replied: "In Bethlehem in Judea, . . . *for this is what the prophet has written*: But you, Bethlehem, in the land of Judah, are by no means least among the rulers of Judah; for out of you will come a ruler who will be the shepherd of my people Israel" (Matthew 2:5). As such, Micah 5:2 is a predictive prophecy that is directly and specifically fulfilled with the birth of Christ in Bethlehem as chronicled in Matthew 2:5.

Typological prophecy is somewhat more complex.[1] If we ask whether Isaiah 7:14 is fulfilled with the virgin birth of Christ as chronicled in Matthew 1:23, the answer is yes and no. Izzy was right to contend that Isaiah 7:14 is fulfilled with the birth of Maher-Shalal-Hash-Baz. But he was wrong to suppose that Isaiah 7:14 was not fulfilled with the birth of Messiah. Why? Because when Matthew writes, "All this took place to fulfill what the Lord had said through the prophet: 'The virgin with be with child and will give birth to a son, and they will call him Immanuel'—which means, 'God with us'" (Matthew 1:22–23), he is speaking of typological rather than predictive fulfillment.

So what is typology? A *type* is a person, event, or institution in redemptive history that prefigures a corresponding but greater reality. The greater reality in which it finds fulfillment is referred to as an *antitype*. The writer of Hebrews specifically employs the notion of *antitype* in referring to the greatness of the heavenly sanctuary of which the holy temple was merely a type or a shadow: "Christ did not enter a man-made sanctuary that was only a copy of the true one [antitype]; he entered heaven itself, now to appear for us in God's presence" (Hebrews 9:24). Consequently, the antitype of the majestic temple is found in the Master Teacher.

In the book of Hebrews, as in the rest of the New Testament, the Old Testament history of Israel is interpreted as a succession of types that find ultimate fulfillment in the life, death, and resurrection of Jesus. One cannot fully grasp the meaning of the New Testament apart from familiarity with the redemptive history and literary forms of the Old Testament. Likewise, the New Testament shines light on the Old Testament and illumines the more complete significance of God's redemptive work in and through the nation of Israel. This relationship between the Testaments is in essence typological.

The New Testament's typological interpretation of the Old Testament, though often implicit in allusions to the Hebrew Scriptures, is made explicit in Paul's epistles. The apostle explains to the Corinthian church that the experiences of Israel prefigured the experiences of the believer under the new covenant as "examples [types] and were written down as warnings for us, on whom the fulfillment of the ages has come" (1 Corinthians 10:11). In his letter to the Romans, Paul refers to Adam as a "pattern" (literally, type) of Jesus Christ (Romans 5:14). He likewise taught the believers at Colossae that the dietary laws, religious festivals, and Sabbath of the old covenant were "a shadow of the things that were to come; the reality, however, is found in Christ" (Colossians 2:17).

The interpretive principle of typology is particularly pervasive in the Gospels. Jesus' successful resistance of temptation in the desert after forty days of fasting is a direct typological contrast with the disobedience of the Israelites that resulted in their forty years of wilderness wanderings (Matthew 4:1–11; Mark 1:12–13; Luke 4:1–13). In remaining faithful to his Father, Jesus did what Israel was unable to do. Jesus is thus true Israel and is revealed as the antitype of the Hebrew prophets through his preaching of repentance, his ministry of healing, his concern for the poor and the social outcasts, and his death near Jerusalem (Luke 13:33). Though like the prophets in these ways, Jesus is demonstrated to be greater than all the previous prophets in the manner of his miraculous ministry, his claims to be God, and the vindication of those claims in his resurrection.

This, of course, is not to confuse the biblical principle of typology with an allegorical method of biblical interpretation that ignores or rejects the historical nature of the Old Testament narratives. On the contrary, typology is firmly rooted in concrete realities and always involves historical correspondence and intensification. As K. J. Woollcombe has aptly pointed out, "Typological exegesis is the search for linkages between events, persons or things *within the historical framework of revelation*, whereas allegorism is the search for a secondary and hidden meaning underlying the primary and obvious meaning of a narrative."[2] Or, as German scholar Leonhard Goppelt explains, "The historicity of what is reported and the literal meaning of the text are of no consequence for allegorical interpretation, but for typology they are foundational."[3] A type must therefore be a historical person, event, or institution that prefigures another reality in redemptive history that is yet future.

Furthermore, biblical typology, as evidenced in the writings of the New Testament, always involves a heightening of the type in the antitype. It is not simply that Jesus replaces the temple as a new but otherwise equal substitute. No, Jesus is far greater than the temple! It is not as though Jesus is simply another in the line of prophets with Moses, Elijah, Isaiah, and Jeremiah. No, Jesus is much greater than the prophets! It is not as though the new covenant replaces the old covenant as a more modern but equivalent alternative. No, the new covenant is far greater than the old covenant—"a better covenant" (Hebrews 7:22)—rendering the old "obsolete" (Hebrews 8:13). The type, thus, is so heightened, escalated, or intensified in the antitype that by contrast it loses its own weight and significance.

Finally, I should note that antitypes themselves may also function as types of future realities. Communion, for example, is the antitype of the Passover meal. Each year the Jews celebrate Passover in remembrance of God's sparing the firstborn sons in the homes of the Israelite families that were marked by the blood of the Passover lamb (Luke 22; cf. Exodus 11–12). Jesus' celebration of the Passover meal with his disciples on the night of his arrest symbolically points to the fact that he is the ultimate Passover Lamb "who takes away the sin of the world" (John 1:29). Though the Last Supper and the corresponding sacrament of Communion serve as the antitype of the Passover meal, they also point forward as types to ultimate fulfillment in "the wedding supper of the Lamb" (Revelation 19:9; cf. Luke 22:15–18). On that glorious day the purified bride—true Israel—will be united with her Bridegroom in the new heaven and the new earth (Revelation 21:1–2). Thus, fulfillment of the promise is itself a guarantee of the final consummation of the kingdom of God. Says Goppelt, this already-but-not-yet typological fulfillment is indicative of "an eschatological tension in NT typology. Salvation has come in Christ; therefore, the church possesses what the fathers longed for. This salvation is hidden with Christ and is coming; therefore, the church, together with the fathers, waits for the perfect antitypes to be revealed."[4]

In sum, then, typology involves a divinely intended pattern of events encompassing both historical correspondence and intensification. As Dr. E. Earle Ellis explains, "Typology views the relationship of Old Testament events to those in the new dispensation not as a 'one-to-one' equation or correspondence, in which the old is repeated or continued, but rather in terms of two principles, historical correspondence and escalation."[5]

Understanding typology in general is essential to grasping the surpassing significance of typological prophecy in particular. Such understanding elucidates the manner in which Isaiah's virgin-birth prophecy finds fulfillment in the near-future birth of Maher-Shalal-Hash-Baz as well as ultimate fulfillment in the far-future birth of Messiah—fulfillment that entails a divinely intended pattern of events encompassing both historical correspondence and intensification.

As we will now see, the splendor of typological prophecy stands in stark contrast to sub-biblical notions such as double-fulfillment, which supposes that Isaiah foresees both the virginal conception of Maher-Shalal-Hash-Baz and the virginal conception of Messiah as twin mountain peaks juxtaposed one in front of the other. Izzy was right to point out that the conception of Maher-Shalal-Hash-Baz was hardly virginal. Moreover, Isaiah's prophecy is replete with definitive time markers such as, "*Before* the boy knows enough to reject the wrong and choose the right, the land of the two kings you dread will be laid waste" (Isaiah 7:16). Only through sleight of mind can Isaiah 7:14 be doubled and driven into the distant future.

As with double-fulfillment, single-fulfillment does violence to the biblical text. Indeed, Isaiah 7:14 does not constitute a direct prediction about the Messiah at all. Though Mary gave birth to Jesus as a virgin, Isaiah *did not* predict the virgin birth of Jesus. As we will now see, when Matthew says the virgin birth of Jesus is the fulfillment of Isaiah's prophecy, he speaks of typological fulfillment, not predictive fulfillment.

ISAIAH 7:14/MATTHEW 1:23

Isaiah 7 opens with breathtaking intrigue. Ahaz, monarch of the tiny kingdom of Judah, is "shaken, as the trees of the forest are shaken by the wind" (7:2). He is in mortal terror of kings Rezin of Syria and Pekah of Israel, who even now plot his ruin. Isaiah exhorts Ahaz to trust the Lord with all his heart and lean not on his own understanding. "Keep calm and don't be afraid. Do not lose heart because of these two smoldering stubs of firewood" (7:4).

Though the faithless Ahaz greatly tried God's patience, the ever faithful Almighty provided a sign guaranteeing Rezin and Pekah would come to ruin: "The virgin will be with child and will give birth to a son, and will call him Immanuel," promised Isaiah. And "before the boy knows enough to reject the wrong and choose the right, the land of the two kings you dread will be laid waste" (7:14–16).

What God promised came to pass. Isaiah "went to the prophetess, and she conceived and gave birth to a son" (Isaiah 8:3). Before the boy knew how to say, "My father or my mother," Syria and Samaria were laid waste by superior Assyrian forces. Despite God's providential care, Ahaz sought favor from King Tiglath-Pileser III of Assyria with resources pilfered from the temple treasury. Worse still, he abandoned temple sacrifice, going so far as to sacrifice his own sons to the gods of Tiglath-Pileser.

As a consequence of sin, the salvation Ahaz experienced was only temporary. Ahaz was reduced to a mere puppet king, his every move controlled by an evil Assyrian empire. One hundred and fifty years later, the temple itself suffered destruction and all Jerusalem lay in ruin. Yet God was not done with the people of the promise. Seven hundred years after faithless

Ahaz, Matthew saw the temporary salvation of Judah as a type of the eternal salvation that God's people would experience through Jesus, the Christ. While Izzy's contention that the Hebrew word *almah* has nothing to do with virginity is right, it is also wholly irrelevant. Matthew recognized a historical pattern of events that found quintessential fulfillment in the miraculous virgin birth of Messiah. Isaiah's wife gave birth to Maher-Shalal-Hash-Baz in a fashion common to all humanity. Thus, though she did not give birth as a virgin, Mary most certainly did.

Even apart from the tapestry of typology, Izzy would do well to recognize that belief in the virgin birth of Jesus Christ is not merely based on blind faith. As noted, miracles are not only possible but necessary in order to make sense of the universe in which we live. According to modern science, the universe had a beginning and is unfathomably fine-tuned to support life. The origin of life, information in the genetic code, irreducible complexity in biological systems, and the phenomenon of the human mind pose intractable problems for solely natural explanations. Thus, reason forces us to look beyond the natural world to a supernatural Designer who miraculously intervenes in the affairs of his created handiwork.

If we accept the evidential basis for believing that an uncaused first cause created the universe, we should have no problem opening our minds to the possibility of an actual virginal conception. Sadly, it has become all too common for modern people to buy into a unique brand of fundamentalism that values rhetoric and emotional stereotypes over reason and evidential substance. Those who suppose that the virgin birth is mythological would be well served to carefully consider the evidences just as they would be wise to open their minds to the possibility that Jesus is the antitype who intensifies all the types in the tapestry of the Old Testament.

HOSEA 11:1/MATTHEW 2:15

A further example of typological prophecy that has stumbled seekers and solidified more than a few skeptics in suspicion of the Scriptures is Hosea

11:1: "When Israel was a child, I loved him, and out of Egypt I called my son." It no doubt makes skeptics like Izzy dizzy to hear Christians pretend Hosea's prophecy is fulfilled in Immanuel rather than Israel. Yet that is precisely what Matthew contends. "[Joseph] got up, took the child and his mother during the night and left for Egypt, where he stayed until the death of Herod. *And so was fulfilled what the Lord had said through the prophet*: *'Out of Egypt I called my son'*" (Matthew 2:14–15).

In context, the Magi came to Jerusalem from the east and asked, "Where is the one who has been born king of the Jews? We saw his star in the east and have come to worship him" (2:2). When Herod heard this, he called together the chief priests and the teachers of the law, and asked them where Christ was to be born. They replied by citing the prophet Micah, who predicted that Jesus was to be born in Bethlehem. Thus, Herod gave orders to "kill all the boys in Bethlehem and its vicinity who were two years old and under" (2:16). But an angel of the Lord appeared to Joseph and urged him to "take the child and his mother and escape to Egypt. Stay there until I tell you, for Herod is going to search for the child to kill him" (2:13).

Here, as in Isaiah 7:14, historical correspondence between Israel's sojourn in Egypt and the sojourn of Immanuel in Egypt is not random but is a divinely intended pattern of events intensified in Christ. As pointed out by R. C. H. Lenski, God "might have arranged for the transfer of the holy family to Babylon by the aid of the magi. Abstractly considered it would have made no difference from what foreign land God would recall Jesus."[6] Instead, "God brought about the first sojourn and made that first sojourn a factual prophecy of the second, which he also brought about. The first is thus a divinely intended type of the second. It is *not* accidental that the angel sent Joseph to Egypt and to no other land."[7]

First we note the reason for exile in Egypt. The extraordinary evil of Jacob's sons exiled Joseph in Egypt, just as the extravagant evil of Herod exiled Jesus there. Furthermore, we note God's providential care for the royal seed of Abraham whereby Immanuel like Israel is preserved in the midst of sojourn in Egypt. Finally, beyond historical correspondences there is a corresponding escalation of type in antitype. Immanuel did what Israel could not. Israel succumbed to the wiles of the world, the flesh, and the devil during her desert sojourn, whereas Immanuel, true Israel, triumphed over every trial and temptation.

And even that is but grasping a thread on the underside of the tapestry of typology. For in the type is impregnated a pattern by which the majesty of the antitype may be more fully appreciated. Jacob and his sons were designated sons of God by adoption. Jesus is designated the Son of God in unique and absolute fashion. Says Lenski:

> Read apart from the antitype, this designation had only its ordinary meaning, but read in conjunction with the antitype, Jesus, "my son" becomes highly significant. Deuteronomy 32:18 states that Israel was begotten as Jehovah's son, and this is a fatherhood which exceeds that of Abraham and of Jacob (Isa. 63:16) and thus points to the miraculous begetting of the Son Jesus "of the Holy Spirit" (Matt. 1:20; Luke 1:35). We now see how Matthew connects "my son" in Hosea and Israel's early sojourn in Egypt as a true type and a divinely intended prophecy of "my Son," the Messiah, who likewise must sojourn in Egypt. Both had to leave the Holy Land, and all the Messianic hope connected with them seemed to be utterly lost in far-off Egypt. Yet, "did call out of Egypt" places the sure hand of God behind all these hopes. Israel returned from Egypt for its mission, and so did this greater Son, Jesus.[8]

The overarching point here is to underscore the need to make careful distinctions between predictive prophecies such as Micah 5:2, which finds fulfillment in Jesus' birthplace in Bethlehem (Matthew 2:5), and typological prophecies such as Hosea 11:1, which are typologically fulfilled in Christ (Matthew 2:15). Failure to recognize the difference has led more than a few to outright doubt and disbelief. While it is incredible to realize that the birthplace of Jesus is accurately prophesied centuries in advance, it is obviously perplexing to look up Matthew's citation of Hosea 11:1 and find it to reference Israel rather than Immanuel. Only when the elegance of typology is comprehended is the mystery of Scripture more fully apprehended.

A helpful analogy may be found in the genealogy we encounter at the beginning of Matthew's gospel. As is the case with typology, a failure to recognize that there's a whole lot more going on than a literalistic recapitulation of generations will lead to an unnecessary suspicion of the text. At first blush Matthew's genealogy appears to be absurd—even contradictory to the genealogy presented by Luke. Further examination reveals it to be ingeniously constructed to highlight the person and work of Jesus Christ.

Matthew, writing to a primarily Jewish audience, emphasizes that Jesus Christ is the seed of Abraham and the legal heir of David, the long-awaited King of Israel who would ultimately restore his people from exile. As such, Matthew records fourteen generations from Abraham to David, fourteen from David to the exile, and fourteen from the exile to the Christ (Matthew 1:17). As a former tax collector, Matthew thus skillfully organizes the genealogy of Jesus into three groups of fourteen, the numerical equivalent of the Hebrew letters in King David's name $(4 + 6 + 4 = D + V + D)$. As such, he simultaneously highlights the most significant names in the lineage of Jesus and artistically emphasizes our Lord's identity as Messiah who forever sits upon the throne of David.

Luke, writing to a primarily Gentile audience, extends his genealogy past Abraham to the first Adam, thus highlighting that Christ, the Second Adam, is the Savior of all humanity. Calling Adam "the son of God" (Luke 3:38) and strategically placing the genealogy between Jesus' baptism and the desert temptation, Luke masterfully reveals Jesus as *Theanthropos*— the God-Man. While Luke's genealogy stretches from the first Adam to the Second, in concert with the gospel of Matthew, only mountain peaks in the lineage are accounted for.

Thus, the common objection from literalists on the left that the genealogies are deficient in number is rendered as obtuse and meaningless as are dissimilarities between them.[9]

JEREMIAH 31:15/MATTHEW 2:18

A final illustration that serves to underscore the criticality of distinguishing between predictive and typological prophecy is found in Matthew's quotation of Jeremiah: "When Herod realized that he had been outwitted by the Magi, he was furious, and he gave orders to kill all the boys of Bethlehem and its vicinity who were two years old and under, in accordance with the time he had learned from the Magi. Then what was said through the prophet Jeremiah was fulfilled, 'A voice is heard in Ramah, weeping and great mourning, Rachel weeping for her children and refusing to be comforted, because they are no more'" (Matthew 2:16–18).

Apart from typology, Matthew's contention would be laughable. In context, Jeremiah warned the Southern Kingdom of Judah that what happened to Israel in the north would soon happen in the south. Thus, it seems a stretch for Matthew to contend that Jeremiah's words are fulfilled by a first-century slaughter. I can hear Izzy now: "If only people would pay attention to context! Jeremiah's words were *not* fulfilled with the death of infants at the hand of the Roman Herod but with destruction of Israel at the hands of the Assyrian Sargon."

Sans typology there is little hope of getting through to Izzy. Being able to explain the elegance of Matthew's intent, however, opens up a wonderful avenue for communication and witness. What Matthew intends all of us—including Izzy—to understand is that there is historical correspondence between Israel's exile eight centuries prior to the time of Christ and the execution of infants at the advent of Christ. Disobedience lay at the root of both catastrophes. Says Lenski, "Israel's sin caused the Assyrians to carry the ten tribes of the northern kingdom into exile where they entirely disappeared: 'they were not.' It is the same sin that placed a foreign monster, the Idumean Herod, on the Jewish throne at the time of the birth of the Messiah and thus enabled him to slay the children of Bethlehem, so that of them, too, it was true: 'they were not.'"[10]

But Matthew intends much more than just historical correspondence. He intensifies the type in the antitype. Through citing Jeremiah 31 he underscores the glorious reality that God brings blessings out of disaster and life out of death. Jeremiah used the exile of the Northern Kingdom as a warning to the Southern Kingdom that disaster loomed on the horizon. He envisioned Rachel, beloved wife of Jacob and matriarch of Israel, in great mourning for her children—her voice rising from the heights of Ramah at the crossroads of a divided kingdom and reverberating in the ears of those who bore the bitter dregs of disobedience.

For the first-century progeny of Rachel, the sound of her voice was a poignant reminder that though weeping lasts for a night, joy comes in the morning. Thus, immediately following the citation of Rachel's weeping, God promises both "hope" and a "future" (Jeremiah 31:17) for true Israel. Out of the ashes would arise an eternal city that "will never again be uprooted or demolished" (31:40). As such, Matthew's citation of Rachel's mourning is at once enduring comfort for all the bereaved of Bethlehem and a sure reminder that the Lion of the tribe of Judah now stood upon the precipice of history.

As a result of the incarnation, Jesus, not Jerusalem, would be the one around whom all true Israel would now be gathered. The earthly Jerusalem was thus a type that was heightened by the greater reality of the heavenly city where the Babe of Bethlehem is enthroned. It is toward the antitypical heavenly Jerusalem with Jesus on its throne that Israel was now to direct its eschatological gaze. Imbued in Matthew's message were warnings that all who fixate on an earthly Jerusalem with continued temple sacrifices were in slavery to a type. Conversely, all who recognized Messiah in their midst were free to inherit the earth (Matthew 5:5). As such, the one who was preserved in Egypt now leads the true children of Israel into an eternal land of promise in which Herod "is no more."

MATT AND IZZY: TAKE TWO

Matt was zealous for the things of God. He believed God had spoken and focused his energies on learning to read the Bible for all its worth. As he immersed himself in the art and science of biblical interpretation, he became increasingly aware of the profundity of Scripture. It was amazing to think that Micah prophesying seven centuries before Christ was empowered by God to correctly predict that Messiah would be born in Bethlehem.

As amazing as the predictive prophecies were, the elegance of the tapestry of typological prophecy proved quite literally mind-altering. It provided a structure that knit the Old Testament to the New and facilitated the understanding of each through reference to the other. How incredible to discover that Jesus' successful resistance of temptation in the desert after forty days of fasting in the New Testament was a direct typological contrast to the disobedience of the Israelites that resulted in their forty years of wilderness wanderings in the Old. In remaining faithful to his Father, Immanuel did what Israel failed to do!

Given the panoply of typological prophecies made in the Old and fulfilled in the New, Matt loved best the "virgin birth" prophecy of Isaiah 7:14—"Therefore the Lord himself will give you a sign: The virgin will be with child and will give birth to a son, and will call him Immanuel." As far as he was concerned, it was the quintessential expression of a divinely intended pattern of events that encompassed both historical correspondence and intensification.

If ever there was an intoxicating illustration of how a typological prophecy was fulfilled in Christ, this was it. The very first chapter of the very first book of the New Testament chronicles the birth of Jesus, as the glorious fulfillment of what the Lord had said through the prophet Isaiah—"'The virgin will be with child and will give birth to a son, and they will call him Immanuel'—which means, 'God with us'" (Matthew 1:23).

Overflowing with exuberance, Matt shared the prophecy and its typological fulfillment with Izzy, his Jewish coworker. Izzy was dumbfounded. He had always seen this prophecy as one of the greatest weaknesses of the Christian worldview. The Hebrew word *almah* in Isaiah's prophecy had nothing to do with virginity. It simply designated a young woman of marriageable age. If Isaiah had had virginity in mind, he would have used the Hebrew word *betulah*.

Not only so but context precluded the possibility that Isaiah's prophecy was fulfilled in the virgin birth of Jesus Christ. Isaiah did *not* prophesy a virgin birth. He prophesied that the birth of his son Maher-Shalal-Hash-Baz was a sign guaranteeing God's temporal salvation of Judah, in danger of being destroyed by two superpowers to the north.

Matt explained to Izzy that the meaning of *almah* was in essence a "red herring." Moreover, Matt was able to show Izzy how the Jewish gospel writer Matthew saw a historical pattern of events surrounding the birth of Isaiah's son that found quintessential fulfillment in a corresponding historical pattern surrounding the birth of Immanuel. While Isaiah's wife gave birth to Maher-Shalal-Hash-Baz in the fashion common to all humanity, the historical pattern reached a climax in the virgin birth of Messiah. Thus, while Isaiah's wife did not give birth as a virgin, Mary most certainly did!

Izzy's interest was more than piqued—particularly as Matt explained that this was not an isolated example. In the ensuing weeks, Matt was able to show Izzy how the words of Hosea, "When Israel was a child, I loved him, and out of Egypt I called my son" (Hosea 11:1), were typologically fulfilled in Christ. How historical correspondence between Israel's sojourn in Egypt and the sojourn of Immanuel there was not random but was a divinely intended pattern of events intensified in Christ. Izzy slowly glimpsed the possibility of a fulfillment that was multifaceted and majestic. Not shallow and shortsighted. Thus, he was eager to learn more.

Week by week they met at the local Starbucks. Over coffee and bagels they studied the Scriptures together. Izzy was increasingly fascinated by everything from the ingenious construction of Matthew's genealogies to the typology inherent in Herod's slaughter of infants in the vicinity of Bethlehem. At first it seemed a stretch that the words of the prophet Jeremiah could be fulfilled by Herod's first-century slaughter. In time, however, Izzy began to grasp the typological correspondence between Israel's exile and the execution of infants.

Months passed as they flipped through the Scriptures together—Izzy more familiar with the Old, Matt the New. Together they learned. As an Orthodox Jew, Izzy was dedicated to the eternal and unalterable Mosaic law as reinterpreted by rabbis subsequent to the fall of Jerusalem. He was convinced that only through devotion to the complex code of Jewish law (*Halakhah*) could one experience nearness to God. In concert with other Orthodox Jews, he looked forward to a rebuilt temple and a Jewish Messiah who would restore the kingdom to Israel.

Now, however, he was beginning to waver. Matt explained that the temple, priesthood, and sacrifices were forever obsolete as a result of Christ's sacrifice on the cross. He showed Izzy from the Scriptures how the priests had offered sacrifices "at a sanctuary that is a *copy* and *shadow* of what is in heaven. This is why Moses was warned when he was about to build the tabernacle: 'See to it that you make everything according to the *pattern* shown you on the mountain.' But the ministry Jesus has received is as superior to theirs as the covenant of which he is mediator is superior to the old one, and it is founded on better promises" (Hebrews 8:5–6).

Slowly but surely the futility of the sacrificial system in light of the Savior's sacrifice became clear to Izzy. Torah study, like temple sacrifice, found satisfying fulfillment in Jesus. "Day after day every priest stands and performs his religious duties; again and again he offers the same sacrifices, which can never take away sins" (Hebrews 10:11). Jesus, however, "offered for all time one sacrifice for sins" (10:12). Jesus forever did away with the need for sacrifice, fulfilling Torah and rendering the temple null and void.

Izzy was particularly moved by a conversation between Jesus and the woman at Jacob's well in Samaria. "Our fathers," said the Samaritan woman, "worshiped on this mountain, but you Jews claim that the place where we must worship is in Jerusalem." Jesus corrected her faulty presuppositions with a liberating truth: "Believe me, woman, a time is coming when you will worship the Father neither on this mountain nor in Jerusalem. . . . A time is coming and has now come when the true worshipers will worship the Father in spirit and truth" (John 4:20–21, 23).

It finally hit Izzy with the force of an earthquake: what Jesus was saying is that in his own person he replaced temple sacrifice. He is not merely mediator of a new covenant; he is the incarnation of it. Indeed he is the antitype of the whole of the old covenant. Thus to revert back to a sacrificial system was to trample the Son of God underfoot, to treat as an unholy thing the blood of the covenant and to insult the Spirit of grace (Hebrews 10:29; cf. Hebrews 5:11–6:12; Galatians 3–5).

All of the types and shadows of the old covenant, including the holy land of Israel, the holy city Jerusalem, and the holy temple of God, have been fulfilled in the Holy Christ. As such, it is Paradise—a new heaven and a new earth—not Palestine for which our hearts yearn. It is "the Holy City, the new Jerusalem, coming down out of heaven from God, prepared as a bride beautifully dressed for her husband" (Revelation 21:2) upon which we fix our gaze. And it is the Master Teacher, not a majestic temple, that forever satisfies our deepest longings.

A few months later, Izzy found himself on bended knee. Today, he follows Messiah as a reproducing disciple maker. More than once he has used the dazzling star of typological prophecy to demonstrate to family and friends that God has spoken—that the Bible is divine as opposed to being merely human in origin.

14

*A*bomination of Desolation

*The sacred Scriptures come from the fulness of the Spirit; so
that there is nothing in the Prophets or the Law, or the Gospel,
or the Epistles, which descends not from divine majesty.*

—ORIGEN

The legacy of the English Bible had its genesis in the writings of Oxford
theologian John Wycliffe, fondly remembered as "the morning star of the
Reformation." Wycliffe's translations from the 1380s remained the only
English Bible until the invention of movable type in the sixteenth century
and profoundly influenced the legacy of the English Bible. Because he held
the Bible, rather than the pope, to be the exemplar of Christianity and the
sole authority for faith and practice, Wycliffe's writings were condemned
as heresy. Putting Scripture into the hands of the laity was considered such
an outrage against the authority of the Church that forty-four years after
Wycliffe died (1384), Pope Martin V had his bones unearthed and inciner-
ated and the ashes unceremoniously thrown to the wind. Like his ashes,
however, the legacy of Wycliffe's English Bible spread abroad in the ensuing years.

Perhaps no single person made a greater contribution to the legacy of the English Bible than did Oxford/Cambridge scholar William Tyndale. Like Wycliffe, Tyndale defied the papacy and its traditions. He purposed to make the Bible available to the commoner so that "a boy who drives the plough" would be as familiar with the Scriptures as was the pope.[1] Tyndale's work became the basis for a plethora of translations, culminating with the King James Version. After a lengthy imprisonment, Tyndale, like Wycliffe before him, was tried for translating the Bible into the English language. He was martyred October 6, 1536. His body ablaze, he cried out, "Lord, open the King of England's eyes!"[2]

Tyndale's prayer found an answer when King Henry VIII authorized an English translation "of the greatest volume" to be chained to every church pulpit in the land.[3] Due to its size, the first "authorized" English translation came to be known as the Great Bible. The volume and popularity of the Great Bible was such that parishioners far and wide gathered in parishes to experience formal readings from its pages.

Though the Bible was now available to the masses, it remained in chains. Not to protect it from thieves, but to protect it from the unbridled speculations of untrained laity. Luther, however, would have none of it. He believed the Bible to be at once so profound that a theologian could drown in it, and yet so perspicuous that a child could fathom it. Thus, when Catholic humanist Desiderius Erasmus of Rotterdam warned that translation of the Bible into the vernacular of the masses would "unloose a floodgate of iniquity," Luther responded in cryptic fashion, "If a floodgate of iniquity be opened, so be it."[4]

To guard against "the floodgate of iniquity" the Reformers forwarded the "analogy of faith" as the primary principle in the art and science of biblical interpretation. The imperative was to interpret the cloudy in view of the clear—the implicit in view of that which was explicit. The whole of Scripture was to be regarded as greater than the sum of its individual parts. Comprehension of the whole was recognized as impossible, apart from comprehension of individual passages, and comprehension of individual passages impossible apart from comprehension of the whole. Through devoted application of the "analogy of faith," faithful interpretation would prevail over the abominable interpretations of the unstable.

Tragically, the safeguard holding back "the floodgate of iniquity" fell into disuse and disrepair. Thus the Bible was turned and twisted into but a pathetic caricature of itself. Great and glorious passages demonstrating the Bible to be divine rather than merely human in origin were grotesquely twisted to make the Bible appear merely human rather than manifestly divine in origin.

The writings of Bart Ehrman are the classic case in point. Failing to follow the analogy of faith, Professor Ehrman deemed the historical Jesus a false apocalyptic prophet mistaken and misguided in predicting that his generation would experience the end of the world:

> Jesus fully expected that the history of the world as we know it (well, as he knew it) was going to come to a screeching halt, that God was soon going to intervene in the affairs of this world, overthrow the forces of evil in a cosmic act of judgment, destroy huge masses of humanity, and abolish existing human, political and religious institutions. All this would be a prelude to the arrival of a new order on earth, the kingdom of God. *Moreover, Jesus expected this cataclysmic end of history would come in his own generation*, at least during the lifetime of his disciples.
>
> It's pretty shocking stuff, really. And the evidence that Jesus believed and taught it is fairly impressive.[5]

Inconceivably—particularly for a highly touted scholar—Ehrman uses the words spoken by Jesus as he sat on the Mount of Olives surrounded by his disciples as evidence of "a judgment that is universal," which "would affect everyone and everything." Says Ehrman, "This effect is spelled out in language that heightens its cosmic nature: 'the sun will be darkened, and the moon will not give its light, and the stars will be falling from heaven and the powers in the heavens will be shaken' (Mark 13:24–25)."[6]

Had Ehrman been faithful to the "analogy of faith," he may not have "unloosed the floodgate of iniquity." In comparing Scripture with Scripture, it is more than obvious that Jesus used the language of sun, moon, and stars to predict his coming in judgment, not his judgment in coming at the end of time. Ezekiel, Joel, Amos, and Zephaniah all spoke in similar fashion. Using the metaphorical imagery of cosmic disturbances, they predicted judgment in their generations.[7] Listen to the words of Isaiah: "See, the day of the LORD is coming—a cruel day, with wrath and fierce anger—to make the land desolate and destroy the sinners within it. *The stars of heaven and their constellations will not show their light. The rising sun will be darkened and the moon will not give its light*" (Isaiah 13:9–10). To those unfamiliar with biblical language, these words may well be taken to mean that the end of the world was at hand. In reality, Isaiah was prophesying that the Medes were about to put an end to the glories of the Babylonian Empire.

The language of sun, moon, and stars is reminiscent of the epic drama that unfolds as Jesus opens the sixth seal in John's Apocalypse: "*The sun turned black like sackcloth made of goat hair, the whole moon turned blood red, and the stars in the sky fell to earth*, as late figs drop from a fig tree when shaken by a strong wind" (Revelation 6:12–13). The language of John harks back to the Olivet Discourse as the language of Jesus harks back to the language of Isaiah in the Old Testament. In each case, the prophets use final consummation language to describe judgment in their own generation. Contra Ehrman, Jesus, heir to the linguistic riches of the Old Testament prophets, uses cosmic imagery to pronounce judgment on Jerusalem, just as Isaiah did to pronounce judgment on Babylon.

The point here is that far from being undressed as a false prophet, who mistakenly believed that the world would end within the generation of his disciples, Jesus rightly prophesied that his generation would see the destruction of Jerusalem and the Jerusalem temple. When the disciples asked the Master about the time of his coming in judgment, he gave them an unmistakable sign. A sign they could readily process. A sign already emblazoned on the canvas of their consciousness: "When you see standing in the holy place '*the abomination that causes desolation*,' spoken of through the prophet Daniel—let the reader understand—then let those who are in Judea flee to the mountains. Let no one on the roof of his house go down to take anything out of the house. Let no one in the field go back to get his cloak" (Matthew 24:15–18).

As such, the abomination of desolation is yet another dazzling star in the constellation of biblical prophecy.

THE ABOMINATION OF DESOLATION SPOKEN OF BY JESUS

The Olivet Discourse began with Jesus walking away from the very house that afforded the Jewish people their spiritual and sociological significance. He had pronounced seven woes on the Pharisees and then uttered the unthinkable: "*Your* house is left to you desolate" (Matthew 23:38). When Jesus drove the money changers out of the temple and overturned their tables, he designated it "*My* house." Now it was relegated "*Your* house." What was once the dwelling of God was now a mere house of men.

When the disciples called the Master's attention to the magnificence of the temple and its surroundings, he replied, "I tell you the truth, not one stone here will be left on another; every one will be thrown down" (Matthew 24:2). Filled with apocalyptic dread and anxiety, they asked, "*When* will this happen, and *what* will be the sign of your coming and of the end of the age?" (24:3).

In sober response, Jesus pointed his disciples toward the coming abomination: "When you see standing in the holy place 'the abomination that causes desolation,' spoken of through the prophet Daniel—let the reader understand—then let those who are in Judea flee to the mountains. Let no one on the roof of his house go down to take anything out of the house. Let no one in the field go back to get his cloak. How dreadful it will be in those days for pregnant women and nursing mothers! Pray that *your* flight will not take place in winter or on the Sabbath. For then there will be great distress, unequaled from the beginning of the world until now—and never to be equaled again" (24:15–21). "At that time," said Jesus, "the sign of the Son of Man will appear in the sky, and all the nations of the earth will mourn. They will see the Son of Man coming on the clouds of the sky, with power and great glory" (24:30). So as to leave no doubt regarding the time of his coming, Jesus said, "I tell you the truth, *this generation* will certainly not pass away until all these things have happened. Heaven and earth will pass away, but my words will never pass away" (24:34–35).

As noted previously, Bart Ehrman supposes that by this prophecy, Jesus disqualified himself as deity and demonstrated beyond the shadow of a doubt that he was a false prophet. And he is hardly unique. Long before Ehrman, the world-class philosopher and leading intellectual Bertrand Russell summarized the same sentiment in an essay titled "Why I Am Not a Christian." Jesus "certainly thought that His second coming would occur in clouds of glory before the death of all the people who were living at that time."[8] Like Russell, the great missionary physician and New Testament scholar Albert Schweitzer believed that Jesus was a false prophet because he testified that his second coming would occur within the lifetime of his disciples. As Schweitzer explains in his autobiography, "The bare text compelled me to assume that Jesus really announced persecutions for the disciples and, as a sequel to them, the immediate appearance of the celestial Son of Man, and that His announcement was shown by subsequent events to be wrong."[9]

Had these men more carefully considered the language of the Old Testament, they may not have so quickly pronounced Christ a false prophet. When Jesus said, "They will see the Son of Man *coming* on the clouds of the sky, with power and great glory" (24:30), he used the language of the prophets. Who can forget the familiar Old Testament passage in which Daniel sees a vision of "one like a son of man, *coming* with the clouds of heaven. He approached the Ancient of Days and was led into his presence" (Daniel 7:13). Here Christ is clearly not *descending* to earth in his second coming but rather *ascending* to the throne of the Almighty in vindication and exaltation.

As the student of Scripture well knows, "clouds" are a common Old Testament symbol pointing to God as the sovereign judge of the nations. In the words of Ezekiel, "the day of the LORD is near—a day of *clouds*, a time of doom for the nations" (Ezekiel 30:3). Or as the prophet Joel put it, "The day of the LORD is coming. It is close at hand—a day of darkness and gloom, a day of *clouds* and blackness" (Joel 2:1–2). Isaiah spoke in similar fashion respecting Egypt: "See, the LORD rides on a swift cloud and is *coming* to Egypt. The idols of Egypt tremble before him, and the hearts of the Egyptians melt within them" (Isaiah 19:1). Certainly no one is so benighted as to think that *coming* on clouds in this context is anything other than language that denotes judgment. Why then should anyone suggest that Christ's *coming on clouds* in context of the Olivet Discourse would refer to anything other than the judgment Jerusalem would experience within a generation, just as Jesus had prophesied? We must inevitably ask ourselves whether it is indeed credible to suppose that Jesus, "heir to the linguistic and theological riches of the prophets, and himself a greater theologian and master of imagery than them all, should ever have turned their symbols into flat and literal prose."[10]

Like Daniel, Isaiah, Ezekiel, and a host of prophets before him, Jesus employed the language of "clouds" to warn his disciples of judgment that would befall Jerusalem within a generation. Using final consummation language to characterize a near-future event, the Master prophesied, "At that time the sign of the Son of Man will appear in the sky, and all the nations of the earth will mourn. They will see the Son of Man coming on the clouds of the sky, with power and great glory" (Matthew 24:30). Far from predicting his second coming, Jesus prophesied that those who saw standing in the holy place the abomination that causes desolation would likewise see his vindication and exaltation as Israel's rightful king.

Common sense alone should be sufficient to convince the unbiased that redefining the word "coming" to mean "second coming" and the phrase "end of the age" to mean "end of the world" is at best misguided. When Jesus said, "I tell *you* the truth, *this generation* will certainly not pass away until *all these things* have happened," his disciples did not for a moment think he was speaking of his second coming or of the end of the cosmos. As conflicted as they may have been about the character of Christ's kingdom or the scope of his rule, they were not in the least confused about who he was addressing.

"The abomination of desolation" spoken of by Jesus had been prophesied six centuries earlier by Daniel, who wrote, "His armed forces will rise up to desecrate the temple fortress and will abolish the daily sacrifice. Then they will set up the abomination that causes desolation. With flattery he will corrupt those who have violated the covenant, but the people who know their God will firmly resist him" (Daniel 11:31; see also 9:27; 12:31). In 167 BC, Daniel's prophecy became an unforgettable reality when Antiochus IV Epiphanes took Jerusalem by force, abolished temple sacrifices, erected an abominable altar to Zeus Olympus, and violated the Jewish covenant by outlawing Sabbath observance.[11]

Thus, when Jesus referenced the desolation spoken of by the prophet Daniel, everyone in his audience knew precisely what he was talking about. The annual Hanukkah celebration ensured that they would ever remember the Syrian antichrist who desecrated the temple fortress, the pig's blood splattered on the altar, and the statue of a Greek god in the Holy of Holies. Had God not supernaturally intervened, through the agency of Judas Maccabaeus, the epicenter of their theological and sociological identity would have been destroyed, not just desecrated.

In the Olivet Discourse Jesus took the quintessential Jewish nightmare and extended it to cosmic proportions. In the fullness of time what Jesus declared desolate was desolated by Roman infidels. They destroyed the temple fortress, and ended the daily sacrifice. This time the blood that desolated the sacred altar flowed not from the carcasses of unclean pigs but from the corpses of unbelieving Pharisees. This time the Holy of Holies was not merely desecrated by the defiling statue of a pagan god but was manifestly destroyed by the pathetic greed of despoiling soldiers. This time no Judas Maccabaeus intervened. Within a generation, the temple was not just desecrated; it was destroyed! "Not one stone here," said Jesus, "will be left on another; every one will be thrown down" (Matthew 24:2). A generation later, when the disciples saw "Jerusalem being surrounded by armies," they *knew* "its desolation" was near (Luke 21:20). Thus, as Jesus had instructed, they *fled to the mountains* (Matthew 24:16; Luke 21:21).

Those who rejected the prophetic message of Jesus and disregarded the abomination of desolation on the great altar of burnt offering were savagely slaughtered. Some one million fell by the sword. When they saw Jerusalem "surrounded by armies," they should have known "its desolation was near."

THE ABOMINATION THAT CAUSES DESOLATION SPOKEN OF THROUGH DANIEL

Like Jesus, Daniel saw a coming "abomination that causes desolation" (Daniel 9:27; 11:31; 12:11). Jesus saw it four decades prior to the fact; Daniel, four centuries. Looking down the corridor of time he envisioned "a stern-faced king, a master of intrigue" who would cause astounding devastation. "His armed forces will rise up to desecrate the temple fortress and will abolish the daily sacrifice. Then they will set up the abomination that causes desolation. With flattery he will corrupt those who have violated the covenant, but the people who know their God will firmly resist him" (Daniel 11:31–32).

Daniel's depiction was so detailed that biblical skeptics roundly assert the book to be history written after the fact rather than prophecy written beforehand. The third-century philosopher Porphyry took the lead. In a polemic titled "Against the Christians," he summarily dismisses Daniel as a Maccabean fraud: "The book of Daniel was written not by the man whom it is named after, but by someone who lived in Judaea at the time of Antiochus Epiphanes."[12] *The New Oxford Annotated Bible* is equally dismissive: "The author was a pious Jew living under the persecution of Antiochus Epiphanes, 167–164 BC."[13] While this refrain is rabidly regurgitated in the present, reality is, there is little to commend it.

From a Jewish perspective, inclusion of Daniel in the *Tanakh* (T–*Torah*, N–*Nevi'm*, K–*Kethuvim*; i.e., the Law, the Writings, and the Prophets, respectively) has never been in question. From the post-exilic Ezra to Simon the Just, the Great Assembly included Daniel in their canon along with Ezekiel and Esther.[14] The Jewish historian Josephus was likewise certain that Daniel preexisted Alexander's arrival on the stage of history. "When the Book of Daniel was shown to him, which predicted that one of the Greeks would destroy the Persian empire, he [Alexander the Great] thought himself to be the one so designated."[15] Most significantly, the Jewish Jesus had no doubt whatsoever concerning Daniel's prophetic prowess. Indeed, he looked back at "the abomination that causes desolation spoken of by the prophet Daniel" as the basis for prophesying that the temple that had been desecrated by the forces of the Old Testament Antiochus would ultimately be destroyed by the forces of a New Testament Antichrist.[16]

While fundamentalists on the left reject Daniel as authentic prophecy on various grounds, three are of particular note. First, in a case of fundamentalism gone wild, they tout the inclusion of three lone words—*lyre*, *harp*, and *pipes*—as definitive deal breakers for the early dating of Daniel. The argument is simplistic. If Daniel had indeed prophesied prior to the advent of Alexander the Great, these Greek words would not as yet have been absorbed into the Aramaic of Daniel 3. The incredulous presupposition here is that cultural intercourse between Babylon and Athens could not have existed prior to Alexander's Hellenistic campaigns. Such a notion flies in the face of both historical evidence and common sense. As has been well established historically, "Greek culture penetrated the ancient Near East long before the Neo-Babylonian period."[17]

Furthermore, antisupernaturalistic skeptics contend that Daniel's usage of the moniker "Chaldean" is clearly anachronistic. This, however, is far from certain. Since archaeology has established the ethnic use of "Chaldean" in eighth-century BC Assyrian records, it is highly unlikely that the professional usage of "Chaldean" will not likewise be established archaeologically in sixth-century BC Babylonian records as well.[18]

Finally, there is a core issue—namely that of close-mindedness. Fundamentalists who deny that Daniel prophesies the succession of nations, from Babylon in the sixth century to the rise and fall of Antiochus IV Epiphanes and the abomination that causes desolation in the second, begin with an antisupernatural bias and thus reject the possibility of prophecy a priori. Instead of open-minded consideration of both natural and supernatural explanations, they close-mindedly reject the possibility of the latter.

Make no mistake. The raison d'être for this idiosyncratic brand of fundamentalism is this: Daniel so accurately describes details surrounding the abomination of desolation that close-minded fundamentalists from the left cannot fathom this as prophecy. One cannot help but be reminded of Nebuchadnezzar, Darius, Cyrus, and Alexander the Great, all of whom were forced to acknowledge that the God of Daniel is indeed "a revealer of mysteries" (Daniel 2:47).[19] As such, he clearly revealed to his servant Daniel the future havoc that Antiochus would wreak on the Jews, Jerusalem, and the Jewish temple (Daniel 7:8, 24–25; 8:23–25; 9:27; 11:29–35; cf. 1 Maccabees 1:54–64). But he also showed Daniel that a faithful remnant—a people who know their God—would firmly resist him (Daniel 11:32). And most significantly that "the God of heaven will set up a kingdom that will never be destroyed, nor will it be left to another people. It will crush all those kingdoms and bring them to an end, but it will itself endure forever" (Daniel 2:44).

God provided Daniel with a panoramic vision of the rise and fall of kings from the Babylonian Nebuchadnezzar to the Grecian Alexander the Great. Now he revealed painstaking details of a terrible seven-year Tribulation that would befall the saints during the beastly reign of the despotic *Epimanes*. Seven Syrian kings from Seleucus Nicator to Seleucus IV would precede Antiochus IV to the throne. Three others would be uprooted before the deluded madman solidified his despotic rule (Daniel 7:7, 24). *Demetrius*, son of Seleucus IV and heir to the Syrian throne, was robbed of his rightful rule as the hostage of Rome; *Heliodoris*, though he succeeded in murdering Seleucus IV, was ousted from royalty within weeks; and *Antiochus*, baby brother of Demetrius, though coregent for a time, was eventually murdered by the Syrian beast.[20]

Onias III was prince of the covenant when the murderous beast (Antiochus IV) ascended the Syrian throne. He upheld the holy covenant of his God and firmly resisted the Hellenizing ways of the Greco-Syrian despot. However, his brother Joshua, who embraced the Hellenistic moniker Jason, was pleased to sell out his brother for a mess of pottage. He offered Antiochus a large sum of money in exchange for the office of high priest. With Onias in exile, the Jewish nation was rapidly transformed into a microcosm of the Hellenistic culture surrounding it. At the behest of Antiochus, Jason erected a Greek gymnasium, persuaded the Hellenizing populace to swear allegiance to Grecian gods, and effectively transformed Jerusalem into a Greek ghetto. Jason's treacherous betrayal bought him but three years. For an even larger bribe Antiochus transferred the priesthood to the maniacal Menelaus, who subsequently orchestrated the murder of Onias (2 Maccabees 4). All this, however, was but the beginning of tribulation.

The Antiochian horn "started small but grew in power to the south and to the east and toward the Beautiful Land" (Daniel 8:9; cf. 7:8).[21] In arrogance "it set itself up to be as great as the Prince of the host; it took away the daily sacrifice from him, and the place of his sanctuary was brought low. Because of rebellion, the host of the saints and the daily sacrifice were given over to it. It prospered in everything it did, and truth was thrown to the ground" (Daniel 8:11–12; cf. 9:27; 11:30–31). Daniel "heard a holy one speaking, and another holy one said to him, 'How long will it take for the vision to be fulfilled—the vision concerning the daily sacrifice, the rebellion that causes desolation, and the surrender of the sanctuary and of the host that will be trampled underfoot?' He said to me, 'It will take 2,300 evenings and mornings; then the sanctuary will be reconsecrated'" (Daniel 8:13–14; cf. 9:24; 12:11–12).[22]

The murder of Onias marked the beginning of the 2,300 evenings and mornings—as the death of Antiochus marked their end. Turmoil in the priesthood precipitated the first major massacre. "In 170/69 BC, when Antiochus was engaged in his campaign against Egypt, he succeeded in seizing Jerusalem in a surprise attack and obliged his rival to seek refuge in the citadel. It was this success of Jason (according to 2 Maccabees) that was the reason for the king's direct intervention in Jerusalem. Antiochus saw it as a revolt against his sovereignty and decided to punish the rebellious city."[23] Thus, in "169 BC, he marched in person with his army against Jerusalem, executed a bloodbath there, and looted the immense treasures of the Jewish Temple, with the help, it is said, of Menelaus himself. All the valuables amongst them, the three great golden vessels from the inner Temple, the altar of incense, the seven-branched candelabrum, and the table of the shew-bread, were taken back by him to Antioch."[24]

In 168 BC, "Antiochus undertook yet another expedition against Egypt. But this time the Romans confronted him. The Roman general, Popillius Laenas, presented him with a decree of the senate which required him to abandon once and for all his designs upon Egypt if he wished to avoid being regarded as an enemy of Rome. When Antiochus replied that he would like to consider the matter, Popillius gave him the famous brief ultimatum by drawing a circle round him with his staff and ordering him formally *entoutha bouleuou* (make up your mind in here)."[25] Embarrassed and raging as a wild beast, Antiochus purposed to vent his fury on those who remained in covenant with the Jewish God. "He commanded his soldiers to cut down relentlessly everyone they met and to kill those who went into their houses. Then there was massacre of young and old, destruction of boys, women, and children, and slaughter of young girls and infants. Within the total of three days eighty thousand were destroyed, forty thousand in hand-to-hand fighting, and as many were sold into slavery as were killed" (2 Maccabees 5:12–14).

In 167, three years after the murder of Onias, the ultimate sacrilege befell Jerusalem. The armed forces of Antiochus rose up against the temple fortress, abolished the daily sacrifice, and set up an abomination that causes desolation (Daniel 11:31; cf. 9:27; 12:11–12; see 1 Maccabees 1:54). With impunity, Antiochus plundered the temple treasury, dedicated the sanctuary to the Olympian Zeus, and sacrificed a pig on the altar. Hellenized Jews en masse took on the mark of the Greco-Syrian beast. "They sacrificed to idols and profaned the sabbath" (1 Maccabees 1:43). Not only so, but "they erected a desolating sacrilege[26] on the altar of burnt-offering. They also built altars in the surrounding towns of Judah, and offered incense at the doors of the houses and in the streets. The books of the law that they found they tore to pieces and burned with fire" (1:54–56). "Harsh and utterly grievous was the onslaught of evil. For the temple was filled with debauchery and revelling by the Gentiles, who dallied with prostitutes and had intercourse with women within the sacred precincts, and besides brought in things for sacrifice that were unfit. The altar was covered with abominable offerings that were forbidden by the laws. People could neither keep the sabbath, nor observe the festivals of their ancestors, nor so much as confess themselves to be Jews. On the monthly celebration of the king's birthday, the Jews were taken, under bitter constraint, to partake of the sacrifices; and when a festival of Dionysius was celebrated, they were compelled to wear wreaths of ivy and to walk in the procession in honour of Dionysus" (2 Maccabees 6:3–7).

Hellenized Jews willingly honored the god of self-gratification and libido. Those who revered the God of Abraham, Isaac, and Jacob counted not their lives worthy even unto death. The intertestamental books of Maccabees are full of accounts of their sacrifice. "Two women were brought in for having circumcised their children. They publicly paraded them around the city, with their babies hanging at their breasts, and then hurled them down headlong from the wall. Others who had assembled in the caves nearby, in order to observe the seventh day secretly, were betrayed to Philip and were all burned together, because their piety kept them from defending themselves, in view of their regard for that most holy day" (6:10–11).

Second Maccabees 7 broaches the otherworldly martyrdom of seven brothers and their mother willing to die rather than transgress the laws of their ancestors. By torture with whips and thongs, Antiochus sought to have them partake of unlawful swine's flesh. When they refused, he "fell into a rage, and gave orders to have pans and caldrons heated. . . . He commanded that the tongue of their spokesman be cut out and that they scalp him and cut off his hands and feet, while the rest of the brothers and the mother looked on" (2 Maccabees 7:3–4). While yet breathing, Antiochus caused him to be fried in a pan.

"After the first brother had died in this way, they brought forward the second for their sport. They tore off the skin of his head with the hair, and asked him, 'Will you eat rather than have your body punished limb by limb?' He replied in the language of his ancestors and said to them, 'No.' Therefore he in turn underwent tortures as the first brother had done. And when he was at his last breath, he said, 'You accursed wretch, you dismiss us from this present life, but the King of the universe will raise us up to an everlasting renewal of life, because we have died for his laws'" (7:7–9). Likewise, after the third brother had fallen victim to their sport, he "courageously stretched forth his hands, and said nobly, 'I got these [hands] from Heaven, and because of his laws I disdain them, and from him I hope to get them back again" (7:11). The fourth brother, when near death, in like fashion, cried out, "One cannot but choose to die at the hands of mortals and to cherish the hope God gives of being raised again by him. But for you there will be no resurrection to life!" (7:14).

After murdering the fifth and sixth brothers, Antiochus turned a malevolent gaze on the remaining sibling. He "promised with oaths that he would make him rich and enviable if he would turn from the ways of his ancestors, and that he would take him for his Friend and trust him with public affairs" (7:24). Filled with a noble spirit, the mother cried out, "'Do not fear this butcher, but prove worthy of your brothers. Accept death, so that in God's mercy I may get you back again along with your brothers.' While she was still speaking, the young man said, 'What are you waiting for? I will not obey the king's command, but I obey the command of the law that was given to our ancestors through Moses. But you, who have contrived all sorts of evil against the Hebrews, will certainly not escape the hands of God'" (7:29–31).

After rightly regaling him "an unholy wretch" and the "most defiled of all mortals," he yet entreated Antiochus, saying, "Do not be elated in vain and puffed up by uncertain hopes, when you raise your hand against the children of heaven. You have not yet escaped the judgment of the almighty, all-seeing God. For our brothers after enduring a brief suffering have drunk of ever-flowing life, under God's covenant; but you, by the judgment of God, will receive just punishment for your arrogance. I, like my brothers, give up body and life for the laws of our ancestors, appealing to God to show mercy soon to our nation and by trials and plagues to make you confess that he alone is God, and through me and my brothers to bring to an end the wrath of the Almighty that has justly fallen on our whole nation'" (7:34–38). Upon hearing his words, Antiochus fell into a monstrous rage, brutalizing the last of the brothers in a fashion that exceeded all the others. Yet despite horrific torture at the hands of the Syrian beast, the young man and his mother died in integrity, putting their "whole trust in the Lord" (7:40).

The dying prayer of the seventh brother found its answer in the Maccabean revolt. Against all odds, savaged Jews purposed to resist the Syrian juggernaut. The Jewish priest Mattathias, together with his five sons—Judas, Jonathan, John, Simon, and Eleazar—initiated resistance by refusing to make sacrifices to the gods of the Greco-Syrian hordes. With valor they implored the Hasidim ("pious ones") to join them in the battle against Hellenization. When a Hellenizing Jew sacrificed in accordance with the command of Antiochus, "Mattathias and his sons took out broad-bladed knives and cut the man down, also killing the king's officer and his soldiers. After overturning the pagan altar, Mattathias cried out, 'Whoever is zealous for the laws of our country and the worship of God, let him follow me!'"[27]

Matthias died in the spring of 166, but not before he appointed his indomitable son Judas Maccabaeus as leader of the fledgling Jewish resistance forces. Judas "was like a lion in his deeds, like a lion's cub roaring for prey. He searched out and pursued those who broke the law; he burned those who troubled his people. Lawbreakers shrank back for fear of him; all the evildoers were confounded; and deliverance prospered by his hand" (1 Maccabees 3:4–6). Upheld by the hand of the Almighty, he roared to victory after victory against a vastly superior Syrian superpower. In his first year alone, Judas routed the armies of Apollonius and conquered the mighty Seron, commander-in-chief of the Syrian forces, at Beth-horon.

In 165, Antiochus commissioned the royal Lysias, in charge of Syrian affairs from the river Euphrates to the borders of Egypt, to wipe the Jewish race from the face of the earth. "Lysias chose Ptolemy son of Dorymenes, and Nicanor and Gorgias, able men among the Friends of the king, and sent with them forty thousand infantry and seven thousand cavalry to go into the land of Judah and destroy it, as the king had commanded" (3:38–39). However, once again, against all odds, Judas routed the superior Syrians at Emmaus, causing them to flee to the land of the Philistines. In victory Judas Maccabaeus and the Jewish resistance forces offered up hymns and praises extolling the majesty of their mighty God and reveling in the reality that "there is no wisdom, no insight, no plan that can succeed against the LORD. The horse is made ready for the day of battle, but victory rests with the LORD" (Proverbs 21:30–31).

In 164, Lysias made yet another ill-fated attempt to subdue the forces of Judas Maccabaeus. This time he personally invaded Judea, dwarfing ten thousand Jewish resistance fighters with an army of sixty thousand infantry and five thousand cavalry. In the ensuing battle five thousand Syrians succumbed to the sword. "When Lysias saw the rout of his troops and observed the boldness that inspired those of Judas, and how ready they were either to live or to die nobly, he withdrew to Antioch" (1 Maccabees 4:35). Judas immediately took control of all Jerusalem save the Seleucid Acra, recaptured Temple Mount, destroyed the pagan altar of the Olympian Zeus, cleansed the sanctuary, and reconsecrated the temple to Yahweh, God of Israel. Thus it was that on December 14, 164, seven years after

Antiochus had orchestrated Onias's murder and exactly three years after he had desecrated the temple fortress, abolished the daily sacrifice, and set up the abomination that causes desolation, the temple was rededicated and the daily sacrifice restored. "Judas and his men celebrated a great feast which lasted for eight days, and which we continue to observe as the Festival of Lights [Hanukkah]."[28] As the Jewish prophet Daniel foretold, "From the time that the daily sacrifice is abolished and the abomination that causes desolation is set up, there will be 1,290 days" (Daniel 12:11).

Upon hearing that the Jews had regained Jerusalem, the Syrian beast vowed in arrogance,

"I will make Jerusalem a cemetery of Jews." But the all-seeing Lord, the God of Israel, struck him with an incurable and invisible blow. As soon as he stopped speaking he was seized with a pain in his bowels, for which there was no relief, and with sharp internal tortures—and that very justly, for he had tortured the bowels of others with many and strange inflictions. Yet he did not in any way stop his insolence, but was even more filled with arrogance, breathing fire in his rage against the Jews, and giving orders to drive even faster. And so it came about that he fell out of his chariot as it was rushing along, and the fall was so hard as to torture every limb of his body. Thus he who only a little while before had thought in his superhuman arrogance that he could command the waves of the sea, and had imagined that he could weigh the high mountains in a balance, was brought down to earth and carried in a litter, making the power of God manifest to all. And so the ungodly man's body swarmed with worms, and while he was still living in anguish and pain, his flesh rotted away, and because of the stench the whole army felt revulsion at his decay. (2 Maccabees 9:4–9)

As prophesied by Daniel, Antiochus, the antichrist of the Old Testament, was finally dead: "destroyed, but not by human power" (Daniel 8:25). Destroyed by the power and province of the almighty God. Indeed, the death of the Syrian beast may well have been in view when Daniel wrote, "Blessed is the one who waits for and reaches the end of the 1,335 days" (Daniel

12:12). For not only did the death of the abominable Antiochus underscore the sovereign power of God over the nations of the earth; it signaled the soon coming of the Ancient of Days, whose "dominion is an everlasting dominion that will not pass away, and his kingdom is one that will never be destroyed" (Daniel 7:14).

A FUTURE ABOMINATION OF DESOLATION?

The prophesied abomination of desolation by which the temple was desecrated in the Old Testament and destroyed in the New is at once a bloody scar and a brilliant star enlightening our minds to the divine nature of the Scriptures. Still, its light has been darkened and its meaning diminished by modern-day prophecy pundits bent on pinning the tail on a twenty-first-century Antichrist who will allegedly arise out of a revived Roman Empire. The contention is that a third temple will soon be constructed on the very spot where the Muslim Dome of the Rock now stands; that the Antichrist will arrive on the stage of history; and that he will set up the abomination that causes desolation. Some crassly contend that the Antichrist is already in power and identify him as the "Obamanation of desolation."[29]

In reality, there is no need to light the fuse of Armageddon by plotting, planning, or pontificating a twenty-first-century Tribulation temple. Allow me to state it plainly: the age of the temple came to an end with the sacrifice of Jesus. "Such a high priest meets our need—one who is holy, blameless, pure, set apart from sinners, exalted above the heavens. Unlike the other high priests, he does not need to offer sacrifices day after day, first for his own sins, and then for the sins of the people. He sacrificed for their sins once for all when he offered himself. For the law appoints as high priests men who are weak; but the oath, which came after the law, appointed the Son, who has been made perfect forever" (Hebrews 7:26–28).

As Hebrews goes on to explain, the temple was but a type. Thus the priest offers sacrifices "at a sanctuary that is a *copy* and *shadow* of what is in heaven. This is why Moses was warned when he was about to build the tabernacle: 'See to it that you make everything according to the *pattern* shown you on the mountain.' But the ministry Jesus has received is as superior to theirs as the covenant of which he is mediator is superior to the old one, and it is founded on better promises" (Hebrews 8:5–6). Hebrews declares the utter futility of the sacrificial system in light of the Savior's sacrifice. "Day after day every priest stands and performs his religious duties; again and again he offers the same sacrifices, which can never take away sins" (Hebrews 10:11). Jesus, however, "offered for all time one sacrifice for sins" (10:12). As such, Jesus forever did away with the need for sacrifice, rendering the temple obsolete.

Despite the fact that Jesus forever dispensed with the need for temple, priest, and sacrifice two thousand years ago, Zionists are bent on stoking the embers of Armageddon by scheming the construction of yet another temple. As the story goes, a third temple will be built where the Dome of the Rock now stands. Antichrist will desecrate the temple by standing in the Holy of Holies and declaring himself God (2 Thessalonians 2:3–4), thus becoming "the abomination that causes desolation" (Matthew 24:15). Resistance in turn will lead to the greatest holocaust in Jewish history.

The entire rebuilt-temple scenario, like a house of cards, rests on little more than inference. Such inference arises from the faulty assumption that Jesus in the space of several sentences within the Olivet Discourse predicts not simply the destruction of the second temple but the desecration of a third temple as well.[30] Not only is the notion of a third temple an inference imposed on the Scriptures, but the New Testament warns that to revert back to the types and shadows of the old covenant is sheer apostasy (Galatians 3–5; Hebrews 5:11–6:12; 10; 12:14–29).[31] In place of sacrificing holy cows, we are called to celebrate Holy Communion in remembrance of the sacrifice of the holy Christ. As such, Scripture forbids Christians to partake in or encourage the building of a third temple, which would occasion the trampling of the holy Son of God underfoot by counting the blood of the covenant a common thing through the offering of unholy animal sacrifices (Hebrews 10:29).

While Jesus never uttered a single word regarding a third temple, he emphatically pronounced the ruin of the second. After pronouncing seven woes upon the teachers of the law and the Pharisees, calling them "hypocrites," "blind guides," "whitewashed tombs," "snakes," and "a brood of vipers," he departed the temple saying, "O Jerusalem, Jerusalem, you who kill the prophets and stone those sent to you, how often I have longed to gather your children together, as a hen gathers her chicks under her wings, but you were not willing. *Look, your house is left to you desolate*" (Matthew 23:37–38). The Shekinah glory of God, which departed the second temple thus leaving it desolate, forever dwells within the spiritual temple. Indeed, the Shekinah glory of God will never again descend upon a temple constructed of lifeless stones; it forever dwells within "the living Stone—rejected by men but chosen by God" (1 Peter 2:4). As the apostle Peter goes on to explain, "You also, like living stones, are being built into a *spiritual house* to be a holy priesthood, offering *spiritual sacrifices* acceptable to God through Jesus Christ" (2:5).

Incredibly, Peter uses the very language once reserved for national Israel and applies it to spiritual Israel. "But *you*," says Peter, "are a chosen people, a royal priesthood, a holy nation, a people belonging to God, that you may declare the praises of him who called you out of darkness into his wonderful light. Once you were not a people, but now you are *the* people of God" (2:9–10). As such, the type and shadow of the first and first-century temples find their substance not in a Tribulation temple followed by a millennial temple but in a church built out of living stones comprised of Jew and Gentile with Jesus Christ himself the capstone. "For in Scripture it says: 'See, I lay a stone in Zion, a chosen and precious cornerstone, and the one who trusts in him will never be put to shame.' Now to you who believe, this stone is precious. But to those who do not believe, 'The stone the builders rejected has become the capstone'" (2:6–7).

Nowhere is the typological fulfillment of the temple and the rest of the old covenant more directly and dramatically underscored than in the book of Hebrews. "When Christ came as high priest," writes the author of Hebrews, "he went through the greater and more perfect tabernacle that is not man-made, that is to say, not a part of this creation. He did not enter by means of the blood of goats and calves; but he entered the Most Holy Place once for all by his own blood, having obtained eternal redemption"

(9:11–12). Hebrews highlights that not only is Jesus the antitype of the temple and the high priest, but he is the antitypical sacrifice as well: "The blood of goats and bulls and the ashes of a heifer sprinkled on those who are ceremonially unclean sanctify them so that they are outwardly clean. How much more, then, will the blood of Christ, who through the eternal Spirit offered himself unblemished to God, cleanse our consciences from acts that lead to death, so that we may serve the living God!" (9:13–14). Indeed, even the sacred ashes of the red heifer, like the blood of bulls and goats, find their ultimate antitypical fulfillment in the blood of Jesus Christ. It is for this reason that the writer of Hebrews explains in no uncertain terms that to revert to a sacrificial system is to trample the Son of God underfoot, to treat as an unholy thing the blood of the covenant, and to insult the Spirit of grace (Hebrews 10:29; cf. Hebrews 5:11–6:12; Galatians 3–5).

So will there be a third temple and a twenty-first-century abomination of desolation? While Zionist zeal threatens to light the fuse of Armageddon, we can be absolutely certain that the prophecies of Daniel and Jesus already blaze as stars in the constellation of fulfilled prophecy demonstrating that the Bible is divine as opposed to merely human in origin. Like Ehrman, who opened the floodgates of iniquity designating Jesus a false apocalyptic prophet, those who fail to heed the analogy of faith stand in danger of opening the floodgates of iniquity by looking forward to the abomination that causes desolation, which has already come.

15

Resurrection Prophecies

Within this awful volume lies
The mystery of mysteries:
Happiest they of human race,
To whom their God has given grace
To read, to fear, to hope, to pray,
To lift the latch, to force the way;
But better had they ne'er been born,
Who read to doubt, or read to scorn.

—Walter Scott

When I first saw the headline, I was more than a little intrigued: "Scientists Find Fountain of Youth." According to the article, "Shriveled testes grew back to normal." Not only so, "Other organs, such as the spleen, liver and intestines, recuperated from their degenerated state, the Harvard study said. Anti-aging therapies could dramatically affect the rapidly increasing elderly population by treating devastating afflictions, including dementia, stroke, and cardiac failure." There was a gotcha, however. While "the experimental treatment developed by researchers at Harvard Medical School turned weak and feeble old mice into healthy rodents by regenerating their aged bodies," replicating the effect in human beings is hugely problematic. "Mice produce telomerase throughout their lives, but the enzyme is switched off in adult humans, an evolutionary trait that prevents cells from dividing out of control. So the risk of cancer cells prospering would substantially increase."[1]

A headline in *Scientific American* was equally captivating—although not nearly as hopeful: "No Truth to the Fountain of Youth." According to the article, "Efforts to combat aging and extend human life date at least as far back as 3500 BC, and self-proclaimed experts have touted anti-aging elixirs ever since. Indeed, the prospect of immortality has always had universal appeal, spurring Alexander the Great and Ponce de Leon to search for the legendary fountain of youth." The article goes on to say that anyone purporting to offer an anti-aging product today is either mistaken or lying. Why? "Even if science could eliminate today's leading killers of older individuals, aging would continue to occur, ensuring that different maladies would take their place." The article concludes as follows: "It is an inescapable biological reality that once the engine of life switches on, the body inevitably sows the seeds of its own destruction."[2]

For those embracing a Christian worldview, this conclusion rings true. "The living know that they will die" (Ecclesiastes 9:5). "Christianity does not offer a peaceful way to come to terms with death," writes Philip Yancey. "No, it offers instead a way to overcome death. Christ stands for Life, and his resurrection should give convincing proof that God is not satisfied with any 'cycle of life' that ends in death. He will go to any extent—he did go to any extent—to break that cycle."[3]

That is the very message radiating from the lips of righteous Job. Satan wielded the sword of death with devastating fury. He butchered Job's livestock. He murdered Job's children. And if God had permitted him to do so, he would have snuffed out Job's life. The devil's devastation was so complete that Job's wife lost all perspective. With her mind careening out of control, she cried, "Curse God and die!" (Job 2:9). Job, however, saw his plight from the perspective of eternity. "I know that my Redeemer lives, and that in the end he will stand upon the earth. And after my skin has been destroyed, yet in my flesh I will see God; I myself will see him with my own eyes—I, and not another. How my heart yearns within me!" (Job 19:25–27).

Abraham, like Job, yearned for resurrection. By faith he lived like a stranger and an alien in a foreign country "for he was looking forward to the city with foundations, whose architect and builder is God" (Hebrews 11:10). Hebrews goes on to say that by faith Abraham purposed to "sacrifice his one and only son, even though God had said to him, 'It is through Isaac that your offspring will be reckoned'" (11:17–18). Why? *"Abraham reasoned that God could raise the dead"* (11:19). As R. C. H. Lenski observed, "Abraham concluded the full truth, not only that God is able to raise this one dead lad, his son, but is able to raise the dead. Abraham believed the doctrine of resurrection, no less."[4]

Martha, too, believed in the reality of resurrection. Four days after Lazarus had died, Jesus said to Martha, "'Your brother will rise again.' Martha answered, 'I know he will rise again in the resurrection at the last day.' Jesus said to her, 'I am the resurrection and the life. He who believes in me will live, even though he dies; and whoever lives and believes in me will never die'" (John 11:23–26). In saying this Jesus pointed to himself as the very one who would overcome death and the grave and as such ensure that all who put their trust in him would likewise discover the *genuine* fountain of youth.

THE PROPHETIC STAR

Resurrection is without a doubt the brightest star in the constellation of biblical prophecy. While all other prophecies demonstrating the Bible to be divine rather than merely human in origin invoke the supernatural— resurrection embodies it. When the Jews demanded that Jesus prove his authority over temple, priest, and sacrifice, he responded, "Destroy this temple, and I will raise it again in three days" (John 2:19). The Jews thought he was speaking of Herod's temple, which had taken forty-six years to build. "But the temple he had spoken of was his body. After he was raised from the dead, his disciples recalled what he had said. Then they believed the Scripture and the words that Jesus had spoken" (2:21–22).

Context here is crucial. Jesus had just "made a whip out of cords, and drove all from the temple area, both sheep and cattle; he scattered the coins of the money changers and overturned their tables. To those who sold doves he said, 'Get these out of here! How dare you turn my Father's house into a market!'" (2:15–16). The meaning of the passion of the Christ was not lost on his disciples. They had seen his miracles. They knew who he was. And they did not in the least question his authority to do what he did. Collectively they remembered the prophetic words of King David, "Zeal for your house will consume me" (2:17).

The Jewish Sanhedrists, too, knew of the miracles of Jesus. Thus, they did not immediately instruct the temple police to arrest him for civil disobedience. Instead they asked for a miracle: "What miraculous sign can you show us to prove your authority to do all this?" (2:18). With nary a glance Jesus could have caused one of the temple police to fall down dead at his feet and with another cause him to rise again from the dead. Yet he did not so much as countenance the thought. They had the testimony of Moses and the Prophets. Thus, they would not be convinced even if someone rose from the dead.

In place of a sign, Jesus presented a prophecy. Not just *a* prophecy— *the* prophecy. The prophecy demonstrating that the whole of the Law and the Prophets pointed forward to him. The prophecy signifying that the Word of God cannot be broken. The prophetic star shining brightest in the constellation of biblical prophecy. "Destroy this temple," said Jesus, "and I will raise it again in three days" (2:19). Dull of mind and spirit, those who heard the words of Jesus seemed incapable of comprehending them. The Sanhedrists thought the Savior referred exclusively to a sanctuary of glistening gold and luminous limestone. Sadly, the disciples fared no better. Not until Jesus had risen from the dead did they realize that the temple he had spoken of was the temple of his body.

When Jesus uttered the words, "Destroy this temple," he was standing in the shadow of a sanctuary of which he himself was the substance. Instead of bowing to the substance, the temple keepers reveled in its shadow. "It has taken forty-six years to build this temple" they sneered, "and you are going to raise it in three days?" (2:20). Enamored by the picture, they were oblivious to the Person. Sadly, they loved the type and loathed the antitype who had emerged in their midst through the doorway of Old Testament prophecies.

In the end their faithlessness led inexorably to the destruction of not just one, but two temples. First, they murdered the antitype. But in three days he took up his life again, thus fulfilling the greatest of all prophecies: "Destroy this temple and I will raise it again in three days." Their treachery led to the destruction of the type as well. Thus was fulfilled the prophetic words of the antitype as he left the type and was walking away: "I tell you the truth, not one stone here will be left on another; every one will be thrown down" (Matthew 24:2). The sun that daily refracts light from the golden dome of the Muslim mosque that has replaced the type on Temple Mount is an enduring reminder that God has spoken—that his Word cannot be broken.

Jesus made his typological relationship to the earthly sanctuary explicit when he pronounced, "One greater than the temple is here" (Matthew 12:6). This seminal truth was amplified in a conversation between Jesus and a woman at Jacob's well in Samaria. "Our fathers," said the Samaritan woman, "worshiped on this mountain, but you Jews claim that the place where we must worship is in Jerusalem." Jesus corrected her faulty presuppositions with a liberating truth: "Believe me, woman," he said, "a time is coming when you will worship the Father neither on this mountain nor in Jerusalem" (John 4:20–21). In saying this Jesus pointed to himself as the antitypical fulfillment of all that had been spoken by Moses and the prophets. "After he was raised from the dead, his disciples recalled what he had said. *Then they believed the Scripture and the words that Jesus had spoken*" (John 2:22).

Truly, the glorious fulfillment of Christ's prophesied resurrection from the dead—"Destroy this temple and I will raise it again in three days"—is not *a* but *the* prophetic star in the constellation of biblical prophecy.

THE STARRY HOST

Furthermore, when the veil is removed and the brilliant light of *the* prophetic star illumines our minds, a starry host of resurrection prophecies banish the darkness of unbelief and doubt. Daniel likens the resurrection of saints to the glory of the stars: "Multitudes who sleep in the dust of the earth will awake: some to everlasting life, others to shame and everlasting contempt. Those who are wise will shine like the brightness of the heavens, and those who lead many to righteousness, like the stars for ever and ever" (Daniel 12:2–3).

In context, Antiochus IV Epiphanes had purposed to Hellenize the Jews. His armed forces rose up against the temple fortress, abolished the daily sacrifice, and set up an abomination that causes desolation. As noted, he plundered the temple treasury, dedicated the sanctuary to the Olympian Zeus, and sacrificed a pig on the altar. Hellenized Jews en masse took the mark of the beast. They sacrificed to idols, profaned the Sabbath, and honored Dionysius by wearing wreaths of ivy. Those who revered their God, however, looked forward to resurrection. Upon being martyred one saintly victim cried out, "You dismiss us from this present life, but the King of the universe will raise us up to an everlasting renewal of life, because we have died for his laws'" (2 Maccabees 7:7–9). Another, "One cannot but choose to die at the hands of mortals and to cherish the hope God gives of being raised again by him. But for you there will be no resurrection to life!" (7:14). And yet another, "You, who have contrived all sorts of evil against the Hebrews, will certainly not escape the hands of God" (7:31).

Antiochus purposed to make Jerusalem a cemetery for Jews. But the God of Abraham, Isaac, and Jacob promised to resurrect the faithful to everlasting life. Those who were wise and stood firm against the abominable Antichrist would shine like the brightness of the heavens and those who led many to righteousness like the stars. The resurrection envisioned is clear and unambiguous. Daniel speaks here not of the disembodied state that follows death but the bodily resurrection that follows the disembodied state. The martyrs were not promised a mere resuscitation in a veil of tears but a majestic resurrection in a new order of things in which they would shine like the brightness of the starry hosts. The rock cut out, but not by human hands, "will set up a kingdom that will never be destroyed, nor will it be left to another people. It will crush all those kingdoms and bring them to an end, but it will itself endure forever" (Daniel 2:44). The resurrection

Daniel prophesied has not as yet been fulfilled. *The* prophetic star in the constellation of biblical prophecy, however, provides the earnest for all who will one day shine like the brightness of the heavens.

Isaiah, likewise, looks to the resurrection of "a man of sorrows, and familiar with suffering" (Isaiah 53:3), as the earnest of our resurrection on the last day. "After the suffering of his soul," exudes Isaiah, "he will see the light of life and be satisfied" (53:11). In like fashion, our bodies will be resurrected from the dust of the ground. The mortal will be clothed with immortality. Isaiah's prophecy is pregnant with the promise of new birth. "Your dead will live; their bodies will rise. You who dwell in the dust, wake up and shout for joy. Your dew is like the dew of the morning; the earth will give birth to her dead" (Isaiah 26:19). It is from the dust that God created humankind; it is to the dust humankind returns; yet it is also from the dust that our DNA emerges as the pattern for resurrected bodies. The restoration of Israel points forward to the restoration of true Israel, and the restoration of true Israel is the earnest of every individual who realizes in Immanuel the promise of resurrection from the dead.

The typological relationship between the resuscitation of Israel and the resurrection of true Israel is seen with stunning clarity in Ezekiel's vision of dry bones scattered in the recesses of a valley. Dry and discarded, they were in danger of disintegrating into dust. A poignant picture of the people of the promise—wasted and dead in exile and sin. Ezekiel prophesied as he was commanded by God and suddenly "there was a noise, a rattling sound, and the bones came together, bone to bone. I looked," said Ezekiel, "and tendons and flesh appeared on them and skin covered them, but there was no breath in them" (Ezekiel 37:7–8). Again Ezekiel prophesied as he was commanded, and breath entered the bodies; "they came to life and stood up on their feet—a vast army" (37:10).

The interpretation leaves little to the imagination. God would open the graves and restore Israel. "I will put my Spirit in you and you will live, and I will settle you in your own land. Then you will know that I the LORD have spoken, and I have done it, declares the LORD" (37:14). The resurrection of Israel to the land, of course, is but a type of resurrection that finds ultimate fulfillment in the resurrection of the Lord—who is the locus of the land.

As such, the resurrection imagery of Ezekiel finds ultimate resolution in the resurrection of Christ and the resurrection of Christ-ians. The antitype that fulfills the entire mosaic of Old Testament resurrection prophecies left no doubt about this coming resurrection: "Do not be amazed at this, for a time is coming when all who are in their graves will hear his voice and come out—those who have done good will rise to live, and those who have done evil will rise to be condemned" (John 5:28–29).

If Christ had not himself been resurrected, the promise that he will resurrect dry bones in scattered graves would be as empty as the tomb guarantying its fulfillment.

THE STAR OF DAVID

Finally, among the starry hosts of Old Testament resurrection prophecies, the Star of David prophecy is most brilliant of all. I refer neither to the Israeli flag nor to a badge of shame forced on Jews during the Holocaust, but to a bright and morning star in the resurrection prophecies of David. In the first apostolic sermon recorded in the New Testament, Peter zeroed in on this stellar prophecy. It was the day of Pentecost and he had chosen Psalm 16:8–11 as the text. Addressing God-fearing Jews and converts to Judaism from every nation under heaven—Parthians; Medes; Elamites; residents of Mesopotamia, Judea, Capadocia, Pontus, Asia, Phrygia, Pamphylia, Egypt, Libya, Rome; Cretans; and Arabs—he spoke of their culpability in the death of Jesus. "This man was handed over to you by God's set purpose and foreknowledge; and you, with the help of wicked men, put him to death by nailing him to the cross. But God raised him from the dead, freeing him from the agony of death, because it was impossible for death to keep its hold on him" (Acts 2:23–24).

To prove that the death of Christ was in accordance with God's set purpose and foreknowledge—so that sin, the root cause of death, might be atoned for—Peter quoted the Star of David prophecy: "I have set the LORD always before me. Because he is at my right hand, I will not be shaken. Therefore my heart is glad and my tongue rejoices; my body also will rest secure, *because you will not abandon me to the grave, nor will you let your Holy One see decay.* You have made known to me the path of life; you will fill me with joy in your presence, with eternal pleasures at your right hand" (Psalm 16:8–11).

Peter left no doubt that David's words were a direct prophecy regarding the resurrection of Jesus. "I can tell you confidently that the patriarch David died and was buried, and his tomb is here to this day. But he was a prophet and knew that God had promised him on oath that he would place one of his descendants on his throne. Seeing what was ahead, he spoke of the resurrection of the Christ, that he was not abandoned to the grave, nor did his body see decay. God has raised this Jesus to life, and we are all witnesses of the fact" (Acts 2:29–32). Peter's Pentecost sermon was so persuasive—so powerful, so poignant—that despite not having so much as a microphone, three thousand were added to the church that very day.

The apostle Paul, likewise, highlighted the Star of David prophecy as powerful proof that what God had promised a thousand years earlier through the quintessential King of Israel was miraculously fulfilled by the resurrection of the Christ. On the Sabbath, this persecutor-turned-proselytizer had entered the Pisidian synagogue in Antioch. The synagogue rulers invited him to speak. Standing up, he motioned with his hand and spoke of God's providence in raising up Israel as the means through which the message of salvation would be spread throughout the earth. Tragically, the rulers of Jerusalem had not recognized Messiah in their midst. "Though they found no proper ground for a death sentence, they asked Pilate to have him executed. When they had carried out all that was written about him, they took him down from the tree and laid him in a tomb. But God raised him from the dead" (Acts 13:28–30).

This resurrection was not only the fulfillment of a prophecy but also an utterly unique event in the whole of recorded history. Others might have been resuscitated, but their bodies were even now experiencing decomposition and decay. Jesus, however, was resurrected, never to decay. "What God promised our fathers," said Paul, "he has fulfilled for us, their children, by raising up Jesus" (13:32–33). In evidence, Paul quoted the words of the familiar psalm—words no doubt emblazoned upon the hearts of his hearers: *"Nor will you let your Holy One see decay"* (Psalm 16:10). Such words, said

Paul, were obviously not fulfilled in the death of David. "For when David had served God's purpose in his own generation, he fell asleep; he was buried with his fathers and his body decayed. But the one whom God raised up from the dead did not see decay" (Acts 13:36–37).

As with Peter, Paul's sermon struck with combustible force. "On the next Sabbath almost the whole city gathered to hear the word of the Lord" (13:44). The fallout was predictable. "When the Jews saw the crowds, they were filled with jealousy and talked abusively against what Paul was saying" (13:45). However, when the Gentiles heard, "they were glad and honored the word of the Lord; and all who were appointed for eternal life believed" (13:48). As a result, "the word of the Lord spread through the whole region" (13:49).

THE GREATEST FEAT

As it did two thousand years ago, the Star of David prophecy continues to pierce the hearts of the open-minded. Paul made clear in his Pisidian sermon that the resurrection of Jesus Christ was not without witness: "For many days he was seen by those who had traveled with him from Galilee to Jerusalem. They are now his witnesses" (13:31).

In the span of a few hundred years, the small band of witnesses that had traveled with Messiah succeeded in turning the Caesar cult upside down. Why? Because they were utterly convinced that, like their Master, they would one day rise from the grave in glorified, resurrected bodies. Thus, as one after another was put to a terrifying death, those who survived pressed on resilient, resolute, rejoicing.

Resurrection prophecies, of course, would mean little if there was no evidence that they had actually been fulfilled. As such, in 1 Corinthians 15:3–11, Paul provides a four-part argument easily remembered using the acronym F-E-A-T:

> For what I received I passed on to you as of first importance: that Christ died for our sins according to the Scriptures, that he was buried, that

he was raised on the third day according to the Scriptures, and that he appeared to Peter, and then to the Twelve. After that, he appeared to more than five hundred of the brothers at the same time, most of whom are still living, though some have fallen asleep. Then he appeared to James, then to all the apostles, and last of all he appeared to me also, as to one abnormally born. For I am the least of the apostles and do not even deserve to be called an apostle, because I persecuted the church of God. But by the grace of God I am what I am, and his grace to me was not without effect. No, I worked harder than all of them—yet not I, but the grace of God that was with me. Whether, then, it was I or they, this is what we preach, and this is what you believed.

FATAL TORMENT

"Christ died for our sins according to the Scriptures" (1 Corinthians 15:3). The fatal suffering of Jesus Christ as recounted in the New Testament is one of the most well-established facts of ancient history. Even in today's modern age of scientific enlightenment, there is a virtual consensus among New Testament scholars—both conservative and liberal—that Christ died on the cross, that he was buried in the tomb of Joseph of Arimathea, and that his death drove his disciples to despair.[5] While noteworthy scholars have suggested that Jesus may have merely swooned, the evidence clearly points in a different direction.

Medical Realities

Christ's fatal torment began in the Garden of Gethsemane after the emotional Last Supper.[6] There he experienced a medical condition known as *hematidrosis*—tiny capillaries in his sweat glands ruptured, mixing sweat with blood. After being arrested by the temple guard, he was mocked, beaten, and spat upon. The next morning, battered, bruised, and bleeding, he was stripped and subjected to the brutality of Roman flogging—a whip stuffed with razor-sharp bones and lead balls reduced his body to quivering ribbons of bleeding flesh. As Christ slumped into the pool of his own blood, soldiers threw a scarlet robe across his shoulders, thrust a scepter into his hands, and pressed sharp thorns into his scalp. After mocking him, the soldiers took the scepter and repeatedly struck Christ on the head. A heavy wooden beam was thrust upon his bleeding body, and he was led away to "the place of the skull," where he experienced excruciating physical torment in the form of the cross. At "the place of the skull," Roman soldiers drove thick, seven-inch iron spikes through Christ's hands and feet. Waves of pain pulsated through Christ's body as the nails lacerated his nerves. Breathing became an agonizing endeavor as Christ pushed his tortured body upward to grasp small gulps of air. In the ensuing hours he experienced cycles of joint-wrenching cramps, intermittent asphyxiation, and excruciating pain as his lacerated back moved up and down against the rough timber of the cross. And then with his passion complete, Jesus gave up his spirit. Shortly thereafter, a Roman legionnaire drove his spear through the fifth interspace between the ribs, upward through the pericardium, and into Christ's heart. Immediately, there rushed forth blood and water, demonstrating conclusively that Jesus had suffered fatal torment.

Major Swoon Theories

The so-called swoon hypothesis is a leap of faith into a chasm of credulity. As underscored by the late liberal Cambridge scholar John A. T. Robinson, it is so fatally flawed it deserves to be "laughed out of court."[7] First, as recounted by the apostle John, when the soldiers determined Jesus was dead, one of them "pierced Jesus' side with a spear, bringing a sudden flow of blood and water" (John 19:34). As a first-century man, John could not have known what modern science has only recently discovered— namely, that blood and water flowed from Jesus' side due to the fact that the heart is surrounded by a sac of water, called a *pericardium*. As such, water proceeded from the pericardium; blood from the heart. Furthermore, even if Jesus had survived crucifixion, he could never have rolled a massive tombstone uphill out of its gully—especially in his weakened condition and without so much as an edge against which to push from inside the tomb. Finally, crucifixion is death by asphyxiation. As the body hangs downward, the intercostal and pectoral muscles surrounding the lungs halt the normal process of breathing. It is unreasonable to suppose that Jesus could have remained breathless for any protracted period of time.[8]

Medical Verdict

Believing Jesus swooned—rather than suffered fatal torment—must surely stretch credulity beyond the breaking point. It means Christ survived six trials (three civil and three religious), suffered scourging by seasoned Roman soldiers, survived seven-inch iron spikes driven through his hands and feet, survived a spear wound in the side, survived for three days without medical attention, single-handedly rolled away an enormously heavy tombstone, subdued armed guards, strolled around on pierced feet, and seduced his disciples into communicating the myth that he had conquered death and the grave while living out the remainder of a pathetic life in obscurity.

EMPTY TOMB

"He was buried . . . he was raised on the third day according to the Scriptures" (1 Corinthians 15:4). As the reliability of the resurrection is undermined in the media, it is crucial that Christians are prepared to demonstrate that Jesus was buried and that on Easter morning some two thousand years ago, the tomb was indeed empty. The late liberal scholar John A. T. Robinson of Cambridge conceded that the burial of Christ "is one of the earliest and best-attested facts about Jesus."[9] This statement is not merely a dogmatic assertion. It is a defensible argument.

The Facts

As Dr. William Lane Craig points out, liberal and conservative New Testament scholars alike agree that the body of Jesus was buried in the private tomb of Joseph of Arimathea. As a Sanhedrist in the court that condemned Christ to death, Joseph is hardly the figment of a fertile imagination. Furthermore, no alternative burial account appears in the historical record. And the tomb quickly lost significance because the remains of Christ were not there to be venerated. This is significant in that the graves of sages were profoundly reverenced. Finally, the account of Jesus' burial in the tomb of Joseph of Arimathea as put forward in Mark's gospel is far too early to be the stuff of legends.[10]

The Female Factor

To begin with, had Jesus been a typical Jewish sage, he would not have encouraged women to be his disciples. While women served as maids and mothers in Jewish society, they would never have been allowed to follow a Jewish master as disciples.[11] Indeed, even Greek philosophers of the day were reticent to count women as their disciples. It is thus remarkable that the gospel writers highlight women as the heroes of their empty tomb accounts.[12] Furthermore, considering the fact that females in ancient Judaism were routinely considered to be little more than chattel, the empty tomb accounts are powerful evidence that the gospel writers valued truth over cultural correctness. Finally, prior to the coming of Christ, females were so denigrated by society that first-century Jewish males routinely mouthed the mantra, "I thank Thee that I am not a woman."[13] Had the gospel accounts been legendary, males would most certainly have been heroes of the narrative.[14]

The First Response

To begin with, the first response of Jewish antagonists takes the empty tomb for granted. Instead of repudiating the empty tomb, they accused Christ's disciples of stealing his body. Furthermore, had the tomb not been empty, enemies of the resurrection could have easily put an end to the pretense by displaying the remains of Christ. Finally, in the centuries following the resurrection of Christ, the fact of the empty tomb was forwarded by friends and foes alike. The bottom line is this: Christianity could not have endured an identifiable tomb containing the remains of Messiah.[15]

Appearances of Christ

"He appeared to Peter, and then to the Twelve. After that, he appeared to more than five hundred of the brothers at the same time, most of whom are still living, though some have fallen asleep. Then he appeared to James, then to all the apostles, and last of all he appeared to me also, as to one abnormally born" (15:5–7). One thing can be stated with ironclad certainty. The apostles did not merely propagate Christ's teachings; they were absolutely positive that he had appeared to them in the flesh. Although two thousand years removed from the actual event, we, too, can be absolutely confident in Christ's post-resurrection appearances.

Earliest Christian Creed

In 1 Corinthians 15:3–7, the apostle Paul reiterates a Christian creed that can be traced all the way back to the formative stages of the early Christian church. Scholars of all stripes have concluded that this creed can be dated to within mere months of Messiah's murder. Furthermore, the short time span between Christ's crucifixion and the composition of this early Christian creed precludes the possibility of legendary corruption. Finally, as has been aptly noted, the creed is early, free from legendary contamination, unambiguous, specific, and ultimately rooted in eyewitness testimony.[16]

Eyewitness Testimony

Peter, Paul, and the rest of the apostles claimed that Christ appeared to hundreds of people, still alive and available for cross-examination.[17] It would be one thing for the apostles to attribute such supernatural experiences to people who had already died. It is quite another to attribute them to multitudes who were still alive. Furthermore, nothing other than the appearances of Christ can account for the utter transformation of Paul, who abdicated his position as an esteemed Jewish leader, a rabbi, and a Pharisee who had studied under the famed Gamaliel. He gave up the mission to stamp out every vestige of what he considered the insidious heresy of Christianity. In the end, he paid the ultimate price for his faith—martyrdom.[18] Finally, Paul was not alone. Multitudes were radically revolutionized as a result of the post-resurrection appearances of Christ. A prime example is James. Before Christ's appearances, James was embarrassed by his half brother. Afterward, he was willing to die for the notion that his half brother was indeed God.[19]

Extreme Measures

Since reason and rhetoric cannot easily dispense with the post-resurrection appearances of Messiah, extreme measures are often the order of the day. As such, it is argued that devotees of Christ may well have experienced hallucinations, hypnosis, or hypersuggestibility.

Hallucination Hypothesis. According to this hypothesis, the disciples merely saw things they wanted to see. This, however, hardly stands up in the light of cold, hard facts. First, hallucinations are not common and contagious; they are subjective and scarce. Yet Christ appeared to many people over a protracted period of time. Furthermore, hallucinations are relegated to people with certain personality disorders, are stimulated by expectations, and do not stop abruptly. In the case of Christ, he appeared to all kinds of personality types with no expectations, and then the appearances stopped abruptly. Finally, hallucinations in and of themselves would not have led to a belief in resurrection on the part of the disciples in that by their very nature hallucinations do not contain anything new or original. As such, a hallucination could have led to the presumption that Christ had manifested as a disembodied spirit, but not that he had physically resurrected from the dead.[20]

Hypnosis Hypothesis. This is the notion that the disciples were in some sort of an altered state of consciousness as a result of sleep deprivation or suffocating despair over the loss of their Master. In a highly suggestible hypnotic state, the disciples saw what they wanted to see—the appearance of Jesus in the flesh! This, of course, is completely *ad hoc*—in other words, there is not a shred of evidence to substantiate it. While it is true that spiritual leaders, political orators, and dictators have capitalized on crowd dynamics to fool the masses, there is no warrant for suggesting that this is what happened to the disciples. Furthermore, even a cursory reading of the writings of the apostles demonstrates that they had a high regard for the mind. Far from seeking to dull the critical-thinking process, they exhorted one another to be alert and sober minded (1 Thessalonians 5:6; 1 Peter 5:8). While hypnotism is capitalized on in the kingdom of the cults, it is completely foreign to the kingdom of Christ. Finally, Christ's post-resurrection appearances were a material reality so certain that the disciples were willing to die for it.

Hypersuggestibility Hypothesis. This is the notion that the disciples were by nature highly suggestible, and thus susceptible to creating the post-resurrection appearances of Christ out of thin air and then believing them. In response, Dr. Luke comes immediately to mind. Far from hyper-suggestible, Luke was committed to history. Thus, he carefully investigated the details surrounding the post-resurrection appearances of Christ (Luke 1:1–4). Furthermore, hypersuggestibility cannot account for the transformation of Christ's followers into lions of the faith willing to face torture, vilification, and even cruel deaths for the notion that their Messiah had appeared to them in the flesh. Finally, hypersuggestibility—like hallucinations or hypnosis—cannot account for the ironclad certainty that Christ's tomb was found empty as conceded by friends and foes alike.

No one summed up better the consensus of both liberal and conservative scholarship than did Professor Norman Perrin, the late New Testament scholar at the University of Chicago: "The more we study the tradition with regard to the appearances, the firmer the rock begins to appear upon which they are based."[21]

TRANSFORMATION

"For I am the least of the apostles and do not even deserve to be called an apostle, because I persecuted the church of God. But by the grace of God I am what I am, and his grace to me was not without effect. No, I worked harder than all of them—yet not I, but the grace of God that was with me. Whether, then, it was I or they, this is what we preach, and this is what you believed" (1 Corinthians 15:9–11). What happened as a result of the resurrection is unprecedented in human history. In the span of a few hundred years, a small band of seemingly insignificant believers succeeded in turning an entire empire upside down.

The Twelve

The Twelve (minus Judas, plus Paul)[22] were radically revolutionized by the resurrection. Peter, once afraid of being exposed as a follower of Christ by a young woman, after the resurrection was transformed into a lion of the faith. Paul, the ceaseless persecutor of a growing church, became the chief proselytizer of the Gentiles. Peter and Paul, of course, were not alone. Within weeks of the resurrection, not just a few, but an entire community of thousands of Jews, willingly transformed the spiritual and sociological traditions underscoring their national identity.[23]

Traditions

Among the deeply entrenched traditions that were transformed in virtue of the resurrection were the Sabbath, the sacrifices, and the sacraments. In Genesis, the Jewish Sabbath was a celebration of God's work in creation (Genesis 2:2–3). In Exodus, the Sabbath expanded to a celebration of God's deliverance from the oppression of Egypt (Deuteronomy 5:15). In the New Testament epistles, it became a celebration of the "rest" that we have through Christ, who delivers us from sin and the grave (Colossians 2:17; Hebrews 4:1–11). God himself provided the early church with a new pattern of worship through Christ's resurrection on the first day of the week, his subsequent Sunday appearances, and the Spirit's Sunday descent (Matthew 28:1–10; John 20:26ff; Acts 2:1; 20:7; 1 Corinthians 16:2).

For the emerging Christian church, the most dangerous snare was a failure to recognize that Jesus was the substance that fulfilled the symbol of the Sabbath. Furthermore, the Jews had been taught from the time of Abraham that they were to sacrifice animals as the symbol of atonement for their sin. After the resurrection, followers of Christ suddenly stopped sacrificing. They recognized that the new covenant was better than the old covenant because the blood of Jesus Christ was better than the blood of animals (Hebrews 8–10). Jewish believers fully understood that Jesus was the substance that fulfilled the symbol—the sacrificial Lamb that takes away the sin of the world (John 1:29). The writer of Hebrews explains in no uncertain terms that to revert to a sacrificial system is to trample the Son of God underfoot— to treat as an unholy thing the blood of the covenant and to insult the Spirit of grace (Hebrews 10:29; cf., Galatians 3–5; Hebrews 5–6).

Finally, the Jewish rites of Passover and baptism were radically transformed as a result of the resurrection. In place of the Passover meal, believers celebrated the Lord's Supper. Jesus had just been slaughtered in grotesque and humiliating fashion, yet the disciples remembered the broken body and shed blood of Christ with joy. Only the resurrection can account for that. In like fashion, baptism was radically transformed. Prior to the resurrection, Gentile converts to Judaism were baptized in the name of the God of Israel. After the resurrection, converts to Christianity were baptized in the name of Jesus (Acts 2:36–41). In doing so, Christians equated Jesus with Israel's God.

Today

Of one thing I am certain—if twenty-first-century Christians would grasp the significance of resurrection like first-century Christians did, their lives would be totally transformed. Not only in the sense of personal transformation in the present, but in the certainty that one day our lowly bodies will be transformed like unto the glorified body of our Savior (Philippians 3:21). Like the Savior's body, our resurrection bodies will be real, physical, flesh-and-bone bodies, perfectly engineered for "a new heaven and a new earth" (Revelation 21:1). Christ's resurrection was a historical event that took place in our space-time continuum. Likewise, our resurrection will be a historical event that takes place when Christ physically returns and transforms our mortal bodies in a microsecond (1 Corinthians 15:51–52). As there is a one-to-one correspondence between the body of Christ that died and the body that rose, our resurrection bodies will be numerically identical to the bodies we now possess. In other words, our resurrection bodies are not second bodies; rather, they are our present bodies gloriously transformed.

The conclusion of the matter is this. Neither Ponce de León nor Alexander the Great discovered the fountain of youth. It does exist, however. Jesus said, "I am the resurrection and the life. He who believes in me will live, even though he dies; and whoever lives and believes in me will never die" (John 11:25–26). All who put their trust in Jesus can be absolutely certain that they will eternally partake of the fountain of youth. Jesus promised that he would lay down his life and take it up again in three days. His fulfillment of the promise is the guarantee that there is life after life after life.

There is life after life in that the redeemed continue to exist in the presence of the Redeemer. There is life after *life after life* in that just as Jesus rose bodily from the grave, so, too, our bodies will rise immortal, imperishable, incorruptible (1 Corinthians 15). Proof of the resurrection is so certain that millions have willingly laid down their lives, certain that they will take them up again. You can be just as certain. For all who are in Christ, the fountain of youth awaits.

16

Superstar ABCs

I have made a covenant with God that he sends me neither visions, dreams, nor even angels. I am well-satisfied with the gift of the Holy Scriptures, which give me abundant instruction and all that I need to know for this life and for that which is to come.

—MARTIN LUTHER

In golf there are lots of stars, but only a few warrant the moniker "superstar." Jack, Arnie, and Tiger immediately come to mind. They are so famous that last names are completely unnecessary. The NBA, likewise, has a plethora of stars but only one Michael Jordan. In world history, too, there are superstars. Alexander the Great. Aristotle. Augustine. They lit the earth for a brief moment but have long since disintegrated into dust. Only one Superstar endures. One for whom there is no measure. He spoke and a universe of numberless stars leaped into existence. Morning stars together proclaimed his holy birth. One day he will flash across the eastern sky in an epic return to the planet he saved. He is the root and the offspring of David and the bright Morning Star. Where there are S-T-A-R-S in the constellation of biblical prophecy, there is only one enduring superstar. Little wonder, then, that prophecies concerning him outnumber all others.

His *ancestry* was marked and his *birthplace* foretold. Circumstances surrounding his death were prophesied before *crucifixion* was even invented.

The *date of his visitation* was predicted within narrow time parameters. He would work *extraordinary miracles* and *fulfill the Law and the Prophets.* It would be too small for him to bring back only those of Israel, thus he would be a light for the *Gentiles* so that salvation would go out to the ends of the earth. Only the hand of God could have etched a prophetic portrait of the Christ in the Old. Only God could cause it to take on flesh in the New. Only Jesus of Nazareth—the *unique* Superstar—could emerge through the doorway of Old Testament prophecy.

ANCESTRY

He is the Seed of the woman. A metaphor pregnant with meaning. Eve was tempted to do the unthinkable—to take the place of God as arbiter of good and evil. Satan tempted, and the woman tasted temptation's ripened fruit. God authored the potential for evil by providing the woman choice; the woman actualized evil through its exercise. The very passage that references humanity's fall provides—in embryo—the prophetic antidote. As the woman fell, so, too, a woman would bear a Second Adam through whom sin and Satan would be vanquished. In the fullness of time the prophecy was fulfilled through the person and work of a prophesied Savior who crushed the serpent's head (Genesis 3:15). "The woman [Eve] was deceived and became a sinner" (1 Timothy 2:14). The woman (Mary) conceived and brought forth a Savior.

Two thousand years before the Savior was born in Bethlehem, God told Abram to leave his ancestral home in Basra (southern Iraq) and to "go to the land I will show you." God promised Abram, "I will make you into a great nation and I will bless you; I will make your name great, and you will be a blessing. I will bless those who bless you, and whoever curses you I will curse; and all peoples on earth will be blessed through you" (Genesis 12:1–3). From a human perspective, the promise was laughable. Abraham and Sarah did not have children. Thus, Abraham conceived of a natural solution. He slept with Hagar, and she conceived a son named Ishmael, who became the father of twelve rulers. God, however, is hardly limited to natural solutions.

He promised Abraham that Sarah would conceive and bear a son. Abraham "laughed and said to himself, 'Will a son be born to a man a hundred years old? Will Sarah bear a child at the age of ninety?'" (Genesis 17:17). But God was gracious. "Sarah became pregnant and bore a son to Abraham in his old age at the very time God had promised him. Abraham gave the name Isaac to the son Sarah bore him" (Genesis 21:2–3). Thus it was that Immanuel would come through the ancestry of Isaac not Ishmael.

Isaac, like Abraham, had sons who became two nations, one stronger than the other. The older despised his birthright and sold it to the younger for some bread and lentil stew. Thus, Jacob, not Esau, became son of the promise. God confirmed his promise to Jacob in a riveting dream at Bethel. Jacob, whose name God changed to Israel (Genesis 32:28; cf. 35:10), saw a stairway that extended from earth to heaven and heard the voice of God saying, "I am the LORD, the God of your father Abraham and the God of Isaac. I will give you and your descendants the land on which you are lying. Your descendants will be like the dust of the earth, and you will spread out to the west and to the east, to the north and to the south. All peoples on earth will be blessed through you and your offspring" (Genesis 28:13–14).

Israel had twelve sons—the oldest being Reuben. Yet the promise was not to the first son, nor even to the second, Simeon. Nor was the promise to Levi—though Messiah would not only be prophet but priest. "Jacob called for his sons and said: 'Gather around so I can tell you what will happen to you in days to come'" (Genesis 49:1). Israel then spoke these very words: "The scepter will not depart from Judah, nor the ruler's staff from between his feet, until he comes to whom it belongs and the obedience of the nations is his" (49:10). Thus it was that not the first, nor the favorite, but the fourth became son of the promise. Those who reigned from the line of Judah— likened to a lion—ruled in anticipation of the Lion in whom the scepter would find ultimate substance. By identifying Messiah as a descendant of the tribe of Judah, God eliminated the descendants of eleven other tribes.[1]

In time the Judahite dynasty climaxed in a ruler who, despite egregious sins, stands forever in Hebrew history as the quintessential righteous king of Israel. Regrettably, David's descendants, beginning with his own son Solomon, rebelled against God and led Israel into idolatry. Intended to be a city on a hill, a light to the nations pointing forward to the coming of a Second Adam who would redeem true Israel from bondage to sin and death, Israel became a mere microcosm of the surrounding pagan cultures. Though for a brief time it stood as a sacred place foreshadowing a Savior, the city of David became a symbol of spiritual prostitution—a harlot against whom the Old Testament prophets pronounced great woes. The harlotry of Jerusalem resulted in civil war, division of the kingdom, and ultimately the Assyrian exile of the Northern Kingdom of Israel, as well as the Babylonian exile of the Southern Kingdom of Judah.

In the midst of prophesying doom for an apostate Israel, the prophets looked forward to a time in which the house of David would be restored. As such, the prophets foresaw a coming Savior who would deliver true Israel from the wrath that was to come. Indeed, Isaiah prophesied, "The virgin shall conceive and bear a Son, and shall call His name Immanuel" (Isaiah 7:14 NKJV). The near-future fulfillment of Isaiah's words (Isaiah 8) confirmed to his contemporaries that he was a true prophet. The typological fulfillment extended beyond temporal salvation to eternal and ultimate salvation through Jesus—Seed of the woman; descendant of Abraham, of Isaac, of Jacob; Lion of the tribe of Judah; and the One who forever sits upon the throne of David.

On an occasion, "while the Pharisees were gathered together," the progeny of David asked them, "'What do you think about the Christ? Whose son is he?' 'The son of David,' they replied. He said to them, 'How is it then that David, speaking by the Spirit, calls him "Lord"?'" (Matthew 22:41–43). The Pharisees were dumbstruck. The man born of a virgin, standing before them, had manifested supernatural authority over sickness, over the forces of nature, over fallen angels, even over death. And now he was asking a question that rendered them speechless. "If then David calls him 'Lord,' how can he be his son?" (22:45). The force of the question may have been lost on lesser antagonists, but not on the teachers of the law. Without a hint of self-consciousness, Jesus claimed to be Lord of heaven and earth. And no one dared to ask him any more questions. Had Jesus been a Benjamite or even a Levite, he would have immediately been exposed as a fraud. Indeed, had Jesus not been of the house and lineage of David, his antagonists would have been keenly aware that his ancestry did not match that of Messiah.

Considering that they had done everything in their power to undermine Jesus, the obvious would have hardly gone unchallenged.

Instead, as predicted by the Old Testament prophets, the Seed of the woman would be a descendant of Abraham, not Lot. The line would proceed through Isaac, not Ishmael. Through Jacob, not Esau. And the fourth of Jacob's sons, not the first. He would be the legal heir of David, the long-awaited King of the Jews who would ultimately restore true Israel from their exile in sin. As such, Matthew records fourteen generations from Abraham to David, fourteen from David to the exile, and fourteen from the exile to the Christ (Matthew 1:17). The ancestry of Jesus is thus adroitly arranged into three sets of fourteen that correspond to the Hebrew letters in King David's name. One thing is certain. Jesus had to be a Jew. Not just any Jew. He had to be the Jewish descendant of Israel's quintessential king—through Jesse by way of Judah and in the lineage of Jacob. God sovereignly directed the course of human history from the woman Eve who was deceived, to the woman Mary who conceived a Son who alone could emerge through the doorway of Old Testament prophecy.

But there's more. Much, much, more!

BIRTHPLACE

My birthplace was Leiden in the Netherlands—something I did not—could not—plan or prearrange. And as you may well imagine, I still have lots of friends and family members there. Every year, especially during Christmas, lots of packages originating in Holland find their way to my doorstep in the US. Were it not for seven points of identification, they might well end up somewhere else—a factory in China, a hotel in Jakarta, a home in Taiwan. Seven points of identification, however, ensure that the packages leave Holland and arrive on my doorstep. Seven points separate me from six billion options—name, number, street, city, state, zip code, country.

Just as there are points of identification that allow a package to arrive on my doorstep, so, too, there are prophecies that identify Jesus as the only one who can emerge through the doorway of Old Testament prophecy. To make the points memorable, I have associated them with the first seven letters of the alphabet beginning with the afore detailed *ancestry* of Christ. The ancestry of Jesus from Eve to Mary in and of itself marks a very narrow doorway through whom only the offspring of David could emerge. Add to that his birthplace and all possibility of an imposter is eliminated.

Seven hundred years before Jesus was born, the prophet Micah prophesied that the birthplace of Messiah would be Bethlehem. Not just any Bethlehem, but Bethlehem Ephrathah on the outskirts of Jerusalem. Not Bethlehem in Zebulunite territory eleven kilometers northwest of Nazareth. "But you, Bethlehem Ephrathah, though you are small among the clans of Judah, out of you will come for me one who will be ruler over Israel, whose origins are from old, from ancient times" (Micah 5:2). Had Jesus been born anywhere other than Bethlehem Ephrathah, Micah's prophecy and consequently the whole of biblical prophecy would have been disqualified as distinctly divine as opposed to merely mortal in origin. Instead, in concert with the Scriptures, Jesus was born precisely where predicted.

Dr. Luke, ever the meticulous historian, pinpoints the precise circumstances surrounding the birth of the babe of Bethlehem. Caesar Augustus had just issued a decree that a census be taken of the entire Roman world. This was when Quirinius was governor of Syria. As a result, Joseph left Nazareth in Galilee and went to Judea, to Bethlehem, because he belonged to the house and line of David. Had he not belonged to the lineage of David, he would most certainly have ended up somewhere else. So it was, that while Joseph and Mary were in Bethlehem, "the time came for the baby to be born, and she gave birth to her firstborn, a son. She wrapped him in cloths and placed him in a manger, because there was no room for them in the inn" (Luke 2:6–7).

Moreover, the fulfillment of Micah's prophecy is not just attested to by Luke. It was an expectation for all of Israel. When King Herod asked Jews where Jesus would be born, they replied without hesitation: "In Bethlehem in Judea, *for this is what the prophet has written*: 'But you, Bethlehem, in the land of Judah, are by no means least among the rulers of Judah; for out of you will come a ruler who will be the shepherd of my people Israel'" (Matthew 2:6). Thus the prophecy of Micah 5:2 was directly and specifically fulfilled with the birth of Christ in Bethlehem. It was there that the singular superstar of human history was born in the fullness of time. It was there that a star, hundreds of times larger than the earth, stopped over the birthplace of Messiah. It was there that Herod gave orders to have all the boys in Bethlehem and vicinity who were two years old and under ruthlessly murdered (Matthew 2:16). And it was in there, Bethlehem Ephrathah, that the word of the prophet Jeremiah was fulfilled—"A voice is heard in Ramah, mourning and great weeping, Rachel weeping for her children and refusing to be comforted, because they are no more" (Jeremiah 31:15 UPDATED NIV)—a gruesome reality that even the wrath of man will please God's purposes.[2]

Given the significance of Christ's birth in Bethlehem, it should come as no surprise that details surrounding the fulfillment of this extraordinary prophecy are continually under attack. First is the contention that only two gospels deal with Christ's birthplace, and do so quite differently. Luke says Jesus was born in a manger while Matthew says Jesus was born at home. Further, it is argued that there is no record outside the Gospels that Caesar Augustus ordered a worldwide taxation. Therefore, there was no need for Mary and Joseph to register in Bethlehem. Finally, it is suggested that people were known by the place where they were born. Since Jesus is known as Jesus of Nazareth, he must have been born there—not Bethlehem.

Marcus Borg of the highly influential Jesus Seminar consistently champions the notion that Matthew and Luke provide different and contradictory information concerning Christ's birth in Bethlehem. Luke says Jesus was born in a manger (2:6–7), Matthew, at home (1:24–25); therefore, neither can be trusted. Matthew, of course, says nothing of the sort—Borg simply fabricates the notion. Far from being contradictory, differences between gospel accounts are complementary. Luke adds details to Matthew's account, such as Christ's birth taking place in a manger because there was no room for them in the inn. Such differences actually augment authenticity. In the words of historian Dr. Paul Barnett, "The differences in the narratives indicate that not only were Matthew and Luke isolated from each other when they wrote, but also that the sources on which they depended were quite separate. Yet from these underlying source strands we have detailed agreement about where Jesus was born, when, to which parents, and the miraculous circumstances of his conception."[3]

Furthermore, dogmatic assertions by John Dominic Crossan, Robert Funk, Bart Ehrman, and other fundamentalist scholars that there is no record outside of the Gospels that emperor Caesar Augustus ordered a worldwide taxation are also patently false.[4] In truth, Caesar Augustus was known for his census taking—in fact, credible historians do not even debate the issue. The Jewish historian Josephus, for example, refers to a Roman taxation of AD 6,[5] which likely took a lengthy period to complete. It no doubt began with Caesar Augustus around 5 BC and was completed a decade later. Luke notes that the census was completed when Quirinius was governor of Syria. As noted by historian Paul Maier during a live *Bible Answer Man* broadcast, "The Romans took forty years to get a census done in Gaul. For a province 1,500 miles away from Rome in Palestine to take a decade is pretty quick. And since that census would finally come in under Quirinius's administration, it would be called correctly by Luke his census."[6] Given Luke's impeccable credentials as a historian, it would be far more circumspect to give him the benefit of the doubt. One need only remember the experience of the brilliant archaeologist Sir William Ramsay, who set out to disprove Luke's historical reliability. Through his painstaking Mediterranean archaeological trips, he discovered that, one after the other, the historical allusions of Luke proved accurate. If, as Ramsay points out, Luke does not err in referencing a plethora of countries, cities, and islands, there is no reason to doubt him concerning this census.[7] The common contention that men were taxed where they lived and women didn't count is also spurious. Maier cites a first-century Roman census in Egypt in which taxpayers living elsewhere were ordered to return to their homelands for registration.[8] Moreover, a Roman census from Bacchius, Egypt, dated AD 119, historically documents that women and children were registered by their husbands or fathers.[9]

Finally, a word about the misguided conviction that Jesus was born in Nazareth—or in the vernacular of Borg, "The fact that Jesus is known as Jesus of Nazareth points very, very heavily to Nazareth being his birthplace. People in that world were known either as son of so-and-so, or by the village in which they were born."[10] Countless counterexamples undermine this hypothesis. For instance, Irenaeus of Lyons (c. 175–195) was probably a native of Smyrna, where as a boy he studied before moving to Lyons;[11]

Lucian of Antioch (c. 240–312) was born at Samosata but completed his education and eventually led the theological schools at Antioch;[12] Paul of Constantinople (d. c. 351) was a native of Thessalonica and became bishop of Constantinople.[13] These men were born in one place but later moved to the places with which their names became associated, as did Jesus, who was born in Bethlehem but lived the vast majority of his life in Nazareth. History shows that in the broader context of people's lives there are several factors that influence how they are identified. More important, because the Bible says Jesus was born in Bethlehem, we can rest assured that he was born in Bethlehem! Like the choice between Bart and the Bible, the choice between the Bible and Borg is not difficult to make. Borg's dogmatic assertions are consistently suspect, biblical prophecies consistently correct. Just as ancestry can hardly be faked, the place of one's birth is impossible to prearrange.

CRUCIFIXION

There is nothing new about crucifixion. In the sixth century before Christ, the Persian Darius I crucified three thousand political dissidents in Babylon.[14] In the fourth century, crucifixion was employed by the Grecian Alexander the Great.[15] In the second century the Greco-Syrian beast Antiochus IV Epiphanes crucified Jewish stalwarts who refused to be Hellenized.[16] While crucifixion was conceived by Persians, it was popularized and perfected by Romans. To extract every ounce of suffering from victims, Romans invented seat (*sedile*) and foot (*suppedaneum*) supports to cause victims to linger in the throes of death.[17] Crucifixion became so inexpressibly gruesome that the word *excruciating*, literally "out of the cross," was coined to fully codify its horror.

While thousands have suffered the inexplicable horror of crucifixion, Christ's crucifixion remains unique. He suffered more than any human ever had before or has since. He suffered the cumulative sufferings of all humanity. For on the cross the infinite Christ bore the sin and suffering of finite humanity. As the chill of death crept through his body, Christ cried out words uttered by the prophet David a millennium earlier: "*Eloi, Eloi, lama sabachthani?*—which means, 'My God, my God, why have you forsaken me?'" (Matthew 27:46). And then, with the debt of humanity paid in full, Jesus gave up his spirit (John 19:30).

Few today doubt Christ's fatal torment upon the cross. It is one of the most well-established facts of ancient history—conceded by Christ's friends and foes alike.[18] There is, however, fierce opposition to the notion that Christ's crucifixion was predicted by the prophets. No doubt the most ferocious opposition is reserved for the very psalm to which Christ drew attention with his dying words—"My God, my God, why have you forsaken me?" Venom found on the Internet in this regard is quite simply mind-boggling. Psalm 22 does not predict Christ's crucifixion, shout the naysayers, and no amount of evidence will convince them to the contrary.

The problem here, of course, is that such naysayers seem caught in the web of their own fundamentalism. They may be vaguely aware of the power of direct predictive prophecies but remain blithely unaware of the explanatory power inherent in typological prophecy. As such, the word *pierced* in Psalm 22:16 is dismissed as a less-than-imaginative interpolation created by a deliberate mistranslation of the Hebrew word *ka'ari*. As noted, this argument is hardly persuasive. The difference between the Hebrew words *ka'aru* ("pierced") and *ka'ari* ("like the lion") is akin to the difference between a jot and a tittle. Not only so, but the phrase "like the lion" makes no sense in the immediate or broader context of the passage. Most significant, however, is the discovery of a manuscript fragment at Nahal Hever in the region of the Dead Sea. This fragment, a millennium older than the Masoretic text, ended in the longer *vav* ("pierced"), not *yod* ("like the lion")—a mere millimeter of ink making all the difference in the world.

What must be understood here is that the Sovereign who inspired the sacred text likewise fashioned the whole of Old Testament history as a foreshadowing representation of the coming Messiah. Thus the evidential value of Psalm 22 as a foreshadowing of Christ's crucifixion stands. I can think of no place that this typological fulfillment is more beautifully explicated than in Keil and Delitzsch's commentary on the Old Testament. "That David, the anointed of Samuel, before he ascended the throne, had to traverse a path of suffering which resembles the suffering path of Jesus, the Son of David, baptized of John, and that this typical suffering of David is embodied for us in the psalms as in the images reflected from a mirror, is an arrangement of divine power, mercy, and wisdom."[19] It is as though David, persecuted by Saul, sees himself as Christ pierced by the Sanhedrin:

> For as God the Father molds the history of Jesus Christ in accordance with His own counsel, so His Spirit molds even the utterances of David concerning himself the type of the future One, with a view to that history. Through this Spirit who is the Spirit of God and of the future Christ at the same time, David's typical history, as he describes it in the Psalms and more especially in this Psalm, acquires that ideal depth of tone, brilliancy, and power, by virtue of which it (the history) reaches far beyond its typical facts, penetrates to its very root in the divine counsels, and grows to be the word of prophecy: so that, to a certain extent, it may rightly be said that Christ here speaks through David, in so far as the Spirit of Christ speaks through him and makes the typical suffering of his ancestor the medium for the representation of his own future sufferings. Without recognizing this incontestable relation of the matter Ps. xxii cannot be understood nor can we fully enter into its sentiments.[20]

The composite picture of crucifixion presented in the Old Testament is as graphic as it is gruesome. "I am poured out like water, and all my bones are out of joint," writes David (Psalm 22:14). "A band of evil men has encircled me, they have pierced my hands and my feet. I can count all my bones; people stare and gloat over me. They divide my garments among them and cast lots for my clothing" (22:16–18).

Isaiah's words likewise rivet our gaze on the canvas of crucifixion. "He was pierced for our transgressions, he was crushed for our iniquities; the punishment that brought us peace was upon him, and by his wounds we are healed" (Isaiah 53:5). Isaiah's vivid portrayal of a singular Servant of the Lord compels identification with the fatal torment of the Christ (Isaiah 52:13–53:12).[21] He is pictured as a "tender shoot" (53:2) coming up out of the "stump of Jesse" (Isaiah 11:1). "Despised and rejected by men" (Isaiah 53:3), he "took up our infirmities and carried our sorrows" (53:4). For "though he had done no violence, nor was any deceit found in his mouth" (53:9), the Lord "laid on him the iniquity of us all" (53:6), "the punishment that brought us peace was upon him, and by his wounds we are healed" (53:5). "Led like a lamb to the slaughter" (53:7), the Servant of the Lord "bore the sin of many, and made intercession for the transgressors" (53:12).[22]

Isaiah foreshadows the suffering and death of Christ as the aim and the end of all Old Testament sacrifices—the antitype of the sin offering, the trespass offering, the Passover Lamb itself—silent before its shearers.[23] Peter builds on the fulfillment of Isaiah's prophecy in asserting that Christ "himself bore our sins in his body on the tree, so that we might die to sins and live for righteousness; by his wounds you have been healed. For you were like sheep going astray, but now you have returned to the Shepherd and Overseer of your souls" (1 Peter 2:24–25). Zechariah adds this to the portrait: "They will look on me, the one they have pierced, and they will mourn for him as one mourns for an only child, and grieve bitterly for him as one grieves for a firstborn son" (Zechariah 12:10).

Taken in isolation, such passages do little to convince the stiff-necked. In total they have the capacity of turning heads toward truth. John testifies to this very truth, "so that you also may believe. These things happened so that the scripture would be fulfilled: 'Not one of his bones will be broken' [Psalm 34:20][24] and, as another scripture says, 'They will look on the one they have pierced'" (John 19:35–37). Long before crucifixion was invented by the Persians and popularized by the Romans, the prophets portrayed a crucified Christ who died on a cross so that the Scriptures may be fulfilled and multitudes may come to knowledge of the Truth. "After the suffering of his soul, he will see the light of life and be satisfied; by his knowledge my righteous servant will justify many, and he will bear their iniquities" (Isaiah 53:11).

DATE

Date setting is the bane of modern-day controversialists. Even as I write, Harold Camping has forty days before the date of his prophesied Day of Judgment. His headline is ominous: "The End of the World Is Almost

Here! Holy God Will Bring Judgment Day on May 21, 2011."[25] "The Bible gives us the correct and accurate information about that Day," writes Camping. "Holy God is a God of great mercy, compassion, and love. That is why he has given us in advance of the destruction the *exact time* of the Day of Judgment. The Bible tells us in Amos 3:7: 'Surely the Lord GOD will do nothing, but He revealeth his secret unto His servants the prophets.' Consequently, we now can know from the Bible the exact time and many details of God's destruction plan that is to come upon the whole world."[26]

Camping calculates the date in rather ingenious fashion. He begins with the premise that Noah's flood began on the seventeenth day of the second month, in the year 4990 BC, and that seven days before the beginning of the Flood "God commanded Noah to warn the peoples of the world that they had seven days to get into the safety of the ark."[27] He proceeds with the premise that 2 Peter 3:8 teaches that "one day is as 1,000 years." Thus, he supposes that "the seven days referred to in Genesis 7:4 can be understood as 7,000 years." He thus concludes that "God is showing us by the words of 2 Peter 3:8 that He wants us to know that exactly 7,000 years after He destroyed the world with water in Noah's day, He plans to destroy the entire world forever. *Because the year 2011 AD is exactly 7000 years after 4990 BC when the Flood began, the Bible has given us absolute proof that the year 2011 is the end of the world during the Day of Judgment, which will come on the last day of the Day of Judgment.*"[28] In the end, Camping assures devotees that a remnant of two hundred million of them will be raptured May 21, 2011.

By the time this manuscript is published, May 21, 2011, will have come and gone, and Camping's reasoning will once again be exposed for all of its absurdities. Not only does he not know the date of Noah's flood, which gets his calculations off on the wrong foot, but a cursory reading of 2 Peter 3 is enough to persuade the biblically literate that God does not intend to communicate that a day *is* equal to a thousand years. Camping, of course, is not alone in such calculations. As one date after another is proven false, new dates crop up like weeds. Following the failure of Camping's May 21, 2011, date, the next date du jour is set at December 21, 2012, the end of the Mayan calendar—just think Jack Van Impe.[29]

In reality no one knows the time of Christ's return and the end of the world. Pretend prophets continue to tell men what itching ears want to hear. True prophets, in contrast, spoke as they were carried along by the Holy Spirit. It is ironic indeed that Camping cites Amos 3:7 in vindication of his claims. Amos could rightly say, "The Lord GOD will do nothing, but he revealeth his secret unto his servants the prophets" (KJV)—for he was a true prophet of God. Thus he rightly told God's people what the future held in store. Though the nation of Israel would suffer utter destruction, out of judgment would emerge a faithful remnant—a true Israel from "every tribe and language and people and nation" (Revelation 5:9). Though the prophecy of Amos was fulfilled when a remnant of Israel was restored to the land, James saw ultimate fulfillment in the inclusion of both Jews and Gentiles in the church. James made this explicit at the Jerusalem council by quoting the prophet Amos: "After this I will return and rebuild David's fallen tent. Its ruins I will rebuild, and I will restore it, that the remnant of men may seek the Lord, and all the Gentiles who bear my name, says the Lord, who does these things that have been known for all ages" (Acts 15:16–18). Inspired by the Spirit, Amos, the true prophet of God, looked into the future and saw One who would come in the fullness of time and "rebuild David's fallen tent" (Amos 9:10; cf. Acts 15:16).

Unlike Camping, who attempts through esoteric numerology to calculate the exact date of rapture as well as the precise date of Christ's first advent, the prophets provided date parameters that, in concert with ancestry, birthplace, and crucifixion prophecies, further pinpoint Jesus as the prophesied Messiah. Rather than casting aspersions on the Scriptures, they demonstrate that God has indeed inspired the sacred text. In the span of human history the timeframe set by such prophecies is narrow indeed. Christ would not come prior to the last oracle spoken by the prophet Malachi. Nor could he be born after the destruction of the temple in Jerusalem.

Malachi's prophecy in this regard is nothing short of arresting. "See, I will send my messenger, who will prepare the way before me. Then suddenly the Lord you are seeking will come to his temple; the messenger of the covenant, whom you desire, will come, says the LORD Almighty" (Malachi 3:1). Israel in its existing moral degradation was not prepared for the coming of the Christ. Thus, God would send "the prophet Elijah before that great and dreadful day of the LORD" (Malachi 4:5). As such, the whole of the Old Testament ends with the promise of a coming Savior who "will turn the hearts of the fathers to their children, and the hearts of the children to the fathers" (4:6). The prophecy came at a time when Israel, intended to be a light to the nations, was plagued by corrupt priests, wicked practices, and a false sense of security in their privileged relationship to the God of Abraham, Isaac, and Jacob. The nation had become so sinful that God's oracles through the prophets no longer had any impact. Thus, for the four hundred years following Malachi's prophetic condemnations, God remained silent. Only with the coming of Elijah (Malachi 3:1) would God again communicate prophetically with his people. The prophet promised by Malachi who came in the fullness of time was not a literal reincarnation or reappearance of Elijah, but John the Baptist, who came in the spirit and power of Elijah. As Jesus himself explained, Elijah was a type of John the Baptist (Matthew 11:13–14; 17:12–13; Luke 1:17)—that is, Elijah, by performing powerful signs and wonders and through the preaching of repentance, established a pattern of prophetic prowess exemplified by John the Baptist at the climax of human history—a climax in which Jesus alone could emerge through the doorway of Old Testament prophecy. As the Elijah prophesied by Malachi appeared in the person of John the Baptist, so the Lord Almighty would come to his temple in the person of Jesus the Christ.

Malachi thus adds his voice to the throng of Old Testament prophets who foretold the coming of Messiah. As the last of the prophetic voices, Malachi's oracles establish the boundaries that date the coming of Christ. His advent would not occur prior to the last prophecy concerning his coming; he would be preceded by John, who would come in the spirit and power of Elijah; and he would come prior to the destruction of the Jerusalem temple. The prophet Haggai makes this equally plain in prophesying that the coming of Christ would cause the glory of the second temple to surpass the glories of the first. Says Haggai, "The glory of this present house will be greater than the glory of the former house" (2:9). Though Haggai's hearers would have understood his prophecy to refer to the physical temple, which they were in process of constructing, the prophecy finds its ultimate fulfillment in Jesus, the true Temple not built by human hands (Mark 14:58; John 2:13–22).[30]

Extraordinary Miracles

The words *it's a miracle* are not at all foreign to me. I've uttered them more times than I can remember. I find a key that fits a particular keyhole and exclaim, "It's a miracle!" I rediscover a keepsake and shout, "It's a miracle!" I witness the birth of yet another kid and reverentially murmur, "It's a miracle!" There is, however, a huge difference between God's ordinary intrusions into the circumstances of our lives and extraordinary miracles. Make no mistake. The birth of a baby *is* a miracle—but not in the extraordinary sense. Extraordinary miracles were those performed by Christ when he opened the eyes of the blind and unstopped the ears of the deaf. When the lame leaped for joy, and Lazarus emerged from the tomb dressed in the robes of his own funeral. The extraordinary miracles wrought by the Savior were such that the Sanhedrin could not deny them. They knew that they were witnesses to extraordinary miracles. They knew Messiah had emerged through the doorway of Old Testament prophecies. Yet with premeditation and forethought, they attributed these extraordinary miracles to Beelzebub the prince of demons. Thus, their guilt remained (Matthew 12:22–37; John 8:48–58).

Luke recalls how, shortly after his temptation in the wilderness, Jesus went into the synagogue in Nazareth on the Sabbath. There he was handed the scroll of Isaiah. Unrolling it, he found the place where it was written: "The Spirit of the Lord is on me, because he has anointed me to preach good news to the poor. He has sent me to proclaim freedom for the prisoners and recovery of sight for the blind, to release the oppressed, to proclaim the year of the Lord's favor" (Luke 4:18–19). Upon rolling up the scroll again, he sat down to expound the meaning of Isaiah 61. He began the exposition with these words: "Today this scripture is fulfilled in your hearing" (4:21). As Isaiah 61 was the interpretation of Isaiah 40–55, Jesus pointed directly to himself as the Servant of the Lord sent to reverse the oppression of Israel.[31] Not from Roman subjugation but from the ruins of sin. As such, he identified himself as One sent to heal the physically blind so that spiritually they might see. The heart of Christ's message that Sabbath day in Nazareth was impossible to miss. The eschaton (final consummation of all things) had been inaugurated. The miracles he did in their midst attested to the reality that he was the extraordinary miracle worker, the fulfillment of Isaiah's prophecies.

The Jews were intimately acquainted with the prophecies of Isaiah. They knew that the coming of Messiah would be heralded by extraordinary miracles. "Then will the eyes of the blind be opened and the ears of the deaf unstopped," Isaiah had prophesied. "Then will the lame leap like a deer, and the mute tongue shout for joy" (35:5–6). But Isaiah had said far more: "Water will gush forth in the wilderness and streams in the desert. The burning sand will become a pool, the thirsty ground bubbling springs" (35:6–7). Isaiah pointed past the healing of eyes and ears to the healing of the earth. When Messiah came he would inaugurate the eschaton. Yet the consummation of all things would be far grander. Paradise would once again reign upon the planet. True Israel would be gathered from the far reaches of the earth. As the Old Testament prophet "Jonah was three days and three nights in the belly of a huge fish, so the Son of Man will be three days and three nights in the heart of the earth," Jesus had prophesied (Matthew 12:40). In saying this he pointed past the miracles to the ultimate sign and wonder. For though he died, yet would he live. Likewise, the whole of true Israel would be joined with him in resurrection.

As Isaiah had prophesied, Messiah would be an extraordinary miracle worker. Matthew testifies to the fulfillment: "Jesus went through all the towns and villages, teaching in their synagogues, preaching the good news of the kingdom and healing every disease and sickness" (9:35). The physically blind received new sight—as did the spiritually. They looked beyond time and space and saw "the Holy City, Jerusalem, coming down out of heaven from God" (Revelation 21:10).

FULFILL

How high can the bar be set? Messiah had to be a descendant of Abraham, Isaac, and Jacob; descended from the tribe of Judah; one who would forever sit upon the throne of David. Of all the towns and hamlets on the planet, his birthplace could only be Bethlehem Ephrathah. Had Jesus been born anywhere else, he would have been disqualified. He had to be crucified with criminals, be born prior to the destruction of Jerusalem's temple, and be a worker of extraordinary miracles. And as though that were not enough, he had to fulfill all the Law and the Prophets. Put another way, he had to fulfill every aspect of the Old Testament—precept as well as prophecy. "I tell you the truth," said Jesus, "until heaven and earth disappear, not the smallest letter, not the least stroke of a pen, will by any means disappear from the Law until everything is accomplished" (Matthew 5:18). Not a jot—the smallest letter in the Hebrew alphabet; not the least stroke of a pen—a microscopic appendage at the end of a Hebrew letter, would vanish.

In saying this, Jesus singled himself out from every other person on the planet—past, present, and future. He had to fulfill every predictive and typological prophecy pointing to the Messiah, such that his face, and his alone, could appear in the luminous tapestry of Old Testament writings. Not only so, he had to keep the Law perfectly. In a word, he had to manifest the very credential of *sinlessness*. Moses could not do that, nor could Isaiah. When the most righteous man in Israel caught a glimpse of the holiness of God, he cried out in recognition of his own sinfulness, "Woe to me! I am ruined! For I am a man of unclean lips, and I live among a people of unclean lips, and my eyes have seen the King, the LORD Almighty" (Isaiah 6:5). The Pharisees, too, fell far short. They tithed their mint and cumin but neglected the weightier matters of the Law. Even Paul, who wrote two-thirds of the New Testament epistles, recognized how far he lived from the land of sinlessness. "What I do is not the good I want to do," he confessed to Roman devotees, "no, the evil I do not want to do—this I keep on doing" (Romans 7:19). Muhammad, likewise, stood impotent in the face of sinlessness. As such, the Qur'an exhorts him to seek forgiveness for sin.[32]

Only the crystal Christ, the paragon of virtue, the one in all the billions, could claim the credential of sinlessness. Eyewitnesses were adamant. "He appeared so that he might take away our sins," says John. "And in him is *no sin*" (1 John 3:5). Paul, likewise, designates Christ as the one "who had no sin" (2 Corinthians 5:21). Peter affirms the sinlessness of Christ, recognizing it as the fulfillment of Isaiah's prophecy: "He committed no sin, and *no*

deceit was found in his mouth" (1 Peter 2:22; cf. Isaiah 53:9). He "has been tempted in every way, just as we are," writes the author of Hebrews, "yet was without sin" (4:15). Jesus went so far as to challenge antagonists, saying, "Can any of you prove me guilty of sin?" (John 8:46). No just response was uttered—for Christ had come "to fulfill all righteousness" (Matthew 3:15). "He will reign on David's throne . . . establishing and upholding it with justice and righteousness" (Isaiah 9:7). "'The days are coming,' declares the LORD, 'when I will raise up to David a righteous Branch, a King who will reign wisely and do what is just and right in the land'" (Jeremiah 23:5). That king has come: "Righteous and having salvation, gentle and riding on a donkey" (Zechariah 9:9).

Only one among the billions could emerge through the doorway of the Law and the Prophets. Only one would be their fulfillment. "Do not think that I have come to abolish the Law or the Prophets," said the righteous King. "I have not come to abolish them but to fulfill them" (Matthew 5:17). All that we have in the Scripture, to its very jot and tittle, stands forever in Christ. Every divine prophecy, every divine precept.

GENTILES

Though he was a Jew from the house and lineage of David, Jesus is specifically identified in the Old Testament prophetic oracles as a light to the Gentiles. Had the prophets identified him as a parochial Jewish Messiah, Jesus could not have emerged through the doorway of Old Testament prophecies.

James quotes the prophet Amos to demonstrate that inclusion of the Gentiles in the New Testament church is in direct fulfillment of Jesus' messianic mission. Previously, he, along with the disciples, had labored under a grievous misconception. They expected Jesus to establish Israel as a sovereign Jewish state. The notion was so ingrained in their psyches that even as Jesus was about to ascend into heaven, they asked, "Lord, are you at this time going to restore the kingdom to Israel?" (Acts 1:6). Jesus not only corrected their erroneous thinking, but expanded their provincial horizons from a tiny strip of land on the east coast of the Mediterranean Sea to the farthest reaches of the earth. "You will receive power when the Holy Spirit comes on you," said Jesus, as he was about to be taken up into heaven, "and you will be my witnesses in Jerusalem, and in all Judea and Samaria, and to the ends of the earth" (1:8).

In effect, Jesus left his disciples with instructions to exit Jerusalem, embrace the earth, and never again entertain the notion of establishing an earthly Jerusalem. They were no longer permitted to view Israel in exclusivistic, parochial categories; their sights instead had been elevated to an Israel inclusive of Jew and Gentile. At the Jerusalem council, James identified this new covenant reality as the antitypical fulfillment of the well-known prophecy that God would "restore David's fallen tent" so "that the remnant of men may seek the Lord, and all the Gentiles who bear my name" (Acts 15:17; cf. Amos 9:11). James underscored the reality that Abraham was not to be the father of *a* nation, but the father of *many* nations (Genesis 17:5). When God promised Abraham, "I will bless those who bless you, and whoever curses you I will curse; and all peoples on earth will be blessed through you" (Genesis 12:3), such blessings and cursings pertain not simply to the faithful remnant of ethnic Israel, but to true Israel, which consists of every person who through faith has been adopted into the family of God. Only after Peter had experienced the vision of unclean food in Joppa did he comprehend the mystery of the gospel. "I now realize how true it is," said Peter, "that God does not show *favoritism* but accepts men from every nation who fear him and do what is right. You know the message God sent to the people of Israel, telling the good news of peace through Jesus Christ, who is Lord of *all*" (Acts 10:34–36).

Rather than focusing on an exclusively Jewish kingdom, Paul likewise rejoices that Messiah's reign extends to faithful Gentiles throughout the earth who, on account of Christ, "are no longer foreigners and aliens, but fellow citizens with God's people and members of God's household" (Ephesians 2:19). In evidence he quoted Isaiah's epic words: "I have made you a light for the Gentiles, so that you may bring salvation to the ends of the earth" (Acts 13:47; cf. Isaiah 49:6). As Paul said elsewhere, "I am saying nothing beyond what the prophets and Moses said would happen—that the Christ would suffer and, as the first to rise from the dead, would proclaim light to his own people and to the Gentiles" (Acts 26:22–23).

The prophets to whom the apostle appeals identified Messiah with such specificity that only One could emerge. His *ancestry* marked thousands of years prior to his birth. His *birthplace in Bethlehem* likewise foretold. The circumstances surrounding his death prophesied in minute detail before *crucifixion* was ever invented. The *date of his visitation* predicted within a historically narrow timeframe. An *extraordinary miracle worker* who would *fulfill* the Law and the Prophets and a light for the *Gentiles* so that salvation would go out to the ends of the earth. The prophecies concerning him are simply so precise that the probabilities of someone fulfilling them by chance do not exist.

"No prophecy of scripture came about by the prophet's own interpretation," writes Peter. "For prophecy never had its origin in the will of man, but men spoke from God as they were carried along by the Holy Spirit" (2 Peter 1:21). No mere mortal can write history prior to the fact. God, and God alone, could have etched Christ's portrait in the Old and cause it to come in flesh in the New. Predictive prophecy is a principle of biblical reliability that reaches even hard-boiled skeptics!

Prophetic S-T-A-R-S in the constellation of biblical prophecy are powerful proofs that God has spoken, that the Bible is divine rather than merely human in origin. In the words of the Almighty, "I told you these things long ago; before they happened I announced them to you" (Isaiah 48:5). Counterfeit prophecy stars are consistently wrong. In illumined contrast, genuine S-T-A-R-S are infallibly correct.

Memorable Snapshots

Succession of Nations

One of the most significant demonstrations that the Bible is divine rather than merely human in origin is the undeniable reality that Daniel, writing six centuries before the advent of Christ, was empowered by the almighty God to do what no soothsayer or astrologer could. With awe-inspiring precision he predicted a succession of nations from Babylon through the Median and Persian Empires, to the persecution and suffering of the Jews under the second-century Greco-Syrian beast Antiochus IV Epiphanes, including the despot's desecration of the Jerusalem temple, his untimely death, and freedom for the Jews under Judas Maccabaeus. Moreover, as Daniel looked down the corridor of time, he got a glimpse of a kingdom that will itself endure forever. Truly, the succession of nations immortalized by the book of Daniel is a surpassingly spectacular star in the constellation of biblical prophecy.

Typological Prophecy

Predictive prophecy is fairly straightforward. As such, Micah 5:2 is a predictive prophecy directly and specifically fulfilled with the birth of Christ in Bethlehem. Typological prophecy is somewhat more complex in that it involves a divinely intended pattern of events encompassing both historical correspondence and intensification. "Typology views the relationship of Old Testament events to those in the new dispensation not as a 'one-to-one' correspondence, in which the old is repeated or continued, but rather in terms of two principles, historical correspondence and escalation."[33] When Matthew says that the virgin birth of Jesus is the fulfillment of Isaiah's prophecy (7:14), he is speaking of typological rather than predictive fulfillment. Only when the elegance of typology is comprehended can the mystery of Scripture be fully apprehended.

Abomination of Desolation

The prophesied abomination of desolation by which the temple was desecrated in the Old Testament and destroyed in the New is at once a bloody scar and a brilliant star enlightening our minds to the divine nature of the Scriptures. Still, its light has been darkened and its meaning diminished by modern-day prophecy pundits bent on pinning the tail on a twenty-first-century Antichrist who will allegedly arise out of a revived Roman Empire. While Zionist zeal threatens to light the fuse of Armageddon, we can be absolutely certain that the prophecies of Daniel and Jesus already blaze as stars in the constellation of fulfilled prophecy demonstrating that the Bible is divine as opposed to merely human in origin.

Resurrection Prophecies

Resurrection is the brightest star in the constellation of biblical prophecy. While all other prophecies demonstrating the Bible to be divine rather than merely human in origin invoke the supernatural—resurrection embodies it. When the Jews demanded that Jesus prove his authority over temple, priest, and sacrifice, he responded, "Destroy this temple, and I will raise it again in three days" (John 2:19). Christ's fulfillment guarantees that there is life after life after life. Life after life in that the redeemed continue to exist in the presence of the Redeemer; life after life after life in that just as Jesus rose bodily from the grave, a starry host of resurrection prophecies guarantee that we, too, will rise immortal, imperishable, incorruptible. If Christ had not himself been resurrected, the promise that he will resurrect dry bones in scattered graves would be as empty as the tomb guaranteeing its fulfillment.

Superstar ABCs

Every year—especially during Christmas—lots of packages find their way to my doorstep. Were it not for seven points of identification, they might well end up somewhere else. Seven points separate me from six billion options—name, number, street, city, state, zip code, country. Likewise, there are prophecies that identify Jesus as the only one who can emerge through the doorway of Old Testament prophecy. To make the points memorable, I've associated them with the first seven letters of the alphabet. His *ancestry* was marked and his *birthplace* foretold. Circumstances surrounding his death were prophesied before *crucifixion* was invented. The *date of his visitation* was predicted within historically narrow time parameters. He would work *extraordinary miracles* and *fulfill the Law and the Prophets*. It would be too small for him to bring back only those of Israel; thus, he would be a light for the *Gentiles* so that salvation would go out to the ends of the earth. Only the hand of God could have etched a prophetic portrait of the Christ in the Old. Only God could cause it to take on flesh in the New. Only Jesus of Nazareth—the unique Superstar—could emerge through the doorway of Old Testament prophecy.

Scriptural
L–I–G–H–T–S

*L*iteral Principle

*I*llumination Principle

*G*rammatical Principle

*H*istorical Principle

*T*ypology Principle

*S*ynergy Principle

Compare Scripture with Scripture. False doctrines,
like false witnesses, agree not among themselves.

—WILLIAM GURNALL

At this point you are sufficiently equipped to answer the question, *Has God spoken?* As such, you know that you know that the Bible is divine rather than merely human in origin. However, if God has spoken, there is an attendant question—*What has God said?* Answering this question is crucial in that a great many people worldwide discount the Bible as the infallible rule for faith and practice because they mistake its meaning. Thus, despite *manuscript copies*, the *archaeologist's spade*, and *prophetic stars*, they continue to disbelieve the message of the Bible.

As noted in the introduction, no less a luminary than the president of the United States of America is convinced that the Bible "suggests slavery is okay and that eating shellfish is an abomination." Not only so, says Barack Obama; the Bible "suggests stoning your child if he strays from the faith."[1] Christopher Hitchens of *Vanity Fair* is equally nonplussed. Says Hitchens, "The Bible contains a warrant for trafficking in humans, for ethnic cleansing, for slavery, for bride-price and for indiscriminate massacre."[2] Like Hitchens, Oxford professor Richard Dawkins does not consider the Bible a trustworthy standard for life and living. In *The God Delusion* he describes the God of the Bible as "the most unpleasant character in all of fiction: jealous and proud of it; a petty, unjust, unforgiving control-freak; a vindictive, bloodthirsty ethnic cleanser; a misogynistic, homophobic, racist, infanticidal, genocidal, filicidal, pestilential, megalomaniacal, sadomasochistic, capriciously malevolent bully."[3]

The battle against the Bible is not relegated to politicians, publishers, or professors. Punmeister Bill Maher characterizes people who hold that God has spoken and that the Bible contains an accurate record of what he has said as obscurantists. A major reason biblical Christianity is so dangerous, according to Maher, is that "it stops people from thinking."[4] The notion of an afterlife, in Maher's opinion, is just plain "dumb." Says Maher, "Some other human being, whose brain was no better than theirs, told them he knew what happens when you die. And it's pretty silly to believe what some other human tells you when he tells you he knows what happens when you die. Because I promise you, he doesn't. Of course, there are all sorts of questions that we're all scared about. Like what happens when we die? Is there a heaven? Am I on the VIP list when I get there? But to believe what other people tell you is just dumb. To believe in fairy tales for answers we can't possibly know."[5]

Obama, Hitchens, Dawkins, and Maher are representative of a modern culture that considers the Bible increasingly irrelevant. Thus when the Bible is so much as mentioned, it is not uncommon to see expressions of polite exasperation etched on the faces of the masses. After all, the Bible not only condemns homosexuality but also clearly teaches that Sabbath breakers must be put to death. As such, professors, political sages, and public personalities, through magazines, manuscripts, the media—and now most notably through the Internet—are raising doubts in the minds of multiplied millions regarding the notion that God has spoken and that the Bible is a reliable repository of his words.

In this milieu it is absolutely crucial to correct obvious misreadings of the Scripture such as those exemplified above. Thus, in part 4 the memorable subacronym L-I-G-H-T-S will be used to internalize rules in the art and science of scriptural interpretation. In my previous book *The Apocalypse Code: Find Out What the Bible Really Says About the End Times and Why It Matters Today*, I use L-I-G-H-T-S to help people understand apocalyptic passages of Scripture. Here I apply these same rules to reading the Bible as a whole. Our objective is to remember *what* each of the rules represents and *how* to apply them in demonstrating that the Bible is the infallible repository for redemptive revelation. That its message is as measured and meaningful today as it was when the words were first divinely inscribed.

To do so involves a discipline known as *hermeneutics*. In Greek mythology the task of the god Hermes was to interpret the will of the gods. In biblical hermeneutics, the task is to interpret the Word of the God. Simply stated, hermeneutics is the art and science of biblical interpretation. It is a science in that certain rules apply. It is an art in that the more you apply these rules, the better you get at it. We begin with the *L* in scriptural L-I-G-H-T-S.

17

Literal Principle

There can be no falsehood anywhere in the literal sense of Holy Scripture.

—Thomas Aquinas

I walked into my office April 1, and spotted a new book atop my ever-growing stack of books to read. The book, provocatively titled *Jesus, Interrupted*, boasted the subtitle *Revealing the Hidden Contradictions in the Bible*.

My first inclination as I perused its pages was that this must surely be an elaborate April Fool's Day joke. Surely no professor—least of all one tenured as a distinguished professor of religious studies at the prestigious University of North Carolina at Chapel Hill—could suffer from such simplistic, closed-minded, black/white stereotypical fundamentalism. Yet the more I read, the more apparent it became that Professor Bart D. Ehrman was hardly writing tongue-in-cheek. He seemed genuinely distraught over the reality that few pastors and church leaders had followed him in his literalistic, walk-on-all-fours, fundamentalist reading of the biblical text.

In evidence he recalls doing a four-week series in a Presbyterian church in North Carolina in which he revealed the hidden contradictions of the Bible. Upon completion he says, "a dear elderly lady came up to me and asked me in frustration, 'Why have I never heard this before?'" Ehrman recalls gazing at the Presbyterian pastor, wondering, "Why had he never told her?"[1]

Questions raced through Ehrman's mind in staccato fashion. Was the pastor beset by a "patronizing attitude that is disturbingly common? Was he afraid to 'make waves'? Was he afraid that historical information might destroy the faith of his congregation? Was he afraid that church leaders might not take kindly to the dissemination of such knowledge? Did church leaders actually put pressure on him to stick to the devotional meaning of the Bible in his preaching and teaching? Was he concerned about job security?"[2]

In the litany of distasteful motives that flooded through his mind that day, one thought must surely have eluded him. Perhaps the pastor had carefully considered Ehrman's regurgitated "revelations" and found them wanting. Perhaps, unlike some of Ehrman's students at the University of North Carolina, the pastor knew that there was nothing particularly "new" or troubling about Ehrman's "hidden contradictions."

While the Presbyterian pastor might well have seen through Ehrman's apparent contradictions, most Christians in a largely biblically illiterate culture have not. As such, Ehrman is succeeding in his mission to shake the faith of multitudes. As noted, Ehrman appears particularly pleased in his progress in shaking the faith of his students. Some students "resist for a long time," says Ehrman, "but before long, as students see more and more of the evidence, many of them find that their faith in the inerrancy and absolute historical truthfulness of the Bible begins to waver."[3] As this professor gone wild has managed to shake the faith of multitudes in the classroom, he is likewise succeeding in shaking the faith of multitudes in the culture by systematically forwarding the notion that the Bible is not only hopelessly contradictory but a dangerous book in which to believe. The real problem, for Ehrman and multitudes that follow in his train, is a misconstrual of the literal principle of biblical interpretation.

To avoid the dangers of hyperliteralism, one must adeptly employ the *literal principle* of biblical interpretation. Simply stated, the literal principle instructs us to interpret the Word of God just as we interpret other forms of communication—in the most obvious and natural sense. As has been well said, "To interpret the Bible literally is to interpret it as literature."[4] Thus when a biblical author uses a symbol or an allegory, we do violence to his intensions if we interpret him literalistically.

Consider Ehrman's assertion that the gospels of Mark and John chronicle irreconcilable accounts with respect to Christ's cleansing of the temple:

> The Gospel of Mark indicates that it was in the last week of his life that Jesus "cleansed the Temple" by overturning the tables of the money changers and saying, "This is to be a house of prayer . . . but you have made it a den of thieves" (Mark 11), whereas according to John this happened at the very beginning of Jesus' ministry (John 2). Some readers have thought that Jesus must have cleansed the temple twice, once at the beginning of his ministry and once at the end. But that would mean that neither Mark nor John tells the "true" story, since in both accounts he cleanses the temple only once. Moreover, is this reconciliation of the two accounts historically plausible? If Jesus made a disruption in the temple at the beginning of his ministry, why wasn't he arrested by the authorities then?

Ehrman concludes by dogmatically asserting, "Historically speaking, then, the accounts are not reconcilable."[5]

Is Ehrman right? Is this just one more in a litany of errors made by a pseudonymous gospel writer? Or is this just indicative of a professor stuck in a literalistic labyrinth of his own making? First, it is not only uncharitable but unquestionably wrongheaded to suggest that neither Mark nor John (whom Ehrman demeans as "illiterate") could be telling the "true" story had the temple been cleansed twice. As is no doubt obvious to even the most unlettered of Ehrman's students, neither gospel writer provides an exhaustive account of everything Jesus said or did. As the apostle John communicates in hyperbolic parlance (no doubt lost on a wooden literalist), "Jesus did many other things as well. If every one of them were written down, I suppose that even the whole world would not have room for the books that would be written" (John 21:25).

Furthermore, the gospel of John itself provides a more than historically plausible insight as to why Jesus might not have been arrested during an initial temple cleansing. The proverbial straw that broke the camel's back leading to the arrest and trial of Jesus would quite logically have resulted from a late, not an early, temple cleansing. Not only so, but as the gospel of John makes clear, the Jewish leaders did not arrest Jesus in the early stages of his ministry for fear of the multitudes who were in awe of Christ's teachings and miracles (John 7; Mark 12:12).

Finally, as even a cursory reading reveals, John not only orders his gospel by theme (e.g., seven signs, seven-day opening, seven-day account of the passion) but presents a more highly developed Christology than that offered in the Synoptics. As such, John says that the Word became flesh and made his dwelling among us (1:14), which fulfills the Old Testament promise that God's glory would again return to his temple (Malachi 3:1). Moreover, John reinterprets the meaning of Passover by revealing Jesus as the quintessential Passover lamb (1:29, 36). As such, it could be logically (and charitably) surmised that John might introduce his account of Christ's temple cleansing early in his gospel narrative—and within a context in which Jesus is revealed as the substance that fulfills the types and shadows of temple, priest, and sacrifice. While such a notion does not sit well with a fundamentalist reading of literature, it accords nicely with a nuanced and highly sophisticated reckoning of time particular to the ancients (i.e., a *kairological* interpretation, which reckons time not in terms of our familiar chronological ordering but in terms of a quality of purpose in which an event is said to occur at just the right time [cf. Genesis 1–2]). In other words, even if there was only one temple cleansing, one might logically assume that John communicates it kairologically as opposed to chronologically.[6]

Ehrman, of course, is not alone in his literalistic proclivities. It is not uncommon to hear skeptical professors on university campuses assert that the Bible cannot be the infallible repository of redemptive revelation on the pretext that Genesis chapter 1 contradicts Genesis chapter 2.[7] How? In chapter 1, the creation of plants precedes the creation of animals, which precedes the creation of man; whereas in chapter 2 the creation of man is followed by the creation of plants and animals.

In response, we should first note that it is highly unlikely that an author would forget what was written within the span of several sentences. Moreover, given the sophistication of the literary genres employed in Genesis, one is immediately alerted to the possibility of a deeper purpose within the narrative. Tragically, our postmodern culture does not appreciate literature the way our ancestors did. We do science well, but we don't do literature well. We know how to read Sagan and Dawkins, but we seem ill equipped to read Shakespeare and Dante. Rather than mining the Bible for all its wealth, fundamentalists from the left insist on forcing language into a literalistic labyrinth from which nothing but nonsense can emerge.

Furthermore, even a cursory reading of Genesis 1 and 2 is enough to discern that the author has a different purpose in one than he does in the other. Chapter 1 presents a *hierarchy* of creation memorably associated with days of the week. Chapter 2 focuses on the crowning jewels of God's creation mandated to be in right relationship with their Creator as well as the whole of creation. As such, the land is depicted as barren until man arrives to cultivate it; and animals are depicted as being created and brought to the first man in order to help him realize his need for a suitable helpmate, which culminates in God's creation of woman. In both chapters, the depiction of a chronological order of creation events is merely a literary device employed to facilitate the author's primary concern, which is to reveal God's purposes in creation.

Finally, one must remember that the language of Scripture is a heavenly condescension so that we might apprehend both the nature and purposes of an infinite God. Those concerned with chronology need look no further than God's revelation in the book of nature. Indeed, those who tenaciously follow evidence wherever it leads will read both the book of Scripture and the book of science with an open mind.

What is important to recognize here is that a literalistic method of interpretation often does as much violence to the text as does a spiritualized interpretation that empties the text of objective meaning. To avoid either extreme, one must adeptly employ the literal principle of biblical interpretation, paying careful attention to *form, figurative language,* and *fantasy imagery.*

Form

To interpret the Bible literally, we must pay special attention to what is known as form (genre). In other words, to interpret the Bible as literature, it is crucial to consider the kind of literature we are interpreting. Just as a legal brief differs in form from a prophetic oracle, so, too, there is a difference in genre between Leviticus and Revelation.

Recognizing form is particularly important when considering writings that are difficult to categorize, such as Genesis, which is largely a historical narrative interlaced with symbolism and repetitive poetic structure.

If Genesis were reduced to an allegory conveying merely abstract ideas about temptation, sin, and redemption, devoid of any correlation with actual events in history, the very foundation of Christianity would be destroyed. If the historical Adam and Eve did not eat the forbidden fruit and descend into a life of habitual sin resulting in death, there is no need for redemption. Conversely, if we consider Satan to be a slithering snake, we would not only misunderstand the nature of fallen angels, but we might also suppose that Jesus triumphed over the work of the devil by stepping on the head of a serpent (Genesis 3:15) rather than through his passion on the cross (Colossians 2:15).

A literal-at-all-costs method of interpretation is particularly troublesome when it comes to books of the Bible in which visionary imagery is the governing genre. For example, in the book of Revelation the apostle John sees an apocalyptic vision in which an angel, swinging a sharp sickle, gathers grapes into "the great winepress of the wrath of God." The blood flowing out of the winepress rises as high as "the horse bridles, by the space of a thousand and six hundred furlongs" (Revelation 14:19–20 KJV).

Interpreting apocalyptic imagery in a woodenly literal sense inevitably leads to absurdity. Far from merely communicating that twenty-first-century Israel would be submerged in a literal river of blood, John is using the apocalyptic language of Old Testament prophets to warn his hearers of massive judgment and destruction of the land of Israel that "must soon take place" (Revelation 1:1). As Isaiah and Joel used the language of sickles, winepresses, and blood to symbolize judgment against the enemies of Israel's God (Isaiah 26:20–21; 34:1–17; 63:1–3; Joel 2:29–31; 3:8–17), so John now uses the genre of the prophets to signify the impending doom of apostate Israel.

The student of Scripture immediately recognizes that the symbolic imagery used by John is multifaceted and masterful. John does not merely recapitulate the apocalyptic imagery of the prophets and apply them to the current crisis. He reconfigures and expands them to cosmic proportions as the King of kings and Lord of lords treads the winepress of the fury of the wrath of God Almighty (Revelation 19:15–16). Once he lay prostrate before his creation in the pool of his own blood, but now the blood flowing from the winepress signifies judgment for the unrepentant who cried out, "Let his blood be on us and on our children!" (Matthew 27:25).

And even then the symbolism is not exhausted. In the tapestry of Revelation's imagery, the blood-splattered robe of Christ is emblematic not only of grapes of wrath but of blood that flowed from Immanuel's veins. The point here is to underline in red the need to seriously consider form in order to rightly interpret the Scriptures.

FIGURATIVE LANGUAGE

It is crucial to recognize that figurative language abounds in Scripture. Such language differs from literal language, in which words mean exactly what they say. Figurative language requires readers to use their imagination to comprehend what the author is driving at. In fact, we might well say that figurative language is the principal means by which God communicates spiritual realities to his children. In other words, God communicates spiritual realities through means of earthly, empirically perceptible events, persons, or objects—what might best be described as living metaphors. There are a wide variety of ways in which the inspired authors of the biblical text employ figurative language. Three of the most basic literary terms used to classify these figures of speech are *metaphor*, *simile*, and *hyperbole*.

Metaphor

A metaphor is an implied comparison that identifies a word or phrase with something that it does not literally represent. Far from minimizing biblical truth, a metaphor serves as a magnifying glass that identifies truth we might otherwise miss. This identification creates a meaning that lies beyond a woodenly literal interpretation and thus requires an imaginative leap in order to grasp what is meant. For example, when Jesus said, "I am the bread of life" (John 6:48), he was obviously not saying that he was literally the "staff of life" (i.e., physical bread). Rather he was metaphorically communicating that he is the "stuff of life" (i.e., the essence of true life).

Simile

Like a metaphor, a simile draws a comparison between two things, but whereas the comparison is *implicit* in a metaphor, it is *explicit* in a simile. Similes employ words such as "like" or "as" in making the comparison. Note, for example, the similes the apostle John uses in his description of Jesus: "Among the lampstands was someone '*like a son of man*' dressed in a robe reaching down to his feet and with a golden sash around his chest. His head and hair were white *like wool*, as white *as snow* and his eyes were *like blazing fire*" (Revelation 1:13–14).

Comparisons such as parables or allegories beginning with the word *like* are simply extended similes. A classic case in point is the parable of the mustard seed: "What shall we say the kingdom of God is *like*, or what parable shall we use to describe it? It is *like* a mustard seed, which is the smallest seed you plant in the ground. Yet when planted, it grows and becomes the largest of all garden plants, with such big branches that the birds of the air can perch in its shade" (Mark 4:30–32).

As with metaphors, the danger is to interpret similes in a woodenly literal fashion. The kingdom of God is obviously not like a mustard seed in every way. Nor did Jesus intend to make his parables "walk on all fours." A kingdom does not look like a mustard seed, nor is a mustard seed the smallest seed in the kingdom. Rather the kingdom of God is like a mustard seed in the sense that it begins small and becomes large. As noted previously, this is precisely the error made by Ehrman—an error that led him to the unwarranted conclusion that the Bible itself is erroneous.

Hyperbole

Hyperbole is a figure of speech that employs exaggeration for effect or emphasis. Etymologically it is defined as exaggerated "overcasting" or extravagant "overshooting." If you step onto a scale and exclaim, "Oh my goodness, I weigh a ton!" you are obviously not intending to say that you literally weigh two thousand pounds. While hyperbole is commonly used in our culture, it is virtually ubiquitous in the Bible. This is particularly true of prophetic passages. In prophesying Jerusalem's destruction, Jesus said, "For then there will be great distress unequaled from the beginning of the world until now—and never to be equaled again" (Matthew 24:21). In doing so, he was not literally predicting that the destruction of Jerusalem would be more cataclysmic than the catastrophe caused by Noah's flood. Rather he was using apocalyptic hyperbole to underscore the distress and devastation that would be experienced when Jerusalem and its temple were judged.

FANTASY IMAGERY

Apocalyptic passages in Scripture are replete with fantasy imagery, such as an enormous red dragon with seven heads and ten horns (Revelation 12:3), and a beast that resembled a leopard with feet like a bear and a mouth like a lion (Revelation 13:2). What is distinct about such fantasy images is that they do not correspond to anything in the real world. While fantasy images are unreal, they provide a realistic means by which to ponder reality. In *How to Read the Bible for All Its Worth*, Dr. Gordon Fee provides us with an apt contrast between the fantasy imagery used in apocalyptic portions of Scripture and the figurative images used elsewhere in the Bible. As Fee explains, the non-apocalyptic prophets and Jesus "regularly used figures of speech but most often it involved real images, for example, salt (Matthew 5:13), vultures and carcasses (Luke 17:37), silly doves (Hosea 7:11), half-baked cakes (Hosea 7:8), et al. But most of the images of the apocalyptic belong to fantasy, for example, a beast with seven heads and ten horns (Revelation 13:1), a woman clothed with the sun (Revelation 12:1), locusts with scorpions tails and human heads (Revelation 9:10), et al." Fee goes on to note that "the fantasy may not necessarily appear in the items themselves (we understand beasts, heads, and horns) but in their unearthly combination."[8]

Throughout the ages Christian writers from John Bunyan to J. R. R. Tolkien and C. S. Lewis have emulated the biblical use of fantasy imagery to underscore the cardinal truths of a Christian worldview. Puritan writer William Gurnall uses the "otherworldly" image of a man's head on a beast's shoulders to highlight the reality that righteousness without truth is abhorrent. As Gurnall puts it, "An orthodox judgment coming from an unholy heart and an ungodly life is as ugly as *a man's head would be on a beast's shoulders*. The wretch who knows the truth but practices evil is worse than the man who is ignorant."[9] Gurnall thus used an imaginary troll to portray an invisible truth.

In sum, in order to read the biblical text for all its worth, it is crucial to read the Bible as literature, paying close attention to form, figurative language, and fantasy imagery. And in doing so, we must ever be mindful that, though the Bible must be read as literature, it is not merely literature. Instead, the Scriptures were uniquely inspired by the Spirit. Thus, we must fervently pray that the Spirit, who inspired the text, illumines our minds to riches buried in the tapestry of the text.

18

*I*llumination Principle

Unless God's word illumines the way, the whole life of men is wrapped
in darkness and mist, so that they cannot but miserably stray.

—JOHN CALVIN

During the heyday of *Larry King Live*, I could not help but tune in as one of the greatest interviewers of all time engaged the most prominent people on the planet—presidents, pastors, politicians, and prominent personalities. One of the regulars was the punmeister Bill Maher, who has made a veritable cottage industry out of ridiculing the Bible. Maher characterizes himself as a "rationalist" who is far too intellectually advanced to believe in biblical fairy tales. In evidence he routinely goes off on the "talking snake" of Genesis. Whether he is on *Larry King Live* or just doing one of his stand-up routines, he can't help getting back to the "talking snake."[1]

As a fundamentalist from the left, caught up in the labyrinth of his own laughter, Maher seems blithely unaware of the literal principle of biblical interpretation. Thus, he embraces a literalistic-at-all-costs method of interpretation, which is particularly troublesome when it comes to reading books of the Bible in which visionary imagery is the governing genre.

When the Bible variously describes Satan as a "dragon" or an "ancient serpent," Maher's fundamentalist mind forces him into a host of literalistic absurdities. As should be obvious, the symbolism of a dragon or a snake is not designed to tell us what Satan *looks* like but to teach us what Satan *is* like.

The real problem, of course, is not merely that Maher interprets the Scriptures in a woodenly literalistic fashion. It is that his heart has not been illumined by the Spirit. As such, the issue is not intellect but illumination. "The way of the wicked is like deep darkness," proverbs Solomon. "They do not know what makes them stumble" (Proverbs 4:19). This is precisely what I am driving at with the *I* in L-I-G-H-T-S. Illumination comes only from the Spirit of God. It is that grace by which the Holy Spirit sheds divine light upon the inspired text. While it is crucial to defend the Bible as divine in an age in which it is under siege, only the Spirit removes the veil so that the blind may truly see.

Illumination does not end when the veil is lifted and the spiritually blind receive sight, however. The spiritually sighted are in need of illumination throughout the duration of their lives. Truly, we do not as yet know the treasures that may be mined from the biblical text. Such mining is not dependent upon degrees. It is directly proportional to our diligence. As we dig, the Spirit will continue to illumine our minds. "We have not received the spirit of the world," says Paul, "but the Spirit who is from God, that we may understand what God has freely given us" (1 Corinthians 2:12).

The Spirit of truth provides insights that permeate the mind as well as *illumination* that penetrates the heart. Far from supplanting the scrupulous study of Scripture, the Holy Spirit provides us with insights that can only be spiritually discerned. Put another way, the Holy Spirit illumines what is *in* the text; illumination does not go *beyond* the text. In this way the Holy Spirit helps us to *exegete* (draw out of) rather than *eisegete* (read into) Scripture.

Nothing should take precedence over getting into the Word and getting the Word into us. If we fail to eat well-balanced meals on a regular basis, we will eventually suffer the physical consequences. Likewise, if we do not regularly feed on the Word of God, we will suffer the spiritual consequences.

Physical meals are one thing; *spiritual meals* are quite another. The sub-acronym M-E-A-L-S will serve to remind you that the Spirit will illumine your heart and mind as you *memorize, examine, apply, listen,* and *study* the Bible for all its worth. The Word of God is the sword of the Spirit. When we grasp it, his illuminating power will flood our being.

Memorize

One of the best things that happened to me as a new believer was being told that all Christians memorize Scripture. By the time I found out that not all of them did, I was already hooked. Now, as I look back, I can say truthfully that nothing compares with the excitement of memorizing Scripture. God has called us to write his Word on the tablet of our hearts (Proverbs 7:1–3; cf. Deuteronomy 6:6), and with the call he has provided the ability. Your mind is like a muscle. If you exercise it, you will increase its capacity to remember and recall. If you don't, like a muscle, it will atrophy. Here are some practical tips to get you started:

- Set goals. He who aims at nothing invariably hits it.
- Make goals attainable. If your goals are unrealistic, you will undoubtedly become discouraged and give up.
- Memorize Scripture passages with a family member or friend. Memorizing with someone else is enjoyable and will also make you accountable.
- Use normally unproductive time to review what you have memorized, such as while waiting in lines, or falling asleep.

There's no time like the present to get started! And a good place to begin is Psalm 119. In fact, committing verse 11 to memory may well encourage you to make Scripture memorization a lifestyle: "I have hidden your word in my heart that I might not sin against you." While you're at it, you may also wish to consider memorizing Joshua 1:8. These wonderful words remind us that memorization facilitates meditation. "Do not let this Book of the Law depart from your mouth; meditate on it day and night, so that you may be careful to do everything written in it. Then you will be prosperous and successful." If you want true prosperity, there it is!

EXAMINE

In Acts 17:11 we read that the Bereans *examined* the Scriptures daily to see if what Paul was teaching was true. For that they were commended as being noble in character. There is an extremely important lesson to be learned here. The Bereans were not *condemned* for examining what Paul said in light of Scripture. Rather, they were *commended*. Ultimate authority was placed not in the revelation of men but in the revelation of the Word. I cannot overemphasize the importance of examining the Word of God. Examination requires the use of our minds, and the Bible exhorts believers to use their minds to honor God. Jesus taught that the first and greatest commandment is to love God with all our hearts, souls, and minds (Matthew 22:37). Peter beckoned believers to prepare their minds for action (1 Peter 1:13). Paul urged Christians to test all things (1 Thessalonians 5:21) and to be transformed by the renewing of their minds in order to discern the will of God (Romans 12:2).

Examining the Scriptures may take discipline and dedication, but the dividends are dramatic. The Bereans examined the Bible daily, and so should we. Here's how you can get going:

- *Find your secret place.* Find a place where you can drown out the static of the world and hear the voice of your heavenly Father as he speaks to you through the majesty of his Word.
- *Pray.* Pray that Jesus Christ will become ever more real to you through the examination of his Word.
- *Read thoughtfully.* Ask the Holy Spirit to give you understanding as you carefully reflect upon the meaning of God's words (2 Timothy 2:7). Buried in the texts are all sorts of precious gems. It is up to you to mine their wealth.

- *Read systematically. The Legacy Reading Plan* (see the appendix; also available online at Equip.org) provides an innovative approach to reading through sixty-six love letters—one book at a time—for the rest of your life. It is unique in that it requires you to process *books* of the Bible rather than piece together *bits* of books.

APPLY

As wonderful and worthwhile as it is to memorize and examine Scripture, it's simply not enough! We must also take the knowledge we have gleaned from the Word of God and *apply* it to every aspect of our daily lives. Wisdom is the *application* of knowledge. This is precisely what Jesus emphasized in concluding his majestic Sermon on the Mount:

> Therefore everyone who hears these words of mine and puts them into practice [or applies them] is like a wise man who built his house on the rock. The rain came down, the streams rose, and the winds blew and beat against that house; yet it did not fall, because it had its foundation on the rock. But everyone who hears these words of mine and does not put them into practice [does not apply them] is like a foolish man who built his house on sand. The rain came down, the streams rose, and the winds blew and beat against that house, and it fell with a great crash. (Matthew 7:24–27)

James uses irony to drive home the same principle. In essence, he says that anyone who hears the Word and does not *apply* it is like a man who looks in a mirror and sees that his face is dirty, but doesn't wash it: "Do not merely listen to the word, and so deceive yourselves. Do what it says. *Anyone who listens to the word but does not do what it says is like a man who looks at his face in a mirror and, after looking at himself, goes away and immediately forgets what he looks like.* But the man who looks intently into the perfect law that gives freedom, and continues to do this, not forgetting what he has heard, but doing it—he will be blessed in what he does"

(James 1:22–25). In God's view, obedience is always better than sacrifice (1 Samuel 15:22).

LISTEN

In order for us to apply God's directions to our everyday lives, we must learn to *listen* carefully as God speaks to us through his Word. Like Samuel, we should say, "Speak, LORD, for your servant is *listening*" (1 Samuel 3:9). As Jesus so wonderfully stated, "My sheep *listen* to my voice; I know them, and they follow me" (John 10:27).

One of the most amazing aspects of Scripture is that it is alive and active, not dead and dull. Indeed, God still speaks today through the mystery of his Word. The Holy Spirit illumines our minds to what is revealed in Scripture. As is well said, the Holy Spirit makes us "wise up to what is written, not beyond it." Before I became a Christian, reading the Bible was like reading someone else's mail. Now, however, the Scriptures have become sixty-six love letters from God, addressed directly and specifically to me.

While we *listen*, we must also "test the spirits." As John, the apostle of love, warns, "Do not believe every spirit, but test the spirits to see whether they are from God, because many false prophets have gone out into the world" (1 John 4:1). Satan's foremost strategy is to disguise himself as an angel of light (2 Corinthians 11:14). His slickest slogan is, *Feel, don't think*. God's Spirit, on the other hand, illumines our minds so that we may understand what he has freely given us (1 Corinthians 2:12).

STUDY

Scripture exhorts us to study to show ourselves approved to God, workmen who do not need to blush with embarrassment, correctly handling the Word of Truth (2 Timothy 2:15). In *examining* Scripture, it is typically best to start with one good translation and then stick with it. This will provide you with consistency as well as help you in the process of memorizing

Scripture. In *studying*, however, it is best to use a number of good Bible translations. A number of Bible translations should be avoided at all costs. Among them are the New World Translation, which reflects the cultic concepts of the Jehovah's Witnesses,[2] and the Lamsa translation, which is doctrinally biased and highly esoteric. To aid in your study of Scripture, here are some other practical tools.

1. *Study Bible.* There are some excellent study Bibles on the market today, including the *Student Bible*, the *NIV Study Bible*, and *The Legacy Study Bible*—the latter's wide margins enable you to chronicle thoughts that touch your heart and inform your mind as you study the Scriptures for all they're worth. This particular study Bible also contains vital background information for every book of the Old and New Testaments. Included is *The Legacy Reading Plan*, which equips you to read the Bible in books as opposed to bits (see appendix).

2. *Commentary.* A Bible commentary serves as a system of checks and balances through which you can evaluate your insights by the insights of others. There are a variety of good commentaries available today, such as the *International Bible Commentary*, edited by F. F. Bruce.

3. *Exhaustive concordance.* An exhaustive or complete concordance is an indispensable tool. With it you can find every citation of every word used in the Bible, along with a half-sentence excerpt to help you recognize the verse. With most concordances, such as *Strong's*, you can also compare English words with the original Hebrew, Aramaic, and Greek.

4. *Bible dictionary.* A good Bible dictionary will give you access to information about the history, culture, people, places, and events in Scripture. One of the best conservative volumes is the *Nelson's New Illustrated Bible Dictionary*, edited by Ronald F. Youngblood;[3] another good choice is the *New International Bible Dictionary*, edited by J. D. Douglas.[4]

5. *Memorable Keys to Essential Christian D-O-C-T-R-I-N-E.* This is a memorable guide to doctrines that form the dividing line between the kingdom of Christ and the kingdom of the cults. This pocket-sized

flip chart enables you to master the main and plain things of historic Christianity in minutes—and remember them for a lifetime.

6. *The Complete Bible Answer Book, Collector's Edition*. This beautiful leather-bound volume is designed to answer questions that stumble seekers and solidify skeptics in opposition to a biblical worldview—and was born out of two decades of hosting the nationally syndicated *Bible Answer Man* radio broadcast. I took my impromptu answers and chiseled them until only the gem emerges.

7. *Additional tools*. Some other tools worth considering include *Vine's Complete Expository Dictionary of Old and New Testament Words*, by W. E. Vine;[5] and introductions to the science and art of biblical interpretation, such as my book *The Apocalypse Code*,[6] R. C. Sproul's *Knowing Scripture*,[7] or James Sire's *Scripture Twisting*.[8]

Jesus said, "I am the bread of life. He who comes to me will never go hungry, and he who believes in me will never be thirsty" (John 6:35). It is my passionate prayer that the acronym M-E-A-L-S will remind you daily to nourish yourself with the Bread of Life.

19

Grammatical Principle

The word of God is deeper than a flannelgraph. It demands the closest possible scrutiny. It calls for the most excellent scholarship. It makes the finest point of technical analysis worth the effort. The yield of such effort is truth.

—R. C. SPROUL

When Jesus came to Caesarea Philippi, he asked his disciples the mother of all questions: "Who do you say I am?" His disciples asked a similar question: "Who is this? Even the wind and the waves obey him!" (Mark 4:41). Jesus left no doubt as to the correct answer. He claimed he was God in human flesh. On one occasion, he was so direct, the Jews picked up stones. "But Jesus said to them, 'I have shown you many great miracles from the Father. For which of these do you stone me?' 'We are not stoning you for any of these,' replied the Jews, 'but for blasphemy, because you, a mere man, claim to be God'" (John 10:32–33).

Jehovah's Witnesses, like first-century Jewish Sanhedrists, do not believe that Jesus Christ is God. In their view he was created by God as the archangel Michael, during his earthly sojourn he became a mere man, and after his crucifixion he was re-created an immaterial spirit creature.

From their perspective the tiny little letter *a* makes all the difference in the world. Jesus Christ was not God, they say—he was *a* god (John 1:1 NWT). God created him as his *firstborn* and he became a junior partner in the creation of all *other* things (Colossians 1:15 NWT).

The moment they commence their grammatical gyrations, our baloney detectors should register red. Is it true that Jesus Christ was just *a* god? Does the designation *firstborn* substantiate their contention? Does the word *other*—as in, he is the Creator of all *other* things—help buttress their denial of unique deity? To answer such questions we now turn to the grammatical principle of biblical interpretation.

Thankfully, you and I were hardwired for language from birth. From infancy onward, speech patterns are unconsciously absorbed and then modified in accord with unspoken rules of grammar. Even at age three, children display grammatical genius that enables them to master complex speech constructions and internalize sophisticated laws of language.[1] Before children learn the laws of language in grade school, they are already able to apply them in their own speech and can readily recognize their abuse in the speech patterns of nonnative speakers. In time even complex grammatical instructions and multiple word meanings become second nature. It shouldn't surprise us, then, that the basic principles of language that we unconsciously absorb in early childhood and consciously internalize from grade school onward are foundational to the grammatical principle of biblical interpretation.

As with any literary work, a thorough understanding of the Bible cannot be attained without a grasp of the basic rules of grammar that govern the relationships and usages of words, including *syntax*, *style*, and *semantics*. When it comes to interpreting Scripture, neither we nor the Witnesses should suppose that the rules of grammar mysteriously change.

SYNTAX

Syntax concerns the proper word order of sentences (or, in the biblical languages, the relationships of words in a sentence). Indeed, we use the very arrangement of words—syntax—to communicate meaning. If we mistake the sequencing of words in a sentence, we may well mistake the intended meaning as well. Such is the case with the Watchtower rendition of John 1:1. "In [the] beginning the Word was, and the Word was with God, and the Word was *a* god."[2] Their argument is simple. If a definite article does not appear before the noun—in this case *theos* (God)—then the noun is to be modified by an indefinite article.[3] To wit their rendering: "the Word was *a* god" as opposed to "the Word was God."

Suffice it to say, Jehovah's Witnesses do not live up to their own rule. If they did, John 1:6 should read as follows: "There came a man sent from *a* god; his name was *a* John." It does not take an expert on Greek syntax to recognize that this is utter nonsense. One thing is certain. The New World Translation of the Watchtower Society does not apply their convolution consistently. Statistically, they apply it less than 10 percent of the time. Worse yet, their grammatical gyrations obscure John's genius. As Greek scholar Daniel Wallace has aptly said, "The construction the evangelist chose to express this idea was the most *concise* way he could have stated that the Word was God and yet was distinct from the Father."[4]

So why tamper with the syntax? Why insert a tiny little letter before the word *God* in the text of John 1:1? Because just like a sin'tax, syntax makes a devastating difference! Instead of Christ being the Creator of *all* things, Christ is, of all things, created. Instead of being equal and eternal with the Father, he is recast as a mere creation. Instead of a consistent Christology, John's gospel becomes convoluted. Think Thomas. After Jesus demonstrated the power to lay down his life and take it up again, Thomas did not identify him as "a god" but as "my God" (John 20:28).[5] And this is not an isolated example. Anyone reading through the fourth gospel with a truly open mind sees Christ repeatedly identified as God. Jesus said it best: "I and the Father are one" (John 10:30; cf. 5:23; 8:58).

Before moving to *style*, allow me to make one additional point regarding the significance of syntax. In Titus 2:13, Greek syntax renders Jesus Christ, "*the great God* and Savior of us." Thus, translators of the New International Version correctly chronicle Paul exhorting Titus to be patient as he awaits "the blessed hope—the glorious appearing of *our great God* and Savior, Jesus

Christ." Not so with Watchtower translators. Playing fast and loose with syntax, they obliterate Paul's meaning rendering the text "the happy hope and glorious manifestation of the great God *and of our* Savior Christ Jesus." Again, a small alteration in syntax making all the difference in the world.

STYLE

In 1604, King James I of England commissioned a translation of the Bible destined to become preeminent among English Bibles. For the next four hundred years the King James Version, completed in 1611, would be the most cherished Bible among the English-speaking people of the world. KJV translators were the leading academicians of prestigious institutions such as Oxford, Cambridge, and Westminster, including Lancelot Andrewes (*Preces Privatae*), who began studying Greek at age six. Their mission "to deliver God's book unto God's people in a tongue which they could understand"[6] was carried out not only with enduring reverence for the divine Author but with linguistic artistry and stylistic majesty. Their legacy may be found in the ethos, mores, civil liberties, art, language, science, and jurisprudence of Western civilization.

The King James Version would likely have remained preeminent among English Bible translations were it not for the discovery of earlier and better manuscripts; progress in our knowledge and understanding of the original biblical languages; and *style*. Newer translations of the English Bible, including the New King James Version, no longer find it necessary to endlessly repeat conjunctions such as *and*. Instead, connective words, such as *however*, *but*, and *for*, are substituted where permitted by our knowledge and understanding of the original language.

The evolution of our English language has led to significant stylistic changes as well. *Gay* clothing (James 2:3 KJV) meant "fine" clothing in Elizabethan English. In modern English the word *gay* has taken on a decidedly connotative meaning. *Prevent* (1 Thessalonians 4:15 KJV) meant "go before" or "precede." *Leasing* (Psalm 4:2 KJV) meant "falsehood." And who today could figure out what Paul meant in saying "from thence we fetched a compass" (Acts 28:13 KJV), now translated in modern Bibles as "we circled around"?

In addition to word meanings, there have been significant stylistic changes in verb forms and spelling as well. *Weareth the gay clothing* is now rendered *wearing the fine clothing*. The *e* has been dropped from words such as *poore* and *footstoole* and the *v* in *vnto* has been replaced by a *u*. Myriad other examples could be set forth, but suffice it to say modern-day English is decidedly different in style from Elizabethan English.

Also noteworthy is the matter of translation styles. A good word-for-word translation is the New American Standard Bible (NASB). Although somewhat stilted, it is excellent for purposes of study. A great thought-for-thought translation is the New International Version (NIV). It is both reliable and readable. The New King James Version (NKJV) is a superior translation in that it preserves the legacy of a common English Bible while taking into consideration manuscripts discovered since the commissioning of the original King James Version (KJV) in 1604 and its initial completion in 1611.

Tragic but true, translators of the New World Translation (NWT) use style as a pretext for changing, as opposed to preserving, the meaning of the biblical text. A classic example can be found in their stylistic changes to Colossians 1:15–20. In the foreword the New World Bible Translation Committee notes that "brackets enclose words inserted to complete or clarify the sense in the English text."[7] You can almost hear them purring: *Don't worry, we are not changing the substance; we're only smoothing out the style.*

In truth, the addition of the bracketed word *other*, added four times in the space of two verses, makes an enormous difference in substance. By virtue of adding the word *other*, Jesus is reduced from the self-existent, uncreated Creator of all things to a creature who was himself created. One thing is certain: this is not merely an inadvertent oversight on the part of Watchtower translators. They knew precisely what they were doing. Their own Kingdom Interlinear Translation of the Greek Scriptures translates the word *panta* as "all (things)"[8]—not "all *other* things." The venerable Greek scholar Bruce M. Metzger finds a particular irony in the Watchtower tampering of the Colossians text: "The ancient Colossian heresy which Paul had to combat resembled the opinion of the modern Jehovah's Witnesses, for some of the Colossians advocated the Gnostic notion that Jesus was the first of many other created intermediaries between God and men. For the true meaning of Paul's exalted description of the Son of God, therefore, the above translation must be read without the fourfold addition of the word 'other.'"[9]

SEMANTICS

To say something is a mere matter of semantics can be a dangerous thing, particularly in an era of political correctness. David Howard, a former top aide to District of Columbia mayor Anthony A. Williams, found out the hard way. Though more than a decade ago now, I still vividly remember when Howard used the word *niggardly* to describe the difficulty of managing a miserly budget. Reaction was palpable. In a *Washington Post* article titled "D.C. Mayor Acted 'Hastily,' Will Rehire Aide," staff writer Yolanda Woodlee notes that "Williams, whose quick acceptance of David Howard's resignation last month led to a national debate over racial sensitivity and political correctness, indicated in a statement yesterday that he had made a mistake."[10]

As a result of the furor, "political pundits and linguists alike debated whether an employee's resignation should be accepted merely because a colleague did not understand a word used in a conversation."[11] Despite the fact that the word *niggardly* predates the n-word and is clearly not etymologically or semantically related, Ronald Walters, a professor of political science at the University of Maryland, saw its use as an example of "racial insensitivity." Says Walters, "The mayor can't afford to have an aide in a town that is 63 percent black making this kind of mistake." NAACP chairman Julian Bond, however, expressed chagrin at having to "censor" one's language in order to accommodate "people's lack of understanding."[12]

Racial semantics are ever-changing. At one time the words *negro* and *colored* were perfectly acceptable, as evidenced by the United Negro College Fund (UNCF) and the National Association for the Advancement of Colored People (NAACP). Today the preferred designations are *black* and *people of color*.[13] Same-sex designations are likewise in a state of flux. Joe

Kort, a gay and lesbian studies professor at Wayne State University, says that "using the term homosexual to describe a lesbian or gay individual is offensive and is like using the 'n-word' to describe African-Americans." The correct words to use, says Kort, "are gays and lesbians or GLBT (gay, lesbian, bisexual, and transgender) community." Even words like "sexual preference and alternative lifestyle are no longer considered appropriate," according to Kort. "Preference implies that sexuality is a choice—which it's not—and for gays and lesbians, heterosexuality is the 'alternative' lifestyle. The correct term is sexual and romantic orientation."[14]

Stop for a moment and consider what it was that spawned the national debate over racial sensitivity and political correctness a decade ago—a debate that continues in ever-heated fashion to the present day. In essence it was a matter of semantics—*the science of meaning*. David Howard used a word that sounded a lot like a racial slur, and a politically correct culture revved into overdrive. It is instructive to note that the Christian church is not immune to such semantic warfare. Let Ezekiel mention the word *rosh* and the imaginations of end-time sensationalists go wild. Just as *niggardly* sounds a lot like the n-word, *rosh* sounds enough like Russia to implicate it as the villain in sensationalistic end-time scenarios. The notion is not new. It was first popularized by the *Scofield Reference Bible* in 1917 and has since spawned a host of semantic jungle masters.[15] For his part, Mark Hitchcock, a relative latecomer in the pin-the-tail-on-the-Antichrist sweepstakes, has made the rosh/Russia argument a pillar in sensationalistic end-time speculations. As such, he interprets "*rosh* as a proper noun referring to a specific place—Russia."[16] The facts, of course, say otherwise. Just as the word *niggardly* predates the n-word by more than a century and is not semantically linked, so, too, the word *Russia* is not a derivation of *rosh*. As documented by credible historians and linguists, the word *Russia* is an eleventh-century Viking word and as such should not be semantically linked to the Hebrew word *rosh*.[17]

As should be obvious at this point, there is no *just* in "It's *just* a matter of semantics." Semantics has not only the potential to launch a war of words but also the power to implicate Russia in a war to end all wars. Not only so, but semantics continues to be the driving force behind some of the most prolific cults in modern history. For the aforementioned Jehovah's

Witnesses, *firstborn* is the magic word. In a semantic twist that defies all logic, they render Jesus the firstborn of Jehovah. Their pretext is Colossians 1:15—which allegedly communicates that Jesus is first in a sequence of births. Their reasoning is simplistic: because *firstborn* sounds like *the first one born*, Jesus must be "the eldest in Jehovah's family of sons."[18]

This, however, is far from true. Words are not univocal—they are equivocal. As such, they have a range of meanings directly dependent on the context in which they are used. Even a cursory reading of Colossians 1 should be enough to convince the open-minded that rather than a sequence of birth, Paul has preeminence of birth in mind. Such usage is firmly established in the Old Testament. For example, Ephraim is referred to as the Lord's "firstborn" (Jeremiah 31:9) even though Manasseh was born first (Genesis 41:51). Likewise, David is appointed the Lord's "firstborn, the most exalted of the kings of the earth" (Psalm 89:27) despite being the youngest of Jesse's sons (1 Samuel 16:10–13). While neither Ephraim nor David was the first one born in his family, both were firstborn in the sense of preeminence or "prime position."

Furthermore, Paul refers to Jesus as the firstborn over all creation, not the firstborn in creation. As such, "He is before *all things*, and in him *all things* hold together" (Colossians 1:17). As previously noted, the force of Paul's language is such that the Witnesses, who ascribe to the ancient Arian heresy that the Son is not preexistent and coeternal with the Father, have been forced to insert the word *other* (e.g., "all other things") into their deeply flawed New World Translation of the Bible in order to demote Christ to the status of a created being.

Finally, as the panoply of Scripture makes plain, Jesus is the eternal Creator, who spoke and the limitless galaxies leaped into existence. In John chapter 1, he is overtly called "God" (1:1). In the first chapter of Hebrews, he is said to be the one who "laid the foundations of the earth" (1:10). And in the very last chapter of the Bible, Christ refers to himself as "the Alpha and the Omega, the First and the Last, the Beginning and the End" (Revelation 22:13). Indeed, the whole of Scripture precludes the semantic sleight of hand that renders Christ anything other than the preexistent sovereign of the universe.

Is it true that Jesus Christ was just *a* god? Does the word *other*—as in, he is the creator of all *other* things—belong in the biblical text? Does *first-born* mean first in a sequence of births? Such questions and a host of others are answered through the proper application of the grammatical principle of biblical interpretation. Familiarity with syntax, style, and semantics, along with some plain old common sense, will serve you well in your quest to mine the Bible for all its wealth.

20

*H*istorical Principle

*Every thinking man, when he thinks, realizes that the teachings of
the Bible are so interwoven with our whole civic and social life that it
would be literally impossible for us to figure what life would be if those
teachings were removed. We would lose almost all the standards by
which we now judge both public and private morals; all the standards
to which we, with more or less resolution, strive to raise ourselves.*

—PRESIDENT THEODORE ROOSEVELT

I can still remember the feeling of disbelief I experienced as I tried to
absorb the intent of Barack Obama's historic "Call to Renewal" address.
Particularly as he posed the following series of penetrating questions:

Which passages of Scripture should guide our public policy? Should we
go with Leviticus, which suggests slavery is okay and that eating shellfish
is abomination? How about Deuteronomy, which suggests stoning your
child if he strays from the faith? Or should we just stick to the Sermon on
the Mount—a passage that is so radical that it's doubtful that our own
Defense Department would survive its application? So before we get carried away, let's read our Bibles![1]

The implication of Obama's questions is hard to mistake: God has not spoken. The Bible cannot possibly be divine. No God worthy of worship would teach that slavery is okay. What parent in his right mind would stone a child who strays away from the faith? Calling consumption of shellfish an abomination is just plain silly. And the Sermon on the Mount? Way too radical! "If God has spoken, then followers are expected to live up to God's edicts, regardless of the consequences," Obama intoned. "To base one's own life on such uncompromising commitments may be sublime; to base our policy making on such commitments would be a dangerous thing."[2]

Perhaps the real danger is a failure to apprehend the biblical message—a danger that has led to untold pain and tragedy. Think of devotees of the Watchtower Society who pay the ultimate physical price through refusing vaccinations, organ transplants, and blood transfusions because they do not know how to rightly divide the Word of Truth.[3] Think about a woman I wrote about in *Christianity in Crisis 21st Century*, who had migrated into the Word of Faith movement. When a lump appeared in her breast, she purposed to deny the symptoms and thus rejected medical treatment. Even as the tumor continued to grow, she stood her ground. It wasn't until the tumor had become a weeping sore consuming most of her breast that she finally sought medical attention. By that time, it was far too late. She thought she understood God's Word.[4] Like Obama, she was way off target.

To suggest that God's Word teaches parents to stone a child who strays from the faith displays a disturbing misapprehension of the message of Deuteronomy. Its legal remedies are prescribed within the context of a theocracy—not a modern-day democracy. As even the most cursory perusal of context makes plain, the son in question (not child) is morally culpable of extravagantly wicked behavior that threatens the health and safety of the entire community (Deuteronomy 21:18–21; cf. Exodus 20:12; Proverbs 1:8–19). Thus, the prescribed punishment was hardly for adolescent decadence. Rather, it applied to adult degeneracy.

Furthermore, the parents' desire to spare their own son served as a built-in buffer against an unwarranted or frivolous enforcement of the law. Likewise, ratification by the elders precluded a precipitous judgment on the part of the parents. Thus, the standard of evidence prescribed by the

Mosaic law exceeds that of modern jurisprudence. For modern-day "progressives" to claim the moral high ground over ancient Deuteronomic laws is the height of hypocrisy. Far from resembling the civility of the Mosaic law, our culture reflects the carnality of Israel's neighbors who sacrificed their sons and daughters to appease their gods. Indeed, for almost four decades now, Western civilization, standing in the shadow of the Bible, has sanctioned the systematic slaughter of innocent children, guilty of nothing more than being fully human.

Obama's comments concerning slavery are equally deplorable. Far from extolling the virtues of slavery, the Bible denounces slavery as sin. The New Testament goes so far as to put slave traders in the same category as murderers, adulterers, perverts, and liars (1 Timothy 1:10). Moreover, slavery within the Old Testament context was sanctioned due to economic realities rather than racial or sexual prejudices. Because bankruptcy laws did not exist, people would *voluntarily* sell themselves into slavery. A craftsman could thus use his skills in servitude to discharge a debt. Even a convicted thief could make restitution by serving as a slave (Exodus 22:3). While Scripture as a whole recognizes the reality of slavery, it never promotes the practice of slavery. In fact, it was the application of biblical principles that ultimately led to the overthrow of slavery, both in ancient Israel and in the United States of America. Israel's liberation from slavery in Egypt became the model for the liberation of slaves in general. In America, many are beginning to wake up to the liberating biblical truth that God has created all people with innate equality (Genesis 1:27; Acts 17:26–28; see also Galatians 3:28).[5]

The entire discussion thus far highlights the significance of the historical principle of biblical interpretation. Unless and until we understand the historical context of any given book in the Bible, whether the Old Testament Leviticus or the New Testament Sermon on the Mount, we have little hope of grasping its meaning. Put another way, in order to properly evaluate biblical texts, we must take into account their historical legacy. Indeed, the acronym L-E-G-A-C-Y is an apt way of remembering factors to consider in determining the historical viability and meaning of sacred Scripture.

We begin with the *L* in the subacronym L-E-G-A-C-Y, which reminds us of the significance of *location*.

LOCATION

To begin with, it is important to know the *where* of an ancient manuscript. The location that a text was written as well as the locations referenced in the text provide crucial clues to meaning and historical trustworthiness.

For example, the aforementioned book of Deuteronomy is based on Mosaic messages delivered to the children of Israel east of the Jordan River, on the plains of Moab, at the edge of the promised land. The Israelites had survived forty years of wilderness wanderings. The question was, would they survive prosperity in the land of promise? If so, adherence to the laws of YHWH was crucial. Israel was in transition from the edge to entry into the land of promise. Thus, it was all the more crucial that they embrace the civility of Mosaic law and inoculate themselves against the carnality of Canaanite culture. Just over the border, wickedness was reaching its full measure as parents sacrificed their sons and daughters to Molech, a bull-headed deity with a human body and a belly that burned like the horrors of hell. Children as old as four were placed in the white-hot arms of the monster. "As the flame burning the child surrounded the body, the limbs would shrivel up and the mouth would appear to grin as if laughing, until it was shrunk enough to slip into the cauldron."[6]

The land of Canaan was at the point of no return. And Israel would be the ax of her judgment. They were called to smash their sacred stones and to burn their idols in the fire. The aim of God's wrath was not the obliteration of the righteous but the obliteration of wickedness that had reached its full measure. For four hundred years God had shown mercy—now judgment was on their border (Genesis 15:13–16, cf. Leviticus 18:24–28). Those who imagine that God was precipitous need only think back on the judgment of Sodom. For ten righteous people, God would have spared the city. But there were none. "Far be it from you," said Abraham, "to kill the righteous with the wicked, treating the righteous and the wicked alike. Far be it from you! Will not the Judge of all the earth do right?" (Genesis 18:25). God's martial instructions are qualified by his moral intentions to spare the repentant.[7] As the author of Hebrews explains, "By faith the prostitute Rahab, because she welcomed the spies, was not killed with those who were disobedient" (Hebrews 11:31). Not only were she and her family spared; she was reckoned as true Israel and came to hold a privileged position in the lineage of Jesus Christ (Matthew 1:5).

Ironically, the loudest protests against God's judgment on Canaanites come from those who clamor for the right to terminate the lives of unborn children living in the warmth of their mothers' wombs. While the very thought causes the faithful to recoil in horror and disbelief, they are no longer located on the border of Canaanite country. Nor are they governed by the laws of an ancient theocratic kingdom. "The weapons we fight with are not the weapons of the world. On the contrary, they have divine power to demolish strongholds," says Paul. "We demolish arguments and every pretension that sets itself up against the knowledge of God" (2 Corinthians 10:4–5).

Location makes all the difference in the world. Without considering the location of a biblical missive, we might well mistake its meaning.

ESSENCE

As with location, the historical principle of biblical interpretation underscores the need to grasp the essence of Scripture's grand metanarrative—a metanarrative that is as multifaceted as it is majestic. Adam falls into a life of perpetual sin and is banished from Paradise. He is relegated to restlessness and wandering, separated from intimacy and fellowship with his Creator. The very chapter that references the Fall, however, records the divine plan for restoration of fellowship (Genesis 3). The plan takes on definition with God's promise to make Abram a great nation through which "all peoples on earth will be blessed" (Genesis 12:3). Abram's call, therefore, constitutes the divine antidote to Adam's fall. God would make Abram not just the father of a nation, but *Abram* would become *Abraham*—"a father of *many* nations" (Genesis 17:5). For as God promised Abraham real estate, he likewise promised him a future royal Seed who would lead true Israel into Paradise restored (Genesis 12:7; 13:15; 24:7; Galatians 3:16).

A microcosm of the grand metanarrative is encapsulated in Genesis 22. Here the father of faith is instructed to sacrifice the son of the promise. Not a notion conjured up by the child sacrifices of pagan Canaanites but a direct command from the Father above to the father of faith, who "reasoned that God could raise the dead" (Hebrews 11:19). Thus Abraham left Beersheba and took the three-day journey to the place in Jerusalem where a temple would one day stand—his sacrifice already accomplished through the willingness to relinquish his firstborn son. Whether Jehovah-jireh would allow a human sacrifice was forever settled by the rustling of a ram in the thicket. Animal sacrifices, not human sacrifice, would point forward to the divine sacrifice, who three days later would raise himself from the dead. In doing so, he would become the earnest of all who will one day rise from death to live in the New Jerusalem coming down out of heaven from God.

The point here is to underscore the need to apprehend the essence of a biblical worldview. Apart from that we may well miss the import of the historical narrative set forth in Genesis. Obama again provides the classic case in point. From his perspective, the Genesis narrative may be subjectively sublime but is publicly pernicious.[8] "It is fair to say that if any of us saw a twenty-first-century Abraham raising the knife on the roof of his apartment building, we would call the police; we would wrestle him down; even if we saw him lower the knife at the last minute, we would expect the Department of Children and Family Services to take Isaac away and charge Abraham with child abuse," writes Obama in *The Audacity of Hope*.[9]

What he seems to be blithely unaware of is that this narrative can hardly be recast in twenty-first-century vernacular. To anachronistically rip a narrative out of its Ancient Near Eastern context and use it as a demonstration of the superiority of modern pluralist assumptions is at best misguided. Not only so, who can miss the irony of a pompous twenty-first-century politician who thinks it enlightened to allow an abortionist to plunge the knife into the most innocent among us under cover of democratic pluralism, yet smugly raise his eyebrows at an ancient who puts away the knife at the command of an Almighty who does not abide human sacrifice? If a "progressive" misses the essence of this historical narrative, he might also mischaracterize the Sermon on the Mount as "so radical that it's doubtful that our own Defense Department would survive its application."[10] In essence, however, the Sermon on the Mount is a schoolmaster driving us from self-righteousness to a Savior who alone can fulfill all the Law and the Prophets. Obama says the problem is "folks haven't been reading their Bibles."[11] I suspect the real problem is that "progressives" have little concept of the historical principle of biblical interpretation and thus haven't been reading the Bible for all its worth.

GENRE

Whenever I think of the word *genre*, the name Bill Maher immediately flashes across my mind. Somehow the two have become hardwired together in my brain. Perhaps it's because Maher says the funniest things—particularly when it comes to genre. He may not know how to pronounce the word, but he absolutely gets the concept. He confessed to once believing that the earth was only five thousand years old. Since graduating the sixth grade, however, he has become somewhat more enlightened.[12] At least so he says. For Maher old myths may have died hard but it seems they are continually replaced by new ones—many connected directly to genre. He now proudly pontificates that "the Bible was not meant to be history. It was not meant to be literal. They were parables. People read it back then and read into it something that was not literal. We're the dummies who read it literally."[13]

Is he right? Is the Bible merely parabolic? Is it true that the Bible was not meant as history? The answer is found in the word *genre*. Grasping genre— or form—is crucial in understanding what a text means by what it says. In other words, to interpret the Bible as literature, it is crucial to consider the kind of literature you are interpreting. As a legal brief differs in form from a prophetic oracle, there is a difference in genre between Leviticus and Revelation. Where visionary imagery is the governing genre, it is foolhardy to interpret literalistically. Conversely, where historical narrative is pre-eminent, it is imperative not to overspiritualize. Even historical narratives, however, can employ richly symbolic imagery, metaphors, and wordplays. In fact, the biblical writers frequently use historical objects or events to teach spiritual realities.

Maher is right to associate parables with the Bible—to do so exclusively, however, is absurd. Perhaps the most familiar of Old Testament parables is associated with Israel's quintessential king. In many pagan nations the king was an untouchable. Arrogant in power, prosperity, and prestige. But Israel was different. She was a nation not only of potentates but also of priests and of prophets. Thus, when David violated the wife of a soldier named Uriah and subsequently had him terminated on the front lines of battle, he was not above accountability in the kingdom. Fearing the potential force of the king's wrath, however, the prophet Nathan engaged David with the subtlety of a parable about two men in a certain town, one rich and the other poor:

> "The rich man had a very large number of sheep and cattle, but the poor man had nothing except one little ewe lamb he had bought. He raised it, and it grew up with him and his children. It shared his food, drank from his cup and even slept in his arms. It was like a daughter to him. Now a traveler came to the rich man, but the rich man refrained from taking one of his own sheep or cattle to prepare a meal for the traveler who had come to him. Instead, he took the ewe lamb that belonged to the poor man and prepared it for the one who had come to him." (2 Samuel 12:2–4)

Upon hearing the parable, David was overwhelmed with righteous indignation. With nary a moment's reflection, the king pronounced judgment. "As surely as the LORD lives, the man who did this deserves to die!" (12:5). In a flash, David found himself staring into the bony finger of the prophet and heard the words by which he would be delivered from denial. "You are the man!" (12:7). The parable proved to be unparalleled in power. Though he would live to see the consequences of his sin, the king repented and was restored to fellowship with God.

No one applied the power of parable with greater effect than Jesus. Luke 16 chronicles the parable of a rich man and "a beggar named Lazarus, covered with sores and longing to eat what fell from the rich man's table" (Luke 16:20–21). In time both died, their roles immediately reversed. The beggar found himself comforted in Abraham's bosom; the rich man experiencing the foretaste of eternal torment. Too late he paid attention to the beggar lying by his gate; too late he postponed repentance; too late he heeded the testimony of the Law and Prophets. Too late; too late; too late! Like a heat-seeking missile, Christ's parable hit its mark—perhaps the heart of a punmeister will be next.

The point here is to acknowledge that the use of parables in the Bible is extensive. But that is hardly the extent of the matter. Scripture is a treasure chest abounding in literary genres ranging from poetry and psalms to historical narratives, didactic epistles, and apocalyptic revelations. To believe as Maher did that the earth is five thousand years old is no doubt related to a miscomprehension of the genres of Genesis. While Genesis most certainly is a historical narrative, it is interlaced with symbolism and repetitive poetic structure. One must ever remember that the language of Scripture is a heavenly condescension so that we might apprehend both the nature and purposes of an infinite God. Indeed, those who tenaciously follow evidence wherever it leads will read both the book of Scripture and the book of science with an open mind. What they will discover is that Genesis is not designed to answer the age question—that question is answered in God's other book, the book of nature.

Failure to consider genre leads to a host of unintended consequences. This is particularly so when it comes to apocalyptic portions of Scripture. When Jesus says that the stars will fall from the sky, he hardly intends to be taken literally. One star would obliterate the earth—let alone a hundred billion stars. Instead, the heir to the linguistic riches of the Old Testament prophets and a greater prophet than them all, used the symbolism of stars to pronounce judgment within his own generation. Failure to consider genre may lead to laughs in a comedy routine; from an eternal perspective, however, the effect is not nearly as funny.

AUTHOR

Bart Ehrman has become a master at mining gold from sensationalistic claims. *In Misquoting Jesus: The Story Behind Who Changed the Bible and Why*, he set his sights on copyists whose dark and duplicitous deeds were fueled, he says, "by anti-Jewish sentiment."[14] In his current offering, *Forged: Writing in the Name of God: Why the Bible's Authors Are Not Who We Think They Are*, the villains are the biblical authors themselves. And all of this, he contends, has been concealed by Christianity. Bart "dares to call it what it was: literary forgery," screams the cover copy, "a practice that was as scandalous then as it is today."[15] The takeaway, of course, is that God has not spoken. Scripture cannot be trusted.

While paper mills continue churning to the contrary, Ehrman's repertoire contains little more than regurgitated sophistry, selling, sensationalism, and an unhealthy dose of Scriptorture. He asserts that neither Revelation nor the gospel of John could have been written by the apostle John.[16] How does he know? Simple! In Revelation 4, John never identifies himself as one of the apostles seated around the throne of God![17] At times, Bart's comedy routine surpasses even that of the irreverent Bill Maher. His students, no doubt, are continually in stitches. Can anyone seriously imagine an "Ehrman version" of Revelation 4:4: "Surrounding the throne were twenty-four elders. They were dressed in white and had crowns of gold on their heads. And I, John, son of Zebedee, was third from the left, the apostle sitting next to James"? Such reasoning is not just silly; it represents a new low in idiosyncratic conjecture.

What should be noted here is that there is nothing particularly new about Ehrman's conspiracy theories. The theory that Revelation was written pseudonymously was dispensed with long ago by credible scholarship. As Revelation scholar G. K. Beale has well said, "If an unknown author were attempting to identify himself with a well-known Christian figure like the apostle John, he would probably call himself not just 'John' but 'John the apostle.' This the author does not do. Indeed, there is little information about the author other than his self-identification as a servant, a fellow believer, a witness for Christ, and one who is suffering exile for that witness (Revelation 1:1, 9–10)." Beale goes on to say that the scholarly consensus is that Revelation was not written pseudonymously but is "a personal self-reference to a real John."[18]

Pseudonymity was largely practiced by writers who lacked credibility.[19] Thus they borrowed the monikers of authentic eyewitnesses to the life and times of Christ to create an air of credibility. In sharp contrast, the book of Revelation (not to mention the gospel of John[20]) provides ample internal evidence that it was written by a Jew intimately acquainted with the historical events and locations he wrote about. Only a handful of extremists today even countenance the possibility that Revelation could have been written pseudonymously—among them, of course, Bart Ehrman. Yet even he allows for the possibility only if one subscribes to the further notion that the apostle John actually claimed to have authored Revelation. Then, says Ehrman, "the book would probably have to be considered pseudonymous."[21]

One of the reasons I think it is helpful to read the biblical authors sequentially is that even though they wrote "as they were carried along by the Holy Spirit" (2 Peter 1:21), their personalities and proclivities are clearly evident in their writings. For example, John, and John alone, identifies Jesus as the Word or *Logos* (Revelation 19:13; John 1:1, 14). Likewise, John alone identifies Jesus as the true witness (Revelation 2:13; 3:14; John 5:31–47; 8:14–18), and it is John who most exploits the Mosaic requirement of two witnesses (Revelation 11:1–12; John 8:12–30). Other examples include Jesus' invitation to all who are thirsty to come to him and drink (Revelation 22:17; John 7:37) and Jesus' reference to his having received authority from his Father (Revelation 2:27; John 10:18). Fact is, the fingerprints of the apostle are all over his writings.

While I present a full accounting of the evidence against pseudonymity charges by Ehrman in my book *The Apocalypse Code*,[22] the point here is to emphasize that knowing who wrote a text is crucial in establishing historical reliability. This is particularly crucial today as a new breed of biblical scholars seeks to disseminate the notion that the Bible is merely the product of historical winners who preferred the dark anti-Semitic overtones of manuscripts such as the gospel of John over more racially sensitive gospels such as the gospel of Judas. Ironically, while we do not know who authored the gospel of Judas, we do know that it was written pseudonymously.[23] In sharp contrast, canonical gospels such as John provide ample internal evidence that they were authored by Jews intimately acquainted with the locations and events they recorded.[24]

Context

As with *location, essence, genre,* and *author,* comprehending the *context* in which a book of the Bible was written is crucial in ascertaining its authority and making sense of its meaning. Ezekiel immediately comes to mind. Without understanding the historical context in which his prophetic oracles were written, one has little chance of understanding his message.

Ezekiel prophesied during an extraordinarily dark period of Judah's history. He was born into the priesthood in Jerusalem right around the time that Josiah found the book of the Law in the temple (622 BC)—a time in which spiritual renewal broke out in the land. Reformation, however, was short-lived. By the time of Josiah's death (609 BC) the idolatrous practices of the past had returned with a vengeance. In contrast to the king, the people of the kingdom craved intimacy with foreign gods on the threshing floors of perverse temples. Like Hosea and Jeremiah, Ezekiel pictured Jerusalem as a great prostitute whose promiscuity dwarfed that of even her sisters, Sodom and Samaria. Thus, the ax of God's judgment fell. In short order, Ezekiel found himself on the dusty plains of Babylon, warning fellow exiles that the worst lay right around the corner. In 586 BC the unthinkable happened: the gilded city and its golden temple were desecrated and destroyed.

Without the historical backdrop, it is virtually impossible to understand the meaning of Ezekiel's prophecies. His oracles begin with a warning that judgment of the city and the temple was waiting in the wings (Ezekiel 4–7). Yet Jerusalem was not alone. Ezekiel prophesied the destruction of nations like Tyre, who saw the fall of Jerusalem as a pathway to her own prosperity. Thus, Tyre would be scraped bare as a rock and its rubble thrown into the midst of the sea (Ezekiel 26). The climax of Ezekiel's prophecies highlights both the resuscitation of Israel and the resurrection of true Israel. Ezekiel prophesied as he was commanded, and suddenly "there was a noise, a rattling sound, and the bones came together, bone to bone. I looked," said Ezekiel, "and tendons and flesh appeared on them and skin covered them, but there was no breath in them." Again Ezekiel prophesied as he was commanded, and breath entered the bodies: "they came to life and stood on their feet—a vast army" (37:7–10). The interpretation leaves little guesswork. God would unlock the abode of the dead and reinvigorate Israel. "I will put my Spirit in you and you will live, and I will settle you in your own land. Then you will know that I the LORD have spoken, and I have done it, declares the LORD" (37:14).

The temple, too, would arise from the ashes. Ezekiel envisioned the glory of the Lord reentering the temple just as he had seen it leave in his earlier vision. Cyrus was God's chosen to "rebuild my city and set my exiles free" (Isaiah 45:13). Likewise, Cyrus would say of the temple, "Let its foundations be laid" (Isaiah 44:28). In his vision, Ezekiel saw the river of the water of life flowing out from under the threshold of the temple in the direction of the Arabah, bringing new life to the barren and healing to the nations. No longer would there be any curse. The presence of the Lord would never again depart, and his servants would never again fail to serve him (Ezekiel 37:21–28; 39:25–29).

Apart from historical context, we would be hard-pressed to understand Ezekiel's prophecy. We must ever be mindful of the fact that Ezekiel was prophesying from the dusty environs of a refugee camp in the south of Babylon near the river Kebar (1:3). From there the priest looked into the eastern sky and longed for the glory of the Lord to return to a temple that had vanished into the rocks that once surrounded it. He yearned for the promise of a temple whose glory would exceed even that of Solomon's temple.[25] In the Spirit he looked forward to events that would take place a generation later, a time when Zerubbabel would rebuild the glorious temple (Haggai 1:1–2:9; Ezra 3:1–13), when Ezra would rebuild the spiritual condition of the returning exiles (Ezra 8:1–20; Nehemiah 8:1–18), and when Nehemiah would challenge his fellow countrymen to arise and rebuild the shattered wall of Jerusalem (Nehemiah 1–7). The point here is that we must not presume that Ezekiel longed for a third or even a fourth temple when a second temple has not as yet arisen from the ashes.

Furthermore, we dare not presume that Ezekiel looked into the twenty-first century and there saw the reemergence of a temple on the very spot where the Dome of the Rock now stands. Nor suppose that beneath the temple's rocky foundation there are fountains that feed a fantastic reservoir containing an inexhaustible supply of water. Or even that fish of every kind will one day swim through the fresh waters of a once Dead Sea (Ezekiel 47:1–12). For just as historical context precludes the possibility that Ezekiel looked forward to a third or fourth temple, the apocalyptic context precludes the possibility that Ezekiel spoke in woodenly literal language. Even Herod's forty-six-year refurbishing efforts could not cause the glory of the second temple to attain to that of the first. The second temple, like the one that preceded it, was but a pale reflection of the One to whom it pointed. As Peter makes plain, it is in Christ alone, the living Stone, and in his body the church that the temple was fully and finally fulfilled (1 Peter 2:4–7). And the water flowing to the Arabah (Ezekiel 47:8)? Listen to the words of Messiah: "If anyone is thirsty, let him come to me and drink. Whoever believes in me, as the Scripture has said, streams of living water will flow from within him" (John 7:37–38). John likewise saw the river of the water of life "as clear as crystal, flowing from the throne of God and of the Lamb down the middle of the great street of the city" (Revelation 22:1–2). The land is now the Lord, Jerusalem now Jesus, and the limestone temple a living Temple, with Jesus Christ its cornerstone.

Finally, let me emphasize here that we dare not interpret Ezekiel's prophecies in any context that is foreign to that which is given to us by Christ and his apostles.[26] The magnifying glass through which we read the Law and the Prophets must ever remain in the hands of New Testament writers. Their typological interpretation of the Old Testament stands as the ultimate corrective to misinterpretations of the words of Ezekiel. The coming of Christ has forever rendered the notion of another earthly temple obsolete. It is the Savior and the saved who now form the sanctuary in which the Spirit of the living God resides. To suppose that the Shekinah glory will return to a shrine in Jerusalem is to regress from substance to shadow and thus impugn the finished work of Christ. It is Paradise—a new heaven and a new earth—not Palestine for which Ezekiel ultimately yearned. It is "the Holy City, the new Jerusalem, coming down out of heaven from God, prepared as a bride beautifully dressed for her husband" (Revelation 21:2) upon which he fixed his apocalyptic gaze. It is the Master Teacher, not a majestic temple, that would forever satisfy the deepest yearnings of a prophet exiled in dusty environs of a dry and thirsty land.

YEARS

Finally, of paramount significance to the historical principle of biblical interpretation is when a text was recorded. Consider the book of Daniel. Can we rightly conclude it was written in the midst of the sixth-century-BC Babylonian captivity? Or are we relegated to the notion that it was written four hundred years later during the Antiochian crisis? The answer to this question makes all the difference in the world. If Daniel was written six centuries before Christ, it shines as a brilliant star in the constellation of biblical prophecy. If it is relegated to the time of Antiochus, it is merely history written after the fact. As previously demonstrated, the arguments for a late dating of Daniel are less than compelling.[27] The core issue appears to be that of close-mindedness. Fundamentalists who deny that Daniel prophesies the succession of nations, from Babylon in the sixth century to the abomination that causes desolation in the second, begin with an antisupernatural bias and thus reject the possibility of prophecy a priori. Instead of open-minded consideration of both natural and supernatural explanations, they close-mindedly reject the possibility of the latter.

Furthermore, consider the Gospels. If a gospel narrative is written hundreds of years after the events it records, it is far less reliable than if it is written early. For this reason alone, late pseudonymous gospels such as the second-century Thomas or third-century Judas were precluded from canonical consideration.[28] The notion that they did not make it into the canon because they were out of line with the direction historical winners wanted to take their newly minted religious notions is simply false. The inflammatory suggestion that the gospel of John was canonized because the early Christian church preferred its dark anti-Semitic overtones over more racially sensitive gospels such as Judas is based largely on antihistorical sophistry. Had Professor Ehrman and ilk heeded the historical principle of biblical interpretation as codified by the L-E-G-A-C-Y acronym, they may not have succumbed to such vindictive prejudice. Anti-Semitism had nothing to do with the canonization of John. Early dating, eyewitness attestation, and extrabiblical corroboration did.

Finally, a word with respect to dating the Apocalypse of John. If it was written in the mid-90s or later, as Professor Ehrman supposes, it seems incredible that there would be no mention of the most apocalyptic event in Jewish history. Imagine writing a thesis on the future of terrorism in America and failing to mention the tragic events of 9/11. Or consider an even more formidable obstacle—that Christ would make an apocalyptic prophecy concerning the destruction of the Jewish temple and that John, writing long after the fact, would fail to mention its fulfillment. If this interpretation is correct—if the Apocalypse of John was written prior to the events of AD 70—the Jerusalem holocaust is already in our rearview mirror. But if not, we may well anticipate Jerusalem's devastation as a future catastrophe. The macro issue here cannot be passed over lightly. Determining *when* a text was written has enormous ramifications.

In sum, failure to properly apprehend the historical principle of biblical interpretation as codified in the L-E-G-A-C-Y acronym can lead to a host of dangerous implications ranging from the life-and-death decision of a Watchtower devotee who refuses a blood transfusion based on a fatalistically flawed understanding of the biblical text to President Barack Obama's mistaken notion that the Bible suggests that slavery is okay. Conversely, proper application of the historical principle leads to the enhancement of life and liberty for all who grasp how to properly mine the Bible for all its wealth.

21

Typology Principle

The Bible appears like a symphony orchestra, with the Holy
Ghost as its Toscanini; each instrument has been brought willingly,
spontaneously, creatively, to play his notes just as the great conductor
desired, though none of them could ever hear the music as a whole.

—J. I. PACKER

I was born in Holland shortly after the conclusion of World War II. As I grew up, I heard my parents recount horrifying details of this tragic epic in human history. On one occasion my mother and one of her brothers barely missed a bus from Schiedam to Rotterdam—a bus destroyed minutes later by direct strike of a German bomb. They still have vivid recollections of smoldering bodies, which, but for the space of moments, would have been their own. My mother saw survival as no mere accident. Thus she, along with her family, devoted themselves heart and soul to the Dutch Resistance Movement—refusing to give in to either racial discrimination against Jews or Nazification of the populace. In exile, Queen Wilhelmina rightly described Adolf Hitler as "the arch-enemy of mankind"[1] and was herself rightly described by Winston Churchill as "the only real man among the governments in exile."[2]

After the war, we immigrated to Canada to begin a brand-new life. Within a decade my father experienced a crisis of a different sort. This time an enemy ravaged him from the inside. For all intents and purposes, doctors gave up on him. Apart from a miracle, he would shortly experience his own mortality. During those dark days my father prayed for God's intervention—not because he was not ready to die but because he was quite certain that he had not accomplished the purpose for which he had been created. He was certain that God had called him to be a pastor, but he had not yet responded to the call. On his deathbed, he pleaded for one more chance at life—one more opportunity to fulfill his destiny. The Lord saw my father's tears, heard his prayers, and healed him. Not long after he regained his strength, Dad began making changes. He resigned from a comfortable position as a design draftsman engineer, sold our home in a Canadian suburb, moved the family to an inner-city neighborhood in Michigan, and began studying to be a pastor at Calvin College and Seminary.

One of the unintended consequences of immigration to the United States was the experience of yet another form of racism. This time it was not of the Aryan superrace variety that my family stood fast against in Holland. This time it was an American segregationist variety postulating a difference among human beings based on skin pigmentation. I still have memories of walking through an all-black neighborhood to an all-white school and encountering a concept of race completely foreign to my experience. In the process I developed friends for whom racism was a day-by-day reality.

It was in school that I encountered a connection between the racism my parents experienced during the war and the racism experienced by my inner-city friends. Both were equally animated by the same idea—an intellectual revulsion that Harvard scientist Ernst Mayr once categorized as "the most fundamental of all intellectual revolutions in the history of mankind."[3] Sir Julian Huxley called it "the most powerful and the most comprehensive idea that has ever arisen on earth."[4] The twentieth century cannot be comprehended apart from the intellectual revolution it produced. It has shaped the worldview of hundreds of millions of people— noteworthy among them Adolf Hitler. Said soul mate Sir Arthur Keith, "The German Fuhrer, as I have consistently maintained, is an evolutionist;

he has consciously sought to make the practices of Germany conform to the theory of evolution."[5]

Reason devoid of revelation led oft-quoted eighteenth-century Scottish empiricist philosopher David Hume to render blacks "naturally inferior to the whites." "Negroes," writes Hume, never "discovered any symptoms of ingenuity." While one of them might at first appear erudite, in the end he is only "like a parrot, who speaks a few words plainly."[6] In like fashion, nineteenth-century English naturalist Charles Darwin reasoned inequality to be self-evident truth. As such, he subtitled his magnum opus *The Preservation of Favored Races in the Struggle for Life*. As Darwin puts it elsewhere, "The more civilized so-called Caucasian races have beaten Turkish hollow in the struggle for existence. Looking to the world at no very distant date, what an endless number of the lower races will have been eliminated by the higher civilized races throughout the world."[7] Incredibly, Darwin apologist Richard Dawkins has cleverly attempted to absolve his exemplar from overt racism. Says Dawkins, "The misunderstanding of the Darwinian struggle for existence as a struggle between groups of individuals—the so-called 'group-selection' fallacy—is unfortunately not confined to Hitlerian racism. It constantly resurfaces in amateur misinterpretations of Darwinism, and even among some professional biologists who should know better."[8] This Dawkinsian slight of mind would be humorous if it were not so pathetic.

One need only read the corpus of Darwin's work to recognize that his *Preservation of Favored Races in the Struggle for Life* hypothesis clearly involves "races," not merely "individuals within races." In *The Descent of Man*, for example, Darwin writes, "At some future period, not very distant as measured by centuries, the civilized races of man will almost certainly exterminate, and replace, the savage races throughout the world. At the same time the anthropomorphous [i.e., most human-looking] apes . . . will no doubt be exterminated. The break will then be rendered wider, for it will intervene between man in a more civilized state, as we may hope, than the Caucasian, and some ape as low as a baboon, instead of as at present between the negro or Australian and the gorilla."[9]

The dichotomy between races and groups of individuals who share common characteristics is little more than a distinction without a difference. Characteristics that groups of individuals share in common are a function of genetics. While Darwin may have been largely ignorant of genetics, the same cannot be said for Dawkins. Indeed, genetics is precisely what grounds his concept of race. The "professional biologists" demeaned by Dawkins should better be commended. It takes great courage in today's politically correct climate to call things as they are. Moreover, to excuse the overt racism (and sexism) in Darwin's writings is itself inexcusable—particularly when such excuses flow from the pen of a man who has the temerity to castigate those who do not believe in his evolutionary hypothesis as "ignorant," "stupid," "insane," "wicked," "tormented," "bullied," or "brainwashed."[10]

Darwin's knighted bulldog Sir Thomas Huxley was no less benighted than his evolutionary descendant. "No rational man, cognizant of the facts," writes Huxley, "believes the average Negro is the equal, still less the superior of the white man. It is simply incredible to think that he will be able to compete successfully with his bigger-brained and smaller-jawed rival in a contest which is to be carried on by thoughts and not by bites."[11] Or consider Dr. John L. Down, who labeled Down syndrome "'Mongoloid idiocy' because he thought it represented a 'throwback' to the 'Mongolian stage' in human evolution."[12]

Lest we suppose this to be the mere prejudice of nineteenth-century scientists, consider the pseudoscience of eugenics. Eugenics hypothesized that the gene pool was being corrupted by the less-fit genes of inferior people. For evolution to succeed, it is as crucial that the unfit die as that the fittest survive. If the unfit survived indefinitely, they would continuously infect the fit with their less-fit genes. The result is more fit genes would be corrupted and evolution compromised.[13] As the late Michael Crichton points out, the theory of eugenics postulated that "the best human beings were not breeding as rapidly as the inferior ones—the foreigners, immigrants, Jews, degenerates, the unfit, and the 'feeble minded.' . . . The plan was to identify individuals who were feeble minded—Jews were agreed to be largely feeble-minded, but so were many foreigners, as well as blacks—and stop them from breeding by isolation in institutions or by sterilization."[14]

The logical progression from evolution to eugenics is hardly surprising. What is breathtaking, however, is the vast rapidity with which this baseless theory was embraced by the cultural elite. Crichton notes that its supporters ranged from President Theodore Roosevelt to Planned Parenthood founder Margaret Sanger. Eugenics research was funded through philanthropies such as the Carnegie and Rockefeller foundations and carried out at prestigious universities such as Stanford, Harvard, Yale, and Princeton.

Legislation to address the concern posed by eugenics was passed in blue states ranging from New York to California. Eugenics was even backed by the National Academy of Sciences and the American Medical Association. Those who resisted eugenics were considered backward and ignorant. Those like Margaret Sanger, the birth mother of Planned Parenthood, who embraced eugenics, were considered enlightened. German scientists who gassed the "feeble-minded," too, were considered forward-thinking and progressive and were rewarded with grants from such institutions as the Rockefeller Foundation right up to the onset of World War II.

It wasn't until the ghastly reality of eugenics reached full bloom in the genocidal mania of German death camps that it quietly vanished into the night. Indeed, after World War II few institutions or individuals would even own up to their insidious belief in eugenics. Nor did the cultural elite ever acknowledge the obvious connection between eugenics and evolution. Eugenics has faded into the shadowy recesses of history. The tragic consequences of the evolutionary dogma that birthed it, however, are yet with us today.

The point here is that ideas have consequences. Evolution has birthed its fair share of aberrations—racism among the most insidious of its progeny. But could the Bible be likewise a proponent of racism? What if God himself is a racist, as presumed by Oxford professor Richard Dawkins? What if Christopher Hitchens is right? What if the Bible contains a warrant for ethnic cleansing? Reality is, this contention is not produced out of whole cloth. A host of Christian popularists weave heavily into its fabric. Christian Zionist Michael Evans is among them. He is absolutely adamant in the prejudice that Palestine belongs exclusively to those who are racially and religiously Jewish. Palestinians, on the other hand, are deemed by Evans to be "a tainted and brainwashed people."[15] His basis? The Bible! Faith teacher John Hagee is equally explicit: "God has given Jerusalem *only* to the Jews." Displacing Arabs in order to make room for Jews he rationalizes as a biblical mandate. Says Hagee, "I am saying to those of you who are running this nation in Washington, D.C., if you are forcing Israel to give up land through our State Department, you stop! You are bringing the wrath and judgment of God to the United States of America."[16] Like their forefathers who considered the Bible the basis for believing blacks bore the curse of Canaan,[17] modern-day Zionists use the Bible as a pretext for racial segregation in the Middle East.

Is this justified? Does the Bible separate people on the basis of race? Is Jerusalem exclusively for Jews? Does the God of the Bible provide a rationale for racism? The answer is emphatically: No! Racism is a horrendous evil. Particularly when rationalized on the basis of the Bible. Understanding the typology principle, once again, is key. As previously noted, a *type* (from the Greek word *typos*) is a person, event, or institution in the redemptive history of the Old Testament that prefigures a corresponding but greater reality in the New. As my friend Stephen Sizer aptly notes, "The failure to recognize this principle is the basic hermeneutical error which Christian Zionists make and from which flow the other distinctive doctrines that characterize the movement."[18]

Nowhere is this more clearly seen than in misinterpretations regarding the promise God made to Abraham: "To your descendants I give this land, from the river of Egypt to the great river, the Euphrates" (Genesis 15:18). Christian Zionists are convinced that such promises are unconditional and as yet unfulfilled. As such, they are convinced that Israel will soon control not only the West Bank, Gaza, and Golan, but Iraq, Jordan, and Lebanon. Says John Hagee, "The Royal Land Grant that God, the original owner, gave to Abraham, Isaac, and Jacob and their seed forever, includes the following territory which is presently occupied by Israel, the West Bank, all of Lebanon, one half of Syria, two-thirds of Jordan, all of Iraq, and the northern portion of Saudi Arabia."[19] Put another way, Israel will soon possess an area of land at least thirty times its present size.

This, however, is far from biblical. Abraham was not promised a country thirty times its present size. He was promised the cosmos! As Paul, Apostle to the Gentiles, underscores, "Abraham and his offspring received the promise that he would be *heir of the world*" (Romans 4:13). Thus, while Christian Zionists hyperventilate over tiny areas of land such as the Golan or Gaza, God promises them the globe. The late Dr. John Gerstner highlights the irony when with tongue firmly planted in cheek he opines, "This certainly does make it hard on the Jews! When they might have had a glorious piece of real estate on the Mediterranean, all they end up with under this interpretation is Christ."[20]

Ironically, Zionists such as John Hagee place far more emphasis on returning Jewish pilgrims to the land than in turning Jewish people to the Lord. Says Hagee, "Let us put an end to this Christian chatter that 'all the Jews are lost' and can't be in the will of God until they convert to Christianity!"[21] What's the rationale? From his perspective, Jews may well be saved under the old covenant, but apparently the new covenant need not apply.[22] To suggest as he does that Jews are somehow entitled to building settlements in Gaza and yet excluded from the blessed salvation of the gospel might well be regarded as the height of anti-Semitism. Worse still is his preoccupation with herding Jews into the land, since he is convinced that two-thirds of the Jewish population in Palestine will soon die in unbelief in a holocaust beyond compare.[23]

Of course, both the idea that Jews in the twenty-first century will endure a holocaust for the first-century sins of their fathers and the ideology that Jews have a divine right to the land based on race are decidedly unbiblical. Our heavenly Father is not pro-Jew; he is pro-justice. He is not pro-Palestinian; he is pro-peace. Only a gospel of peace and justice through faith in Jesus Christ is potent enough to break the stranglehold of anti-Semitism and racism fueled in part by a failure to comprehend the typology principle of biblical interpretation. This is made explicit through a vision of unclean food experienced by Peter in Joppa. After he encountered the Gentile centurion Cornelius, Peter comprehended its import. "I now realize how true it is," said Peter, "that God does not show *favoritism* but accepts men from every nation who fear him and do what is right. You know the message God sent to the people of Israel, telling the good news of peace through Jesus Christ, who is Lord of *all*" (Acts 10:34–36). Race is simply of no consequence. When Peter along with the rest of the disciples inquired, "Lord, are you at this time going to restore the kingdom to Israel?" (Acts 1:6), Jesus reoriented their thinking from a restored Jewish state to a kingdom that knows no borders or boundaries. "My kingdom," he reiterated before Pilate, "is not of this world" (John 18:36).

As our Lord typologically fulfilled and thus heightened the reality of the Law, so, too, he fulfilled and thus heightened the reality of the land. The writer of Hebrews makes clear that the rest the descendants of Abraham experienced when they entered the land is but a type of the rest we experience when we enter an eternal relationship with the Lord. The land may have provided temporal rest for the *physical* descendants of Abraham, but the Lord provides eternal rest for the *spiritual* descendants of Abraham (Hebrews 3–4). In the fore-future the promise was fulfilled when the children of Israel entered the promised land. In the far future the promise is typologically fulfilled in the Lord, who is the locus of the land. In the final future the promise of the land will be fully and finally consummated when Paradise lost is reconstituted as Paradise restored. Canaan is thus typological of a renewed cosmos.

Accordingly, Abraham was anything but a Zionist. Like Isaac and Jacob, he viewed living in the promised land in the same way a stranger would view living in a foreign country. Why? Because as the writer of Hebrews makes plain, "He was looking forward to a city with foundations, whose architect and builder is God" (11:10). As such Abraham looked beyond binding borders and boundaries to a day in which the meek would "inherit the earth" (Matthew 5:5; cf. Psalm 37:11, 22). While Christian Zionists see the fact that Jerusalem is now completely in the hands of the Jews as validation for biblical theology, nothing could be further from the truth. Even if one ignores the typological fulfillment of Jerusalem in Jesus, the old covenant promise of return to the land is inviolately conditioned upon belief and faithfulness. There is therefore no warrant for Christian Zionists' claims that the recapturing of Jerusalem by modern Israel signifies the preliminary fulfillment of God's promises to Abraham.[24]

While one may rightly defend the right of the secular state of Israel to exist, the contention that the modern state of Israel is a fulfillment of biblical prophecy is indefensible. History, like the New Testament, reveals that the Holy City—turned harlot city—is superseded by the holy Christ. Jesus is thus the antitype who fulfills all of the typology vested in Jerusalem. Thus, while Jerusalem remains an important historical site as the typological City of David and the birthplace of Christianity, there is neither biblical nor historical warrant for treating it as the object of our eschatological hope. It is in Jesus, not Jerusalem, that we come face-to-face with the glory and presence of the living God.

Biblical Christianity is fixated not on an earthly Jerusalem but on a heavenly "city with foundations, whose architect and builder is God" (Hebrews 11:10). The apostle John got a glimpse of this antitypical Holy City when the Spirit showed him "the Holy City, Jerusalem, coming down out of heaven from God. It shone with the glory of God, and its brilliance was like that of a very precious jewel, like a jasper, clear as crystal" (Revelation 21:10–11). As John gazed upon the splendor of this heavenly Jerusalem, his mind must surely have flashed back to the words of King Jesus as he stood before Pilate. "My kingdom," Jesus had said, "is not of this world. If it were, my servants would fight to prevent my arrest by the Jews. But now my kingdom is from another place" (John 18:36). The quintessential point of understanding for John as well as for the rest of the disciples began to dawn at the time of Christ's post-resurrection appearances. Previously they had been under the same misconceptions as modern-day Christian Zionists. They had expected Jesus to establish Jerusalem as the capital of a sovereign Jewish empire. The notion was so ingrained in their psyches that even as Jesus was about to ascend into heaven, they asked, "Lord, are you at this time going to restore the kingdom to Israel?" (Acts 1:6)

Jesus not only corrected the disciples' erroneous thinking but also expanded their horizons from a tiny strip of land on the east coast of the Mediterranean to the farthest reaches of the earth. "You will receive power when the Holy Spirit comes on you"—said Jesus, as he was about to be taken up into heaven—"and you will be my witnesses in Jerusalem, and in all Judea and Samaria, *and to the ends of the earth*" (1:8). In effect, Jesus left his disciples with instructions to exit Jerusalem, embrace the earth, and never again entertain the thought of establishing an earthly Jerusalem. The disciples were no longer permitted to view Israel in exclusivistic parochial categories; their sights instead must be elevated to an *inclusive* Israel. From a truly biblical perspective, true Israel consists of people from "from every tribe and language and people and nation" (Revelation 5:9). Indeed, the apostle Paul underscores the reality that Abraham was to be the father not of *a* nation but of *many* nations through whom all the world would be blessed (Genesis 17:5; Romans 4:16–18). When God promised Abraham, "I will bless those who bless you, and whoever curses you I will curse; and all peoples on earth will be blessed through you" (Genesis 12:3), such blessings and cursings pertained not simply to the faithful remnant of ethnic Israel but to true Israel, consisting of every person who through faith has been adopted into the family of God.

At this point the significance of the typology principle should be manifestly clear. When Christopher Hitchens implicates God as a racist bent on ethnic cleansing, he most surely does so on a misunderstanding of biblical hermeneutics. He may be correct in asserting that "the anti-Semite Balfour had tried to bribe the Jews with the territory of another people in order to seduce them from Bolshevism and continue the diplomacy of the Great War,"[25] but that is hardly a correct basis for impugning the God of the Bible. Whatever Balfour's motivations or beliefs, the Bible does not view people from the perspective of race but rather regards them as the seed of Abraham and heirs according to the promise on the basis of relationship.

Understanding the typology principle of biblical interpretation forever dispenses with any thought of racism. Abraham was promised a royal Seed through whom "*all* peoples on earth" would be blessed (Genesis 12:3, 7; cf. Galatians 3).

22

Synergy Principle

Explain the Scriptures by the Scriptures.

—CLEMENT OF ALEXANDRIA

The atmosphere was electric. The president of the United States was about to address a gathering of radio talk show hosts in the White House. As he entered the hall, they all stood and applauded. All, that is, except one—a Jewish woman with strikingly blond hair, dressed in a bright green jacket. Her presence seemed to rattle the president. He lost his train of thought several times before turning on his heel and speaking directly to the still seated talk show host.

The president wondered out loud whether she might be an MD—or maybe a doctor of psychology, theology, or even social work. Unfazed, the striking Jewess pointed to her PhD in English literature. The president found her response less than amusing. A PhD in English literature was impressive but hardly a basis for counseling a needy public on the pressing issues of life.

The real issue came to the fore quickly. Homosexuality, it turned out, was the bone of contention. The PhD called it an "abomination." For the president, *that* was the real abomination! The PhD smartly diverted authority from herself to the Scriptures. Clarification only further opened the floodgates.

Words riveted in his memory burst forth like venom—the first words emanating in a virtual snarl—*Leviticus 18:22!* Catching himself, the president quickly donned the cloak of Colombo and asked whether Leviticus 18:22 might be comparable to Exodus 21:7. After all, if the condemnation of homosexuality wasn't a problem for the PhD, perhaps selling his youngest daughter into slavery as sanctioned by Exodus 21:7 would not be problematic either. And maybe, he mused, he could get a good price to boot—after all, she spoke fluent Italian, was good at doing dishes, and was a student of Georgetown University.

And what about his chief of staff? Perhaps in accordance with Exodus 35:2 he should put him to death for habitually working on the Sabbath. Should he throw the first stone or have the police do it on his behalf?

Now in full command, the president pressed on with unrepressed sarcasm. Should the Washington Redskins or the Fighting Irish of Notre Dame be forced to wear gloves while handling a football since Leviticus 11:7 forbids touching dead pigskin? Should his brother be stoned for planting different crops side by side? Should he burn his mother to death for wearing garments made of different threads?

The president's parting shot hit with a sniper's precision. No one—not even a vaunted PhD—was to remain seated when the president of the United States was in the room.

As he paused to catch his breath, a hush invaded the rotunda. The once self-assured talk show host rose slowly to her feet, her face reddened in shame. Her quick wit and commanding presence had vanished. The president had rendered her speechless. The Bible that she used to berate GLBTs had effectively beaten her into submissive silence.[1]

Imagine the humiliation you would feel if you were standing in her shoes. What would you—what could you—have said? Had the president of the United States really demonstrated the Bible to be outdated and absurd? Should it, like the sexual mores it promotes, be relegated to the scrap heap of history? Do the very Scriptures that condemn homosexuality commend slavery? Should football be outlawed because touching pigskin makes one "unclean"? Must we kill those who work on the Sabbath? And what's up with stoning men for planting different crops side by side or burning women for wearing clothing made of two different threads?[2]

As sermons go, this one was smokin'! From its original air date to the present, I can think of no more effective sermon ever aired on television. There was no mistaking its message: no matter how much evidence you produce to demonstrate that God has spoken or that the Bible is divine rather than merely human in origin—*what* God has said is clearly outdated and irrelevant in a modern age of scientific enlightenment. The expression of polite exasperation etched on the faces of the audience was a perfect crescendo to the rhetorical skills of the president as he plunged verbal daggers into the antiquated pages of an outdated text. A Bible that teaches homosexuality is an abomination and slavery is okay has no standing on the vanguard of the twenty-first-century enlightenment.

During its heyday (September 22, 1999–May 14, 2006), *The West Wing* was among the most popular shows on television. It received rave reviews from diverse audiences ranging from political science professors to White House staffers. Judging from arguments adduced in *The Audacity of Hope*, even President Barack Obama was tuned in. If so, he was hardly alone. More than eleven million households[3] watched as NBC employed the Dr. Jenna Jacobs character to caricature Dr. Laura Schlessinger as a rude and bigoted religious talk show host. The tirade of President Josiah Bartlet (played by Martin Sheen) was hardly original, however. It was lifted in large part from a widely circulated e-mail that appears on gay/lesbian websites in which many of the same questions were posed to none other than Dr. Laura.[4] Millions sat in their living rooms and applauded her humiliation. Right-wing bigots like Dr. Laura and, by implication, orthodox Jews and evangelical Christians, were finally put in their place. Multitudes more were shaken in their faith. They wondered whether the Bible had indeed been exposed as antiquated and absurd.

Today, a little more than a decade after its original airing, President Bartlet's diatribe serves as a perfect illustration for illumining the import of the *synergy principle* of biblical interpretation. Indeed, this maxim may rightly be deemed the principle imperative of the art and science of biblical interpretation. Simply stated, the whole of Scripture is greater than the sum of its individual passages. You cannot comprehend the Bible as a whole without comprehending its individual passages, nor comprehend its individual passages apart from comprehending the Bible as a whole. We do a grave injustice to the majesty of the most significant book in the history of Western civilization if we rip passages out of their historical contexts or fail to grasp the context of Scripture as a whole. As should become plain in the following pages, proper understanding of the *synergy principle* renders the president's tirade as slick in style but dreadfully deficient in substance.

SLAVERY

When confronted with the issue of slavery, NBC's version of Dr. Laura was left speechless. While I have already adequately addressed the issue of slavery,[5] the hubris of President Bartlet's tantrum compels me to add some additional remarks here.

First is an issue of grammar. As we have seen, words are not univocal; they're equivocal. As such, to read anachronistic modern meanings into an Ancient Near Eastern context is hardly enlightened. Someone unfamiliar with Elizabethan English, for example, might well mistake the phrase *gay clothing* as having sexual overtones. Likewise, someone unfamiliar with Scandinavian etymology may mistake the word *niggardly* as a racial slur, or, as in the present case, read a modern prejudice into the Ancient Near Eastern word *slave*. In the New World a *slave* may have been a commodity or property denuded of rights and privileges. Not so in ancient Israel. There a *slave* was akin to a *subject* or a *servant*. As such, when a Christian calls herself a slave or a bondservant of Christ, we do not for a moment mistake her meaning. While we would never call a modern presidential aide a slave, an ancient Israelite vassal king, with all the pomp and circumstance of monarchy, could so be designated. In other words, in ancient Israel *slavery* denoted subordination in social standing, not ownership.

Furthermore, as aptly underscored by apologist Glenn Miller, Mosaic law was far-reaching in its "initiatives designed to *preclude* someone having to consider voluntary slavery as an option."[6] Said Moses, "There should be no poor among you, for in the land the LORD your God is giving you to possess as your inheritance, he will richly bless you, if only you fully obey the LORD your God and are careful to follow all these commands I am giving you today" (Deuteronomy 15:4–5). Even a cursory overview of Mosaic initiatives should suffice to moderate modern superiority complexes: do not be tightfisted but give generously and every seventh year forgive your debtors their debts (Deuteronomy 15); reserve the seventh year of the planting cycle for the poor among you (Exodus 23; Leviticus 25); leave the margins around your fields unharvested so that the needy are not deprived of food (Leviticus 19); exempt the poor from interest payments (Leviticus 25); every third year you must dedicate your Levitical tithe to the poor (Deuteronomy 14). In short, Israel was adjured to remember the harsh conditions of her own captivity in Egypt so that she would not likewise abuse the alien, the poor, or the downtrodden in her midst.

Finally, Exodus 21 hardly supposes that a modern-day president should consider selling his well-to-do daughter as a slave. This passage is not intended to indulge the elite; it is intended to protect the poor. In contrast to a Hugh Hefner playmate easily dispensed with after being substantially used up, Mosaic law intended to protect the dignity of women placed in less-than-ideal circumstances. As such, Exodus 21 stipulates the legal rights of an impoverished woman who becomes a servant member of a well-to-do household. One would think that the initiatives of the Mosaic law would quell the bravado of modern-day presidents who immorally enslave our children and theirs to a crushing burden of debt.[7]

Instead of reading anachronistic prejudices into the text of Scripture, in *West Wing* fashion, we would be well served to read the Bible synergistically. Just as former speaker of the house Nancy Pelosi had no hope of comprehending the provisions of Obamacare apart from reading its two thousand–plus pages, so we do no justice to Torah Law without careful consideration of its complexities. We can no more read New World realities into Ancient Near Eastern legalities than we can read Torah legalities into New Covenant realities. We must ever be mindful that the whole of Scripture is greater than the sum of its individual parts. We cannot grasp the Bible as a whole without grasping its individual passages, nor its individual passages without grasping the Bible as a whole.

SABBATH

For more than two decades I've conducted live *Bible Answer Man* radio broadcast sessions in churches, conferences, and radio rallies all around the world. Late in the evening, as I come to the end of autographing books and interacting with attendees, a group of Adventists invariably waits in the wings, ready to engage me on the subject of Sunday worship. For them the issue is crystal clear: those who persist in worshipping on Sunday have taken on the "mark of the beast" (Revelation 13:17; 14:9, 11; 16:2). No matter what I say to the contrary, they remain resolute in their convictions. The only hope I have of erasing the mark from my forehead is altering my day of worship.

President Bartlet takes Torah legalities even more seriously. As such, he foolishly supposes that the Bible provides an imperative for stoning his chief of staff, and thereafter killing himself, for violating the proscriptions of Exodus 35:2. Answering the question of Sabbath observance may pose somewhat of a problem for Orthodox Jews, but it poses no problem whatsoever for Christians who believe that Christ is the substance that fulfills the symbol of the Sabbath. Once again, synergy, the principle imperative of biblical hermeneutics, precludes all such nonsense.

To begin with, as the president of the United States would surely know, America holds to a democratic, not a theocratic, form of government. Thus, Sabbath breaking may have had serious ramifications within ancient Judaism, but it is not a warrant for killing people today. Not even the Jewish House majority leader Eric Cantor would suggest killing the president's chief of staff for violating the seventh-day Sabbath. There is no more warrant for killing a Sabbath breaker today than there is for killing GLBTs. In fact, the mechanisms required to carry out the death penalty under Mosaic law are no longer extant. Indeed, the very Jews who believed that Christ was worthy of death for violating the law of Moses had to convince Roman authorities to crucify him.

Furthermore, while Jews may have a hard time explaining why Mosaic penalties no longer apply (at least in spirit), the rationale for Christians is found in Christ. As the apostle Paul explains, "Christ redeemed us from the curse of the law by becoming a curse for us" (Galatians 3:13). Such redemption from the curse of the law is available to all regardless of ethnicity or gender. Says Paul, "The law was put in charge to lead us to Christ that we might be justified by faith. Now that faith has come, we are no longer under the supervision of the law. You are all sons of God through faith in Christ Jesus, for all of you who were baptized into Christ have clothed yourselves with Christ. There is neither Jew nor Greek, slave nor free, male nor female, for you are all one in Christ Jesus. If you belong to Christ, then you are Abraham's seed, and heirs according to the promise" (3:24–29). Paul admonishes Colossian Christians not to judge (much less kill) anyone by what they "eat or drink" or by whether or not they observe "a religious festival, a New Moon celebration or a Sabbath day. These are a shadow of the things that were to come; the reality, however, is found in Christ" (Colossians 2:16–17). Religious rites inexorably bow to redemptive realities.

Finally, while some Christian traditions have denounced Sunday worship as the end-time mark of the beast (which likewise cannot be understood apart from Old Testament referents), there are good, biblical reasons that millions of Christians gather on the first day of the week for worship. In remembrance of the resurrection, thousands of Jews willingly gave up a theological tradition that had given them their national identity. God himself had provided the early church with a new pattern of worship through Christ's resurrection on the first day of the week as well as the Holy Spirit's descent on Pentecost Sunday. Moreover, Scripture provides us with the ever-escalating emphasis that is invested in the typology of the Sabbath-day celebration. In Genesis, the Sabbath was a celebration of God's work in creation (Genesis 2:2–3; Exodus 20:11). After the Exodus, the Sabbath expanded to a celebration of God's deliverance from oppression in Egypt (Deuteronomy 5:15). And as a result of the resurrection, the Sabbath became a celebration of the "rest" we have through Christ, who delivers us from sin and the grave (Hebrews 4:1–11). For the emerging Christian church, the most dangerous snare was a failure to recognize that Jesus was the substance that fulfilled the symbol of the Sabbath.

Once again, the synergy principle proves to be of paramount importance.

SWINE

President Bartlet proceeds to make his biggest mess by addressing the subject of swine. Sarcastically, he suggests that players for the Washington Redskins, Notre Dame, or West Point may become ceremonially unclean by touching a football made of the skin of a dead pig—this despite the reality that the footballs used in college and professional ranks are not made of pigskin. Rather, they are made of cowhide, the skin of a kosher animal. Ironically, the president has just dressed down the PhD for not having her degree in psychology, theology, or medicine.[8] Therefore, he implies that she is not qualified to speak on matters of personal faith and morals. It appears, however, that the president has not been properly briefed and, thus, despite his PhD in economics, he appears less than qualified to pontificate on this subject.

To begin with, the fact that Dr. Jenna's PhD is in English literature rather than psychology is no warrant for intimating that she is ill equipped to properly interpret literary documents. At face value, it appears she has a better grasp of biblical hermeneutics than that displayed by the president. If indeed the president had an adequate understanding of the rich tradition of biblical Judaism, he would have no doubt been far more restrained in his diatribe against the Scriptures. At best, he proved himself a master at rhetoric and emotional stereotypes rather than reason and evidential substance.

Furthermore, there is a quantum difference between enduring moral principles such as those regarding same-sex proclivities and temporary ceremonial practices relegated to a particular historical context. The distinction between clean and unclean animals symbolized the distinction between that which was holy and that which was unholy within the context of a theocracy. As seen previously, the ceremonial symbolism of the law was fulfilled in Christ, who makes the unclean clean. Thus, as Scripture declares, we are not to "call anything impure that God has made clean" (Acts 10:15; cf. Matthew 15:11; Mark 7:15, 19; 1 Timothy 4:3–5).

Finally, we should note that President Bartlet's obscurantism vis-à-vis theocratic laws respecting "pigskin" applies likewise to President Obama, who supposes the Bible teaches "that eating shellfish is an abomination."[9] Jesus made this plain when he rebuked the Pharisees and the teachers of the law for fastidiously holding on to traditions of men. "'Don't you see that nothing that enters a man from the outside can make him "unclean"?' said Jesus. 'For it doesn't go into his heart but into his stomach, and then out of his body.' (In saying this, Jesus declared all foods 'clean'" (Mark 7:18–19).[10] Jesus' point here that food is not the source of moral defilement, but rather moral defilement comes from the heart, was for the disciples a principle that explains why Gentile Christians need not observe traditional Jewish dietary scruples (Acts 11:1–18; Romans 14:1ff; Colossians 2:16; 1 Timothy 4:1–4).

As such, they rightly heeded the principle of scriptural synergy—realizing that the symbol of ceremonial legalities was fulfilled in the substance of their Master.

SEEDING AND SEWING

The West Wing's final attempt to invalidate Scripture involved the injunction against seeding "different crops side by side" and sewing garments together "from two different threads." The president succeeds in raising the emotional level of his argument by relating these Levitical laws to his brother and his mother. Once again, however, he sidesteps the primary rule of hermeneutics and seduces an audience of eleven million with emotive rhetoric. Nowhere in Scripture is there any suggestion that we should kill family members for failing to heed Levitical laws regarding seeding and sewing.

Furthermore, Scripture simply uses the object lessons of seeding crops and sewing clothes to illustrate the spiritual and social distinctions between the kingdom of darkness and the kingdom of light. The mixing of different things was associated with the very syncretistic pagan practices that Israel had been warned to avoid. As such, Scripture provides myriad illustrations to underscore the principle of undivided loyalty. In Deuteronomy, for example, the Israelites were commanded not to plow with an ox and a donkey yoked together (22:10). Paul, writing to the Corinthians, uses this common-sense principle to underscore that as a donkey and an ox do not work together synergistically in the process of plowing, so, too, a believer and an unbeliever do not harmonize well in the process of living. Thus, says Paul, "Do not be yoked together with unbelievers. For what do righteousness and wickedness have in common? Or what fellowship can light have with darkness? What harmony is there between Christ and Belial? What does a believer have in common with an unbeliever?" (2 Corinthians 6:14–15).

Finally, the highly complex nature of Mosaic laws can hardly be relegated to simplistic, superficial sound bites. Devoid of context, the twenty-first-century mind can only with great difficulty grasp the significance of biblical illustrations, metaphors, or figures of speech. A golfer living in the twenty-first century knows precisely what I mean when I speak of "draining a snake on the eighteenth hole."[11] To someone living in a context or culture in which golf is not played, however, it makes little or no sense. Similarly, the civil and ceremonial significance of Mosaic laws makes little sense to someone who has never read the Bible synergistically.

SAME-SEX SEXUALITY

Everything thus far is but prologue to the main point of this celebrated *West Wing* episode. Namely, because the Bible is wrong respecting issues ranging from slavery to seeding and sewing, it must be wrong when it comes to same-sex sexuality. In other words, there is no credence to the notion of unclean foods or unclean animals; thus, there is no credibility to biblical prohibitions against homosexuality.

This, however, is far from true. Through faithful application of the *synergy principle*—what the Reformers dubbed "the analogy of faith," and the primary rule in the art and science of biblical interpretation—we immediately recognize a quantum difference between a temporary type and an enduring ethical edict. The former is fulfilled and escalated in the antitype, and thus abrogated. The latter applies universally to all people, in all places, at all times. As such, it is more than a little messed up for President Obama to say that Leviticus "suggests slavery is okay and that eating shellfish is an abomination."[12] As previously demonstrated, complex codes regarding the propriety of human relationships are hardly reducible to superficial sound bites—especially by those prone to imposing New World realities on ancient biblical meanings and mores. Obama's mischaracterizations regarding shellfish are more subtle, but they are equally misleading. He is right in suggesting that Leviticus characterizes the eating of shellfish as "an abomination." He is wrong in isolating this injunction from its biblical context. The distinction between clean and unclean foods symbolized the difference between that which was holy and that which was unholy within the context of an ancient theocratic form of government. Consequently, from a New Testament perspective, it is as morally appropriate to eat shellfish as it is to eat steak.

I would be remiss here if I did not explicitly address the biblical perspective regarding same-sex sexuality. For a male to have same-sex intercourse with another man as though the latter were not male but female was distinctly forbidden in the Old Testament context (Leviticus 18; 20). Dr. Robert A. J. Gagnon astutely observes that the proscriptions of Leviticus are grounded in "transcultural creation structures," and that "the closest analogies appear in the proscriptions to incest, adultery, and bestiality—forms of sexual behavior that continue to be rejected by contemporary communities of faith."[13] Says Gagnon, "Neither the male anal cavity (the orifice for expelling excrement) nor the mouth (the orifice for taking in food) are likely candidates for what God intended as a receptacle for the male penis."[14] The process by which a "passive partner made himself 'available' for the penis and sexual desire of the active partner" was considered by Jewish philosopher Philo of Alexandria an exploitive step toward feminization. "Moreover, in line with the Levitical prohibitions, Philo and Josephus regarded both partners as worthy of death, not just the active partner, because both were willing participants in this gender-bending activity."[15]

Furthermore, the common suggestion that "Jesus was, or might have been, personally neutral or even affirming of homosexual conduct is revisionist history at its worst."[16] All available evidence speaks to the contrary.

While Jesus did not directly address incestuous, intergenerational, inter-species, or same-sex sexuality, he clearly reaffirmed every jot and tittle of enduring moral law. Paul, likewise, derived his proscriptions against same-sex sexuality in Romans 1, 1 Corinthians 6, and 1 Timothy 1 from the creation order of Genesis and the prohibitions of Leviticus, and he contended that "even Gentiles without access to the direct revelation of Scripture have enough evidence in the natural realm to discover God's aversion to homosexual behavior."[17] In the book of Romans, Paul describes both the perversion and the penalty: "Their women exchanged natural relations for unnatural ones. In the same way the men also abandoned natural relations with women and were inflamed with lust for one another. Men committed indecent acts with other men, and *received in themselves the due penalty for their perversion*" (1:26–27).

We would do well to recognize that the Bible does not condemn homosexuality in an arbitrary and capricious fashion. Rather it carefully defines the borders of human sexuality so that our joy may be complete. It does not require an advanced degree in physiology to appreciate the fact that the human body is not designed for homosexual relationships. Spurious slogans and sound bites do not change the scientific reality that same-sex-sexuality relationships are devastating not only from a psychological but also from a physiological perspective.

While there are attendant moral and medical problems with sexual promiscuity in general, it would be homophobic in the extreme to obscure scientific realities concerning same-sex sexuality. It is a hate crime of un-paralleled proportions to attempt to keep a whole segment of the population in the dark concerning such issues. We should rather model the behavior of our Lord toward all who are lost through speaking truth—and speaking it in love. Says Gagnon, "The church can and should recapture Jesus' zeal for all the 'lost' and 'sick' of society, including those engaged in homosexual prac-tice. Concretely, this means visiting their homes, eating with them, speaking and acting out of love rather than hate, communicating the good news about God's rule, throwing a party when they repent and return home, and then reintegrating them fully into communities of faith."[18]

While at first blush it may appear that the president portrayed on

The West Wing is a benevolent intellectual and the Dr. Laura caricature, a bigoted ignoramus, quite the opposite is the case. Rather than fall for rhetoric and emotional stereotypes, such as those presented by NBC, we must commit ourselves to becoming so familiar with the truth that when a counterfeit looms on the horizon, we will recognize it instantaneously. At worst, we should be aware that answers exist. At best, we should be prepared to give an answer to everyone who asks us to give the reason for the hope that we have—and to do this with gentleness and respect.

The imperative here is to engage ourselves heart and soul in mining the Bible for all its wealth. Familiarity with the *literal* principle, *illumination* principle, *grammatical* principle, *historical* principle, *typology* principle, and *synergy* principle is axiomatic in the quest. The ultimate code breaker resides not in subjective flights of fancy but in examining Scripture in light of Scripture.

Memorable Snapshots

Literal Principle

To interpret the Bible literally means to interpret it in the most obvious and natural sense. Put another way, "to interpret the Bible literally is to interpret the Bible as literature." Thus when a biblical author uses a symbol or an allegory, we do violence to his intentions if we interpret him literalistically. A literalistic method of interpretation often does as much violence to the text as does a spiritualized interpretation that empties the text of objective meaning. To avoid either extreme, one must adeptly employ the literal principle of biblical interpretation, paying careful attention to *form*, *figurative language*, and *fantasy imagery*. And in doing so, we must ever be mindful that, though the Bible must be read as literature, it is not merely literature; it is divinely inspired literature.

Illumination Principle

Illumination is that grace by which the Holy Spirit sheds divine light upon the inspired text. While it is crucial to defend the Bible as divine in an age in which it is under siege, only the Spirit removes the veil so that the blind may truly see. Illumination does not end when the veil is lifted and the spiritually blind receive sight, however. The spiritually sighted are in need of illumination throughout the duration of their lives. Truly, we do not as yet know the treasures that may be mined from the biblical text. Such mining is not dependent upon academic degrees. It is directly proportional to our diligence. As we dig, the Spirit will continue to illumine our minds. "We have not received the spirit of the world," says Paul, "but the Spirit who is from God, that we may understand what God has freely given us" (1 Corinthians 2:12).

Grammatical Principle

Thankfully, you and I were hardwired for language from birth—from infancy onward, speech patterns are unconsciously absorbed and then modified in accord with unspoken rules of grammar. Even at age three, children display grammatical genius that enables them to master complex speech constructions and internalize sophisticated laws of language. It shouldn't surprise us, then, that the basic principles of language that we unconsciously absorb in earthly childhood and consciously internalize from grade school onward are foundational to the grammatical principle of biblical interpretation. As with any literary work, a thorough understanding of the Bible cannot be attained without a grasp of the basic rules (grammar) that govern the relationships and usages of words, including *syntax*, *style*, and *semantics*.

Historical Principle

Christianity is historical and evidential. Thus, the biblical text is best understood when one is familiar with the customs, culture, and historical context of biblical times. Such background information is extremely helpful in drawing out the full meaning of any given text. Unless and until we understand the historical context of any given book of the Bible, whether the Old Testament Leviticus or the New Testament Sermon on the Mount, we have little hope of grasping its meaning. Put another way, in order to properly evaluate biblical texts, we must take into account their historical legacy. Indeed, the acronym L-E-G-A-C-Y is an apt way of remembering factors to consider in determining the historical viability and meaning of sacred Scripture—*location, essence, genre, author, context, years.*

Typology Principle

A *type* is a person, event, or institution in the redemptive history of the Old Testament that prefigures a corresponding but greater reality in the New. A type is thus a copy, a pattern, or a model that signifies an even greater reality. The greater reality to which it points and in which it finds its fulfillment is referred to as an *antitype*. As such, the writer of Hebrews specifically employs the word *antitype* to refer to the greatness of the heavenly sanctuary of which the holy temple is merely a shadow. In Hebrews, as in the rest of the New Testament, the history of Israel is interpreted as a succession of types that find ultimate fulfillment in the life, death, and resurrection of our Lord. In sum, typology involves a divinely intended pattern of events encompassing both historical correspondence and intensification.

Synergy Principle

Scriptural synergy—what the Reformers referred to as the *analogy of faith*—may rightly be deemed the principal imperative in the art and science of biblical interpretation. Simply stated, it means that the whole of Scripture is greater than the sum of its individual passages. You cannot comprehend the Bible as a whole without comprehending its individual passages, and you cannot comprehend its individual passages without comprehending the Bible as a whole. Scriptural synergy demands that individual passages may never be interpreted in such a way as to conflict with the whole of Scripture. The biblical interpreter must keep in mind that all Scripture, though communicated through various human instruments, has one single Author. And that Author does not contradict himself, nor does he confuse his servants.

Conclusion

"Western civilization was born out of reasonable faith. And because this is so, its revelations rightly illumine and elucidate human reason. Revelations in the books of nature and of knowledge lead us beyond the darkness of imago Darwinii to the dignity of imago Dei."

Invincible in power and majesty, the glory of the nations. An empire great in size and savage strength. Ruler with iron fist. Not for a mere hundred years but for the better part of a millennium. For six hundred years, the city of Rome towered above the nations. Adorned by seven wonders, she sparkled in vain pomp and circumstance, with invincibility so certain she bore the moniker "Eternal."

And then, the unthinkable: Alaric and his Arian hordes breached the walls and sacked the immortal city. Pagan Romans looked in utter disbelief at statues of ancient deities who had proved impotent to save. Christians wondered if, indeed, the end of the world was now at hand.

Rome did not fall all at once. A generation would pass before a new breed of masters would hold sway in Europe. The Romans dubbed them barbarians in that they had little mastery over Greek and Latin. Yet they were hardly barbarian in the modern sense.

The Roman historian Tacitus provided balance to his critique of the victorious Vandals, Franks, Angles, Goths, and Saxons by noting their liberty from Roman vices and their respect for women and children. Though the Germanic invaders seized empty land and property belonging to emperors, they largely left the inhabitants unmoved. Indeed, in one of the greatest ironies of history, the invaders surrendered their culture, religion, and native tongues to that of the inhabitants.

It would not be long before the Germanic invaders, infatuated by the grandeur and glory of Roman ways, engaged the empire's Christian belief structure as well. As noted by historian Bruce Shelley, Europe owes more to Christianity than most have acknowledged. "When the barbarians destroyed the Roman Empire in the West, it was the Christian Church that put together a new order called Europe. The church took the lead in rule by law, the pursuit of knowledge, and the expressions of culture. The underlying concept was Christendom, which united empire and church."[1] The foundational principle undergirding the new world order was codified in a singular word—*revelation*.

Indeed, Augustine, arguably the greatest theologian of the Christian epoch, believed revelation to be the necessary precondition for all knowledge. No matter how keen a man's eyesight, he can see nothing if confined to pitch-black darkness. As light is axiomatic to seeing, so revelation is needed for knowing.[2]

The realization that revelation is axiomatic for knowledge led medieval thinkers to crown theology the queen of the sciences. Peter Paul Rubens personified this elegantly in his seventeenth-century painting *The Triumph of the Eucharist*. Seated in a chariot propelled by angelic beings is theology—queen of the sciences. Walking alongside are philosophy, the wise and grizzled veteran, and science, a newcomer in the cosmic conversation. Theology is never absent philosophy and science. But philosophy and science absent revelation leads inexorably to the blind ditch of ignorance.[3]

This is precisely why Greek philosophers were hardly a match for Christian theologians. While they were ingenious with respect to laws of logic, they were woefully ignorant respecting divine revelation. Aristotle, ignoring the revelation "In the beginning God," embraced the implausibility of an eternal universe. Greeks and Romans likewise rejected the one true

God who spoke the universe into existence. Instead they variously entreated human gods or gods made in the likeness of humanity. Not so with early Christian theologians such as Augustine. His God was neither human nor fashioned in the likeness of humanity. His God was an omniscient, omnipotent deity, who has the will and power to reveal himself.

BOOK OF NATURE

The new world order that arose from the impotence of Greco-Roman thought was grounded in the premise that God has revealed himself as Creator and sustainer of the universe in the book of nature. No one made this point more eloquently or emphatically than did the apostle most responsible for spreading the Christian ethic throughout the Roman Empire. "For since the creation of the world," says Paul, "God's invisible qualities—his eternal power and divine nature—have been *clearly seen*, being *understood from what has been made*, so that men are without excuse. . . . Although they claimed to be wise, they became fools and exchanged the glory of the immortal God for images" (Romans 1:20, 22).

The fool in mind here is not one who lacks mental acumen. Socrates, Plato, and Aristotle were all brilliant thinkers. Through rigorous reason they codified the laws of logic and established a foundation for Western philosophy. No, the fool is one whose mind is blinded by superstitious preconceptions. As such, Aristotle posited a god who was merely an essence and transformed planets into beings capable of emotions such as anger. Even Plato, who contra Aristotle believed that the universe came into being at a point in time, was severely hampered through neglect of revelation. As such, he held fastidiously to a belief in ideal shapes—the very superstition "that prevented Copernicus from entertaining the thought that planetary orbits might be elliptical, not circular."[4]

Again, the problem was not that Christian apologists from Augustine to Aquinas dwarfed the intellects of pagan philosophers such as Aristotle. The basic laws of reason were as accessible to one as to the other. It was the failure to apply the explanatory power of revelation to the mysteries of life that trapped pagan thinkers in the intellectual cul-de-sac of their own making. Thus, ingenuities ranging from capitalism to chemistry would forever remain beyond their ken.[5]

To comprehend the full impact that attends neglect of revelation, one need only look eastward to Islam. Like Christianity, Islam holds to God's transcendence, but unlike Christianity, it shirks the notion that God has revealed himself in time and space. History bears eloquent testimony to the consequences. In place of ingenuity, intellectual stagnation. In place of science, superstition. In place of human equality, enslavement.

As social scientist Rodney Stark aptly notes, "Islamic scholars achieved significant progress only in terms of specific knowledge, such as certain aspects of astronomy and medicine that did not necessitate any general theoretical basis. And, as time passed, even this sort of progress ceased." Even the Rasa'il, says Stark, that "great encyclopedia of knowledge produced by early Muslim scholars, fully embraced the Greek conception of the world as a huge, conscious living organism having both intellect and soul."[6] Thus observations in conflict with Aristotle's arguments were largely dismissed as "incorrect or an illusion."[7]

Unlike the followers of Caesar or Muhammad, followers of Christ were more than willing to dispute the works of the Greek philosophers. "Many of the great scientists of the sixteenth and seventeenth centuries often paid lip service to their 'debts' to Aristotle and others, but their actual work negated almost everything the Greeks had said about how the world works."[8]

Aristotle and his devotees idealized the world in terms of how it ought to be. Christian thinkers turned pages in the book of nature and discovered how it really was. Luther went so far as to say that "any potter has more knowledge of nature" than was written in the books of Aristotle.[9]

Such gravitas is not without warrant. The organization and complexity of the physical universe bear eloquent testimony to the existence of an uncaused First Cause and Intelligent Designer. Ocean tides caused by the gravitational pull of the moon are a classic case in point. If the moon were significantly larger, devastating tidal waves would submerge large areas of land. If the moon were smaller, tidal motion would cease and the oceans would stagnate and die. From its tides to its temperatures to even the tilt of its axis (23.5 degrees from perpendicular to the plane of its orbit), Earth is an unparalleled planetary masterpiece of precision and design. As "any potter" readily perceives, the universe is not an illusion; it did not spring out of nothing (nothing comes from nothing; nothing ever could); and it has not eternally existed (the laws of thermodynamics and Big Bang cosmology tell us that the universe came into existence a finite time ago). Thus the only philosophically plausible possibility left to any perceptive potter is that the universe was made by an unmade Cause greater than itself.

This is precisely why science did not—indeed, could not—emerge from Greek philosophy any more than it could have evolved within the dreary environs of philosophical naturalism. Men of science were, of necessity, also men of God. As committed to revelation as they were to reason.

Leonardo da Vinci, widely considered to be the real founder of modern science, was deeply committed to the light of revelation.[10] Robert Boyle, the father of modern chemistry as well as the greatest physical scientist of his generation, was an able apologist for the reality of revelation. Sir Isaac Newton, a prodigious intellect who developed calculus, discovered the law of gravity, and designed the first reflecting telescope, humbly bowed before the guiding principle of revelation. Louis Pasteur, well known for the process of pasteurization and for utterly demolishing the concept of spontaneous generation, underscored the power of revelation and undermined the evident absurdities of Darwinian predilections.

Other intellects gracing the doorway of science include Johannes Kepler (scientific astronomy), Francis Bacon (scientific method), Blaise Pascal (mathematician and philosopher), Carolus Linnaeus (biological taxonomy), Gregor Mendel (genetics), Michael Faraday (electromagnetics), and Joseph Lister (antiseptic surgery).

Rather than reveling in Dawkinsian[11] rhetoric and emotional stereotypes, such men were deeply committed to divine revelation and empirical science. As such, they not only unpacked revelations within the book of nature but were illumined by the light of biblical revelation.

BOOK OF KNOWLEDGE

As God has revealed his divine power and eternal nature within the book of nature, so, too, he has revealed his divine purposes through the book of knowledge. The Bible commences with the immortal words: "In the beginning God created the heavens and the earth" (Genesis 1:1) and continues with the revelation that the God who created the universe created humankind in his image and likeness (1:26). As such, humanity, in a finite way, shares God's communicable attributes, including personality, morality, and rationality. Such attributes in turn provide the capacity to enjoy fellowship with God and to develop meaningful relationships with one another. More to the point, they equip human beings to carry out the cultural mandate to "rule creation in such a way that it would come to realize its full potential."[12]

At first blush this may not seem earthshaking. Upon closer examination, it is transformational. Greek thinkers had little concept of forward progress. Aristotle, as noted, believed himself to be living during the climax of progress. Not so with Augustine, who held to the biblical maxim "It is the glory of God to conceal a matter; to search out a matter is the glory of kings" (Proverbs 25:2).

To search out that which God has concealed involves the faculty of reason. Reason itself, however, is singularly insufficient. While truth may be comprehended by reason, the fountainhead of truth is revelation. Without divine disclosure we are but blind men grasping at the trunk of the proverbial elephant.

My personal experience illustrates the point. When I was fourteen, my parents purchased an encyclopedia set called the *Book of Knowledge*. In it I discovered an evolutionary paradigm that dispensed with the need for a rational Creator who ordered the cosmos in accordance with his nature. In place of a Creator, the *Book of Knowledge* posited chance. Says biologist Jacques Monod, winner of the prestigious Nobel Prize, "Chance alone is at the source of every innovation, of all creation in the biosphere. Pure chance, absolutely free but blind, is at the very root of the stupendous edifice of evolution."[13]

It wasn't until I was twenty-nine that I realized such reasoning to be a departure from knowledge into a dangerous world of antiknowledge. What makes an Australian aborigine the equal of a Tiger Woods? Or what makes a human embryo the moral equivalent of President Obama? Or why suppose a woman to be the equal, much less the superior, of a man? Why not pontificate, as Darwin did, that man can attain "to a higher eminence, in whatever he takes up, than can woman—whether requiring deep thought, reason, or imagination, or merely the use of the senses and hands"?[14]

The answer is revelation. Reason sans revelation led scientists to postulate that blacks are inferior to whites and women inferior to men. Never reason informed by revelation. As God's book of knowledge reveals, we are created in the *imago Dei* ("image of God"—Genesis 1:27; Acts 17:29). And that makes all the difference in the world. The *imago Dei* ensures a Down syndrome child is afforded the same dignity given a distinguished scientist. The *imago Darwinii* leads in quite an opposite direction. This point is amplified by none other than the late Stephen Jay Gould, who observed that the highly regarded evolutionary notion of recapitulation (ontogeny recapitulates phylogeny) served as a basis for Dr. Down labeling Down syndrome "'Mongoloid idiocy' because he thought it represented a 'throwback' to the 'Mongolian stage' in human evolution."[15] As Gould points out, the term "'Mongoloid' was first applied to mentally defective people because it was then commonly believed that the Mongoloid race had not yet evolved to the status of the Caucasian race."[16]

Thankfully, Gould decried "recapitulation's responsibility for the racism of the post-Darwinian era."[17] As he puts it, "Recapitulation provided a convenient focus for the pervasive racism of white scientists; they looked to the activities of their own children for comparison with normal, adult behavior in lower races."[18]

For neo-Darwinians like Richard Dawkins, the *imago Dei* is little more than a troublesome myth. As such, a human being has no more intrinsic value than a banana. Nor is humanity the crowning jewel of God's creation. In time a far more sophisticated life form will supplant humankind, courtesy of the evolutionary paradigm. As hippos transitioned into whales, humans will inevitably transition into whatever. The fact that there is scant fossil evidence for this fundamentalist fervor seems of little consequence. Nor is molecular evidence to the contrary a stumbling block. His mind being darkened, Dawkins blindly swallows an ocean. Skin becomes impermeable to water; eye protection mechanisms appear like magic; as do changes in the brain, diving and emerging mechanisms, a respiratory system that prevents the bends, lactation system, sonar, and so on. Indeed Dawkins, enamored by reason sans revelation, has long ago departed the world of science and waded into an illusory land of science fiction.

The problem for Dawkins is that reason without revelation has left him impotent in the quest to read the book of nature for all its worth. Likewise, he is ill equipped to read God's book of knowledge. His fundamentalist reading of Scripture is simply breathtaking. Failing to recognize that Scripture is inspired literature, but literature nonetheless, he persists in pressing the language of the biblical text into a wooden, literal labyrinth.[19] Even worse, he perpetuates the false dichotomy between faith and reason.[20]

In truth, Western civilization was born out of reasonable faith. And because this is so, its revelations rightfully illumine and elucidate human reason. Moreover, revelation encapsulated within its pages leads us beyond the darkness of *imago Darwinii* and to the dignity of *imago Dei*.

BEGOTTEN OF FLESH

The ultimate expression of the *imago Dei* resides in the One begotten of flesh. To Epicurean and Stoic philosophers in Athens, this was the height of absurdity. The ruminations of an incoherent "babbler." To Muslim philosophers it was even worse. Blasphemous. God "begetteth not, nor is he begotten" (Sura 112:3). Thus Islam dogmatically denounces the Christian declaration of Christ's unique deity as the unforgiveable sin of *shirk*.

Modern thinkers are similarly persuaded. *New York Times* columnist Nicholas Kristof sees the incarnation as reflective of the way "American Christianity is becoming less intellectual and more mystical over time." "The heart is a wonderful organ," says Kristof, "but so is the brain."[21] Ironically, while smirking at incarnation, he swallows the odd predilection that nothing created everything.

Those who have a truly open mind resist following in this train. Miracles are not only possible, but they are necessary in order to make sense of the universe in which we live. According to modern science, the universe not only had a beginning, but it is unfathomably fine-tuned to support life. Not only so, but the origin of life, information in the genetic code, irreducible complexity of biological systems, and the phenomenon of the human mind pose intractable difficulties for merely natural explanations. Thus, reason forces us to look beyond the natural world to a supernatural Designer who intervenes in the affairs of his created handiwork. Which is precisely what incarnation entails.

The Apostle to the Gentiles captures the quintessence of revelation when he describes Christ as "the image of the invisible God" (Colossians 1:15). "For by him," says Paul, "all things were created: things in heaven and on earth, visible and invisible, whether thrones or powers or rulers or authorities; all things were created by him and for him. He is before all things, and in him all things hold together" (1:16–17). Not only that, but as Paul puts it, "God was pleased to have all his fullness dwell in him, and through him to reconcile to himself all things, whether things on earth or things in heaven, by making peace through his blood shed on the cross" (1:19–20).

This is the apex of divine revelation—God with us. As Christian scholars have ably communicated, the Infinite has progressively revealed himself in accordance with our finitude. Thus, prior to Immanuel the books of nature and knowledge revealed his glory. But in the incarnation, "We have seen his glory, the glory of the One and Only, who came from the Father, full of grace and truth" (John 1:14).

Remarkably, this glorious revelation, like the others, is apprehended through reason. Indeed, reason constrains us to believe. The one begotten of flesh demonstrated that he was God by manifesting the credential of sinlessness. While the Qur'an exhorts Muhammad to seek forgiveness for his sins, the Bible exonerates Messiah, saying Jesus "had no sin" (2 Corinthians 5:21). And this is not a singular statement. John declares, "And in him is no sin" (1 John 3:5), and Peter says Jesus "committed no sin, and no deceit was found in his mouth" (1 Peter 2:22). Jesus himself went so far as to challenge his antagonists, asking, "Can any of you prove me guilty of sin?" (John 8:46).

Jesus demonstrated supernatural authority over sickness, the forces of nature, fallen angels, and even death itself. *Matthew 4* records that Jesus went throughout Galilee teaching, preaching, "and healing every disease and sickness among the people" (4:23). *Mark 4* documents Jesus rebuking the wind and the waves saying, "Quiet! Be still!" (4:39). In *Luke 4* Jesus encountered a man possessed by an evil spirit and commanded the demon to "Come out of him!" (4:35). And in *John 4*, Jesus told a royal official whose son was close to death, "Your son will live" (4:50).

Ultimately, Jesus demonstrated power over death through the immutable fact of his resurrection. Christianity simply could not have survived an identifiable tomb containing the corpse of Christ. What happened as a result of the resurrection is unprecedented in human history. In the span of a few hundred years, a band of seemingly insignificant believers succeeded in turning an entire empire upside down. Not just through fierce devotion to the Great Commission but through faithful dedication to the Great Commandment. Put another way, not just by saving souls but by redeeming minds. As Charles Malik so ably puts it, "The problem is not only to win souls but to save minds. If you win the whole world and lose the mind of the world, you will soon discover you have not won the world. Indeed it may turn out that you have actually lost the world."[22]

So where does that leave us today? A day in which we stand in the shadow of the Bible; a day in which we yet benefit from its blessings but are blithely unaware of its source; a day in which we have more Bibles than at any other time in human history; a day in which you can go to church color-coordinated with your Bible and yet remain strangely unaware of what is divinely etched in its pages.

It leaves us on the cusp of a civilization that, like the Roman Empire, is either poised for ruin or ready for revival. And you, not pagans, are the deciding factor. Pagans adequately exercise their job description—that of being pagan. The question is, are you exercising your job description—that of being an ambassador for Christ? "We are therefore Christ's ambassadors," says Paul, "as though God were making his appeal through us" (2

Corinthians 5:20). Truth is, most of us have failed in our ambassadorial commission. We remain secret agents who have never blown our cover within a lost and dying empire.

You have just read a volume that answers the question *has God spoken?* in the affirmative. Our challenge is to build a lighthouse in the midst of the gathering darkness; to be change agents in the culture rather than a microcosm of the culture; to be transformed by the renewing of our minds rather than conformed to the culture.

Make no mistake: we will either drift into the spiritual malaise of a biblically bankrupt Europe, or we will experience revival like that of the persecuted church in China. You will ultimately be the difference-maker—not as an individual but as a member of the body of Christ.

My challenge to you is this: get into the Word and get the Word into you. Memorize, meditate, and mine the Bible for all its wealth. Stem the tide of darkness by ever being ready to provide proof of the Bible's divine inspiration.

Appendix:
The Legacy Reading Plan

If I live to be the age my father was when he died, I will have the privilege of reading through the Bible eighteen more times. If I live longer, so much the better! Reading through the Bible in one year at any age is a daunting proposition. Thus, the Legacy Reading Plan is strategically designed to empower you to "eat the elephant" one book at a time. The format is specifically formulated to make your time in God's Word the best it can be. Indeed, the acronym L-E-G-A-C-Y is a memorable reminder to make this next year a year of breakthrough.

LOCATION

Do you have a secret place—a location where you can drown out the static of the world and hear the voice of your heavenly Father as he speaks to you through the majesty of his Word? For some it may be the sauna; for others a study. We are all unique creations of God. Thus, your secret place may be a sedan. The point is, we all desperately need a place away from the invasive sounds of the world so we can hear the sounds of another place—another voice. So begin your Legacy Reading Plan by locating *your* secret place.

ESSENCE

The Legacy Reading Plan is unique in that it requires you to process books of the Bible rather than piecing together bits of books. The goal is to comprehend the essence God is communicating by reading each biblical book as a whole. The exceptions are Psalms and Proverbs. Psalms constituted a hymnbook or devotional guide for ancient Israel. Likewise, our goal will be to meditate on three individual psalms each week, thus progressing through the book of Psalms once each year. Because the book of Proverbs is replete with principles for successful daily living, the Legacy Reading Plan is one chapter of Proverbs each day, thus progressing through Proverbs once a month.

GENRE

To understand Scripture in the sense in which it is intended, it is important to pay special attention to the *genre* we are reading. In other words, to interpret the Bible as literature, it is crucial to consider the *kind* of literature we are interpreting. As a legal brief differs from a prophetic oracle, there is a difference in genre between Leviticus and Revelation. Genre is particularly significant when considering writings that are difficult to categorize, such as Genesis, which is largely a historical narrative interlaced with symbolism and repetitive poetic structure. During the spring the plan is to read through historical narratives, while the focus for the summer is prophecy.

AUTHOR

As it is essential to read through books rather than bits, so it is helpful to read biblical authors sequentially. As such, the Legacy Reading Plan is grouped by author. This is particularly helpful because even though biblical authors wrote "as they were carried along by the Holy Spirit" (2 Peter 1:21), their personalities and proclivities are clearly evident in their writings. For example, John, and John alone, identifies Jesus as the Word or Logos (John 1; Revelation 19). Likewise, John alone identifies Jesus as the true witness (John 5; Revelation 2), and it is John who most exploits the Mosaic requirement of two witnesses (John 8; Revelation 2).

CONTEXT

Context has an impact on how you contextualize one set of biblical books in relation to another. For this reason, the Epistles are read prior to the Synoptic Gospels in the Legacy Reading Plan. As such, the didactic (teaching) principles of the Epistles will provide a theological context by which you can better understand the gospel narratives. Moreover, because the book of Revelation draws heavily upon the imagery of the Hebrew prophets, the reading of Revelation is placed in close proximity to the Old Testament prophets. And because the Gospels recount the birth and ministry of Christ, the Synoptics and the book of Acts are assigned to the month of December.

YEAR

The overarching objective of the Legacy Reading Plan is to read through the Bible once a year, every year, for the rest of your life. The reading calendar is naturally segmented into seasons and the seasons into months. At the beginning of each year, you know that during the winter your focus will be on the Pentateuch and poetry (249 chapters); in the spring, the historical books (249 chapters); in the summer, the Prophets (250 chapters); and during the fall, the New Testament (260 chapters). Each season is further broken down into months. Thus every January your goal is to read through Genesis and Exodus and every December the Synoptic Gospels and Acts. There are times when you will naturally read ten chapters at a time and others when you will read one or two. More important, you will read the Bible just as you read other literature.

Legacy Reading Plan

HEBREW PENTATEUCH AND HEBREW POETRY

Winter (249 chapters)
Psalms—3 per week
Proverbs—1 chapter per day

January	February	March
Genesis	Leviticus	Job
Exodus	Numbers	Ecclesiastes
	Deuteronomy	Song of Solomon

HEBREW HISTORY

Spring (249 chapters)
Psalms—3 per week
Proverbs—1 chapter per day

April	May	June
Joshua	1 and 2 Kings	Ezra
Judges	1 and 2 Chronicles	Nehemiah
Ruth		Esther
1 and 2 Samuel		

HEBREW PROPHETS

Summer (250 chapters)
Psalms—3 per week
Proverbs—1 chapter per day

July	August	September	
Isaiah	Ezekiel	Hosea	Nahum
Jeremiah	Daniel	Joel	Habakkuk
Lamentations		Amos	Zephaniah
		Obediah	Haggai
		Jonah	Zechariah
		Micah	Malachi

NEW TESTAMENT

Fall (260 chapters)
Psalms—3 per week
Proverbs—1 chapter per day

October	November		December
John	Romans	1 and 2 Timothy	Matthew
1, 2, 3 John	1 and 2 Corinthians	Titus	Mark
Revelation	Galatians	Philemon	Luke
	Ephesians	Hebrews	Acts
	Philippians	James	
	Colossians	1 and 2 Peter	
	1 and 2 Thessalonians	Jude	

Notes

Introduction

1. See Bruce A. McDowell and Anees Zaka, *Muslims and Christians at the Table: Promoting Biblical Understanding Among North American Muslims* (Philipsburg, NJ: P&R Publishing, 1999), 73.
2. Quoted in Joseph Fielding Smith, ed., *The Teachings of the Prophet Joseph Smith* (Salt Lake City: Deseret Book Company, 1976), 194.
3. Journal of Oliver B. Huntington, page 168 of typed copy at Utah State Historical Society, quoted in Jerald Tanner and Sandra Tanner, *Introduction to 3,913 Changes in the Book of Mormon* (Salt Lake City: Utah Lighthouse Ministries, 1996).
4. McDowell and Zaka, *Muslims and Christians at the Table*, 41–42.
5. See Gary R. Habermas, *The Historical Jesus* (Joplin, MO: College Press, 1996), 143–70 (see especially 158); William Lane Craig's opening speech in *Will the Real Jesus Please Stand Up? A Debate Between William Lane Craig and John Dominic Crossan*, ed. Paul Copan (Grand Rapids: Baker Book House, 1998), 26–27.
6. Two DVDs I highly recommend for personal and group study on this issue are *The Bible vs. the Book of Mormon* DVD (Brigham City, UT: Living Hope Ministries, 2003), and *DNA vs. The Book of Mormon* DVD (Brigham City, UT: Living Hope Ministries, 2003), available through Christian Research Institute (www.equip.org).
7. Barack Obama, "News and Speeches: Call to Renewal Key Note Address," June 28, 2006, the transcript of which is available online at http://blog .beliefnet.com/stevenwaldman/2008/11/obamas-historic-call-to-renewa .html; the basic points cited are in slightly edited form in Barack Obama, *The Audacity of Hope: Thoughts on Reclaiming the American Dream* (New York: Vintage, 2006, 2008), 258.
8. See discussion in chapter 22 on pages 265–77.
9. Christopher Hitchens, *God Is Not Great: How Religion Poisons Everything* (New York: Twelve, 2007), 102.

10. Richard Dawkins, *The God Delusion* (New York: Houghton Mifflin Company, 2006), 31.

11. Ibid., 109.

12. Ibid., 136.

13. Bart D. Ehrman, *Misquoting Jesus: The Story Behind Who Changed the Bible and Why* (New York: HarperSanFrancisco, 2005), 9; emphasis in original.

14. Ibid., 10.

15. See, e.g., Bart D. Ehrman, *Jesus: Apocalyptic Prophet of the New Millennium* (New York: Oxford University Press, 1999), 130–31, 244–45; Bart D. Ehrman, *The New Testament: A Historical Introduction to the Early Christian Writings*, 3rd ed. (New York: Oxford University Press, 2004), 128–29.

16. Ehrman, *Misquoting Jesus*, 10.

17. Ibid., 12; emphasis in original.

18. Bart D. Ehrman, *Forged: Writing in the Name of God—Why the Bible's Authors Are Not Who We Think They Are* (New York: HarperOne, 2011), 5.

19. Ibid., 250.

20. Quoted in Cathleen Falsani, "The God Factor," *Chicago Sun-Times*, October 24, 2004, News 16.

21. *Larry King Live*, CNN, January 28, 2004.

22. *Politically Incorrect*, ABC, January 24, 2002.

23. Hank Hanegraaff, *The Face That Demonstrates the Farce of Evolution* (Nashville: Thomas Nelson, 1998).

24. Hank Hanegraaff, *Resurrection* (Nashville: W Publishing Group, 2000).

Part One: Manuscript C-O-P-I-E-S

1. Bart D. Ehrman, *Jesus, Interrupted: Revealing the Hidden Contradictions in the Bible (and Why We Don't Know About Them)* (New York: HarperOne, 2009), 6.

2. See Ehrman, *Jesus, Interrupted*, author bio, back inside flap.

3. Bart D. Ehrman, *Misquoting Jesus: The Story Behind Who Changed the Bible and Why* (New York: HarperSanFrancisco, 2005), 10.

4. Ibid., inside cover.

5. See discussion (and notes) in chapter 2 on pages 20–21.

6. Dan Vergano and Cathy Lynn Grossman, "Long-Lost Gospel of Judas Recasts 'Traitor,'" *USA Today*, April 6, 2006, http://www.usatoday.com/news/religion/2006-04-06-judas_x.htm (accessed March 17, 2011).

7. Ibid.

8. See "The Gospel of Judas," *National Geographic Channel*, aired April 16, 2006, http://channel.nationalgeographic.com/channel/gospelofjudas/index.html (accessed July 7, 2006). Also available at YouTube, "The Gospel of Judas, the Hidden Story of the Betrayal of Christ 6/8 (Dutch subs)," http://

www.youtube.com/watch?v=7KSQJwqkXFs; and YouTube, "The Gospel of Judas, the Hidden Story of the Betrayal of Christ 7/8 (Dutch subs)," http://www.youtube.com/watch?v=rWvH-s7r1GQ (accessed March 21, 2011).

9. Dan Brown, *The Da Vinci Code: A Novel* (New York: Doubleday, 2003); Michael Baigent, Richard Leigh, and Henry Lincoln, *Holy Blood, Holy Grail* (New York: Delacorte Press, 1982); William Klassen, *Judas: Betrayer or Friend of Jesus?* (Minneapolis: Fortress Press, 2004).

10. See Brown, *The Da Vinci Code*, 231ff.

11. Baigent, Leigh, and Lincoln, *Holy Blood, Holy Grail*; Michael Baigent, *The Jesus Papers: Exposing the Greatest Cover-Up in History* (New York: HarperSanFrancisco, 2006).

12. Quoted in Stacy Meichtry, "New Views of Judas Reflect New Views on Evil," Religion News Service, April 6, 2006, online at http://religionnews.com /ArticleofWeek040606.html (accessed December 18, 2006).

13. Funk was interviewed in *Peter Jennings Reporting: The Search for Jesus*, ABC, aired June 26, 2000.

14. Ehrman, *Misquoting Jesus*, 9–10.

15. Ehrman, *Jesus, Interrupted*, 7.

16. The apostle Paul affirmed that "all Scripture is inspired by God" (2 Timothy 3:16). The biblical doctrine of verbal plenary inspiration is that "God superintended the very choice of words in the Holy Volume so that it may be truly said to be entirely God's Word without admixture of human error." But God did so in such a way as to use and conserve the biblical authors' unique personalities and literary styles. (The quote is from R. Laird Harris, *Inspiration and Canonicity of the Scriptures*, revised edition [Greenville, SC: A Press, 1995], 12.)

Chapter 1: Copyist Practices

1. Paul D. Wegner, *A Student's Guide to Textual Criticism of the Bible* (Downers Grove, IL: IVP Academic, 2006), 140–42.

2. Kenneth L. Barker, "Copying the Old and New Testament Manuscripts," http://helpmewithbiblestudy.org/5Bible/TransCopyingTheOTNT Manuscripts_Barker.aspx (accessed March 17, 2011).

3. Dr. Craig Evans explains, "Prior to the discovery of the [Dead Sea Scrolls], the oldest complete Hebrew Bible was the Leningrad Codex, which dates to AD 1008. . . . It is easy to see why scholars were excited about the Scripture scrolls from the Dead Sea, for they date back to the first and second centuries BC and represent a large amount of the Hebrew [Old Testament]" (Evans, *Holman QuickSource Guide to the Dead Sea Scrolls*, 266, 267.) Evans's book is a fabulous introduction to the Dead Sea Scrolls.

4. See R. Laird Harris, *Can I Trust My Bible? Important Questions Often*

Asked About the Bible . . . with Some Answers by Eight Evangelical Scholars,
"How Reliable Is the Old Testament Text?" (Chicago: Moody Press, 1963),
124–25; compare Millar Burrows, *The Dead Sea Scrolls* (London: Secker
and Warburg, 1956), 303–14. Gleason Archer concurs: "Even though the
two copies of Isaiah discovered in Qumran Cave 1 near the Dead Sea
in 1947 were a thousand years earlier than the oldest dated manuscript
previously known (AD 980), they proved to be word for word identical with
our standard Hebrew Bible in more than 95 percent of the text. . . . The
five percent of variation consisted chiefly of obvious slips of the pen and
variations in spelling" (Gleason L. Archer Jr., *A Survey of Old Testament
Introduction*, revised and expanded [Chicago: Moody, 1994], 29).

5. Barker, "Copying the Old and New Testament Manuscripts."

6. Bruce M. Metzger, *The Text of New Testament: Its Transmission, Corruption,
and Restoration*, 3rd ed. (New York: Oxford University Press, 1992), 17–18.

7. My references in this volume to "fundamentalists on the left" have nothing
to do with politics.

8. Bart D. Ehrman, *Misquoting Jesus: The Story Behind Who Changed the Bible
and Why* (New York: HarperSanFrancisco, 2005), inside front cover.

9. Ibid., 207.

10. Ibid., 193.

11. Ibid., 194.

12. Ibid.; emphasis in original.

13. The alteration as depicted by Ehrman consists of three words, which are
found in two manuscripts. Another five manuscripts contain one of the
three variant words, increasing the ambiguity (see Donald A. Hagner, *Word
Biblical Commentary, vol. 33b: Matthew 14—18* [Dallas: Word Books, 1995],
825–26).

14. Quoted in Stacy Meichtry, "New Views of Judas Reflect New Views on Evil,"
Religion News Service, April 6, 2006, online at http://religionnews.com
/ArticleofWeek040606.html (accessed December 18, 2006).

15. Funk was interviewed on *Peter Jennings Reporting: The Search for Jesus*,
ABC, aired June 26, 2000.

16. John Dominic Crossan interviewed on *Peter Jennings Reporting: The Search
for Jesus*, ABC, aired June 26, 2000.

17. Ehrman, *Misquoting Jesus*, 10.

18. Ibid., inside cover.

19. Timothy Paul Jones explains that most variations consist of "differences
in spelling, word order, or the relationships between nouns and definite
articles—variants that are easily recognizable and, in most cases, virtually
unnoticeable in translations! For example, the Greek words for 'we' (*h meis*)
and the plural 'you' (*hymeis*) look similar, and copyists frequently confused
them. But does it ultimately matter whether 'you . . . are children of

promise' or 'we . . . are children of promise' (Galatians 4:28)?" (*Misquoting Truth: A Guide to the Fallacies of Bart Ehrman's* Misquoting Jesus [Downers Grove, IL: InterVarsity Press], 43.)

Chapter 2: Oral Culture

1. Bart D. Ehrman, *Jesus: Apocalyptic Prophet of the New Millennium* (New York: Oxford University Press, 1999), 52; cf. Bart D. Ehrman, *Jesus, Interrupted: Revealing the Hidden Contradictions in the Bible (And Why We Don't Know About Them)* (New York: HarperOne, 2009) 147.

2. Bart D. Ehrman, *Peter, Paul, and Mary Magdalene: The Followers of Jesus in History and Legend* (New York: Oxford University Press, 2006), 259.

3. C. S. Lewis forwarded his famous trilemma argument thusly: "I am trying here to prevent anyone saying the really foolish thing that people often say about Him: I'm ready to accept Jesus as a great moral teacher, but I don't accept His claim to be God. That is the one thing we must not say. A man who was merely a man and said the sort of things Jesus said would not be a great moral teacher. He would either be a lunatic—on the level with a man who says he is a poached egg—or else he would be the Devil of Hell. You must make your choice. Either this was, and is, the Son of God: or else a madman or something worse. You can shut Him up for a fool, you can spit at Him and kill Him as a demon; or you can fall at His feet and call Him Lord and God. But let us not come with any patronizing nonsense about His being a great human teacher. He has not left that open to us. He did not intend to" (*Mere Christianity* [New York: HarperCollins, 1952, 1980], 52).

4. Plato, *Phaedrus*.

5. Paul Barnett, *Jesus & the Rise of Early Christianity: A History of New Testament Times* (Downers Grove, IL: InterVarsity Press, 1999), 162.

6. Rainer Riesner, "Jesus as Preacher and Teacher," in *Jesus and the Oral Gospel Tradition*, ed. Henry Wansbrough (Sheffield: JSOT, 1991), 202.

7. Ibid.

8. Ibid., 203.

9. Ibid., 204.

10. Ibid., 205.

11. Scripture quotations are Ehrman's translation, Ehrman, *Jesus, Interrupted*, 51.

12. See Ehrman, *Jesus: Apocalyptic Prophet of the New Millennium*, 130–31; and Bart D. Ehrman, *The New Testament: A Historical Introduction to the Early Christian Writings*, 3rd ed. (New York: Oxford University Press, 2004), 128–29.

13. Ehrman mistakenly assumes that Luke is writing long after Mark, after the events of AD 70, and so is attempting to relieve Jesus of falsely prophesying that the high priest himself would remain alive to see the fulfillment of the

prophecy. But the "you" in the original Greek at Mark 14:62 is plural, so in no way should Christ's words be construed to require that the individual Caiaphas remain alive to see the prophesied events fulfilled; rather, it is sufficient that the generation at large that condemned Christ to death remain alive to see the events prophesied (Mark 13:30), which is precisely what happened in AD 70 with divine judgment on Israel through destruction of Jerusalem and the temple at the hands of the Roman general Titus.

Moreover, Luke could not expect his literal-minded Gentile readers to know that "coming on clouds" means having the sovereign authority of Yahweh himself and has nothing to do with physically riding on a moving cloud (though Ehrman should know this!). So, Luke simply omitted it, recognizing that its meaning is already captured in the readily understood allusion to Psalm 110:1. Luke often translates Jewish allusions for the sake of his Gentile audience. For another example, instead of the very Jewish, "When you see standing in the holy place 'the abomination that causes desolation,' spoken of through the prophet Daniel—let the reader understand—then let those who are in Judea flee to the mountains" (Matthew 24:15–16), Luke writes the Gentile-friendly, "When you see Jerusalem being surrounded by armies, you will know that its desolation is near. Then let those who are in Judea flee to the mountains" (Luke 21:20–21). New Testament historian N. T. Wright explains, "Luke (21.20) has cashed out the apocalyptic imagery in Matthew (24.15) and Mark (13.14) in terms of Jerusalem's being surrounded with armies. This for his gentile readers makes far more sense: faced with a cryptic allusion to Daniel, they would not be in a position to obey the command of Mark 13.14b, 'Let the reader understand.' Luke's reading of Mark is quite clear: all this language refers to the fall of Jerusalem, which is to be understood in terms of the scriptural background of the predicted destruction of Babylon" (N. T. Wright, *Jesus and the Victory of God* [Minneapolis: Fortress Press, 1996], 359).

14. For further discussion on the legitimacy of distinguishing the essential voice of Jesus from a literal transcription of Christ's spoken words (or from words made up out of whole cloth and attributed to Jesus), see Darrell L. Bock, "The Words of Jesus in the Gospels: Live, Jive, or Memorex?" in Michael J. Wilkins and J. P. Moreland, eds., *Jesus Under Fire* (Grand Rapids: Zondervan, 1995).

15. I first heard this metaphor from New Testament scholar N. T. Wright. If we are not conscious of the music of the Old Testament playing in the background as we play that of the New Testament, we will steep ourselves in cacophony. "Let him who has ears to hear . . ."

16. Ehrman insists that Acts 4:13 means that John, like Peter, was illiterate (*Misquoting Jesus*, 39). In truth, as Dr. Craig Blomberg explains in his review of Ehrman's book *Misquoting Jesus*, "One surprising factual error

occurs when Ehrman insists that Acts 4:13 means that Peter and John were illiterate (the term *agrammatos* "unlettered" in this context means not educated beyond the elementary education accessible to most first-century Jewish boys)." (Craig L. Blomberg, Review Entry # 0206 *Bart D. Ehrman. Misquoting Jesus: The Story Behind Who Changed the Bible and Why* in Richard S. Hess, ed., *Denver Journal: An Online Review of Current Biblical and Theological Studies*, vol. 9, 2006, at http://www.denverseminary.edu /article/misquoting-jesus-the-story-behind-who-changed-the-bible-and- why [accessed March 18, 2011].) Moreover, if Paul admonished Timothy to study the Scriptures (2 Timothy 2:15), *a fortiori* would the original apostles have devoted themselves to such study (cf. Acts 6:2).

17. Information and quote in this paragraph come from Gary R. Habermas, *The Historical Jesus: Ancient Evidence for the Life of Christ* (Joplin, MO: College Press, 1996), 153–54.

18. Gary R. Habermas and Antony G. N. Flew, *Did Jesus Rise from the Dead?* (San Francisco: Harper & Row, 1987), 86.

19. See William Lane Craig, *Reasonable Faith: Christian Truth and Apologetics*, 3rd ed. (Wheaton, IL: Crossway Books, 2008), 360ff. See also note 25 (this page).

20. Habermas, *The Historical Jesus*, 154; Craig, *Reasonable Faith*, 362.

21. Paul received this creed from the believing community (1 Corinthians 15:3), perhaps from Peter and James in Jerusalem (Galatians 1:18–19), if not sooner (see Habermas, *The Historical Jesus*, 155).

22. C. H. Dodd, "The Appearances of the Risen Christ: A study in the form criticism of the Gospels," in *More New Testament Studies* (Manchester: University of Manchester, 1968), 128; as quoted in Craig, *Reasonable Faith*, 379.

23. Ehrman, *Peter, Paul, and Mary Magdalene*, 259.

24. See Craig, *Reasonable Faith*, 379–80; Josephus, *Antiquities of the Jews*, 20:200.

25. Although legend can, under certain circumstances, emerge relatively quickly, the solid historical bedrock pertaining to Jesus persisted through the brief period from Jesus to the writing of not only Paul's letters but the canonical gospels. As the eminent New Testament scholar Richard Bauckham explains in his landmark work *Jesus and the Eyewitnesses*, "The Gospels were written within living memory of the events they recount." Moreover, says Bauckham, "Oral transmission is quite capable of preserving traditions faithfully, even across much longer periods than that between Jesus and the writing of the Gospels." Bauckham convincingly shows that the testimony of the eyewitnesses to the ministry and work of Jesus forms the solid ground on which the four canonical gospels are closely based, and that those eyewitnesses "remained accessible sources and authoritative guarantors of their own testimony throughout the period between Jesus and the writing of the Gospels" (Richard Bauckham, *Jesus and the Eyewitnesses: The Gospels as Eyewitness Testimony* [Grand Rapids: Eerdmans, 2006], 7, 240, 241). See

also Michael R. Licona, *The Resurrection of Jesus: A New Historiographical Approach* (Downers Grove, IL: IVP Academic, 2010), 584–85, 588–600, and the section on the historical bedrock pertaining to Jesus (277–463). Licona's massive book may well be the most important work on the resurrection and historiography today. For a lay-level treatment on legendary development, see Gary R. Habermas and Michael R. Licona, *The Case for the Resurrection of Jesus* (Grand Rapids: Kregel, 2004), 84–92. Another fine accessible work that offers a devastating critique of the Gnostic and apocryphal gospels as distortions of the historical record and demonstrates that the canonical gospels of Matthew, Mark, Luke, and John are not only reliable but are by far the best sources for understanding the historical Jesus is Craig A. Evans, *Fabricating Jesus: How Modern Scholars Distort the Gospels* (Downers Grove, IL: InterVarsity Press, 2006). For a brief, accessible article concerning approaches that critical scholars apply to the gospel texts, such as the criteria of authenticity, in order to demonstrate the reliability of the four biblical gospels, see Gary Habermas, "Recent Perspectives on the Reliability of the Gospels," *Christian Research Journal*, 28, 1 [2005]: 22–31, http://www.equip.org/PDF/JAR011.pdf (accessed March 21, 2011).

Chapter 3: Papyrus and Parchment

1. Bart D. Ehrman, *Misquoting Jesus: The Story Behind Who Changed the Bible and Why* (New York: HarperSanFrancisco, 2005), 11.
2. "According to Ibn Abbās, Muhammad said the black stone came down from Paradise and at the time of its descent it was whiter than milk, but that the sins of the children of Adam have caused it to be black, by their touching it" (Thomas Patrick Hughes, *Dictionary of Islam: A Cyclopedia of the Doctrines, Rites, Ceremonies, and Customs, Together with the Technical and Theological Terms of the Muslim Religion* [Chicago, IL: KAZI Publications, Inc., 1994], 154–55).
3. See the fascinating work in this area by Gary Habermas, "The Shroud of Turin and Its Significance for Biblical Studies," *Journal of the Evangelical Theological Society* 24.1 (1981): 47–54, http://works.bepress.com/gary_habermas/1; "Historical Epistemology, Jesus' Resurrection, and the Shroud of Turin," http://www.shroud.com/pdfs/habermas.pdf (both accessed March 22, 2011).
4. James R. White, *The King James Only Controversy: Can You Trust Modern Translations?* (Minneapolis, MN: Bethany House Publishers, 2009), 77–78.
5. This is the number I've had in my head for a while. But the actual number of extant Greek New Testament manuscripts is ever growing. As of January 2006, New Testament scholar Daniel Wallace documented 5,745 (J. Ed Komoszewski, M. James Sawyer, Daniel B. Wallace, *Reinventing Jesus: What*

the Da Vinci Code *and Other Novel Speculations Don't Tell You* [Grand Rapids: Kregel, 2006], 77). For an updated catalog of manuscripts, see the website of the Institute for New Testament Textual Research in Muenster, Germany, http://egora.uni-muenster.de/intf/institut/profil_en.shtml.

6. Most scholars date P52 from about AD 110 to 125. See, e.g., Philip W. Comfort, "Texts and Manuscripts of the New Testament," in *The Origin of the Bible*, ed. Philip Wesley Comfort (Wheaton, IL: Tyndale House Publishers, 1992), 179; Kurt Aland and Barbara Aland, *The Text of the New Testament: An Introduction to the Critical Editions and to the Theory and Practice of Modern Textual Criticism*, rev. ed., Erroll F. Rhodes, trans. (Grand Rapids: Eerdmans, 1989), 76. Most of the details I convey concerning the biblical manuscripts are found in Comfort, "Texts and manuscripts of the New Testament"; Komoszewski, Sawyer, and Wallace, *Reinventing Jesus*; and Bruce M. Metzger, *The Text of New Testament: Its Transmission, Corruption, and Restoration*, 3rd ed. (New York: Oxford University Press, 1992).

7. F. F. Bruce, *The Books and the Parchments: How We Got Our English Bible* (Grand Rapids: Revell, 1950), 178.

8. As noted, God preserved the written text of the New Testament through the church's practice of copying and widely distributing the manuscripts.

9. See Comfort, "Texts and Manuscripts of the New Testament."

10. See Ibid., 193.

11. See F. F. Bruce. *The Books and the Parchments* (Old Tappan, NJ: Fleming H. Revell Company, 1984), 168–69; F. F. Bruce, *The New Testament Documents: Are They Reliable?* (Grand Rapids: Wm. B. Eerdmans Publishing Co., 1981), 11; Bruce M. Metzger, *The Text of New Testament: Its Transmission, Corruption, and Restoration*, 3rd ed. (New York: Oxford University Press, 1992), 34; Komoszewski, Sawyer, Wallace, *Reinventing Jesus*, 106; Paul Barnett, *Is the New Testament Reliable? A Look at the Historical Evidence* (Downers Grove, IL: InterVarsity Press, 1986), 44–46; Paul D. Wegner, *A Student's Guide to Textual Criticism of the Bible* (Downers Grove, IL: IVP Academic, 2006), 40; Lee Strobel, *The Case for Christ: A Journalist's Personal Investigation of the Evidence for Jesus* (Grand Rapids: Zondervan, 1998), 60–61; Lee Strobel, *The Case for the Real Jesus: A Journalist Investigates Current Attacks on the Identity of Christ* (Grand Rapids: Zondervan, 2007), 83–84; note also that "Oxford's most important manuscript of classical philosophy is the Clarke Plato (MS. E. D. Clarke 39), the oldest surviving manuscript for about half of Plato's dialogues, which was acquired by the University in 1809: it was written in Constantinople in AD 895" (University of Oxford: Bodleian Philosophy Faculty Library, "Manuscripts and Rare Books," http://www.bodleian.ox.ac.uk/philosophy/collections/manuscripts [accessed March 21, 2011]).

12. The only known manuscript of the gospel of Judas is written in Coptic and is dated to c. AD 280. The circumstances surrounding its unveiling are suspicious, but it was probably discovered in Upper Egypt. See "The Gospel of Judas," National Geographic Channel, aired April 16, 2006. For a good analysis of the gospel of Judas, see N. T. Wright, *Judas and the Gospel of Jesus: Have We Missed the Truth About Christianity?* (Grand Rapids: Baker Book House, 2006).

13. Cf. Daniel B. Wallace, "The Gospel of John: Introduction, Argument, Outline," online at http://www.bible.org/page.asp?page_id=1328 (accessed July 7, 2006).

14. The early Church Fathers say Paul was martyred under Nero. Writing in the early fourth century, Eusebius cites Dionysius of Corinth (writing c. AD 170), Tertullian (writing c. AD 200), and Origen (writing c. AD 230–250). See Gary R. Habermas and Michael R. Licona, *The Case for the Resurrection of Jesus* (Grand Rapids: Kregel Publications, 2004), 56–59, 224; cf. Ben Witherington, *The Paul Quest: The Renewed Search for the Jew of Tarsus* (Downers Grove, IL: InterVarsity Press, 1998), 324–27.

15. Acts ends with Paul under house arrest in Rome. With the emphasis Luke puts on Paul's ministry in Acts, it is inexplicable that he did not record Paul's execution under Nero if Acts was written after Paul's death.

16. New Testament scholar Craig Blomberg offers this argument for the dating of Mark, Luke, and Acts in Craig L. Blomberg, *The Historical Reliability of the Gospels* (Downers Grove, IL: InterVarsity Press, 1987), 12–18; and in Lee Strobel, *The Case for Christ: A Journalist's Personal Investigation of the Evidence for Jesus* (Grand Rapids: Zondervan, 1998), 32–34.

17. See Leon Morris, *The First Epistle of Paul to the Corinthians: An Introduction and Commentary* (Leicester, England: InterVarsity Press, 1985), 31; John A. T. Robinson, *Redating the New Testament* (Eugene, OR: Wipf and Stock Publishers, 2000, previously published by SCM Press, 1976), 54; Bart D. Ehrman, *The New Testament: A Historical Introduction to the Early Christian Writings*, 3rd ed. (New York: Oxford University Press, 2004), 288.

18. John A. T. Robinson, *Redating the New Testament* (Eugene, OR: Wipf and Stock, 2000, originally published by SCM Press, 1976), 13.

19. These are not instances of the informal logical fallacy known as the argument from silence. Rather, the unacknowledged event in each case is so significant as to warrant the expectation of its being mentioned. Thus, these are instances of a cogent argument from significant or "pregnant" silence.

20. Even when fundamentalists on the left are forced to concede the historical reliability of New Testament accounts, they are prone to misinterpreting their historical meanings. As such, Professor Ehrman attributes apocalyptic sophistry to Jesus. Ehrman holds that the historical Jesus was an apocalyptic prophet who was not only mistaken but misguided in predicting that his

generation would experience the end of the world. Why? Because according to Ehrman the apocalyptic Jesus "urged his followers to abandon their homes and forsake families for the sake of the Kingdom that was soon to arrive. He didn't encourage people to pursue fulfilling careers, make a good living, and work for a just society for the long haul; for him, there wasn't going to be a long haul. The end of the world as we know it was already at hand." (Bart D. Ehrman, *Jesus: Apocalyptic Prophet of the New Millennium* [New York: Oxford University Press, 1999], 244).

In point of fact Jesus did not predict the end of the world within a generation! Rather Jesus was predicting an apocalypse now—within a generation the Jews would experience the destruction of their city and its temple. Thus, when Jesus told followers that within a "generation" they would see him "coming on the clouds of heaven," he was using an Old Testament judgment metaphor. While Ehrman seems oblivious to the import of Jesus' words, Caiaphas and the council that condemned Christ were not! Far from saying that the end of the world was at hand, Jesus employed the Old Testament symbolism of clouds to warn the council that just as judgment had fallen on Egypt, so, too, judgment would fall on Jerusalem (Matthew 24:34; 26:64).

Clouds were a common Old Testament symbol that pointed to God as the sovereign judge of the nations. For example, Isaiah writes, "See, the Lord rides on a swift cloud and is coming to Egypt" (19:1). Historical context should have been sufficient to ascertain that Jesus was not giving Caiaphas a dissertation on the end of the space/time continuum. Rather, Jesus was prophesying that those who would not bow the knee before the living Temple in their midst would experience the demolition of a physical temple that had become the object of their idolatry.

John made the point explicit in Revelation when he wrote, "Look, he is coming with the clouds, and every eye will see him, even those who pierced him" (Revelation 1:7). Caiaphas and the council would see Christ coming with the clouds as Judge of earth and sky. Christ was not saying the council would see him riding a cloud-chariot of sorts but that he would understand that Jesus was indeed who he claimed to be—"seeing" is an obvious metaphor for comprehension and understanding. As such, with the destruction of Jerusalem and the temple, they would understand that Jesus had indeed ascended to the right hand of power as the Judge of heaven and earth.

21. Quoted in John A. T. Robinson, *Redating the New Testament*, 360.
22. Conjoining the argument for the early dating of the New Testament with the argument from oral culture outlined in Chapter 2 (and notes) dramatically bolsters the historical credibility of the original New Testament writings (the words of which are well-conserved within the extant manuscripts).

Chapter 4: Internal Evidence

1. The first five books of the Bible are collectively known as the five books of Moses, the Torah ("law"), or Pentateuch ("five-volumed book").

2. Two DVDs I highly recommend for personal and group study on this issue are *The Bible vs. the Book of Mormon* DVD (Brigham City, UT: Living Hope Ministries, 2003), and *DNA vs. The Book of Mormon* DVD (Brigham City, UT: Living Hope Ministries, 2003), available through Christian Research Institute (www.equip.org).

3. See William M. Ramsay, *The Bearing of Recent Discovery on the Trustworthiness of the New Testament,* reprint ed. (Grand Rapids: Baker Book House, 1953); *St. Paul the Traveler and the Roman Citizen* (Grand Rapids: Baker Book House, 1962).

4. For more on the archaeological evidence for these pools, see chapter 8, pages 71–78.

5. Daniel B. Wallace, "The Gospel of John: Introduction, Argument, Outline," online at http://www.bible.org/page.asp?page_id=1328 (accessed July 7, 2006). For further discussion of the evidence that the apostle John is the author of the gospel of John, see Craig L. Blomberg, *The Historical Reliability of John's Gospel: Issues and Commentary* (Downers Grove, IL: InterVarsity Press, 2001), 22–41.

6. For further study concerning the gospel of Thomas, see Craig A. Evans, *Fabricating Jesus: How Modern Scholars Distort the Gospels* (Downers Grove, IL: InterVarsity Press, 2006), 52–77; and the relevant discussion in Gregory A. Boyd, *Cynic Sage or Son of God?* (Wheaton: BridgePoint, 1995). For more on the gospel of Judas, see Evans, *Fabricating Jesus,* 240–45; N. T. Wright, *Judas and the Gospel of Jesus: Have We Missed the Truth About Christianity?* (Grand Rapids: Baker Book House, 2006).

7. Simon Greenleaf, *The Testimony of the Evangelists: The Gospels Examined by the Rules of Evidence* (Grand Rapids: Kregel Classics, 1995; originally published 1874), 31–32.

8. See 1 Corinthians 15:5, where the original apostles, minus Judas, are referred to as the Twelve (which further evidences the very early date for this creed).

9. Contrast, for example, Mark 14:66–72 with Acts 2:14ff. Regarding the martyrdom of Peter, see Clement of Rome (c. AD 30–100), *First Epistle to the Corinthians,* chap. 5; Tertullian (c. AD 160–225), *On Prescription Against Heretics,* chap. 36; Eusebius (c. AD 260–340), *History of the Church,* Book 2:25; Book 3:1; in Book 3:1 Eusebius is quoting Origen (c. AD 185–254) concerning Peter's crucifixion.

10. Paul L. Maier, *In the Fullness of Time: A Historian Looks at Christmas, Easter, and the Early Church* (Grand Rapids: Kregel, 1991), 333–34. The late first-century or early second-century document *1 Clement* 5 tells us that Paul was beheaded during Nero's reign.

11. Ibid., 203–5; 218–20. Christian philosopher and apologist J. P. Moreland explains that animal sacrifices, keeping the Law, the Sabbath, non-Trinitarian monotheism, and the view of a human messianic political king who would deliver Jews from Gentile oppression and establish the Davidic kingdom without concept of a crucified (let alone rising) messiah formed the core beliefs of first-century Judaism, which were radically altered by the early Jewish church in the wake of the incomparable life, death, and resurrection of Jesus of Nazareth(J. P. Moreland, *Scaling the Secular City: A Defense of Christianity* [Grand Rapids, Baker Book House, 1987], 179–80).

12. William Lane Craig's opening speech in *Will the Real Jesus Please Stand Up? A Debate Between William Lane Craig and John Dominic Crossan*, ed. Paul Copan (Grand Rapids: Baker Book House, 1998), 26–27; William Lane Craig, "Did Jesus Rise from the Dead?" in eds. Michael J. Wilkins and J. P. Moreland *Jesus Under Fire* (Grand Rapids: Zondervan, 1995), 147–48.

13. Quoted in Lee Strobel, *The Case for Christ: A Journalist's Personal Investigation of the Evidence for Jesus* (Grand Rapids: Zondervan, 1998), 217–18; emphasis in original.

14. Bart Ehrman, *Jesus, Interrupted: Revealing the Hidden Contradictions in the Bible (and Why We Don't Know About Them)* (New York: Harper One, 2009), 8.

15. Scripture quotations are Ehrman's translation. Ehrman, *Jesus, Interrupted*, 41; emphasis added.

Chapter 5: External Evidence

1. See Gary R. Habermas, *The Historical Jesus* (Joplin, MO: College Press, 1996), 187–228 (esp. 224–28). Additionally, in evaluating the relative merits of the ancient Jewish and pagan references to Christ and his followers, the following are helpful: *Josephus: The Essential Works: A Condensation of* Jewish Antiquities *and* The Jewish War, trans. and ed. Paul L. Maier (Grand Rapids: Kregel, 1994); Robert E. Van Voorst, *Jesus Outside the New Testament: An Introduction to the Ancient Evidence* (Grand Rapids: Eerdmans, 2000); John P. Meier, *A Marginal Jew: Rethinking the Historical Jesus*, vol. 1 (New York: Doubleday, 1991), 56–111.

2. *Josephus: The Essential Works: A Condensation of* Jewish Antiquities *and* The Jewish War, trans. and ed. Paul L. Maier (Grand Rapids: Kregel, 1994), inside cover.

3. Ibid., 284.

4. Ibid., 269–70.

5. Maier translates the standard text of *Antiquities* 18:63 as follows: "About this time lived Jesus, a wise man, if indeed one ought to call him a man. For he was the achiever of extraordinary deeds and was a teacher of those who accept the truth gladly. He won over many Jews and many of the Greeks.

He was the Messiah. When he was indicted by the principal men among us and Pilate condemned him to be crucified, those who had come to love him originally did not cease to do so; for he appeared to them on the third day restored to life, as the prophets of the Deity had foretold these and countless other marvelous things about him. And the tribe of Christians, so named after him, has not disappeared to this day." (Ibid., 282.)

6. Ibid., 284; cf. Geza Vermes, "Jesus in the Eyes of Josephus," *Standpoint*, Jan/Feb 2010, http://www.standpointmag.co.uk/node/2507/full (accessed April 11, 2011).

7. Tacitus, *Annals* 15.44; emphasis added. Primary source information on Christ and Christianity in ancient Jewish and pagan writings can be found in C. K. Barrett, *The New Testament Background: Selected Documents* (New York: The Macmillan Company, 1957); Darrell L. Bock and Gregory Herrick, *Jesus in Context: Background Readings* (Grand Rapids: Baker Academic, 2005); *Josephus: The Essential Works*, Maier; and Van Voorst, *Jesus Outside the New Testament*.

8. Tacitus, *Annals* 15.44, emphasis added.

9. "Greekling" means Hadrian was enthralled with Greek culture.

10. Darrel L. Bock, *Studying the Historical Jesus: A Guide to Sources and Methods* (Grand Rapids: Baker Academic, 2002), 47–49.

11. *Twelve Caesars*, Nero 16.2.

12. *Twelve Caesars*, Claudius 25.4.

13. Pliny, *Letter to Trajan*, 96.

14. Ibid.

15. Habermas, *The Historical Jesus*, 198.

16. Pliny, *Letter to Trajan*, 96.

17. See "The Gospel of Judas," *National Geographic Channel*, aired April 16, 2006. For a good discussion concerning the gospel of Judas, see N. T. Wright, *Judas and the Gospel of Jesus: Have We Missed the Truth about Christianity?* (Grand Rapids: Baker Book House, 2006).

18. Van Voorst, *Jesus Outside the New Testament*, 58–64.

19. Ibid., 122–29.

20. Ibid., 104–20.

21. "How Firm a Foundation," words by John Rippon, 1787.

Chapter 6: Science of Textual Criticism

1. Eldon Jay Epp and Gordon D. Fee, *Studies in the Theory and Method of New Testament Textual Criticism* (Grand Rapids: William B. Eerdmans, 1993), 3.

2. James R. White, *The King James Only Controversy: Can You Trust Modern Translations?* (Minneapolis: Bethany House, 1995, 2009), 78; emphasis in original.

3. Ibid. See also the excellent discussion in J. Ed Komoszewski, M. James
    Sawyer, Daniel B. Wallace, *Reinventing Jesus: What the* Da Vinci Code *and
    Other Novel Speculations Don't Tell You* (Grand Rapids: Kregel, 2006), part 2.
4. Peter Ruckman, *The Christian's Handbook of Manuscript Evidence*
    (Pensacola: Pensacola Bible Press, 1990), 126; quoted in White, *The King
    James Only Controversy*, 28.
5. Bart D. Ehrman, *Misquoting Jesus: The Story Behind Who Changed the Bible
    and Why* (New York: HarperSanFrancisco, 2005), 10.
6. Philip Schaff, *Companion to the Greek Testament and the English Version*, 3rd
    ed. (New York: Harper, 1883), as quoted in Norman L. Geisler and William
    Nix, *A General Introduction to the Bible*, rev. ed. (Chicago: Moody, 1986), 474.
7. Archibald T. Robertson, *An Introduction to the Textual Criticism of the New
    Testament* (Nashville: Broadman, 1925), 22, as quoted in Geisler and Nix, *A
    General Introduction to the Bible*, 474.
8. White, *The King James Only Controversy*, 67. Komoszewski, Sawyer, and
    Wallace concur: "Although the quantity of textual variants among the New
    Testament manuscripts numbers in the hundreds of thousands, the *quality*
    of these variants as changes in meaning pales by comparison. Only about 1
    percent of the variants are both meaningful and viable. And . . . these do not
    affect foundational beliefs." Thus, they conclude, "First, there is virtually no
    need for conjecture about the original wording. That is, the wording of the
    original text is almost always to be found in the extant (remaining) copies.
    Second, any uncertainty over the wording of the original New Testament
    does not have an impact on major teachings of the New Testament. The
    deity of Christ certainly is not affected by this. There is simply no room for
    uncertainty about what the New Testament originally taught" (*Reinventing
    Jesus*, 63, 117; emphasis in original).
9. Bruce M. Metzger, *A Textual Commentary on the Greek New Testament*
    (Stuttgart, Germany: United Bible Societies, 1971), 716.
10. Quoted in White, *The King James Only Controversy*, 100.
11. Ibid., 102.
12. Metzger, *A Textual Commentary of the Greek New Testament*, 16–17.
13. Ehrman, *Misquoting Jesus*, 64.
14. Merrill C. Tenney, *The Gospel of John*, in *The Expositor's Bible Commentary*,
    vol. 9, Frank E. Gaebelein, gen. ed. (Grand Rapids: Zondervan, 1981), 89.
15. Craig L. Blomberg, *Jesus and the Gospels* (Nashville: Broadman & Holman,
    1997), 75.

Part Two: Archaeologist's S-P-A-D-E

1. *The Book of Mormon* (Salt Lake City: The Church of Jesus Christ of Latter-
    day Saints, 1987), introduction; emphasis added.

2. Ibid.
3. Ibid.
4. Ibid.
5. Ibid.
6. The claim that the Book of Mormon was written in "reformed Egyptian" is found in Mormon 9:32.
7. Paul L. Maier, "Archaeology: Biblical Ally or Adversary?" *Christian Research Journal* 27, 2 (2004), http://www.equip.org/PDF/DA111.pdf.
8. See William M. Ramsay, *The Bearing of Recent Discovery on the Trustworthiness of the New Testament*, repr. ed. (Grand Rapids: Baker Book House, 1953); *St. Paul the Traveler and the Roman Citizen* (Grand Rapids: Baker Book House, 1962).
9. Jeffrey L. Sheler, "Is the Bible True?" *U.S. News and World Report*, October 25, 1999, 58; reprinted from Jeffrey L. Sheler, *Is the Bible True?* (San Francisco: HarperSanFrancisco, 1999).
10. Jeffrey L. Sheler, *Is the Bible True?* (San Francisco: HarperSanFrancisco, 1999), 111.

Chapter 7: Steles and Stones

1. James K. Hoffmeier, "Out of Egypt," *Biblical Archaeology Review* (Jan/Feb 2007), online at http://members.bib-arch.org/publication.asp?PubID=BSBA&Volume=33&Issue=1&ArticleID=7 (accessed June 21, 2010).
2. J. Maxwell Miller and John H. Hayes, *A History of Ancient Israel and Judah* (Louisville, KY: Westminster John Knox Press, 1986), 78.
3. Thomas L. Thompson, *The Mythic Past: Biblical Archaeology and the Myth of Israel* (New York: Basic Books, 1999), 78.
4. Philip Davies, "The Intellectual, the Archaeologist and the Bible," in *The Land I Will Show You: Essays in Honor of J. Maxwell Miller*, ed. J. A. Dearman and M. P. Graham (Sheffield: JSOT Press, 2001), 247; as quoted in James K. Hoffmeier, *Ancient Israel in Sinai: The Evidence for the Authenticity of the Wilderness Tradition* (New York: Oxford University Press, 2005), 6.
5. Nahum M. Sarna, revised by Hershel Shanks, "Israel in Egypt: The Egyptian Sojourn and the Exodus," *Ancient Israel*, 1999, http://members.bib-arch.org/publication.asp?PubID=BSBKAI&Volume=0&Issue=0&ArticleID=2 (accessed June 21, 2010).
6. Sir Alan Gardiner, "The Geography of the Exodus," in *Recueil d'études égyptologiques dediées à la mémoire de Jean-François Champollion* (Paris: Bibliothèque de l'école des hautes études, 1922), 205; as quoted in Sarna and Shanks, "Israel in Egypt."
7. Sarna and Shanks, "Israel in Egypt."

8. Jeffrey L. Sheler, *Is the Bible True?* (New York: HarperSanFrancisco, 1999), 80.

9. Hoffmeier, as quoted in Kevin D. Miller, "Did the Exodus Never Happen?" *Christianity Today*, September 7, 1998, http://www.christianitytoday.com /ct/1998/september7/8ta044.html (accessed July 1, 2010).

10. Kevin D. Miller, "Did the Exodus Never Happen?" *Christianity Today*, September 7, 1998, http://www.christianitytoday.com/ct/1998 /september7/8ta044.html (accessed July 1, 2010).

11. *The Exodus Revealed: Searching for the Red Sea Crossing*, Questar Discovery Media Prod., 2002, DVD, cited in http://worldview3.50webs.com/exodus .html; cf. also discussion in John H. Walton, Victor H. Matthews, and Mark W. Chavalas, *The IVP Bible Background Commentary: Old Testament* (Downers Grove, IL: InterVarsity Press, 2000], 186.

12. Sheler, *Is the Bible True?* 81; cf. Exodus 2:10. "The name Moses is from the Egyptian *ms(w)*, meaning 'to beget.' . . . Wordplay occurs in that the closest Hebrew root means 'to draw out'" (John H. Walton, Victor H. Matthews, and Mark W. Chavalas, *The IVP Bible Background Commentary: Old Testament* [Downers Grove, IL: InterVarsity Press, 2000], 78).

13. Maier, "Archaeology: Biblical Ally or Adversary?"

14. Alfred J. Hoerth, *Archaeology and the Old Testament* (Grand Rapids: Baker Book House, 1998), 228.

15. Ibid.

16. Maier, "Archaeology: Biblical Ally or Adversary?"

17. Margaret S. Drower, *Flinders Petrie: A Life in Archaeology* (Madison, WI: University of Wisconsin Press, 1995), 221.

18. Daniel Lazare, "False Testament: Archaeology Refutes the Bible's Claim to History," *Harper's*, March 2002, 40, http://harpers.org /archive/2002/03/0079105.

19. Thomas L. Thompson, "On Reading the Bible for History: A Response," *Journal of Biblical Studies* 1:3 (2001), http://journalofbiblicalstudies.org /Issue3/Short_Study/on_reading_the_bible_for_history.htm (accessed June 30, 2010). Archaeologists Neil Asher Silberman and Israel Finkelstein write, "David and Solomon are such central religious icons to both Judaism and Christianity that the recent assertions of radical biblical critics that King David is 'no more a historical figure than King Arthur,' have been greeted in many religious and scholarly circles with outrage and disdain. Biblical historians such as Thomas Thompson and Niels Peter Lemche of the University of Copenhagen and Philip Davies of the University of Sheffield, dubbed 'biblical minimalists' by their detractors, have argued that David and Solomon, the united monarchy of Israel, and indeed the entire biblical description of the history of Israel are no more than elaborate, skillful ideological constructs produced by priestly circles in Jerusalem in post-exilic or even Hellenistic times" (Neil Asher Silberman and Israel

Finkelstein, *The Bible Unearthed: Archaeology's New Vision of Ancient Israel and the Origin of Its Sacred Texts* [New York: Touchstone, 2002], 128).

20. See, e.g., Kenneth A. Kitchen, "The Patriarchal Age: Myth or History?" *Biblical Archaeology Review* (March/April 1995), http://members.bib-arch .org/publication.asp?PubID=BSBA&Volume=21&Issue=2&ArticleID=3 (accessed July 1, 2010).

21. John Noble Wilford, "From Israeli Site, News of House of David," *New York Times*, August 6, 1993, http://www.nytimes.com/1993/08/06/world /from-israeli-site-news-of-house-of-david.html?scp=3&sq=Avraham%20 Biran&st=cse (accessed June 30, 2010).

22. Ibid.

23. Michael D. Lemonick, "Are the Bible's Stories True?" *Time*, June 24, 2001, http://www.time.com/time/printout/0,8816,133539,00.html (accessed June 30, 2010).

24. Ibid.

25. Wilford, "From Israeli Site, News of House of David."

26. Sheler, *Is the Bible True?* 61.

27. See William M. Ramsay, *St. Paul the Traveler and Roman Citizen*, ed. Mark Wilson (Grand Rapids: Kregel, 2001).

28. André Lemaire, "'House of David' Restored in Moabite Inscription," *Biblical Archaeology Review* (May/June 1994): 30–34, 36–37. http://members.bibarch .org/publication.asp?PubID=BSBA&Volume=20&Issue=3&ArticleID=2 (accessed June 30, 2010).

29. In what follows, I draw from the helpful discussion in Hoerth, *Archaeology and the Old Testament*, 306–10.

30. Hoerth, *Archaeology and the Old Testament*, 308.

31. Siegfried H. Horn, "Why the Moabite Stone Was Blown to Pieces," *Biblical Archaeology Review*, May/June 1986, http://members.bib-arch .org/publication.asp?PubID=BSBA&Volume=12&Issue=3&ArticleID=3 (accessed September 15, 2010).

32. Paul L. Maier, *In the Fullness of Time: A Historian Looks at Christmas, Easter, and the Early Church* (Grand Rapids: Kregel, 1991), 145. In what follows, I draw from Maier.

33. See Ibid., 146.

34. See Josephus, *Antiquities of the Jews*, 18:3.1.

35. Sheler, *Is the Bible True?* 112.

Chapter 8: Pools and Fools

1. Bart D. Ehrman, *Forged: Writing in the Name of God—Why the Bible's Authors Are Not Who We Think They Are* (New York: HarperOne, 2011), 5.

2. Ibid., 8.

3. Bart D. Ehrman, *Jesus, Interrupted: Revealing the Hidden Contradictions in the Bible (and Why We Don't Know About Them)* (New York: HarperCollins, 2010), 106, cf. 112–23. Ehrman writes, "We have numerous Gospels, letters, treatises, and apocalypses that claim to be written by people who did not write them. The authors who called themselves Peter, Paul, John, James, Philip, Thomas, or—pick your name!—knew full well they were not these people. They lied about it in order to deceive their readers into thinking they were authority figures. Some of these writings made it into the Bible. There are New Testament letters claiming to be written by Peter and Paul, for example, and James and Jude. But these books were written by other, unknown authors living after the apostles themselves had died" (*Forged*, 262).

4. See Ehrman, *Forged*, 55–56.

5. Ehrman, *Jesus, Interrupted*, 81.

6. Craig L. Blomberg, *The Historical Reliability of John's Gospel: Issues and Commentary* (Downers Grove, IL: InterVarsity Press, 2001), 23.

7. See endnote 16 (page 300) for chapter 2.

8. See fuller discussion against the claim that the New Testament is anti-Semitic in chapter 1 on pages 14–15.

9. See fuller discussion concerning the early dating of the New Testament in chapter 3 on pages 28–31.

10. Daniel B. Wallace, "The Gospel of John: Introduction, Argument, Outline," online at http://www.bible.org/page.asp?page_id=1328 (accessed March 24, 2011); see also John A. T. Robinson, *Redating the New Testament* (Eugene, OR: Wipf and Stock Publishers, 2000, originally published by SCM Press, 1976), 277–78.

11. Thomas H. Maugh II, "Biblical Pool Uncovered in Jerusalem," *Los Angeles Times*, August 9, 2005, A8.

12. Ibid.

13. See Hershel Shanks, "The Siloam Pool: Where Jesus Cured the Blind Man," *Biblical Archeology Review* 31, no. 5, Sep/Oct (2005): 16–23.

14. See Alfred J. Hoerth, *Archaeology and the Old Testament* (Grand Rapids: Baker Book House, 1998), 348–49; cf. Brian T. Arnold and Bryan E. Beyer, *Readings from the Ancient Near East* (Grand Rapids: Baker Academic, 2002), 146–47.

15. Hank Hanegraaff, *The Prayer of Jesus: Secrets to Real Intimacy with God* (Nashville: Thomas Nelson, 2001).

16. See Timothy McGrew and Lydia McGrew, "The Argument from Miracles: A Cumulative Case for the Resurrection of Jesus of Nazareth," in *The Blackwell Companion to Natural Theology*, William Lane Craig and J. P. Moreland, eds., (West Sussex, UK: Wiley-Blackwell, 2009), 600.

17. Ibid.

18. Shimon Gibson, *The Final Days of Jesus: The Archaeological Evidence* (New York: HarperCollins, 2009), 74–75.

Chapter 9: Assyrian Archaeology

1. The Assyrian captivity of the Northern Kingdom of Israel occurred in 722 BC. The Babylonian captivity of the Southern Kingdom of Judah began in 606 BC, with the destruction of Jerusalem and Solomon's temple in 586 BC.

2. See section on Sennacherib's prism in Bill T. Arnold and Bryan E. Beyer, *Readings from the Ancient Near East: Primary Sources for Old Testament Study* (Grand Rapids: Baker Academic 2002), 146–47.

3. Lucian of Samosata, *Charon or Seeing the Sights*, quoted in Magnus Magnusson, *Archaeology of the Bible* (New York: Simon and Schuster, 1977), 175.

4. There are three known hexagonal clay prisms celebrating Sennacherib's military campaigns dated to the early seventh century BC containing very similar inscriptions (Taylor's Prism, discovered in 1830 by Charles Taylor at Nineveh and housed in the British Museum; Sennacherib's Prism, Oriental Institute of Chicago; and the Jerusalem Prism, Israel Museum in Jerusalem). Additionally, fragments from eight other prisms thought to contain similar text have been discovered as well. For further information, see http://www.britishmuseum.org/explore/highlights/highlight_objects /me/t/the_taylor_prism.aspx (accessed March 24, 2011).

5. Quoted in Alfred J. Hoerth, *Archaeology and the Old Testament* (Grand Rapids: Baker Book House, 1998), 348.

6. See Arnold and Beyer, *Readings from the Ancient Near East*, 146–47.

7. Herodotus, *Histories* 2:141:5, online at http://old.perseus.tufts.edu /GreekScience/hdtbk2.html (accessed December 18, 2011).

8. Josephus, *Antiquities*, 10:1:5.

9. William W. Hallo and K. Lawson Younger, eds., *The Context of Scripture: Canonical Compositions from the Biblical World*, vol. 1 (Leiden: Brill Academic Press, 1997), 137, cited by Ralph W. Klein at http://fontes.lstc .edu/~rklein/Documents/Assins.htm.

10. Cited by Rusty Russell, Bible History Online, http://www.bible-history .com/empires/prism.html.

11. Ibid.

12. See "The Black Obelisk of Shalmaneser III," British Museum, http://www .britishmuseum.org/explore/highlights/highlight_objects/me/t/black_ obelisk_of_shalmaneser.aspx (accessed March 24, 2011).

13. Ibid.

14. James Orr, *The Problem of the Old Testament: Considered with Reference to Recent Criticism* (New York: Charles Scribner's Sons, 1906), 399.

15. Ibid., 398.
16. C. F. Keil and F. Delitzsch, *Commentary on the Old Testament in Ten Volumes*, vol. 7 (Grand Rapids: Eerdmans, 1976), 374 (vol. 1).
17. Ibid., 375.
18. James Maxwell Miller and John Haralson Hayes, *A History of Ancient Israel and Judah* (Louisville, KY: Westminster John Knox Press, 1986), 338.
19. Ibid.
20. Albert Ten Eycke Olmetead, *Western Asia in the Days of Sargon of Assyria* (Lancaster, PA: Press of the New Era Printing Company, 1908), 1.

Chapter 10: Dead Sea Scrolls

1. See Tacitus, *Histories* 1:2–3.
2. Josephus, *Jewish War* 6, in trans. and ed. Paul L. Maier *Josephus: The Essential Works* (Grand Rapids: Kregel, 1988), 371.
3. See the full dreadful account in Josephus, *Jewish War* 6.
4. Dr. Craig Evans, an expert on the Dead Sea Scrolls, thinks it wholly plausible the first Dead Sea Scrolls (DSS) were unearthed in the third century and that a second discovery may have taken place five or six centuries later: "It is certainly possible that Origen possessed a manuscript that belonged to the original group of DSS. The second discovery of DSS may have taken place in the late eighth or early ninth century. In a letter to Sergius, the bishop of Elam, Timotheus I, the Nestorian patriarch of Selucia, mentioned manuscripts found in a cave near Jericho. . . . Jericho was certainly more widely known than the defunct Qumran community, and so Timotheus may have chosen to mention Jericho in order to give Sergius a general idea of where the discovery had taken place. . . . In modern times, the first scroll was discovered in the late nineteenth century, not in the region of the Dead Sea but in a synagogue in Cairo Egypt. . . . The scroll discovered in the Cairo genizah became known as the Damascus Document" (Craig A. Evans, *Holman QuickSource Guide to the Dead Sea Scrolls* [Nashville: Holman Reference, 2010], 33–34).
5. Jeffrey L. Sheler, *Is the Bible True? How Modern Debates and Discoveries Affirm the Essence of the Scriptures* (New York: HarperSanFrancisco, 1999), 130.
6. Ibid., 134.
7. Evans, *Guide to the Dead Sea Scrolls*, 39.
8. My principal source for the information presented in this paragraph, as well as the information discussed within the purview of my S-I-G-N-S acronym, is Evans, *Guide to the Dead Sea Scrolls*.
9. See R. Laird Harris, *Can I Trust My Bible? Important Questions Often Asked About the Bible . . . with Some Answers by Eight Evangelical Scholars*,

"How Reliable Is the Old Testament Text?" (Chicago: Moody Press, 1963), 124–25; compare Millar Burrows, *The Dead Sea Scrolls* (London: Secker and Warburg, 1956), 303–14. Gleason Archer concurs: "Even though the two copies of Isaiah discovered in Qumran Cave 1 near the Dead Sea in 1947 were a thousand years earlier than the oldest dated manuscript previously known (AD 980), they proved to be word for word identical with our standard Hebrew Bible in more than 95 percent of the text. . . . The five percent of variation consisted chiefly of obvious slips of the pen and variations in spelling" (Gleason L. Archer Jr., *A Survey of Old Testament Introduction*, revised and expanded [Chicago: Moody, 1994], 29).

10. At 7'1" Shaq may have been even larger than Goliath!

11. Evans, *Guide to the Dead Sea Scrolls*, 272–73.

12. Ibid., 275.

13. Rabbi Tovia Singer, "Why Didn't the Red Ribbon on the Head of the Scapegoat Turn White in 30 C.E.?" http://www.outreachjudaism.org/like-a -lion.html (accessed August 9, 2010).

14. Michael L. Brown, *Answering Jewish Objections to Jesus*, vol. 3 (Grand Rapids: Baker Book House, 2003), 125.

15. Robert Jamison, A. R. Fausset, and David Brown, *A Commentary Critical, Experimental, and Practical on the Old and New Testaments*, vol. 3 (Grand Rapids: Wm. B. Eerdmans, 1973), 546.

16. Martin Luther, *Lectures on Genesis*. Philip Edgcumble Hughes notes, "According to Genesis 11, Abraham was a direct descendant of Shem, and Jerome considers it appropriate that in meeting his ancestor he should have paid him tithes and been blessed by him. This judgment is repeated in the commentators of the following centuries. Luther in his day describes it as 'the general opinion' which is founded on 'the general conviction of Hebrews.' 'Even though not much depends on whether their conviction is right or wrong,' he says, 'I gladly agree with their opinion.' The identification of Melchizedek with Shem pleases him, he adds, 'because there was no greater patriarch at the time, especially in spiritual matters'" (Philip Edgcumble Hughes, [Grand Rapids: Eerdmans, 1988], 244).

17. Ed Decker, *Decker's Complete Handbook on Mormonism* (Eugene, OR: Harvest House, 1995), 282. See Doctrine and Covenants 27:8–14.

18. Norman Geisler and Thomas Howe, *When Critics Ask: A Popular Handbook on Bible Difficulties* (Wheaton, IL: Victor, 1992), 47.

19. Evans, *Guide to the Dead Sea Scrolls*, 359.

20. Ibid., 360.

21. Ron Rhodes, *Christ Before the Manger: The Life and Times of the Preincarnate Christ* (Grand Rapids: Baker Book House, 1992, repr. Wipf and Stock, 2002), 248.

Chapter 11: *Epic of Gilgamesh*

1. Binary Spider, http://www.youtube.com/watch?v=KsmW-X1GWgk, YouTube (accessed March 22, 2011).

2. Bart D. Ehrman, *Jesus, Interrupted: Revealing the Hidden Contradictions in the Bible (and Why We Don't Know About Them)* (New York: Harper One, 2009), 10.

3. The notion that Mount Everest was 29,055 feet tall at the time of the Flood is false. Given the science of plate tectonics, it is clear that Everest is significantly higher today than it would have been at the time of the Flood.

4. In conveying the history of the discovery of the Epic, I draw from David Damrosch, "Epic Hero: How a Self-taught British Genius Rediscovered the Mesopotamian Saga of Gilgamesh—after 2,500 Years," *Smithsonian*, May 2007, http://www.smithsonianmag.com/history-archaeology /gilgamesh.html; see also The British Museum, "Austen Henry Layard (1817–94), archeologist," http://www.britishmuseum.org/explore /highlights/article_index/a/austen_henry_layard_1817-94.aspx; and The British Museum, "Hormuzd Rassam (1826–1910), archaeologist," http:// www.britishmuseum.org/explore/highlights/article_index/h/hormuzd _rassam_18261910.aspx.

5. Damrosch, "Epic Hero."

6. Ibid.

7. Ibid.

8. In addition to the epic itself, I consulted the following in composing the summary of the story: New World Encyclopedia, "Gilgamesh, Epic of," http://www.newworldencyclopedia.org/entry/Epic_of_Gilgamesh; Academy for Ancient Texts, "Epic of Gilgamesh," http://www.ancienttexts .org/library/mesopotamian/gilgamesh; Michael McGoodwin, "Epic of Gilgamesh: Summary" (2001, revised 2006), http://www.mcgoodwin.net /pages/otherbooks/gilgamesh.html (accessed August 19, 2010); and The British Museum, "The Flood Tablet, Relating Part of the Epic of Gilgamesh," http://www.britishmuseum.org/explore/highlights/highlight_objects/me/t /the_flood_tablet.aspx (accessed March 23, 2011).

9. Unless otherwise indicated, quotations of the Epic are from *The Ancient Near East*, vol. 1: *An Anthology of Texts and Pictures*, ed. James B. Pritchard (Princeton: Princeton University Press, 1958); and *Ancient Near Eastern Texts Relating to the Old Testament*, 3rd ed., James B. Pritchard, ed., (Princeton: Princeton University Press, 1969); both as quoted in Alfred J. Hoerth, *Archaeology and the Old Testament* (Grand Rapids: Baker Book House, 1998), 192–94.

10. Academy for Ancient Texts, "The Epic of Gilgamesh, Tablet XI, The Story of the Flood," http://www.ancienttexts.org/library/mesopotamian/gilgamesh /tab11.htm (accessed March 23, 2011).

11. I consulted the following helpful sources in comparing and contrasting the Epic with the biblical account: Alfred J. Hoerth, *Archeology and the Old Testament* (Grand Rapids: Baker Book House, 1998), 191–96 (Hoerth is particularly helpful); Nozomi Osanai, *A Comparative Study of the Flood Accounts in the Gilgamesh Epic and Genesis*, online at http://www .answersingenesis.org/home/area/flood/introduction.asp (accessed April 14, 2011); Gleason L. Archer, *A Survey of Old Testament Introduction*, revised and expanded (Chicago: Moody Press, 1994), 220–23; Howard Vos, *Baker Encyclopedia of the Bible*, vol. 2, ed. Walter A. Elwell (Grand Rapids: Baker Book House, 1988), 798–800; John Walton, *Chronological and Background Charts of the Old Testament* (Grand Rapids: Zondervan, 1994), 81. For helpful comments on the Genesis Flood, see C. F. Keil and F. Delitzsch, *Commentary on the Old Testament in Ten Volumes*, vol. 1 (Grand Rapids: Eerdmans, 1976), 140–50.

12. Hoerth, *Archeology and The Old Testament*, 196.

13. Michael D. Lemonick, "Are the Bible's Stories True? Archeology's Discoveries," *Time*, December 18, 1995, http://www.time.com/time /magazine/article/0,9171,983854-6,00.html (accessed March 23, 2011).

Part Three: Prophetic S-T-A-R-S

1. This quote is commonly attributed to Rudhyr and captures the essence of his teaching (see Dane Rudhyr, "The Birth Chart as a Celestial Message from the Universal Whole to an Individual Part," http://www.khaldea.com /rudhyar/astroarticles/celestialmessage.shtml [accessed March 24, 2011]).

2. Joyce Wadler, Angela Blessing, Dirk Mathison, Margie Bonnett Sellinger, "The President's Astrologers: The Reagans Have Been Sneaking Peeks at the Stars for a Long, Long Time," *People*, May 23, 1988, vol. 29, no. 2, http:// www.people.com/people/archive/article/0,,20099022,00.html (accessed March 24, 2011); cf. "Good Heavens! An astrologer dictating the President's schedule?" *Time*, May 16, 1988, http://www.time.com/time/magazine /article/0,9171,967389,00.html#ixzz1HUiBulZt (accessed March 24, 2011).

3. William Dyrness, "The Age of Aquarius," in Carl E. Armerding and W. Ward Gasque, eds., *A Guide to Biblical Prophecy* (Peabody, MA: Hendrickson Publishers, 1989), 19; see also William A. Dyrness, "Astrology," in William A. Dyrness and Veli-Matti Karkkainen, *Global Dictionary of Theology* (Downers Grove, IL: IVP Academic, 2008), 81.

4. Dyrness, "The Age of Aquarius," 19.

5. See Tom Harris, "How Nostradamus Works," http://science.howstuffworks .com/science-vs-myth/extrasensory-perceptions/nostradamus.htm (accessed February 2, 2010).

6. Ibid.

7. "False Prophecy," http://www.snopes.com/rumors/nostradamus.asp (accessed February 2, 2010).

8. This (false) prophecy is recorded in the book of Mormon scripture known as *Doctrine and Covenants* (130:12–17). For further study, see my booklet *The Mormon Mirage: Seeing Through the Illusion of Mainstream Mormonism* (Charlotte, NC: Christian Research Institute, 2008).

9. Ernest R. Sandeen, *The Roots of Fundamentalism: British and American Millenarianism 1800–1930* (Chicago: The University of Chicago Press, 1970), 51.

10. Hal Lindsey, *The Late Great Planet Earth* (Grand Rapids: Zondervan, 1970).

11. Dyrness, "The Age of Aquarius," 23.

12. John Walvoord, *Israel in Prophecy* (Grand Rapids: Zondervan, 1968), 107, 113–14, quoted in Timothy P. Weber, *On the Road to Armageddon: How Evangelicals Became Israel's Best Friend* (Grand Rapids: Baker Book House, 2004), 149; emphasis added.

13. Hal Lindsey with C. C. Carlson, *The Late Great Planet Earth* (Grand Rapids: Zondervan, 1970 [40th printing May 1974]), 110.

14. Tim LaHaye and Thomas Ice, *Charting the End Times* (Eugene, OR: Harvest House, 2001), 63.

15. Tim LaHaye and Jerry B. Jenkins, *Are We Living in the End Times?* (Wheaton: Tyndale, 1999), 146.

16. LaHaye and Ice, *Charting the End Times*, 58.

17. Hal Lindsey with C. C. Carlson, *The Late Great Planet Earth* (Grand Rapids: Zondervan, 1970), 53, 54.

18. The year 1948 plus forty years (a generation) equals 1988; minus a seven-year tribulation equals 1981 for the date of the "secret rapture."

19. Weber, *On the Road to Armageddon*, 173.

20. *Jack Van Impe Presents*, Trinity Broadcasting Network, May 30, 2007.

21. Ibid.

Chapter 12: Succession of Nations

1. Josephus, *Antiquities* 10:186.

2. *Antiquities*, 10.11.7. Cf. F. F. Bruce, *The Canon of Scripture* (Downers Grove, IL: InterVarsity Press, 1988), 32–36; James Patrick Holding, "The Authenticity of Daniel: A Defense," http://www.tektonics.org/af/danieldefense.html (accessed March 24, 2011).

3. For further defense of the sixth-century authorship of the book of Daniel, see chapter 14 on pages 153–54.

4. See Alfred J. Hoerth, *Archaeology and the Old Testament* (Grand Rapids: Baker Book House, 1998), 376–77.

5. For discussion concerning the dominance of Media within the Ancient Near

East at this time, see Robert J. M. Gurney, *God in Control: An Exposition of the Prophecies of Daniel* (Worthing, West Sussex, England: H. E. Walter Ltd., 1980, revised 2006), chapter 5; the 2006 revised version is available online at http://www.biblicalstudies.org.uk/book_god-in-control_gurney.html (accessed February 14, 2011); and John H. Walton, "The Four Kingdoms of Daniel," *Journal of the Evangelical Theological Society* 29.1 (1986): 25–36, http://www.biblicalstudies.org.uk/article_daniel_walton.html (accessed April 7, 2011).

6. In fleshing out my interpretation of Daniel's prophecies of the succession of four kingdoms (Babylon, Media, Medo-Persia, Greece), I am particularly indebted to R. J. M. Gurney, *God in Control.* Though I do not agree with Gurney at every point (e.g., the seventy weeks' prophecy of Daniel 9:24–27), I am convinced he is on the right track. Likewise, John H. Walton, "The Four Kingdoms of Daniel"; and C. Marvin Pate and Calvin B. Haines Jr., *Doomsday Delusions: What's Wrong with Predictions About the End of the World* (Downers Grove, IL: InterVarsity Press, 1995), 63–75. See also Milton S. Terry, *Biblical Hermeneutics: A Treatise on the Interpretation of the Old and New Testaments* (Grand Rapids: Academie Books Zondervan, repr., n.d.), 418–26; Milton S. Terry, *Biblical Apocalyptics: A Study of the Most Notable Revelations of God and of Christ in the Canonical Scriptures* (New York: Eaton and Mains, 1898; repr. Eugene, OR: Wipf and Stock, 2001), 181–212; F. W. Farrar, *The Book of Daniel* (London: Hodder and Stroughton, 1895). Though contra Terry and Farrar, as noted, I hold that the prophet Daniel wrote the book that bears his name in Babylon during the sixth century BC (see chapter 14).

7. See Gurney, *God in Control*, chapter 3, and Walton, "The Four Kingdoms of Daniel," 25–36.

8. See Delitzsch's discussion in C. F. Keil and F. Delitzsch, *Commentary on the Old Testament in Ten Volumes*, vol. 7 *Isaiah* (Grand Rapids: Eerdmans, 1976), 219 (second volume).

9. T. Cuyler Young Jr., "Cyrus," in *The Anchor Bible Dictionary*, vol. 1, ed. David Noel Freedman (New York: Doubleday, 1992), 1231.

10. Quote from the Cyrus cylinder, in Pierre Briant, trans. by Peter T. Daniels, *From Cyrus to Alexander: A History of the Persian Empire* (Winona Lake, IN: Eisenbrauns, 2002), 44.

11. Cf. A. R. Millard, "Persia," in *New Bible Dictionary*, ed. J. D. Douglas et al., 2nd ed. (Wheaton, IL: Tyndale, 1962), 914–16; and F. F. Bruce, *New Testament History* (New York: Doubleday-Galilee, 1980), 1–19.

12. *Josephus: The Essential Works: A Condensation of* Jewish Antiquities *and* The Jewish War, trans. and ed. Paul L. Maier (Grand Rapids: Kregel, 1994), 188 (*Antiquities* 11).

13. Ibid.

14. Ibid., 187.

15. Ashuruballit II, last king of the Assyrian Empire, reigned from Harran from 612 BC (fall of Nineveh) to 609. Haran, last capital of the Assyrian Empire, finally and fatally fell to the Babylonians in 609, marking the end of Assyrian supremacy.

16. C. F. Keil, *Biblical Commentary on the Book of Daniel*, in C. F. Keil and F. Delitzsch, *Commentary on the Old Testament in Ten Volumes*, vol. 9 (Grand Rapids: Eerdmans, 1976), 289. Elam was not only significant as the birthplace of King Cyrus, who founded the Medo-Persian Empire, but as the site of the future Persian palace.

17. Most of the details I convey concerning Alexander the Great are found in Curtius Rufus, *The History of Alexander*, trans. John Yardley (New York: Penguin, 2001); Peter Green, *Alexander of Macedon 356–323 B.C.: A Historical Biography* (Berkeley: University of California Press, 1992).

18. R. D. Milns, "Alexander the Great," in *The Anchor Bible Dictionary*, vol. 1, ed. David Noel Freedman (New York: Doubleday, 1992), 146.

19. Ezekiel's prophecies regarding Tyre can be accurately dated to the time of Nebuchadnezzar's final assault on Jerusalem (586)—twelve years after he had been taken to Babylon in 598.

20. Edward Robinson, *Biblical Researches in Palestine and the Adjacent Regions: A Journal of Travels in the Years 1838 & 1852* (London: John Murray, Albermarle Street, 1856), 463, online at http://books.google.com (accessed February 2, 2011).

21. For additional information on the history of Tyre, cf. Trudy Ring, Robert M. Salkin, Sharon La Boda, *International Dictionary of Historic Places: Middle East and Africa* (Chicago: Fitzroy Dearborn Publishers, 1996), 711ff.

22. Josephus, *The Essential Works*, trans. and ed. Maier, 202 (*Antiquities* 11:331).

23. Ibid.

24. Ibid., 202–3.

25. The battle of Ipsus (301 BC) was the most significant battle fought following the death of Alexander the Great. Antigonus Monophtalmus attempted to reunite the Greek Empire under his rule. His defeat at Ipsus spelled the end of a united Greek Empire and led to a fractured and brittle empire that in time would give way to Rome.

26. Alexander the Great did not have a plan of succession in place prior to his untimely death in 323 BC; thus, tremors of confusion rippled through the Greco-Macedonian Empire. Out of the chaos eventually emerged the Ptolemies in the south and the Seleucids in the north. The first of the ten horns spoken of by Daniel (7:7) was Seleucus I Nicator (Daniel 11:5) who began to rule in 312 c. BC. He was followed successively by six kings (Antiochus I Soter [280–261 BC], Antiochus II Theos [261–246 BC], Seleucus II Kallinikos [246–226 BC], Seleucus III Keraunos [226–223 BC],

Antiochus III the Great [223–187 BC], Seleucus IV Philopator [187–176 BC]; list comes from F. W. Farrar, *The Book of Daniel* [London: Hodder and Stroughton, 1895], 241). As R. Gurney explains, the next three were plucked up by the roots in startling fashion in fulfillment of Daniel 7:8: "While I was thinking about the horns, there before me was another horn, a little one, which came up among them; and three of the first horns were uprooted before it. This horn had eyes like the eyes of a human being and a mouth that spoke boastfully" (UPDATED NIV). Antiochus IV Epiphanes took control of the Seleucid Empire and proved to be not only the worst Jewish nightmare but spelled the beginning of the end of the Greek Empire (Gurney, *God in Control*, chapter 5).

27. Gleason L. Archer Jr., *Daniel*, in *The Expositor's Bible Commentary*, vol. 7, Frank E. Gaebelein, gen. ed. (Grand Rapids: Zondervan, 1985), 136.

28. The following insights may be instructive to those opting for a succession of nations from Babylon to Medo-Persia to Greece, culminating with the Roman Empire. First, Rome is never explicitly mentioned in the book of Daniel. Instead the empires explicitly dealt with are Babylon, Media, Persia, and Greece. Furthermore, the culmination of Daniel's concerns—the very thing that caused Daniel's face to turn pale (7:28), that exhausted him and caused him to become ill (8:27)—were prophecies concerning the Greek kingdom, culminating at "the time of the end" (8:17, 19; 11:35, 40; 12:4, 9) with "the abomination of desolation" (9:27; 11:31; 12:11 ; cf. 1 Maccabees 1:54) exacted upon Israel by the Syrian despot Antiochus IV Epiphanes, the "little horn" (7:8; 8:9). Finally, Daniel is clearly concerned with the succession of kingdoms from a singularly Jewish perspective. Thus he views fulfilled prophecy in much the same way that Jeremiah and Isaiah do. In Jeremiah 51:11 Babylon is overthrown by the Medes, not the Medo-Persians; likewise, in Isaiah 13:17–18 Babylon is overthrown by Medes, not Medo-Persians. Moreover, from the perspective of the book of Daniel, Darius the Mede is the successor of Babylon's kings—indeed, he is the one who threw Daniel into the lions' den. Even the great Cyrus was a Mede, while Persians are not spoken of independently of Media. Media is clearly seen within the book of Daniel as a kingdom unto itself that is subsumed by the much greater Persia at a later stage (Daniel 8:3).

29. A Jubilee era comprises "seven sabbaths of years" or "a period of forty-nine years," followed by the proclamation of "liberty throughout the land" in the fiftieth year—the year of Jubilee (Leviticus 25:8, 10).

Chapter 13: Typological Prophecy

1. I am especially indebted to two excellent articles concerning typological prophecy in general and the nature of the relationship between Isaiah 7:14 and Matthew 1:22–23 in particular: James M. Hamilton Jr., "The Virgin

Will Conceive: Typology in Isaiah and Fulfillment in Matthew, the Use of Isaiah 7:14 in Matthew 1:18–23," Tyndale Fellowship Biblical Theology Study Group July 6–8, 2005, online at http://www.swbts .edu/resources/SWBTS/Resources/FacultyDocuments/Hamilton /TheVirginWillConceive.7_19_05.pdf (accessed March 23, 2011); and Duane A. Garrett, "Type, Typology," in *Evangelical Dictionary of Biblical Theology*, ed. Walter A. Elwell (Grand Rapids: Baker Book House, 1996), 785–87.

2. K. J. Woollcombe, "The Biblical Origins and Patristic Development of Typology," in G. W. H. Lampe and K. J. Woollcombe, *Essays on Typology*, part of the Studies in Biblical Theology series (Naperville, IL: Alec R. Allenson, Inc., 1957), 40; emphasis in original.

3. Leonhard Goppelt, *Typos: the Typological Interpretation of the Old Testament in the New*, trans. Donald H. Madvid (Grand Rapids: Eerdmans, 1982), 18.

4. Ibid., 175.

5. E. Earle Ellis, "Foreword" to Goppelt, *Typos*, x.

6. R. C. H. Lenski, *Commentary on the New Testament: The Interpretation of St. Matthew's Gospel* (Peabody, MA: Hendrickson, repr. 2001, originally published 1943), 77.

7. Ibid., 78.

8. Ibid., 78–79; cf. Exodus 4:22.

9. Matthew traces his genealogy through David's son Solomon, while Luke traces his genealogy through David's son Nathan. It may be that Matthew's purpose is to provide the legal lineage from Solomon through Joseph, while Luke's purpose is to provide the natural lineage from Nathan through Mary. It could also be that Matthew and Luke are both tracing Joseph's genealogy—Matthew, the legal line, and Luke, the natural line. As such, the legal line diverges from the natural in that Levirate Law stipulated if a man died without an heir, his genealogy could legally continue through his brother (Deuteronomy 25:5–6). Obviously, the fact that there are a number of ways to resolve dissimilarities rules out the notion that the genealogies are contradictory. For further study, see Craig L. Blomberg, *Jesus and the Gospels* (Nashville: Broadman & Holman, 1997), 199, 207–8.

10. Lenski, *Commentary on the New Testament: The Interpretation of St. Matthew's Gospel*, 81–82.

Chapter 14: Abomination of Desolation

1. See David Ireson, "Ploughboy Notes: "The Gospel Truth," The Tyndale Society website, http://www.tyndale.org (accessed April 14, 2011).

2. See "The Life of William Tyndale," http://www.tyndale.org/; cf. Paul Jackson, "William Tyndale: Victoria Embankment Gardens," http://www .tyndale.org/TSJ/2/jackson.html (accessed April 14, 2011).

3. Cf. "The Life of William Tyndale," http://www.tyndale.org.

4. Desiderius Erasmus and Martin Luther, *Discourse on Free Will*, trans. Ernst F. Winter (New York: Continuum, 2006), 96; cf. R. C. Sproul, "The Word of God in the Hands of Man," *Tabletalk*, April 1, 2009, http://www.ligonier .org/learn/articles/word-god-hands-man (accessed April 7, 2011).

5. Bart D. Ehrman, *Jesus: Apocalyptic Prophet of the New Millennium* (New York: Oxford University Press, 1999), x; emphasis added.

6. Ibid., 159–60.

7. See, e.g., Ezekiel 32:7 (judgment on Egypt); Joel 2:10, 31; Amos 5:18–20 (judgment on Israel); Zephaniah 1:14–18 (judgment on Judah).

8. Bertrand Russell, *Why I Am Not a Christian: and other essays on religion and related subjects*, ed. Paul Edwards (New York: Simon and Schuster, 1957), 16. Russell also wrote that "there are a great many texts [in the Gospels] that prove" that Jesus believed he would return within the lifetime of his original hearers, but he cites only two: "I tell you the truth, you will not finish going through the cities of Israel before the Son of Man comes" (Matthew 10:23), and "I tell you the truth, some who are standing here will not taste death before they see the Son of Man coming in his kingdom" (Matthew 16:28; cf. Luke 9:27). Other texts Russell might have had in mind include: "And so upon you will come all the righteous blood that has been shed on earth, from the blood of righteous Abel to the blood of Zechariah son of Berekiah, whom you murdered between the temple and the altar. I tell you the truth, all this will come upon this generation" (Matthew 23:35–36); "I tell you the truth, this generation will certainly not pass away until all these things have happened" (Matthew 24:34); and "But I say to all of you: In the future you will see the Son of Man sitting at the right hand of the Mighty One and coming on the clouds of heaven" (Matthew 26:64).

There is no question that the Lord Jesus indicates in these passages that at least some of his disciples as well as enemies would remain alive until the prophesied events unfolded. What Russell missed through his negligent dismissal of Scripture was a correct understanding of what Jesus actually predicted would happen within the near future: not his bodily return to earth in the second coming but his coronation as the true King by his death, resurrection, and ascension to the right hand of God, the manifestation of his kingdom through the power of the Holy Spirit, and climactically his vindication in the judgment on unbelieving Israel in the destruction of Jerusalem and the temple (AD 70).

Russell and others, such as C. S. Lewis, who have struggled with the implications of such passages of Scripture, are also cited in Gary DeMar, *Last Days Madness: Obsession of the Modern Church* (Atlanta: American Vision, 1999, 4th rev. ed.), 46–49; and R. C. Sproul, *The Last Days According to Jesus: When Did Jesus Say He Would Return?* (Grand Rapids: Baker Book House, 1998), 12–13.

9. Albert Schweitzer, *Out of My Life and Thought: An Autobiography* (New York: Henry Holt and Company, 1933), 7.

10. George B. Caird, *Jesus and the Jewish Nation* (London: Athlone Press, 1965), 22; quoted in N. T. Wright, *Jesus and the Victory of God*, vol. 2, *Christian Origins and the Question of God* (Minneapolis: Fortress, 1996), 341.

11. See 1 Maccabees 1–4; 2 Maccabees 4–5.

12. Malchus Porphyry, *Against the Christians* from Attalus, "Porphyrius: Comments on Daniel," http://www.attalus.org/translate/daniel.html (accessed March 24, 2011).

13. Bruce M. Metzger and Roland E. Murphy, eds., *The New Oxford Annotated Bible* (New York: Oxford University Press, 1991), 1126OT.

14. Cf. Wilhem Barcher, "Synagogue, The Great," *Jewish Encyclopedia*, http://www.jewishencyclopedia.com/view.jsp?artid=1214&letter=S (accessed March 24, 2011).

15. *Josephus: The Essential Works: A Condensation of* Jewish Antiquities *and* The Jewish War, trans. and ed. Paul L. Maier (Grand Rapids: Kregel, 1994), 202 (*Antiquities* 11:331).

16. Moreover, in a sweeping statement recorded in Matthew 23:35 and also Luke 11:51 in which he refers to the "first and last murders recounted in the Old Testament," Jesus attests to the same canon we know as our Old Testament Scriptures (Kaiser, *The Old Testament Documents*, 38).

17. Gerhard F. Hasel, "The Book of Daniel and Matters of Language: Evidences Related to Names, Words, and the Aramaic Language," *Andrews University Seminary Studies* 19, no. 3 (1981): 215, http://www.auss.info/auss_publication_file.php?pub_id=632&journal=1&type=pdf (accessed November 23, 2010). See W. F. Albright, *From Stone Age to Christianity*, 2nd ed. (New York: Johns Hopkins Press, 1957), 337; E. M. Yamauchi, *Greece and Babylon* (Grand Rapids: Baker Book House, 1967), 94; Gleason L. Archer Jr., *A Survey of Old Testament Introduction*, rev. ed. (Chicago: Moody Press, 1994), 431.

18. See Hasel, "The Book of Daniel and Matters of Language," 212.

19. Daniel 2:47 and 4:8–9 reflect Nebuchadnezzar's words that Daniel's God is the "God of gods"; for Darius's confession, see Daniel 6:26–27; concerning Cyrus, see *Josephus: The Essential Works: A Condensation of* Jewish Antiquities *and* The Jewish War, Paul L. Maier, trans. and ed. (Grand Rapids: Kregel, 1994), 188 (*Antiquities* 11:1); and regarding Alexander the Great, see *Josephus: The Essential Works*, Maier, 202 (*Antiquities*, 11:331).

20. See Robert J. M. Gurney, *God in Control: An Exposition of the Prophecies of Daniel* (Worthing, West Sussex, England: H. E. Walter Ltd, 1980, revised 2006), chapter 3; the 2006 revised version is available online at http://

www.biblicalstudies.org.uk/book_god-in-control_gurney.html (accessed February 14, 2011). Historical information concerning the Seleucid kings found in J. C. McCann Jr., "Seleucus," in Geoffrey W. Bromiley, ed., *The International Standard Bible Encyclopedia*, vol. 4 (Grand Rapids: Eerdmans, 1988), 385–86; John Whitehorne, "Seleucus," in David Noel Freedman, ed., *The Anchor Bible Dictionary*, vol. 5 (New York: Doubleday, 1992), 1076–77.

21. The image of the little horn appears only in Daniel 7 and 8. The temptation is to presuppose that the little horn in chapter 7 refers to someone different from the one depicted in chapter 8, which is almost universally recognized as Antiochus. Exegetically, however, both "little horn" images refer to the same person; and because chapter 8 so clearly refers to Antiochus, then so must chapter 7. Indeed, I think the plain and natural reading of the text should lead any rational reader to the same conclusion. What prevents many from embracing this conclusion is the preconception that the Roman Empire (or revived Roman Empire) must be in view (see discussion in Gurney, *God in Control*, chapter 4, http://www.biblicalstudies.org.uk/pdf/gic/chapter-4.pdf; cf. John E. Goldingay, "The Book of Daniel: Three Issues," *Themelios*, 2, 2, [1977], 45–49, http://s3.amazonaws.com/tgc-documents/journal-issues/2.2_Goldingay.pdf [accessed April 15, 2011], though I disagree with Goldingay's second-century BC dating for the book of Daniel).

22. John Goldingay compares Daniel 8:13–14 and Daniel 9:24: "A coherent understanding of [Daniel 9:24] emerges, then, if we take it as a restatement of the visionary promises of chapter 8. Like that vision, it looks forward from the time of Daniel himself to the Antiochene crisis, and promises God's deliverance. There is no reason to refer it [9:24] exegetically to the first or second coming of Christ" (John E. Goldingay, *Daniel*, Word Biblical Commentary, vol. 30 [Dallas: Word, 1989], 260).

23. Emil Schürer, *The History of the Jewish People in the Age of Jesus Christ*, vol. 1, revised by Geza Vermes, Fergus Millar, and Matthew Black (Edinburgh, Scotland: T&T Clark, 1973), 150.

24. Ibid., 151.

25. Ibid., 151–52.

26. I.e., "abomination of desolation" (see Brenton's translation in Sir Lancelot Charles Lee Brenton, *The Septuagint with Apocrypha: Greek and English* (Peabody, MA: Hendrickson Publishers, 1986 [originally published by Samuel Bagster & Sons, Ltd., London, 1851]).

27. Josephus, *Antiquities*, in Paul L. Maier, trans. and ed., *Josephus: The Essential Works* (Grand Rapids: Kregel, 1988), 212 (*Antiquities* 12:265).

28. Ibid., 213 (*Antiquities* 12:327).

29. A quick Google search reveals many examples.

30. Jim Combs, "The Olivet Discourse," in Tim LaHaye, gen. ed., *Tim LaHaye Prophecy Study Bible* (Chattanooga, TN: AMG Publishers, 2000), 1039.

31. I should note that the warning passages in Hebrews must be read in light of the entire book of Hebrews in order to see that they are largely warnings against returning to the types and shadows of the old covenant. Hebrews was written to Jewish believers who in the midst of suffering doubted the sufficiency of Christ's atoning sacrifice for sin and were being tempted to separate from the larger body of Christ and to return to the Judaism of unbelieving Israel.

Chapter 15: Resurrection Prophecies

1. Deborah Hastings, "Scientists Find Fountain of Youth . . . in Mice," November 29, 2010, aolnews.com, http://www.aolnews.com/2010/11/29 /scientists-find-fountain-of-youth-in-mice (accessed March 24, 2011).
2. S. Jay Olshansky, Leonard Hayflick, and Bruce A. Carnes, "No Truth to the Fountain of Youth," *Scientific American*, December 29, 2008, online, http:// www.scientificamerican.com/article.cfm?id=no-truth-to-the-fountain-of -youth (accessed March 24, 2011).
3. Philip Yancey, *Where Is God When It Hurts?* (Grand Rapids: Zondervan, 1977), 247. I recommend this book to anyone struggling with pain.
4. R. C. H. Lenski, *Commentary on the New Testament: The Interpretation of the Epistle to the Hebrews and of the Epistle of James* (Peabody, MA: Hendrickson, repr., 2001 [1966]), 402.
5. See Gary R. Habermas, *The Historical Jesus* (Joplin, MO: College Press, 1996), 143–70 (esp. 158); William Lane Craig's opening speech in *Will the Real Jesus Please Stand Up? A Debate Between William Lane Craig and John Dominic Crossan*, ed. Paul Copan (Grand Rapids: Baker Book House, 1998), 26–27.
6. The following medical data and descriptions concerning Christ's fatal torment adapted from C. Truman Davis, "The Crucifixion of Jesus: The Passion of Christ from a Medical Point of View," *Arizona Medicine* (March 1965): 183–87; and William D. Edwards, Wesley J. Gabel, and Floyd E. Hosmer, "On the Physical Death of Jesus Christ," *Journal of the American Medical Association* (March 21, 1986): 1455–63.
7. Quoted in Gary R. Habermas, *The Historical Jesus* (Joplin, MO: College Press, 1996), 71.
8. See Habermas, *The Historical Jesus*, 72–74.
9. John A. T. Robinson, *The Human Face of God* (Philadelphia: Westminster, 1973), 131, quoted in William Lane Craig's opening address in *Will the Real Jesus Please Stand Up?* 27. And as scholar D. H. Van Daalen has noted, "It is extremely difficult to object to the empty tomb on historical grounds; those who deny it do so on the basis of theological or philosophical assumptions" (William Lane Craig, "Contemporary Scholarship and the

Historical Evidence for the Resurrection of Jesus Christ," *Truth* 1 [1985]: 89–95, from the Leadership University website at http://www.leaderu. com/truth/1truth22.html; see William Lane Craig, "Did Jesus Rise from the Dead?" in Michael J. Wilkins and J. P. Moreland, eds., *Jesus Under Fire* [Grand Rapids: Zondervan, 1995], 152).

10. Information in this paragraph comes from William Lane Craig's opening address in Copan, ed., *Will the Real Jesus Please Stand Up?* and Craig, "Did Jesus Rise from the Dead?" in Wilkins and Moreland, eds., *Jesus Under Fire*, 146–49.

11. See Craig S. Keener, *The IVP Bible Background Commentary: New Testament* (Downers Grove, IL: InterVarsity Press, 1993), 210. See Luke 8:1–3.

12. William Lane Craig as interviewed by Lee Strobel in Lee Strobel, *The Case for Christ: A Journalist's Personal Investigation of the Evidence for Jesus* (Grand Rapids: Zondervan, 1998), 217–18.

13. *Nelson's New Illustrated Bible Dictionary*, Ronald F. Youngblood, gen. ed., (Nashville: Thomas Nelson Publishers, 1995), 1318.

14. See William Lane Craig, *Reasonable Faith: Christian Truth and Apologetics*, 3rd ed. (Wheaton, IL: Crossway Books, 2008), 367–69.

15. The points in this paragraph come from Craig, "Did Jesus Rise from the Dead?" in Wilkins and Moreland, eds., *Jesus Under Fire*, 146–53.

16. The points in this paragraph come from Habermas, *The Historical Jesus*, 152–57; and Craig, *Reasonable Faith*, 362.

17. See 1 Corinthians 15:6. Paul received this creed from the believing community (15:3), perhaps from Peter and James in Jerusalem (Galatians 1:18–19), if not sooner (see Habermas, *The Historical Jesus*, 155).

18. See Acts 22:3–4; 26:1–32; 1 Corinthians 11:16–33. *1 Clement* 5 tells us that Paul was beheaded during Nero's reign. For further study, see Paul L. Maier, *In the Fullness of Time: A Historian Looks at Christmas, Easter, and the Early Church* (Grand Rapids: Kregel, 1991), 333–34.

19. See Craig, *Reasonable Faith*, 379–80; Josephus, *Antiquities of the Jews*, 20:200.

20. See Gary R. Habermas, "Explaining Away Jesus' Resurrection: Hallucination—the Recent Revival of Theories," *Christian Research Journal* 23:4 (2001), online http://www.equip.org/PDF/DJ923.pdf (accessed March 24, 2011).

21. Norman Perrin, *The Resurrection According to Matthew, Mark, and Luke* (Philadelphia: Fortress, 1977), 80, as quoted in William Lane Craig's opening address in Copan, ed., *Will the Real Jesus Please Stand Up?* 28.

22. See 1 Corinthians 15:5, in which the original apostles, minus Judas, are referred to as the Twelve (cf. John 20:24).

23. Cf. J. P. Moreland, *Scaling the Secular City: A Defense of Christianity* (Grand Rapids, Baker Book House, 1987), 179–80. See also note 11, page 307.

Chapter 16: Superstar ABCs

1. A note of caution concerning the Messianic fulfillment of Genesis 49:10 is in order here. Although this prophecy was indeed fulfilled in Jesus Christ, many Christian apologists forward an urban legend to make the case. The story line is something like this. Not until just after the birth of Christ were the Jews for the first time denied self-governance, including the authority to exercise capital punishment. Not recognizing that the young Christ was already in their midst, the Jews mourned that the scepter had departed prior to the coming of Messiah. Thus the prophecy of Genesis 49:10 had apparently been falsified. In support of this claim, various versions of the following quote from an ancient Jewish Rabbi named Rachmon pop up in books, sermons, and Internet postings: "When the members of the Sanhedrin found themselves deprived of their right over life and death, a general consternation took possession of them; they covered their heads with ashes, and their bodies with sackcloth, exclaiming: 'Woe unto us, for the scepter has departed from Judah and the Messiah has not come.'"

   Although a few cite Josephus's *Antiquities of the Jews* (without a specific reference), most apologists who forward this quote cite the Babylonian Talmud as the source (e.g., "Babylonian Talmud chapter 4:37" or "Babylonian Talmud, San. Chpt. 4, Fol. 37, recto"; Google "Rabbi Rachmon" for a plethora of examples). It turns out that the quote is not found in either the works of Josephus or the Babylonian Talmud.

   Jewish scholar Dr. Michael Brown explains that "the passage simply doesn't exist in the Talmud, let alone in the alleged location in Talmudic tractate Sanhedrin." Moreover, says Brown, "Rabbi Rachmon appears to be a creation as well! Citing him would be like talking about the famous 19th century preacher Charles Sturgood or the like." Well, then, whence came the quote? "Allegedly, from the learned missionary named Raymundus Martini, who, writing in Latin, sometimes cited Talmudic or rabbinic passages not extant in our current editions (or any known edition), and in a rare case of a textual variant, it's possible he had a valid text in front of him. But *if* he claimed this text existed, it was simply a forged text that he found, with no basis historically or textually whatsoever" (personal e-mail correspondence dated February 8, 2011).

   The reality is that it is not necessary to resort to "bibliographic ghosting" in order to demonstrate the fulfillment of Jacob's prophetic blessing over his fourth son, namely, that the scepter would not depart from Judah until Messiah came (for discussion of the meaning of "Shiloh" in Genesis 49:10, see C. F. Keil and F. Delitzsch, *Commentary on the Old Testament*, vol. I [Grand Rapids: Eerdmans, reprinted 1976], 393–400). Through his first advent and exaltation, Jesus Christ fulfilled the prophecy. Judah had not decisively lost ruling authority prior to the coming of

Christ—Judah's loss of power during the Babylonian exile was only temporary (Ezekiel 21:24–27; cf. Zechariah. 6:9–14)—but from the point of view of those who blindly refuse to submit to the lordship of Christ, the first-century judgment of destruction on Jerusalem must indeed represent a decisive departing of the scepter. Moreover, as "the Lion of the tribe of Judah" (Revelation 5:5; cf. Hebrews 7:14), the risen and exalted Christ reigns forever over all creation, and "the obedience of the nations is his" (Genesis 49:10), as multiplied millions of believers from around the globe submit to his lordship.

The lesson from this is clear. In a day in which Internet lies travel halfway round the world before truth has had a chance to put its boots on, we must all consciously heed the command of the apostle: "Test everything. Hold on to the good" (1 Thessalonians 5:21; cf. Acts 17:11). If we will learn to read the Bible for all its worth, titillating stories that have no foundation in reality will not seduce us away from the pure Word of Truth. Rather, the halcyon beauty of the Holy Bible will enthrall and equip us to stand "alert and of sober mind," able to resist the wiles of the evil one, who "prowls around like a roaring lion looking for someone to devour" (1 Peter 5:8 UPDATED NIV).

2. See discussion of this prophecy in chapter 13 on pages 138–40.

3. Paul Barnett, *Is the New Testament Reliable? A Look at the Historical Evidence* (Downers Grove, IL: InterVarsity Press), 119.

4. See *Peter Jennings Reporting: The Search for Jesus*, ABC, aired June 26, 2000; Bart D. Ehrman, *Jesus, Interrupted: Revealing the Hidden Contradictions in the Bible (and Why We Don't Know About Them)* (New York: Harper One, 2009), 32. Robert Funk dogmatically asserts, "Caesar Augustus was the Roman emperor from 27 BCE. to 14 C.E. There is no evidence that he decreed a census of the 'whole civilized world' during his tenure, although the Romans did enroll the non-citizens of individual provinces for tax purposes and military service as circumstances warranted" (Robert Funk, *The Acts of Jesus: What Did Jesus Really Do?* [New York: HarperSanFrancisco, 1998], 520).

5. Josephus, *Antiquities* 18.1.1–2.

6. Paul Maier, interview on the *Bible Answer Man* broadcast November 12, 1999. Dr. Maier further explained, "Quirinius took a census in AD 6 rather than at the time of Christmas, and critics say Luke made a bad error here [in Luke 2:2]. We're not sure that he did. It could be a translation problem. The first reading ideally would be that this is the *first* census when Quirinius is governor of Syria, in which case we're ten years off. However, the word *protos* in Greek can also be translated as follows: 'This was *before* that census taken by Quirinius that everyone knew about.' That's one translation. The one I prefer is, 'This census was *first completed* when Quirinius was governor of Syria.'"

7. See William M. Ramsay, *The Bearing of Recent Discovery on the Trustworthiness of the New Testament*, repr. ed. (Grand Rapids: Baker Book House, 1953); William M. Ramsay, *St. Paul the Traveller and the Roman Citizen* (Grand Rapids: Baker Book House, 1962).

8. Paul L. Maier, *In the Fullness of Time: A Historian Looks at Christmas, Easter, and the Early Church* (Grand Rapids: Kregel, 1991), 4–5.

9. Ibid., 4–5.

10. Marcus Borg interview in *Peter Jennings Reporting: The Search for Jesus*, ABC, aired June 26, 2000.

11. Philip Schaff, *History of the Christian Church*, vol. 2 (Grand Rapids: Eerdmans, 1994), 251; cf. J. D. Douglas, gen. ed., *The New International Dictionary of the Christian Church*, rev. ed. (Grand Rapids: Zondervan, 1978), 516.

12. Douglas, *New International Dictionary of the Christian Church*, 607.

13. Ibid., 756.

14. Maier, *In the Fullness of Time*, 164.

15. Curtius Rufus, *The History of Alexander*, trans. John Yardley (New York: Penguin, 2001), 61.

16. Josepheus, *Antiquities*, 12:242.

17. Cf. Maier, *In the Fullness of Time*, 164–67; J. B. Torrance, *New Bible Dictionary*, ed. J. D. Douglas et al. (Wheaton, IL: Tyndale, 1982), 254; Richard P. Bucher, "Crucifixion in the Ancient World," http://www .orlutheran.com/html/crucify.html; Kaufmann Kohler and Emil G. Hirsch, "Crucifixion," *Jewish Encyclopedia*, http://www.jewishencyclopedia.com /view.jsp?artid=905&letter=C.

18. See FEAT discussion, pages 175–85 in this book. For a more thorough discussion, see my book *Resurrection* (Nashville: W Publishing Group, 2000).

19. F. Delitzsch, *Psalms*, in C. F. Keil and F. Delitzsch, *Commentary on the Old Testament in Ten Volumes*, vol. 5 (Grand Rapids: Eerdmans, 1976), 306 (vol. 1).

20. Ibid., 307–8 (vol. 1).

21. I encourage you to read Isaiah 52:13–53:12 and then go back and read Isaiah 40–55 as a whole to see the progression of thought concerning the identity of the Servant. In 49:3 the Servant is Israel. In 50:4–9 the Servant appears to be the individual prophet. In 49:5–6 the Servant is to bring the knowledge of Israel's God to the nations. Yet in 52:13–53:12, Duane Garrett observes, the Servant "suffers and dies vicariously for the sins of the world but is ultimately vindicated and exalted." What's going on? Garrett explains the typological nature of this prophecy: "Isaiah is not speaking of any one individual but of the ideal of the servant of the Lord. That ideal may have its fulfillment corporately (in Israel) or individually (in, for example, the prophets), but the

ultimate and complete fulfillment is in Christ himself. Thus, not everyone who might be legitimately called a 'servant of the Lord' fulfills every aspect of these prophecies; only Messiah can atone for the sins of the world. Even so, anyone who with patience endures hardship and persecution for God's sake and carries on the task of proclaiming God's message to the nations is properly a 'servant of the Lord' and fulfills this prophecy." In light of this understanding, we can comprehend the apostle Paul's statement, "I fill up in my flesh what is still lacking in regard to Christ's afflictions, for the sake of his body, which is the church. I have become its servant by the commission God gave me to present to you the word of God in its fullness" (Colossians 1:24–25). Thus, as Garrett concludes, this way of reading Isaiah "does not diminish but rather enhances the glory of Christ as the ultimate fulfillment of Servant Songs" (Duane A. Garrett, "Type, Typology," in *Evangelical Dictionary of Biblical Theology*, Walter A. Elwell, ed. [Grand Rapids: Baker Book House, 1996], 786).

22. John Whitacre eloquently sums up the typological view: "Jesus' own life, including his death and resurrection, is the primal pattern that Scripture itself replicates. He is the sun whose rays create shadows both backward and forward in time. Accordingly, he not only fulfills Scripture in the sense of replicating its patterns, he brings Scripture itself to completion by being its central referent" (Rodney A. Whitacre, *John* [Downers Grove, IL: InterVarsity Press, 1999], 462).

23. See Isaiah 53:10–11. The Old Testament sacrifices, including the sin offering (Leviticus 4:1–5:13; 6:24–30; 8:14–17; 16:3–22), the guilt or trespass offering (5:14–6:7; 7:1–6), and the Passover Lamb (Exodus 12) find explicit fulfillment in Christ (e.g., John 1:29; 1 Corinthians 5:7; Ephesians 5:2; Hebrews 9:13–14; 10:10; 12:24; 13:10; 1 Peter 1:2). See Delitzsch's discussion in Keil and Delitzsch, *Commentary on the Old Testament in Ten Volumes*, vol. 7 (second volume).

24. See Exodus 12:46, Numbers 9:12, and Psalm 34:20, recognizing, of course, that in writing, "the scripture would be fulfilled" (John 19:36), the apostle John has in mind a typological interpretation of these passages.

25. "The End of the World Is Almost Here! Holy God Will Bring Judgment Day on May 21, 2011" (Oakland, CA: Family Radio, 2009), 1. Camping also made false predictions concerning the return of Jesus Christ in 1994 (cf. Hank Hanegraaff, "D-Day Declarations," *Christian Research Journal*, 18, no. 2 [1995]: 54 [http://www.equip.org/articles/john-hinkle], and Stephen C. Meyers, "Harold Camping: 1994?" *Christian Research Journal*, 16, no. 3 [1994]:45 [http://www.equip.org/articles/harold-camping-1994-]), and has made the cultic proclamation that the Church Age has ended and that Christians need to flee their churches and fellowship around his teachings (see James White, "Dangerous Airwaves: Harold Camping's Call to Flee the Church," *Christian Research Journal*, 25, no. 1 [2002]: 20–25, 41–43,

[http://www.equip.org/articles/harold-camping] and Gretchen Passantino, "Camping's New Book Continues His Rejection of the Church," *Christian Research Journal*, 25, no. 3 [2003]: 57 [http://www.equip.org/articles /the-end-of-the-church-age-and-after]).

26. "The End of the World Is Almost Here!" 1, 3, emphasis in original.

27. Ibid., 4.

28. Ibid., 5; emphasis in original.

29. *Jack Van Impe Presents*, Trinity Broadcasting Network, May 30, 2007.

30. Some readers may have noticed a proverbial elephant in the room. Namely, I have not used Daniel's "seventy weeks" prophecy to prove that Jesus is the Christ (Daniel 9:24–27). This despite the fact that many apologists view this prophecy as predicting the exact year, even the very day, of Christ's presentation of himself as Israel's Messiah, and therefore consider it to be among the strongest proofs of Christ's identity we have in our apologetic arsenal. The problem here, however, is that there is little agreement among biblical exegetes concerning the seventy-weeks prophecy. To begin with, the Hebrew of these four verses is among the most difficult of the entire Old Testament to translate—note the extensive footnotes containing alternative renderings associated with this passage in most modern translations, and compare and contrast, say, the Revised Standard Version's rendering with that of the New International Version. Other points of contention among interpreters include determining which of the plethora of starting and ending dates for the seventy weeks best fit the data; whether the weeks of "years" should be 365-day solar years, 360-day lunar years, or some other time configuration; and the identity of the figure who "confirm[s] a covenant with many for one week" (Daniel 9:27 NKJV). Moreover, though the New Testament voluminously cites Old Testament prophecies fulfilled in Jesus as evidence that he is indeed the Christ, as F. W. Farrar observes, "Neither our Lord, nor His Apostles, nor any of the earliest Christian writers once appealed to the evidence of this prophecy, which . . . would have been so decisive! If such a proof lay ready to their hand—a proof definite and chronological—why should they have deliberately passed it over, while they referred to other prophecies so much more general, and so much less precise in dates?" (F. W. Farrar, *The Book of Daniel* [London: Hodder and Stroughton, 1895], 287). With this in mind, recall the discussion (and notes) in chapter 14 under the subsection, "The Abomination That Causes Desolation Spoken of Through Daniel," pages 153–62.

To gain an appreciation for how difficult the seventy-weeks prophecy is to interpret, especially in light of the book of Daniel as a whole, compare and contrast the relevant expositions found in the following: C. Marvin Pate and Calvin B. Haines Jr., *Doomsday Delusions: What's Wrong with Predictions About the End of the World* (Downers Grove, IL: InterVarsity

Press, 1995); F. W. Farrar, *The Book of Daniel* (London: Hodder and Stoughton, 1895); Edward J. Young, *The Prophecy of Daniel: A Commentary* (Eugene, OR: Wipf and Stock, 1998, originally published 1949); Milton S. Terry, *Biblical Apocalyptics: A Study of the Most Notable Revelations of God and of Christ in the Canonical Scriptures* (Eugene, OR: Wipf and Stock Publishers, 2001); Gary DeMar, *Last Days Madness: Obsession of the Modern Church*, 4th ed. (Atlanta: American Vision, 1999); Robert J. M. Gurney, *God in Control: An Exposition of the Prophecies of Daniel* (Worthing, West Sussex, England: H. E. Walter Ltd, 1980, revised 2006); the 2006 revised version is available online at http://www.biblicalstudies.org.uk/book_god-in-control_gurney.html (accessed February 14, 2011); Richard L. Pratt Jr., "Hyper-Preterism and Unfolding Biblical Eschatology," in Keith A. Mathison, ed., *When Shall These Things Be? A Reformed Response to Hyper-Preterism* (Phillipsburg, NJ: P & R, 2004); J. Dwight Pentecost, *Things to Come: A Study in Biblical Eschatology* (Grand Rapids: Zondervan, 1958).

31. David W. Pao and Eckhard J. Schnabel, "Luke," in G. K. Beale and D. A. Carson, eds., *Commentary on the New Testament Use of the Old Testament* (Grand Rapids: Baker Academic, 2007), 288.
32. In the Qur'an see 40:55; 47:19; 48:1–2.
33. E. Earle Ellis, "Foreword" to Leonhard Goppelt, *Typos: the Typological Interpretation of the Old Testament in the New*, trans. Donald H. Madvid, (Grand Rapids: Eerdmans, 1982), x.

Part Four: Scriptural L·I·G·H·T·S

1. Barack Obama, "News and Speeches: Call to Renewal Key Note Address" June 28, 2006, the transcript of which is available online at http://blog.beliefnet.com/stevenwaldman/2008/11/obamas-historic-call-to-renewa.html; the basic points cited are in slightly edited form in Barack Obama, *The Audacity of Hope: Thoughts on Reclaiming the American Dream* (New York: Vintage, 2006, 2008), 258.
2. Christopher Hitchens, *God Is Not Great: How Religion Poisons Everything* (New York: Twelve, 2007), 102.
3. Richard Dawkins, *The God Delusion* (New York: Houghton Mifflin, 2006), 31.
4. *Larry King Live*, CNN, January 28, 2004.
5. Ibid.

Chapter 17: Literal Principle

1. Bart D. Ehrman, *Jesus, Interrupted: Revealing the Hidden Contradictions in the Bible (and Why We Don't Know About Them)* (New York: Harper One, 2009), 13.
2. Ibid., 13–14.

3. Ibid., 6.
4. R. C. Sproul, *Knowing Scripture* (Downers Grove: InterVarsity Press, 1977), 48; emphasis added.
5. Ehrman, *Jesus, Interrupted*, 6–7.
6. Both Greek words *chronos* and *kairos* are translated as "time," but with quite different emphases. For related study on *kairos* versus *chronos* as ways of understanding time in the unfolding of redemption, see Oscar Cullmann, *Christ and Time*, trans. Floyd F. Filson (Bloomsbury Street, London: SCM Press LTD, 1951), 39–44.
7. Ehrman himself raises this objection in Ehrman, *Jesus, Interrupted*, 9.
8. Gordon D. Fee and Douglas Stuart, *How to Read the Bible for All Its Worth: A Guide to Understanding the Bible*, 2nd ed. (Grand Rapids: Zondervan Publishing House, 1993), 233.
9. William Gurnall, *The Christian in Complete Armour*, vol. 2, revised and abridged by Ruthanne Garlock et al., (Edinburgh, Great Britain: The Banner of Truth Trust, 1988 [originally published in 1658]), 150.

Chapter 18: Illumination Principle

1. *Larry King Live*, August 19, 2008, cf. Bill Maher, *Religulous*, directed by Larry Charles, Lionsgate, 2008.
2. See discussion concerning the mistranslation practices of the Jehovah's Witnesses in chapter 19 on pages 230–38.
3. Ronald F. Youngblood, ed., *Nelson's New Illustrated Bible Dictionary* (Nashville: Thomas Nelson, 1995).
4. J. D. Douglas, ed., *New International Bible Dictionary* (Grand Rapids: Zondervan, 1999).
5. W. E. Vine, *Vine's Complete Expository Dictionary of Old and New Testament Words* (Nashville: Thomas Nelson, 1996).
6. Hank Hanegraaff, *The Apocalypse Code: Find Out What the Bible REALLY Says About the End Times . . . and Why It Matters Today* (Nashville: Thomas Nelson, 2010).
7. R. C. Sproul, *Knowing Scripture* (Downers Grove, IL: InterVarsity Press, 1977). Originally titled *Knowing God's Word*.
8. James Sire, *Scripture Twisting: 20 Ways the Cults Misread the Bible* (Downers Grove, IL: InterVarsity Press, 1980).

Chapter 19: Grammatical Principle

1. Steven Pinker, *The Language Instinct: How the Mind Creates Language* (New York: HarperPerennial, 1994), 276; see 39–45, 262–76.
2. *New World Translation of the Holy Scriptures* (Brooklyn: Watch Tower Bible and Tract Society of Pennsylvania, 1961); emphasis added.

3. See Daniel B. Wallace, *Greek Grammar Beyond the Basics: An Exegetical Syntax of the New Testament* (Grand Rapids: Zondervan, 1996), 266–67.

4. Ibid., 269; emphasis in original.

5. The Greek of John 20:28 is unambiguous and definitive. Literally, Thomas says to the risen Christ, "the Lord of me and the God of me." As eminent New Testament scholar N. T. Wright explains, "Thomas, who was not present that first evening, acquires his now perpetual nickname by declaring his doubt that the Lord had truly risen, and is then confronted by the risen Jesus inviting him to touch and see for himself. Thomas refuses the invitation, coming out instead with the fullest expression of faith anywhere in the whole gospel" (N. T. Wright, *The Resurrection of the Son of God* [Minneapolis: Fortress, 2003], 664).

6. F. H. A. Scrivener, *The Authorized Edition of the English Bible (1611) Its Subsequent Reprints and Modern Representatives* (Cambridge: At the University Press, 1884), 286.

7. *New World Translation of the Holy Scriptures*, 6.

8. *The Kingdom Interlinear Translation of the Greek Scriptures* (Brooklyn: Watchtower Bible and Tract Society, 1969), 896.

9. Bruce M. Metzger, "The Jehovah's Witnesses and Jesus Christ," *Theology Today* 10, no. 1 (April 1953), 76; online at http://www.newreformationpress.com/freebies/Bruce%20Metzger%20-%20The%20Jehovah's%20Witnesses%20and%20Jesus%20Christ.pdf (accessed February 22, 2011).

10. Yolanda Woodlee, "D.C. Mayor Acted 'Hastily,' Will Rehire Aide, *Washington Post*, February 4, 1999, A1, online at http://www.washingtonpost.com/wp-srv/local/longterm/williams/williams020499.htm (accessed February 22, 2011).

11. Ibid.

12. Ibid.

13. Cf. Joe Kort, "The Terms 'Homosexual' and the 'N-word': The term homosexual is like using the 'N-word,'" *Psychology Today* Blog, October 12, 2008, http://www.psychologytoday.com/blog/gays-anatomy/200810/the-terms-homosexual-and-the-n-word (accessed February 22, 2011).

14. Ibid.

15. For this reference and others concerning *rosh*/Russia, I am indebted to Doug Krieger, "Russia Has a Cameo Appearance in Bible Prophecy," Part XXII, http://www.the-tribulation-network.com/ebooks/rise_or_fall/rise_or_fall_of_american_empire_p22-3.htm (accessed April 8, 2011).

16. Mark Hitchcock, "Gog and Magog," in Tim LaHaye, ed., *Tim LaHaye Prophecy Study Bible* (Chattanooga, TN: AMG Publishers, 2000), 876.

17. See Ralph H. Alexander, *Ezekiel*, in *The Expositor's Bible Commentary*, vol. 6, Frank E. Gaebelein, gen. ed. (Grand Rapids: Zondervan, 1986), 929–30; cf. Carl Friedrich Keil, *Biblical Commentary on the Prophecies of Ezekiel*, vol. 2,

James Martin, trans., in C. F. Keil and F. Delitzsch, *Commentary on the Old Testament in Ten Volumes*, vol. 9 (Grand Rapids: Eerdmans, repr. 1976), 160.

18. *Reasoning from the Scriptures* (Brooklyn: Watchtower Bible and Tract Society of New York, 1985), 408.

Chapter 20: Historical Principle

1. Barack Obama, "News and Speeches: Call to Renewal Key Note Address," June 28, 2006, the transcript of which is available online at http://blog .beliefnet.com/stevenwaldman/2008/11/obamas-historic-call-to-renewa .html; the basic points cited are in slightly edited form in Barack Obama, *The Audacity of Hope: Thoughts on Reclaiming the American Dream* (New York: Vintage, 2006, 2008), 258.

2. Obama, *The Audacity of Hope*, 260.

3. See, e.g., "Mother dies after refusing blood," BBC News, November 5, 2007, http://news.bbc.co.uk/2/hi/uk_news/england/shropshire/7078455.stm; and "Refusing Blood 'Source of Regret'" BBC News, November 6, 2007, http://news.bbc.co.uk/2/hi/uk_news/england/sussex/7080902.stm.

4. See Hank Hanegraaff, *Christianity in Crisis 21st Century* (Nashville: Thomas Nelson, 2009).

5. For further study, see Paul Copan, *Is God a Moral Monster? Making Sense of the Old Testament God* (Grand Rapids: Baker Book House, 2011). See "Curse of Ham," New World Encyclopedia online, http://www.newworldencyclopedia.org/entry/Curse_of_Ham (accessed March 21, 2011). For discussion on Christianity's influence and role in the abolition of slavery in the West, see Alvin J. Schmidt, *How Christianity Changed the World* (Grand Rapids: Zondervan, 2004), 272–91.

6. Kleitarchos, Scholia on Plato's Republic 337A, quoted in Clay Jones, "Killing the Canaanites: A Response to the New Atheism's 'Divine Genocide' Claims," *Christian Research Journal* 33, no. 4 (2010): 32. See Jones's article for a compelling contrast between the atheists' accusation of divine genocide and the biblical case for capital punishment concerning the Canaanites. See also *Is God a Moral Monster?*

7. For this basic biblical principle, see especially Jeremiah 18:7–10 and Ezekiel 18.

8. See the insightful editorial, George Neumayr, "Obama's Campaign-Season Christianity," *American Spectator*, September 30, 2010, online at http://spectator.org/archives/2010/09/30/obamas-campaign-season-christi (accessed March 17, 2010).

9. Obama, *The Audacity of Hope*, 260–61.

10. Ibid., 258.

11. Barack Obama, "News and Speeches: Call to Renewal Key Note Address," June 28, 2006, the transcript of which is available online at http://blog

.beliefnet.com/stevenwaldman/2008/11/obamas-historic-call-to-renewa
.html.

12. Maher quoted in Cathleen Falsani, "The God Factor," *Chicago Sun-Times*, October 24, 2004, News 16.

13. *Politically Incorrect*, ABC, January 24, 2002.

14. Bart D. Ehrman, *Misquoting Jesus: The Story Behind Who Changed the Bible and Why* (New York: HarperSanFrancisco, 2005), 194.

15. Bart D. Ehrman, *Forged: Writing in the Name of God—Why the Bible's Authors Are Not Who We Think They Are* (New York: HarperOne, 2011).

16. Bart D. Ehrman, *The New Testament: A Historical Introduction to the Early Christian Writings*, 3rd ed. (New York: Oxford University Press, 2004).

17. Ehrman, *The New Testament*, 469.

18. G. K. Beale, *The Book of Revelation: A Commentary on the Greek Text* (Grand Rapids: Eerdmans, 1999), 34.

19. Bart Ehrman explains, "Perhaps the most common reason to forge writing in antiquity was to get a hearing for one's own views. . . . If you wrote in your own name (Mark Aristedes, or whatever), no one would be much intrigued or feel compelled to read what you had to say, but if you signed your treatise 'Plato,' then it might have a chance" (Ehrman, *The New Testament*, 373).

20. As noted, in the case of the gospel of John, myriad internal details demonstrate that it was written by someone intimately acquainted with the topography of ancient Palestine. John references the Pool of Bethesda surrounded by five covered colonnades (John 5:2) as well as the Pool of Siloam used by those who were infirm (John 9:7). Archaeology has verified the descriptions and locations of both of these pools. John also correctly notes changes in elevation between Cana in Galilee, Capernaum, and Jerusalem (John 2:11–13). Other examples include the two Bethanys—one less than two miles from Jerusalem on the road to Jericho where Mary, Martha, and Lazarus lived (John 11:18); the other beyond the Jordan River that only an ancient Palestinian could have identified (John 1:28) (Daniel B. Wallace, "The Gospel of John: Introduction, Argument, Outline," online at http://bible.org/seriespage/gospel-john-introduction-argument-outline [accessed, March 24, 2011]; see also John A. T. Robinson, *Redating the New Testament* [Eugene, OR: Wipf and Stock Publishers, 2000, originally published by SCM Press, 1976], 277–78).

Furthermore, the author of the gospel of John was a Palestinian Jew and an eyewitness to the events recorded in his gospel (John 21:24). Thus he had firsthand knowledge of the motivations, meditations, and movements of our Lord and his apostles.

Finally, as Craig Blomberg explains, "every piece of ancient, external evidence, save one, agrees that the author was the apostle John, the son of Zebedee" (Craig L. Blomberg, *The Historical Reliablity of John's Gospel: Issues and Commentary* [Downers Grove: InterVarsity Press, 2001], 23).

21. Ehrman, *The New Testament*, 468.

22. Hank Hanegraaff, *The Apocalypse Code: Find Out What the Bible REALLY Says About the End Times . . . and Why It Matters Today* (Nashville: Thomas Nelson, 2010).

23. See N. T. Wright, *Judas and the Gospel of Jesus: Have We Missed the Truth About Christianity?* (Grand Rapids: Baker Book House, 2006).

24. See also Daniel B. Wallace, "The Gospel of John: Introduction, Argument, Outline," online at http://www.bible.org/page.asp?page_id=1328 (accessed March 24, 2011); John A. T. Robinson, *Redating the New Testament* (Eugene, OR: Wipf and Stock Publishers, 2000, originally published by SCM Press, 1976), 277–78.

25. Ezekiel 10 depicts God's glory departing from the temple corrupted by sin, whereas Ezekiel 43 reveals God's glory filling a new holy temple. Cf. Haggai 2:2–9; Malachi 3:1; and Daniel 9:24–37; 11:31.

26. Colin Chapman, *Whose Land? Whose Promise? The Continuing Crisis over Israel and Palestine* (Grand Rapids: Baker Book House, 2002), 171–72.

27. See pages 114–15; 153–54.

28. Concerning the gospel of Thomas, see Craig A. Evans, *Fabricating Jesus: How Modern Scholars Distort the Gospels* (Downers Grove, IL: InterVarsity Press, 2006), 52–77; and the relevant discussion in Gregory A. Boyd, *Cynic Sage or Son of God?* (Wheaton: BridgePoint, 1995). For more on the gospel of Judas, see Craig A. Evans, *Fabricating Jesus: How Modern Scholars Distort the Gospels* (Downers Grove, IL: InterVarsity Press, 2006), 240–45; N. T. Wright, *Judas and the Gospel of Jesus: Have We Missed the Truth about Christianity?* (Grand Rapids: Baker Book House, 2006).

Chapter 21: Typology Principle

1. "Wilhelmina of the Netherlands," *New World Encyclopedia* online, http://www.newworldencyclopedia.org/entry/Wilhelmina_of_the_Netherlands (accessed March 21, 2011).

2. Ibid.

3. Ernst Mayr, "The Nature of the Darwinian Revolution," *Science*, June 2, 1972, 981.

4. Sir Julian Huxley, *Essays of a Humanist* (New York: Harper & Row, 1964), 125.

5. Arthur Keith, *Evolution and Ethics* (New York: Putnam, 1947), 230, quoted in Henry M. Morris, *The Long War Against God* (Grand Rapids: Baker Book House, 1989), 76.

6. David Hume, *The Philosophical Works*, vol. 3 (Edomnirg, London: Adam

Black and William Tate, 1826), 236n, viewed via books.google.com (March 24, 2011).

7. Letter from Charles Darwin to W. Graham, 3 July 1881, *Life and Letters of Charles Darwin*, vol. 1, 316, cited in Gertrude Himmelfarb, *Darwin and the Darwinian Revolution* (London: Chatto & Windus, 1959), 343.

8. Richard Dawkins, *The Greatest Show on Earth: The Evidence for Evolution* (New York: Free Press, 2009), 62.

9. Charles Darwin, *The Descent of Man*, chap. 6, "On the Affinities and Genealogy of Man," sect. "On the Birthplace and Antiquity of Man," in *Great Books of the Western World*, vol. 49, *Darwin*, Robert Maynard Hutchins, ed. (Chicago: Encyclopaedia Britannica, 1952), 336.

10. Richard Dawkins, "Ignorance Is No Crime," May 14, 2006, http://richarddawkins.net/articles/114 (accessed March 24, 2011).

11. Thomas H. Huxley, *Lay Sermons, Addresses and Reviews* (New York: Appleton, 1871), 20, quoted in Morris, *The Long War Against God*, 60.

12. Henry M. Morris and Gary E. Parker, *What Is Creation Science?* rev. ed. (El Cajon, CA: Master Books, 1987), 67; see also Stephen Jay Gould, "Dr. Down's Syndrome," *Natural History* (April 1980): 142–48.

13. See Marvin L. Lubenow, *Bones of Contention: A Creationist Assessment of the Human Fossils* (Grand Rapids: Baker Book House, 1992), 47.

14. Michael Crichton, *State of Fear* (New York: HarperCollins Publishers, 2004), 576. A concise overview of the history of eugenics is Crichton's "Why Politicized Science Is Dangerous," Appendix 1 from his novel *State of Fear*, 575–80. I follow Crichton in my discussion of eugenics.

15. Michael D. Evans, *The American Prophecies: Ancient Scriptures Reveal Our Nation's Future* (New York: Warner Faith, 2004), 193.

16. *John Hagee Today*, Trinity Broadcasting Network, September 26, 2006.

17. See "Curse of Ham," *New World Encyclopedia* online, http://www.newworldencyclopedia.org/entry/Curse_of_Ham (accessed March 21, 2011).

18. Stephen Sizer, *Christian Zionism: Road-map to Armageddon?* (Leicester, England: Inter-Varsity Press, 2004), 135.

19. John Hagee, *Should Christians Support Israel?* (San Antonio, TX: Dominion Publishers, 1987), 99.

20. John H. Gerstner, *Wrongly Dividing the Word of Truth: A Critique of Dispensationalism* (Brentwood, TN: Wolgemuth & Hyatt Publishers, 1991), 44.

21. Hagee, *Should Christians Support Israel?* 125.

22. See John Hagee, *In Defense of Israel* (Lake Mary, FL: Frontline, 2007), chap. 10. Nothing is clearer in the Bible than the New Testament teaching that salvation, including forgiveness of sins, eternal life, and, to use Hagee's words, being "in the will of God," is by grace alone, through *faith in* Christ alone, and *on account* of Christ alone (see, e.g., John 14:6; Romans 3–4;

Ephesians 2:8–10). The apostle John could not have put it more plainly: "Who is the liar? It is the man who denies that Jesus is the Christ. Such a man is the antichrist—he denies the Father and the Son. No one who denies the Son has the Father; whoever acknowledges the Son has the Father also" (1 John 2:22–23).

23. The amount of time and money that Christian Zionists have invested in relocating Jews to Israel is staggering. As noted by Timothy Weber, John Hagee, for example, claims to have spent $3.7 million to relocate more than six thousand Jews (Timothy P. Weber, *On the Road to Armageddon: How Evangelicals Became Israel's Best Friend* [Grand Rapids: Baker Academic, 2004], 227).

24. The claim that unrepentant modern Israel fulfills prophecies of return from exile contradicts Moses' teaching in Deuteronomy. Colin Chapman explains that Moses directly proclaimed that disobedience against the Lord results in dispersion (Deuteronomy 28:58–64; 29:23–28) and returning to the Land requires repentance: "When you and your children return to the LORD your God and obey him with all your heart . . . *then* the LORD your God will restore your fortunes and have compassion on you and gather you again from all the nations where he scattered you. Even if you have been banished to the most distant land under the heavens, from there the LORD your God will gather you and bring you back. He will bring you to the land that belonged to your fathers, and you will take possession of it. He will make you more prosperous and numerous than your fathers" (Deuteronomy 30:2–5).

Chapman then cites Daniel and Nehemiah as exemplars of genuine repentance who confess the sins of the people (Daniel 9:1–19; Nehemiah 1:4–11). "Thus," writes Chapman, "when God brings the remnant back to the Land, he does so in accordance with the conditions described in Deuteronomy. The people confess their sins corporately at a later stage after the return (Ezra 10:1–4; Nehemiah 9:1–37). But before the return, a significant number of individuals have expressed repentance on behalf of the people."

To those who argue that Ezekiel 33–39 justifies the teaching that repentance and belief will eventually follow the physical reoccupation of the Land, Chapman points out that cleansing and resettling coincide. As the Lord says, "On the day I cleanse you from all your sins, I will resettle your towns, and the ruins will be rebuilt" (Ezekiel 36:33). And, again, Deuteronomy's foundational condition for return is repentance.

Chapman concludes, "If the temple was destroyed in AD 70 and Jews exiled from the Land, as Jesus taught, as a judgment for their failure to recognize him as Messiah (Luke 19:41–44), the repentance required in the terms of Deuteronomy 30 would, from a Christian perspective, mean recognition of Jesus as Messiah. This would be the condition of return.

Peter on the Day of Pentecost could say 'this is that which was spoken of by the prophet' (Acts 2:16). But I have great difficulty in putting the return in the 19th and 20th centuries in the same category as the return in the sixth century [BC]. There are far too many significant differences!" (Colin Chapman, "One Land, Two Peoples—How Many States?" *Mishkan* 26 [1997]; also Colin Chapman, "Ten questions for a theology of the land," in Philip Johnston and Peter Walker, eds., *The Land of Promise: Biblical, Theological and Contemporary Perspectives* [Leicester, England: Apollos (Inter-Varsity Press), 2000], 175–77.)

25. Christopher Hitchens, *Hitch-22: A Memoir* (New York: Twelve, 2010), 379.

Chapter 22: Synergy Principle

1. My description of a scene that occurred during episode 25 of *The West Wing*, "The Midterms" (NBC), aired October 18, 2000.

2. In his diatribe, President Bartlet attempted a classic form of argumentation known as "reduction to absurdity," which assumes the opposite of what one is trying to prove and then goes on to show that such an assumption leads to an obviously absurd conclusion, and, so, the initial assumption must be false. Bartlet tries to show that if we accept the Scriptures as the authority on the moral invalidity of homosexuality, we must also apply to ourselves in contemporary America everything Moses required of ancient Israel. But upholding every one of Moses' laws, when fleshed out with particular examples, seems absurd. The tacit but obvious conclusion is that the outdated Scriptures provide no authoritative or relevant guidance for our lives today in the post-Christian, postmodern world. However, in short, Bartlet's reasoning is fallacious in two main ways. First, he fails to read the Mosaic texts in light of their proper historical context, especially in relation to their fulfillment in Jesus Christ, so as to miss a fundamental teaching of Scripture that some biblical laws are enduring universal moral principles while others are injunctions reserved for application within a particular historical context. Second, he commits one or more fatal factual errors in every premise of his argument.

3. The Associated Press (AP Online), "Prime-Time Nielson Ratings," 25 October 2000.

4. "A Letter to Dr. Laura," anonymous, n.d. One gay/lesbian website posts a note about this episode of *The West Wing*: "On October 18, 2000, NBC aired an episode of . . . *The West Wing* in which the character President Josiah Bartlet . . . absolutely skewers a character named 'Dr. Jenna Jacobs,' who bears striking similarities to our very own, dear, Laura Schlessinger, in a dialogue very similar in theme to the 'Dear Dr. Laura' letter which was wending its way about the net not that many months ago" ("West Wing

Skewers Laura Schlessinger," at http://www.robertslevinson.com
/gaylesissues/features/collect/newsnotes/bl_tidbit0005.htm [accessed March
21, 2011]; previously at www.gaylesissues.about.com). The anonymous "A
Letter to Dr. Laura" contains the following, which were reiterated almost
verbatim by Bartlet, "I would like to sell my daughter into slavery, as it
suggests in Exodus 21:7. In this day and age, what do you think would be a
good price for her?" and "I have a neighbor who insists on working on the
Sabbath. Exodus 35:2 clearly states he should be put to death. Am I morally
obligated to kill him myself?"

5. See discussion in chapter 20 on page 241.

6. Glenn M. Miller, "Good Question . . . Does God condone slavery in the
Bible?" March 18, 2004, http://christianthinktank.com/qnoslave.html
(accessed March 2, 2011).

7. For an excellent discussion of the slavery found in the Bible, see Glenn M.
Miller, "Good Question . . . Does God condone slavery in the Bible?" See
also Paul Copan, *Is God a Moral Monster? Making Sense of the Old Testament
God* (Grand Rapids: Baker Books, 2011).

8. Actually, Dr. Laura's PhD is in physiology from Columbia University
(College of Physicians and Surgeons), New York. And she holds a
postdoctoral certification in marriage, family, and child counseling from
the University of Southern California–Los Angeles.

9. Barack Obama, "News and Speeches: Call to Renewal Key Note Address,"
June 28, 2006, the transcript of which is available online at http://blog
.beliefnet.com/stevenwaldman/2008/11/obamas-historic-call-to-renewa.html.

10. Does Mark 7:19 tell us foods eaten are purged or purified? The differences
in English translations come as the result of a textual variant. Modern
translations like the NASB, NIV, and the ESV follow the oldest and most
reliable Greek manuscript evidence, which reads καθαρίζων [katharizōn],
which is understood as an editorial comment from Mark that "he [Jesus]
declared all foods clean"—literally, "purifying all foods." The KJV and
NKJV®, however, follow the few Greek manuscripts that read καθαρίζον
[katharizon], which is understood as the Lord's conclusion to a rhetorical
question, "thus purging all foods?" Bruce Metzger points out that "the
overwhelming weight of manuscript evidence supports the reading
[katharizōn]. The difficulty of construing this word in the sentence
prompted copyists to attempt various corrections and ameliorations." The
word [katharizōn], therefore, is to be preferred as the way the original text
read, and [katharizon] came as the result of a copyist wrongly presuming
the former to be a mistake and attempting to fix the alleged problem. C. E.
B. Cranfield observes that "he declared all foods clean" is "best explained as
the evangelist's own comment, drawing out the implications of Jesus' words
with an eye on the contemporary problem of what was to be the Church's

attitude to Jesus' ideas about clean and unclean foods." The New Testament writers also observed that with freedom in Christ comes responsibility, and we must never allow our freedom to stumble our weaker brothers and sisters in Christ (1 Corinthians 8; 10:23–33). (Metzger's quote is from Bruce Metzger, A Textual Commentary on the Greek New Testament [Stuttgart, Germany: United Bible Societies , 1971], 95. And Cranfield's is from C. E. B. Cranfield, The Cambridge Greek New Testament Commentary: The Gospel According to St. Mark, C. F. D. Moule, ed. [New York: Cambridge University Press, 1959], 241).

11. In other words, making an extraordinarily long, winding putt.

12. Obama, "Call to Renewal."

13. Robert A. J. Gagnon, *The Bible and Homosexual Practice: Text and Hermeneutics* (Nashville: Abingdon Press, 2001), 157.

14. Ibid., 181.

15. Ibid., 182.

16. Ibid., 228.

17. Ibid., 337.

18. Ibid., 228.

Conclusion

1. Bruce L. Shelley, *Church History in Plain Language* (Nashville: Thomas Nelson, 1995), 61.

2. See R. C. Sproul, *The Consequences of Ideas: Understanding the Concepts That Shaped Our World* (Wheaton, IL: Crossway, 2000), 58–59.

3. Sociologist Rodney Stark notes, "Augustine was heir to the entire legacy of Greek philosophy, and Aquinas and his peers acknowledge their deep debts to Hellenic scholarship. But the antiscientific elements of Greek thought were withstood by Augustine and by the Scholastics, and long before Greco-Roman learning was confined to classics departments, it was *not* the philosophy of scientists. While it is true (and constantly cited by the classicists) that Newton remarked in a letter to Robert Hook in 1675 that 'if I have seen further (than you and Descartes) it is by standing on the shoulders of giants,' such high regard for the ancients is not expressed or reflected in his work or in his usual presentations of self. Instead, Newton and his peers achieved their breakthroughs in obvious opposition to the Greek 'giants.' What the great figures involved in the sixteenth- and seventeenth-century blossoming of science—including Descartes, Galileo, Newton, and Kepler—did confess was their absolute faith in a creator God, whose work incorporated rational rules awaiting discovery.

"The rise of science was not an extension of classical learning. It was the natural outgrowth of Christian doctrine: nature exists because it was created by God. In order to honor God, it is necessary to fully appreciate the wonders of his handiwork. Because God is perfect, his handiwork functions in accord with *immutable principles*. By the full use of our God-given powers of reason and observation, it ought to be possible to discover these principles" (Rodney Stark, *The Victory of Reason: How Christianity Led to Freedom, Capitalism, and Western Success* [New York: Random House, 2006], 22–23; emphasis in original).

4. Rodney Stark, *The Victory of Reason: How Christianity Led to Freedom, Capitalism, and Western Success* (New York: Random House, 2006), 19. For an insightful overview of ancient Greek thinking, see "Blessings of Rational Theology," chapter 1 of *The Victory of Reason*.

5. I am particularly indebted to the work of Vishal Mangalwadi and Rodney Stark concerning the historical relationship between revelation and reason in the development of Western civilization. See especially, Vishal Mangalwadi, *Truth and Transformation: A Manifesto for Ailing Nations* (YWAM, 2009); and *The Book That Made Your World: How the Bible Created the Soul of Western Civilization* (Nashville: Thomas Nelson, 2011) (Vishal's lecture series on CD, "Must the Sun Set on the West? An Indian Explores the Soul of Western Civilization" is also excellent); Stark, *The Victory of Reason*; and Rodney Stark, *For the Glory of God: How Monotheism Led to Reformations, Science, Witch-hunts, and the End of Slavery* (Princeton: Princeton University Press, 2003).

6. Stark, *The Victory of Reason*, 21.

7. Ibid.

8. Ibid., 22.

9. Martin Luther, "An Open Letter to the Christian Nobility of the German Nation Concerning the Reform of the Christian Estate," in *Works of Martin Luther: With Introductions and Notes*, (Philadelphia, PA: A. J. Holman Company and Castle Press, 1915), 146.

10. Concerning Leonardo Da Vinci and the following great men of science, see Henry M. Morris, *Men of Science Men of God: Great Scientists of the Past Who Believed the Bible* (El Cajon, CA: Master Books, 1988).

11. A word coined to reflect the idiosyncratic fundamentalist ranting of atheist Richard Dawkins.

12. Millard J. Erickson, *Christian Theology* (Grand Rapids: Baker Book House, 1988), 510.

13. Jacques Monod, *Chance and Necessity* (New York: Vintage, 1972), 112–13.

14. Charles Darwin, *The Descent of Man*, in *Great Books of the Western World*, vol. 49, *Darwin*, Robert Maynard Hutchins, ed. (Chicago: Encyclopedia Britannica, 1952), 566.

15. Stephen Jay Gould, "Dr. Down's Syndrome," *Natural History*, April 1980, 142–48.

16. Henry M. Morris, *Creation and the Modern Christian* (El Cajon, CA: Master Book, 1985), 72.

17. Henry M. Morris, *The Long War Against God* (Grand Rapids: Baker Book House, 1989), 139.

18. Gould, "Dr. Down's Syndrome," 144.

19. Examples abound. Dawkins argues that intelligent people don't get their morals from the Bible, for "if we did, we would strictly observe the sabbath and think it just and proper to execute anybody who chose not to. We would stone to death any new bride who couldn't prove she was a virgin, if her husband pronounced himself unsatisfied with her. We would execute disobedient children." Moreover, says Dawkins, "Jesus' family values, it has to be admitted, were not such as one might wish to focus on. He was short, to the point of brusqueness, with his own mother, and he encouraged his own disciples to abandon their families to follow him" (Richard Dawkins, *The God Delusion* [New York: Houghton Mifflin, 2006], 249–50).

20. Again, examples abound. Dawkins contends that Christian belief is "a persistently false belief held in the face of strong contradictory evidence" (Dawkins, *The God Delusion*, 5). Biblical faith, according to Dawkins, "means blind trust, in the absence of evidence, even in the teeth of evidence." Elsewhere within the same book, he writes, "But what, after all, is faith? It is a state of mind that leads people to believe something—it doesn't matter what—in the total absence of supporting evidence. . . . Faith seems to me to qualify as a kind of mental illness" (Richard Dawkins, *The Selfish Gene*, 2nd ed. [Oxford: Oxford University Press, 2nd ed., 1989], 198, 330).

21. Nicholas D. Kristof, "Believe It, or Not," *New York Times*, August 15, 2003, http://www.nytimes.com/2003/08/15/opinion/believe-it-or-not.html (accessed March 23, 2011).

22. Charles Malik, "The Two Tasks," in William Lane Craig and Paul M. Gould, eds., *The Two Tasks of the Christian Scholar: Redeeming the Soul, Redeeming the Mind* (Wheaton, IL: Crossway, 2007), 63.

Selected Bibliography

Books

Adams, Jay E., and Milton C. Fisher. *The Time of the End: Daniel's Prophecies Reclaimed.* Woodruff, SC: Timeless Texts, 2000.

Aland, Kurt, and Barbara Aland. *The Text of the New Testament: An Introduction to the Critical Editions and to the Theory and Practice of Modern Textual Criticism.* Rev. ed. Erroll F. Rhodes, trans. Grand Rapids: Eerdmans, 1989.

Albright, W. F. *From Stone Age to Christianity: Monotheism and the Historical Process.* 2nd ed. New York: Johns Hopkins Press, 1957.

Alexander, Ralph H. *Ezekiel,* in *The Expositor's Bible Commentary,* vol. 6. Frank E. Gaebelein, gen. ed. Grand Rapids: Zondervan, 1986.

Archer, Gleason L., Jr. *Daniel,* in *The Expositor's Bible Commentary,* vol. 7, Frank E. Gaebelein, gen. ed. Grand Rapids: Zondervan, 1985.

_____. *A Survey of Old Testament Introduction.* Rev. ed. Chicago: Moody Press, 1994.

Arnold, Brian T., and Bryan E. Beyer. *Readings from the Ancient Near East.* Grand Rapids: Baker Academic, 2002.

Baigent, Michael. *The Jesus Papers Exposing the Greatest Cover-Up in History.* San Francisco: HarperSanFrancisco, 2006.

Baigent, Michael, Richard Leigh, and Henry Lincoln. *Holy Blood, Holy Grail.* New York: Delacorte Press, 1982.

Barnett, Paul. *Is the New Testament Reliable? A Look at the Historical Evidence.* Downers Grove, IL: InterVarsity Press, 1986.

_____. *Jesus and the Rise of Early Christianity: A History of New Testament Times.* Downers Grove, IL: InterVarsity Press, 1999.

Barrett, C. K. *The New Testament Background: Selected Documents.* New York: The Macmillan Company, 1957.

Bauckham, Richard. *Jesus and the Eyewitnesses: The Gospels as Eyewitness Testimony.* Grand Rapids: Eerdmans, 2006.

Beale, G. K. *The Book of Revelation: A Commentary on the Greek Text.* Grand Rapids: William B. Eerdmans Publishing Co., 1999.

Blomberg, Craig L. *The Historical Reliability of the Gospels.* Downers Grove, IL: InterVarsity Press, 1987.

_____. *The Historical Reliablity of John's Gospel: Issues and Commentary.* Downers Grove: InterVarsity Press, 2001.

_____. *Jesus and the Gospels.* Nashville: Broadman and Holman, 1997.

Bock, Darrell L. "The Words of Jesus in the Gospels: Live, Jive, or Memorex?" in *Jesus Under Fire*. Michael J. Wilkins and J. P. Moreland, eds., Grand Rapids: Zondervan, 1995.

Bock, Darrell L. *Studying the Historical Jesus: A Guide to Sources and Methods*. Grand Rapids: Baker Academic, 2002.

Bock, Darrell L., and Gregory Herrick, *Jesus in Context: Background Readings*. Grand Rapids: Baker Academic, 2005.

Boyd, Gregory A. *Cynic Sage or Son of God*? Wheaton: BridgePoint, 1995.

Brenton, Sir Lancelot Charles Lee. *The Septuagint with Apocrypha: Greek and English*. Peabody, MA: Hendrickson Publishers, 1986 [originally published by Samuel Bagster & Sons, Ltd., London, 1851].

British Museum, "Austen Henry Layard (1817–94), archeologist," http://www.british museum.org/explore/highlights/article_index/a/austen_henry_layard_1817-94.aspx; and The British Museum, "Hormuzd Rassam (1826–1910), archaeologist http://www. britishmuseum.org/explore/highlights/article_index/h/hormuzd_rassam_1826-1910. aspx (accessed April 12, 2011).

British Museum, "The Flood Tablet, Relating Part of the Epic of Gilgamesh," http://www .britishmuseum.org/explore/highlights/highlight_objects/me/t/the_flood_tablet. aspx (accessed March 23, 2011).

Brown, Michael L. *Answering Jewish Objections to Jesus*, vol. 3, *Messianic Prophecy Objections*. Grand Rapids: Baker Book House, 2003.

Bruce, F. F. *The Books and the Parchments*. Old Tappan, NJ: Fleming H. Revell Company, 1984.

_____. *The New Testament Documents: Are They Reliable*? Grand Rapids: Wm. B Eerdmans Publishing Co., 1981.

_____. *New Testament History*. New York: Doubleday-Galilee, 1980.

Burrows, Millar. *The Dead Sea Scrolls*. London: Secker and Warburg, 1956.

Chapman, Colin. "Ten questions for a theology of the land," in Philip Johnston and Peter Walker, eds., *The Land of Promise: Biblical, Theological and Contemporary Perspectives*. Leicester, England: Apollos Inter-Varsity Press, 2000.

_____. *Whose Land? Whose Promise? The Continuing Crisis over Israel and Palestine*. Grand Rapids: Baker Book House, 2002.

Comfort, Philip W. *New Testament Text and Translation Commentary: Commentary on the variant readings of the ancient New Testament manuscripts and how they relate to the major English translations*. Carol Stream, IL: Tyndale, 2008.

Comfort, Philip Wesley. "Texts and Manuscripts of the New Testament," in *The Origin of the Bible*. Philip Wesley Comfort, ed. Wheaton, IL: Tyndale House Publishers, 1992.

Copan, Paul. *Is God a Moral Monster? Making Sense of the Old Testament God*. Grand Rapids: Baker Book House, 2011.

Craig, William Lane."Did Jesus Rise from the Dead?" in Michael J. Wilkins and J. P. Moreland, eds., *Jesus Under Fire*. Grand Rapids: Zondervan, 1995.

_____. *Reasonable Faith: Christian Truth and Apologetics*, 3rd ed. Wheaton, IL: Crossway Books, 2008.

_____, in *Will the Real Jesus Please Stand Up? A Debate Between William Lane Craig and John Dominic Crossan*. Paul Copan, ed. Grand Rapids: Baker Book House, 1998.

Cranfield, C. E. B. *The Cambridge Greek New Testament Commentary: The Gospel According to St. Mark*. C. F. D. Moule, ed. New York: Cambridge University Press, 1959.

Crichton, Michael. *State of Fear*. New York: HarperCollins Publishers, 2004. "Why Politicized Science Is Dangerous," Appendix 1.

Cullmann, Oscar. *Christ and Time*. Floyd F. Filson, trans. Bloomsburry Street, London: SCM Press LTD, 1951.

Davies, Philip. "The Intellectual, the Archaeologist and the Bible," in *The Land I Will Show You: Essays in Honor of J. Maxwell Miller*. J. A. Dearman and M. P. Graham, eds. Sheffield: JSOT Press, 2001.

Dawkins, Richard. *The God Delusion*. New York: Houghton Mifflin Company, 2006.

_____. *The Greatest Show on Earth*. New York: Free Press, 2009.

_____. *The Selfish Gene*. 2nd ed. Oxford: Oxford University Press, 1989.

Decker, Ed. *Decker's Complete Handbook on Mormonism*. Eugene, OR: Harvest House, 1995.

DeMar, Gary. *Last Days Madness: Obsession of the Modern Church*. 4th rev. ed. Atlanta: American Vision, 1999.

Dembski, William. A. *The End of Christianity: Finding a Good God in an Evil World*. Nashville: B&H Academic, 2009.

Douglas, J. D., gen. ed. *The New International Dictionary of the Christian Church*. Rev. ed. Grand Rapids: Zondervan, 1978.

Drower, Margaret S. *Flinders Petrie: A Life in Archaeology*. Madison, WI: University of Wisconsin Press, 1995.

Eddy, Paul Rhodes, and Gregory A. Boyd. *The Jesus Legend: A Case for the Historical Reliability of the Synoptic Jesus Tradition*. Grand Rapids: Baker Academic, 2007.

Ehrman, Bart D. *Forged: Writing in the Name of God—Why the Bible's Authors Are Not Who We Think They Are*. New York: HarperOne, 2011.

_____. *Jesus: Apocalyptic Prophet of the New Millennium*. New York: Oxford University Press, 1999.

_____. *Jesus, Interrupted: Revealing the Hidden Contradictions in the Bible (and Why We Don't Know About Them)*. New York: HarperOne, 2009.

_____. *Misquoting Jesus: The Story Behind Who Changed the Bible and Why*. San Franciso: HarperSanFrancisco, 2005.

_____. *The New Testament: A Historical Introduction to the Early Christian Writings*. 3rd ed. New York: Oxford University Press, 2004.

_____. *Peter, Paul, and Mary Magdalene: The Followers of Jesus in History and Legend*. New York: Oxford University Press, 2006.

Ehrman, Bart D., and Daniel B. Wallace. "The Textual Reliability of the New Testament: A Dialogue," in *The Reliability of the New Testament: Bart Ehrman and Daniel Wallace in Dialogue*. Robert B. Stewart, ed. Minneapolis: Fortress, 2011.

Elwell, Walter A., ed. *Baker Encyclopedia of the Bible*, vol. 2. Grand Rapids: Baker Book House, 1988.

Epp, Eldon Jay, and Gordon D. Fee. *Studies in the Theory and Method of New Testament Textual Criticism*. Grand Rapids: Eerdmans, 1993.

Erasmus, Desiderius, and Martin Luther. *Discourse on Free Will*. Ernst F. Winter, trans. New York: Continuum, 2006.

Erickson, Millard J. *Christian Theology*. Grand Rapids: Baker Book House, 1988.

Evans, Craig A. *Fabricating Jesus: How Modern Scholars Distort the Gospels*. Downers Grove, IL: InterVarsity Press, 2006.

_____. *Holman QuickSource Guide to the Dead Sea Scrolls*. Nashville: Holman Reference, 2010.

_____. "Textual Criticism and Textual Confidence: How Reliable Is Scripture?" in *The Reliability of the New Testament: Bart Ehrman and Daniel Wallace in Dialogue*. Robert B. Stewart, ed. Minneapolis: Fortress, 2011.

Farrar, F. W. *The Book of Daniel*. London: Hodder and Stoughton, 1895.

Fee, Gordon D., and Douglas Stuart. *How to Read the Bible for All Its Worth: A Guide to Understanding the Bible*. 2nd ed. Grand Rapids: Zondervan, 1993.

France, R. T. *The Evidence for Jesus*. London: Hodder & Stoughton, 2001.

Free, Joseph P. *Archaeology and Bible History*. Revised and expanded by Howard F. Vos. Grand Rapids: Zondervan, 1992.

Funk, Robert W. *The Acts of Jesus: What Did Jesus Really Do?* New York: Harper SanFrancisco, 1998.

Gagnon, Robert A. J. *The Bible and Homosexual Practice: Text and Hermeneutics*. Nashville: Abingdon Press, 2001.

Geisler, Norman. *Systematic Theology*, vol. 1, *Introduction, Bible*. Minneapolis: Bethany House, 2002.

Geisler, Norman, and Thomas Howe. *When Critics Ask*. Grand Rapids: Baker Book House, 1992.

Geisler, Norman L., and William Nix. *A General Introduction to the Bible*. Rev. ed. Chicago: Moody, 1986.

Geisler, Norman L., and Abdul Saleeb. *Answering Islam: The Crescent in Light of the Cross*. 2nd ed. Grand Rapids: Baker Book House, 2002.

Gerstner, John H. *Wrongly Dividing the Word of Truth: A Critique of Dispensationalism*. Brentwood, TN: Wolgemuth & Hyatt Publishers, 1991.

Gibson, Shimon. *The Final Days of Jesus: The Archaeological Evidence*. New York: HarperCollins, 2009.

Goldingay, John E. *Daniel*, Word Biblical Commentary, vol. 30. Dallas: Word, 1989.

Goppelt, Leonhard. *Typos: the typological interpretation of the Old Testament in the New*. Donald H. Madvid, trans. Grand Rapids: Eerdmans, 1982.

Green, Peter. *Alexander of Macedon 356–323 B.C.: A Historical Biography*. Berkeley: University of California Press, 1992.

Greenleaf, Simon. *The Testimony of the Evangelists: The Gospels Examined by the Rules of Evidence*. Grand Rapids: Kregel Classics, 1995.

Gurnall, William. *The Christian in Complete Armour*, vol. 2, revised and abridged by Ruthanne Garlock, Kay King, Karen Sloan, Candy Coan Edinburgh, Great Britain: The Banner of Truth Trust, 1988 [originally published in 1658].

Gurney, Robert J. M. *God in Control: An Exposition of the Prophecies of Daniel*. Worthing, West Sussex, England: H. E. Walter Ltd, 1980, revised 2006, online at http://www .biblicalstudies.org.uk/book_god-in-control_gurney.html (accessed April 14, 2011).

Habermas, Gary R. *The Historical Jesus: Ancient Evidence for the Life of Christ*. Joplin, MO: College Press, 1996.

Habermas, Gary R., and Antony G. N. Flew, *Did Jesus Rise from the Dead?* San Francisco: Harper & Row, 1987.

Habermas, Gary R., and Michael R. Licona. *The Case for the Resurrection of Jesus*. Grand Rapids: Kregel Publications, 2004.

Hagee, John. *In Defense of Israel*. Lake Mary, FL: Frontline, 2007.

_____. *Should Christians Support Israel?* San Antonio, TX: Dominion Publishers, 1987.

Hagner, Donald A. *Matthew 14—18 Word Biblical Commentary*, vol. 33b. Dallas: Word Books, 1995.

Hallo, William W., and K. Lawson Younger, eds., *The Context of Scripture: Canonical Compositions from the Biblical World*, vol. 1. Leiden: Brill Academic Press, 1997.

Hanegraaff, Hank. *The Apocalypse Code*. Nashville: Thomas Nelson, 2007.

_____. *Christianity in Crisis 21st Century*. Nashville: Thomas Nelson, 2009.

_____. *The Complete Bible Answer Book—Collector's Edition*. Nashville: Thomas Nelson, 2008.

_____. *The Covering*. Nashville: W Publishing Group, 2002.

_____. *The Face That Demonstrates the Farce of Evolution*. Nashville: Thomas Nelson, 1998.

_____. *The Mormon Mirage: Seeing Through the Illusion of Mainstream Mormonism*. Charlotte, NC: Christian Research Institute, 2008.

_____. *The Prayer of Jesus*. Nashville: Thomas Nelson, 2001.

_____. *Resurrection*. Nashville: W Publishing Group, 2000.

Hanegraaf, Hank, and Paul L. Maier. *The Da Vinci Code: Fact or Fiction?* Carol Stream, IL: Tyndale, 2004.

Harris, R. Laird. *Inspiration and Canonicity of the Bible*. Grand Rapids: Zondervan, 1957.

Hitchens, Christopher. *God Is Not Great: How Religion Poisons Everything*. New York: Twelve, 2007.

_____. *Hitch 22: A Memoir*. New York: Twelve, 2010.

Hoerth, Alfred J. *Archaeology and the Old Testament*. Grand Rapids: Baker Book House, 1998.

Hoffmeier, James K. *Ancient Israel in Sinai: The Evidence for the Authenticity of the Wilderness Tradition*. New York: Oxford University Press, 2005.

_____. *The Archaeology of the Bible*. UK: Lion Hudson, 2008.

_____. *Israel in Egypt: The Evidence for the Authenticity of the Exodus Tradition*. New York: Oxford University Press, 1996, 1999.

House, H. Wayne. *Chronological and Background Charts of the New Testament*. Grand Rapids: Zondervan, 1981.

Hughes, Thomas Patrick. *Dictionary of Islam: A Cyclopedia of the Doctrines, Rites, Ceremonies, and Customs, Together with the Technical and Theological Terms of the Muslim Religion*. Chicago, IL: KAZI Publications, Inc., 1994.

Hume, David. *The Philosophical Works*, vol. 3. Edomnirg, London: Adam Black and William Tate, 1826.

Huxley, Sir Julian. *Essays of a Humanist*. New York: Harper & Row, 1964.

Jamison, Robert, A. R. Fausset, and David Brown, *A Commentary Critical, Experimental, and Practical on the Old and New Testaments*, vol. 3. Grand Rapids: Wm. B. Eerdmans, 1973.

Jones, Timothy Paul. *Misquoting Truth: A Guide to the Fallacies of Bart Ehrman's Misquoting Jesus*. Downers Grove, IL: InterVarsity Press. 2007.

Kaiser, Walter, Jr. *The Old Testament Documents: Are They Reliable and Relevant?* Downers Grove, IL: IVP Academic, 2001.

Keil, C. F. and F. Delitzsch. *Commentary on the Old Testament in Ten Volumes*, vol. 1, *The Pentateuch*. Grand Rapids: Eerdmans, reprinted 1976.

_____. *Biblical Commentary on the Old Testament in Ten Volumes*, vol. 5, *Psalms*. Grand Rapids: Eerdmans, reprinted 1976.

_____. *Biblical Commentary on the Old Testament in Ten Volumes*, vol. 7, *Isaiah*. Grand Rapids: Eerdmans, reprinted 1976.

_____. *Biblical Commentary on the Old Testament in Ten Volumes*, vol. 9, *Ezekiel, Daniel*. Grand Rapids: Eerdmans, reprinted 1976.

Keener, Craig S. *The IVP Bible Background Commentary: New Testament*. Downers Grove, IL: InterVarsity Press, 1993.

Kennedy, D. James. *Truths That Transform*. Old Tappan, NJ: Revell, 1974.

_____. *Why I Believe*, rev. and expanded. Nashville: Word, 1999.

Kennedy, D. James, and Jerry Newcombe. *The Real Messiah: Prophecies Fulfilled*. Boca Raton, FL: D. James Kennedy Foundation, 2008.

Kitchen, K. A. *Ancient Orient and Old Testament*. Downers Grove, IL: InterVarsity Press, 1966.

Klassen, William. *Judas: Betrayer or Friend of Jesus?* Minneapolis: Fortress Press, 2004.

Komoszewski, J. Ed, M. James Sawyer, and Daniel B. Wallace, *Reinventing Jesus: What the Da Vinci Code and Other Novel Speculations Don't Tell You*. Grand Rapids: Kregel, 2006.

LaHaye, Tim, and Thomas Ice. *Charting the End Times*. Eugene, OR: Harvest House, 2001.

LaHaye, Tim, and Jerry B. Jenkins. *Are We Living in the End Times?* Wheaton: Tyndale, 1999.

Lenski, R. C. H. *Commentary on the New Testament: The Interpretation of the Epistle to the Hebrews and of the Epistle of James*. Peabody, MA: Hendrickson, reprint 2001 [1966].

_____. *Commentary on the New Testament: The Interpretation of St. Matthew's Gospel*. Peabody, MA: Hendrickson, reprint 2001 [1943].

Lewis, C. S. *Mere Christianity*. New York: HarperCollins, 1952, 1980.

Licona, Michael R. *The Resurrection of Jesus: A New Historiographical Approach*. Downers Grove, IL: IVP Academic, 2010.

Lindsey, Hal, with C. C. Carlson. *The Late Great Planet Earth*. Grand Rapids: Zondervan, 1970, 40th printing, May, 1974.

Lubenow, Marvin L. *Bones of Contention: A Creationist Assessment of the Human Fossils*. Grand Rapids: Baker Book House, 1992.

Luther, Martin. "An Open Letter to the Christian Nobility of the German Nation Concerning the Reform of the Christian Estate," in *Works of Martin Luther: With Introductions and Notes*. Philadelphia: A.J. Holman Company and The Castle Press, 1915.

Magnusson, Magnus. *Archaeology of the Bible*. New York: Simon and Schuster, 1977.

Maier, Paul L. *In the Fullness of Time: A Historian Looks at Christmas, Easter, and the Early Church*. Grand Rapids: Kregel, 1991.

_____, trans. and ed. *Josephus: The Essential Works: A Condensation of Jewish Antiquities and the Jewish War*. Grand Rapids: Kregel, 1994.

_____, trans. and commentary. *Eusebius: The Church History*. Grand Rapids: Kregel, 2007.

Malik, Charles. "The Two Tasks," in William Lane Craig and Paul M. Gould, eds., *The Two Tasks of the Christian Scholar: Redeeming the Soul, Redeeming the Mind*. Wheaton, IL: Crossway, 2007.

Mangalwadi, Vishal. *The Book That Made Your World: How the Bible Created the Soul of Western Civilization*. Nashville: Thomas Nelson, 2011.

_____. *Truth and Transformation: A Manifesto for Ailing Nations*. Seattle, WA: YWAM, 2009.

McDowell, Bruce A., and Anees Zaka. *Muslims and Christians at the Table: Promoting Biblical Understanding Among North American Muslims*. Philipsburg, NJ: P&R Publishing, 1999.

McDowell, Josh. *The New Evidence That Demands a Verdict*. Nashville: Thomas Nelson, 1999.

McGrath, Alister. *Dawkins' God: Genes, Memes, and the Meaning of Life*. Malden, MA: Blackwell, 2005.

McGrew, Timothy, and Lydia McGrew. "The Argument from Miracles: A Cumulative Case for the Resurrection of Jesus of Nazareth," in *The Blackwell Companion to Natural Theology*. William Lane Craig and J. P. Moreland, eds. West Sussex, United Kingdom: Wiley-Blackwell, 2009.

McRay, John. *Archaeology and the New Testament.* Grand Rapids: Baker Book House, 1991.

Meier, John P. *A Marginal Jew: Rethinking the Historical Jesus,* vol. 1. New York: Doubleday, 1991.

Metzger, Bruce M. *The Text of the New Testament: Its Transmission, Corruption, and Restoration.* 3rd ed. New York: Oxford University Press, 1992.

_____. *A Textual Commentary of the Greek New Testament.* Stuttgart, Germany: United Bible Societies; 2nd rev. ed., 2005.

Metzger, Bruce M., and Roland E. Murphy, eds. *The New Oxford Annotated Bible.* New York: Oxford University Press, 1991.

Miller, J. Maxwell, and John H. Hayes. *A History of Ancient Israel and Judah.* Philadelphia: Westminster, 1986.

Montgomery, John Warwick, ed. *God's Inerrant Word: An International Symposium on the Trustworthiness of Scripture.* Minneapolis: Bethany Fellowship, 1974.

Moreland, J. P. *Scaling the Secular City: A Defense of Christianity.* Grand Rapids: Baker Book House, 1987.

Morris, Henry M. *Creation and the Modern Christian.* El Cajon, CA: Master Book, 1985.

_____. *The Long War Against God.* Grand Rapids: Baker Book House, 1989.

_____. *Men of Science, Men of God: Great Scientists of the Past Who Believed the Bible.* El Cajon, CA: Master Books, 1988.

Morris, Leon, *The First Epistle of Paul to the Corinthians: An Introduction and Commentary.* Leicester, England: InterVarsity Press, 1985.

Obama, Barack. *The Audacity of Hope: Thoughts on Reclaiming the American Dream.* New York: Vintage, 2006, 2008.

Olmetead, Ten Eycke. *Western Asia in the Days of Sargon of Assyria.* Lancaster, PA: Press of the New Era Printing Company, 1908.

Orr, James. *The Problem of the Old Testament: Considered with Reference to Recent Criticism.* New York: Charles Scribner's Sons, 1906.

Pao, David W., and Eckhard J. Schnabel. "Luke," in *Commentary on the New Testament Use of the Old Testament.* G. K. Beale and D. A. Carson, eds. Grand Rapids: Baker Academic, 2007.

Pate, C. Marvin, and Calvin B. Haines Jr. *Doomsday Delusions: What's Wrong with Predictions About the End of the World.* Downers Grove, IL: InterVarsity Press, 1995.

Pentecost, J. Dwight. *Things to Come: A Study in Biblical Eschatology.* Grand Rapids: Zondervan, 1958.

Pratt, Richard L., Jr. "Hyper-Preterism and Unfolding Biblical Eschatology," in *When Shall These Things Be? A Reformed Response to Hyper-Preteris.* Keith A. Mathison, ed. Phillipsburg, NJ: P & R, 2004.

Provan, Iain, V. Philips Long, and Tremper Longman III. *A Biblical History of Israel.* Louisville, KY: Westminster John Knox Press, 2003.

Ramsay, William M., *The Bearing of Recent Discovery on the Trustworthiness of the New Testament.* Repr. ed. Grand Rapids: Baker Book House, 1953.

_____. *St. Paul the Traveler and the Roman Citizen.* Grand Rapids: Baker Book House, 1962.

Rasmussen, Carl G. *Zondervan Atlas of the Bible.* Rev. ed. Grand Rapids: Zondervan, 2010.

Reasoning from the Scriptures. Brooklyn: Watchtower Bible and Tract Society of New York, 1985.

Rhodes, Ron. *Christ Before the Manger: The Life and Times of the Preincarnate Christ.* Grand Rapids: Baker Book House, 1992. Reprinted by Wipf and Stock, 2002.

_____. *Reasoning from the Scriptures with the Jehovah's Witnesses.* Eugene, OR: Harvest House, 1993.

Riddlebarger, Kim. *A Case for Amillennialism: Understanding the End Times.* Grand Rapids: Baker Book House, 2003.

Riesner, Rainer. "Jesus as Preacher and Teacher," in *Jesus and the Oral Gospel Tradition.* Henry Wansbrough, ed. Sheffield: JSOT, 1991.

Ring, Trudy, Robert M. Salkin, and Sharon La Boda. *International Dictionary of Historic Places: Middle East and Africa.* Chicago: Fitzroy Dearborn Publishers, 1996.

Robinson, Edward. *Biblical Researches in Palestine and the Adjacent Regions: A Journal of Travels in the Years 1838 & 1852.* London: John Murray, Albermarle Street, 1856.

Robinson, John A. T., *Redating the New Testament.* Eugene, OR: Wipf and Stock Publishers, 2000. Previously published by SCM Press, 1976.

Rufus, Curtius. *The History of Alexander,* John Yardley, trans. New York: Penguin, 2001.

Russell, Bertrand. *Why I Am Not a Christian: and other essays on religion and related subjects.* Paul Edwards, ed. New York: Simon and Schuster, 1957.

Sandeen, Ernest R. *The Roots of Fundamentalism: British and American Millenarianism 1800–1930.* Chicago: The University of Chicago Press, 1970.

Schaff, Philip. *History of the Christian Church,* vol. 2. Grand Rapids: Eerdmans, 1994.

Schmidt, Alvin J. *How Christianity Changed the World.* Grand Rapids: Zondervan, 2004.

Schürer, Emil. *The History of the Jewish People in the Age of Jesus Christ,* vol. 1. Revised by Geza Vermes, Fergus Millar, and Matthew Black Edinburgh, Scotland: T&T Clark, 1973.

Scrivener, F. H. A. *The Authorized Edition of the English Bible (1611) Its Subsequent Reprints and Modern Representatives.* Cambridge: At the University Press, 1884.

Sheler, Jeffrey L. *Is the Bible True? How Modern Debates and Discoveries Affirm the Essence of the Scriptures.* New York: HarperSanFrancisco, 1999.

Shelley, Bruce L. *Church History in Plain Language.* Nashville: Thomas Nelson, 1995.

Silberman, Neil Asher, and Israel Finkelstein. *The Bible Unearthed: Archaeology's New Vision of Ancient Israel and the Origin of Its Sacred Texts.* New York: Touchstone, 2002.

Sire, James. *Scripture Twisting: 20 Ways the Cults Misread the Bible.* Downers Grove, IL: InterVarsity Press, 1980.

Sizer, Stephen. *Christian Zionism: Road-map to Armageddon?* Leicester, England: Inter-Varsity Press, 2004.

Smith, Joseph Fielding , ed., *The Teachings of the Prophet Joseph Smith.* Salt Lake City: Deseret Book Company, 1976.

Sproul, R. C. *The Consequences of Ideas.* Wheaton: IL, Crossway Books, 2000.

_____. *Knowing Scripture.* Downers Grove, IL: InterVarsity Press, 1977. Originally titled *Knowing God's Word.*

_____. *The Last Days According to Jesus: When Did Jesus Say He Would Return?* Grand Rapids: Baker Book House, 1998.

Stark, Rodney. *For the Glory of God: How Monotheism Led to Reformations, Science, Witch-hunts, and the End of Slavery.* Princeton: Princeton University Press, 2003.

_____. *Victory of Reason.* New York: Random House, 2006.

Strobel, Lee. *The Case for Christ.* Grand Rapids: Zondervan, 1998.

____. *The Case for the Real Jesus: A Journalist Investigates Current Attacks on the Identity of Christ.* Grand Rapids: Zondervan, 2007.

Tenney, Merrill C. *The Gospel of John,* in *The Expositor's Bible Commentary,* vol 9. Frank E. Gaebelein, gen. ed. Grand Rapids, Zondervan, 1984.

Terry, Milton S., *Biblical Apocalyptics: A Study of the Most Notable Revelations of God and of Christ in the Canonical Scriptures.* Eugene, OR: Wipf and Stock Publishers, 2001.

_____. *Biblical Hermeneutics: A Treatise on the Interpretation of the Old and New Testaments*. Grand Rapids: Academie Books Zondervan, reprint, n.d.

Thompson, Thomas L., *The Mythic Past: Biblical Archaeology and the Myth of Israel*. London: Basic Books, 1999.

Van Voorst, Robert E. *Jesus Outside the New Testament: An Introduction to the Ancient Evidence*. Grand Rapids: Eerdmans, 2000.

Vine, W. E. *Vine's Complete Expository Dictionary of Old and New Testament Words*. Nashville: Thomas Nelson, 1996.

Wallace, Daniel B. *Greek Grammar Beyond the Basics: An Exegetical Syntax of the New Testament*. Grand Rapids: Zondervan, 1996.

Walton, John. *Chronological and Background Charts of the Old Testament*. Grand Rapids: Zondervan, 1994.

Walton, John H., Victor H. Matthews, and Mark W. Chavalas. *The IVP Bible Background Commentary: Old Testament*. Downers Grove, IL: InterVarsity Press, 2000.

Weber, Timothy P. *On the Road to Armageddon: How Evangelicals Became Israel's Best Friend*. Grand Rapids: Baker Book House, 2004.

Webster, William. *Behold Your King: Prophetic Proofs That Jesus Is the Messiah*. Battle Ground, WA: Christian Resources, 2003.

Wegner, Paul D. *A Student's Guide to Textual Criticism of the Bible*. Downers Grove, IL: IVP Academic, 2006.

Whitacre, Rodney A. *John*. Downers Grove, IL: InterVarsity Press, 1999.

White, James R. *The King James Only Controversy*, 2nd ed. Minneapolis: Bethany House, 2009.

Witherington, Ben. *New Testament History: A Narrative Account*. Grand Rapids: Baker Academic 2003.

_____. *The Paul Quest: The Renewed Search for the Jew of Tarsus*. Downers Grove, InterVarsity Press, 1998.

Wright N. T. *Jesus and the Victory of God*. Christian Origins and the Question of God, vol. 2. Minneapolis: Fortress Press, 1996.

_____. *Judas and the Gospel of Jesus: Have We Missed the Truth About Christianity?* Grand Rapids: Baker Book House, 2006.

_____. *The Resurrection of the Son of God*. Christian Origins and the Question of God, vol. 3. Minneapolis: Fortress, 2003.

Yamauchi, Edwin M. *Greece and Babylon*. Grand Rapids: Baker Book House, 1967.

_____. *Persia and the Bible*. Grand Rapids: Baker Book House, 1990, 1996.

Yancey, Philip. *Where Is God When It Hurts?* Grand Rapids: Zondervan, 1977.

Young, Edward J. *The Prophecy of Daniel: A Commentary*. Eugene, OR: Wipf and Stock, 1998, originally published 1949.

Frequently Accessed Bible Encyclopedias and Dictionaries:

The Anchor Bible Dictionary, 6 vols. David Noel Freedman, ed. New York: Doubleday, 1992.

Dictionary of Biblical Imagery. Leland Ryken, James C. Wilhoit, and Tremper Longman III, eds. Downers Grove, IL: InterVarsity Press, 1998.

The International Standard Bible Encyclopedia, 4 vols. Geoffrey W. Bromiley, gen. ed. Grand Rapids: Eerdmans, 1982.

Nelson's New Illustrated Bible Dictionary, revised. Ronald F. Youngblood, gen. ed. Nashville: Thomas Nelson, 1995.

New Bible Dictionary, second ed. J. D. Douglas, ed. Wheaton, IL: Tyndale, 1982.

Articles and Online Resources

Academy for Ancient Texts, "Epic of Gilgamesh," http://www.ancienttexts.org/library /mesopotamian/gilgamesh (accessed March 23, 2011).

Archaeology Odyssey. "Past Perfect: Excavating Nimrud." Spring 1998, 42–46. http:// members.bib-arch.org/publication.asp?PubID=BSAO&Volume=1&Issue=2& ArticleID=14 (accessed July 22, 2010).

Barcher, Wilhem. "Synagogue, The Great," *Jewish Encyclopedia*, http://www.jewish encyclopedia.com/view.jsp?artid=1214&letter=S (accessed March 24, 2011).

Barker, Kenneth L. "Copying the Old and New Testament Manuscripts," http:// helpmewithbiblestudy.org/5Bible/TransCopyingTheOTNTManuscripts_Barker. aspx (accessed March 17, 2011).

Blomberg, Craig L. Review Entry # 0206 *Bart D. Ehrman. Misquoting Jesus: The Story Behind Who Changed the Bible and Why,* in Richard S. Hess, ed., *Denver Journal: An Online Review of Current Biblical and Theological Studies,* Vol. 9, 2006,http://www .denverseminary.edu/article/misquoting-jesus-the-story-behind-who-changed-the -bible-and-why/ (accessed March 18, 2011).

British Museum. "Sennacherib's Prism," http://www.britishmuseum.org/explore /highlights/highlight_objects/me/t/the_taylor_prism.aspx (accessed March 24, 2011).

Butt, Kyle. "Tyre in Prophecy." *Reason and Revelation,* vol. 26 / no. 10 (October 2006): 73–79, http://www.apologeticspress.ws/rr/pdfs/0610.pdf (accessed April 15, 2011).

Byl, John. "On Biblical Units of Measurements," http://www.geocentricity.com/ba1 /no073/bibunits.html (accessed August 6, 2010).

Chapman, Colin. "One Land, Two Peoples—How Many States?" *Mishkan* 26 (1997).

Combs, Jim. "The Olivet Discourse," in Tim LaHaye, gen. ed., *Tim LaHaye Prophecy Study Bible.* Chattanooga, TN: AMG Publishers, 2000.

Damrosch, David. "Epic Hero: How a Self-taught British Genius Rediscovered the Mesopotamian Saga of Gilgamesh—after 2,500 Years," *Smithsonian,* May 2007, http://www.smithsonianmag.com/history-archaeology/gilgamesh.html (accessed April 12, 2011).

Davis, C. Truman. "The Crucifixion of Jesus: The Passion of Christ from a Medical Point of View," *Arizona Medicine* (March 1965): 183–87.

Dawkins, Richard. "Ignorance Is No Crime," May 14, 2006, http://richarddawkins.net /articles/114 (accessed March 24, 2011).

Dyrness, William. "The Age of Aquarius," in Carl E. Armerding and W. Ward Gasque, eds., *A Guide to Biblical Prophecy.* Peabody, MA: Hendrickson Publishers, 1989.

Dyrness, William A. "Astrology," in William A. Dyrness and Veli-Matti Karkkainen, *Global Dictionary of Theology.* Downers Grove, IL: IVP Academic, 2008.

Edwards, William D., Wesley J. Gabel, and Floyd E. Hosmer. "On the Physical Death of Jesus Christ," *The Journal of the American Medical Association* (March 21, 1986): 1455–63.

Encyclopædia Britannica, 2010. "Ancient Iran." Encyclopædia Britannica Online, http:// www.britannica.com/EBchecked/topic/851961/ancient-Iran (accessed October 14, 2010).

Encyclopædia Britannica, 2010. "Antiochus IV Epiphanes." Encyclopædia Britannica Online,http://www.britannica.com/EBchecked/topic/28380/Antiochus-IV-Epiphanes (accessed December 3, 2010).

Encyclopædia Britannica, 2011. "Sargon II." Encyclopædia Britannica Online, http://www .britannica.com/EBchecked/topic/524298/Sargon-II (accessed July 30, 2010).

Falsani, Cathleen. "The God Factor," *Chicago Sun-Times,* October 24, 2004, News 16.

Gardiner, Sir Alan. "The Geography of the Exodus," in *Recueil d'études égyptologiques dediées à la mémoire de Jean-François Champollion*. Paris: Bibliothèque de l'école des hautes études, 1922.

Garrett, Duane A. "Type, Typology," in *Evangelical Dictionary of Biblical Theology*, Walter A. Elwell, ed. Grand Rapids: Baker Book House, 1996.

Goldingay, John E. "The Book of Daniel: Three Issues." *Themelios*, 2, 2, (1977), 45–49, http://s3.amazonaws.com/tgc-documents/journal-issues/2.2_Goldingay.pdf (accessed April 15, 2011).

Gould , Stephen Jay. "Dr. Down's Syndrome," *Natural History* (April 1980).

Gurney, Robert J. M. "The Four Kingdoms of Daniel 2 and 7." *Themelios* 2.2 (January 1977): 39–45, online at http://www.biblicalstudies.org.uk/pdf/daniel-2_gurney.pdf (accessed April 14, 2011).

Habermas, Gary. "Explaining Away Jesus' Resurrection: Hallucination—the Recent Revival of Theories," *Christian Research Journal* 23:4 (2001), http://www.equip.org /PDF/DJ923.pdf (accessed March 24, 2011).

_____. "Historical Epistemology, Jesus' Resurrection, and the Shroud of Turin," http:// www.shroud.com/pdfs/habermas.pdf (accessed March 22, 2011).

_____. "Recent Perspectives on the Reliability of the Gospels," *Christian Research Journal* 28, 1 [2005]: 22–31, http://www.equip.org/PDF/JAR011.pdf (accessed March 21, 2011).

_____. "The Shroud of Turin and Its Significance for Biblical Studies," *Journal of the Evangelical Theological Society* 24.1 (1981): 47–54, http://works.bepress.com/gary_ habermas/1; (accessed March 22, 2011).

Halpern, Baruch. "Erasing History." *Bible Review*, December 1995, 26–35, 47, http:// members.bib-arch.org/publication.asp?PubID=BSBR&Volume=11&Issue=6&Artic leID=7 (accessed April 14, 2011).

Hamilton, James M., Jr., "The Virgin Will Conceive: Typology in Isaiah and Fulfillment in Matthew, the Use of Isaiah 7:14 in Matthew 1:18–23," Tyndale Fellowship Biblical Theology Study Group July 6–8, 2005, http://www.swbts.edu/resources/SWBTS /Resources/FacultyDocuments/Hamilton/TheVirginWillConceive.7_19_05.pdf (accessed March 23, 2011).

Hanegraaff, Hank, "D-Day Declarations," *Christian Research Journal* 18, no. 2 (1995): 54, http://www.equip.org/articles/john-hinkle (accessed April 12, 2011).

Harris, Tom. "How Nostradamus Works," http://science.howstuffworks.com/science-vs -myth/extrasensory-perceptions/nostradamus.htm (accessed February 2, 2010).

Hasel, Gerhard F. "The Book of Daniel and Matters of Language: Evidences Related to Names, Words, and the Aramaic Language," *Andrews University Seminary Studies*, vol. 19, no. 3 (1981): 211–25, http://www.auss.info/auss_publication_file.php?pub_ id=632&journal=1&type=pdf (accessed November 23, 2010).

Hastings, Deborah. "Scientists Find Fountain of Youth . . . in Mice," Nov. 29, 2010, aolnews.com, http://www.aolnews.com/2010/11/29/scientists-find-fountain-of-youth -in-mice (accessed March 24, 2011).

Herodotus, *Histories* 2:141:5, http://old.perseus.tufts.edu/GreekScience/hdtbk2.html (accessed December 18, 2010).

Hitchcock, Mark. "Gog and Magog" in Tim LaHaye, ed., *Tim LaHaye Prophecy Study Bible*. Chattanooga, TN: AMG Publishers, 2000.

Hoffmeier, James K. "Out of Egypt," *Biblical Archaeology Review* (Jan/Feb 2007), http:// members.bib-arch.org/publication.asp?PubID=BSBA&Volume=33&Issue=1&Artic leID=7 (accessed June 21, 2010).

Holding, James Patrick. "The Authenticity of Daniel: A Defense," http://www.tektonics .org/af/danieldefense.html (accessed March 24, 2011).

Horn, Siegfried H., "Why the Moabite Stone Was Blown to Pieces," *Biblical Archaeology Review*, May/Jun 1986, http://members.bib-arch.org/publication.asp?PubID=BSBA &Volume=12&Issue=3&ArticleID=3 (accessed September 15, 2010).

"Issue 200: Ten Top Discoveries." *Biblical Archaeology Review*, Jul/Aug Sep/Oct 2009, 74–96. http://members.bib-arch.org/publication.asp?PubID=BSBA&Volume=35& Issue=4&ArticleID=15 (accessed April 14, 2011).

Kitchen, Kenneth A. "The Patriarchal Age: Myth or History?" *Biblical Archaeology Review* (March/April 1995), http://members.bib-arch.org/publication.asp?PubID=BSBA& Volume=21&Issue=2&ArticleID=3 (accessed July 1, 2010).

Kleitarchos, Scholia, on Plato's Republic 337A, quoted in Clay Jones, "Killing the Canaanites: A Response to the New Atheism's 'Divine Genocide' Claims," *Christian Research Journal*, Vol. 33 / No. 4 (2010): 32.

Kort, Joe. "The Terms 'Homosexual' and the 'N-word': The term homosexual is like using the "N-word," *Psychology Today* blog, October 12, 2008, http://www.psychology today.com/blog/gays-anatomy/200810/the-terms-homosexual-and-the-n-word (accessed February 22, 2011).

Krieger, Doug. "Russian Has a Cameo Appearance in Bible Prophecy," Part XXII, http:// www.the-tribulation-network.com/ebooks/rise_or_fall/rise_or_fall_of_american_ empire_p22-3.htm (accessed April 8, 2011).

Kristof, Nicholas D., "Believe It, or Not," *New York Times*, August 15, 2003, http://www .nytimes.com/2003/08/15/opinion/believe-it-or-not.html (accessed March 23, 2011).

Lazare, Daniel, "False Testament: Archaeology Refutes the Bible's Claim to History," *Harper's*, March 2002, 40, http://harpers.org/archive/2002/03/0079105 (accessed April 12, 2011).

Lemaire, André. "'House of David' Restored in Moabite Inscription," *Biblical Archaeology Review* (May/Jun 1994): 30–34, 36–37. http://members.bib-arch.org/publication.asp ?PubID=BSBA&Volume=20&Issue=3&ArticleID=2 (accessed June 30, 2010).

Lemonick, Michael D. "Are the Bible's Stories True? Archaeology's Evidence." *Time*, June 24, 2001, http://www.time.com/time/printout/0,8816,133539,00.html (accessed June 30, 2010).

Maier, Paul L. "Archaeology: Biblical Ally or Adversary?" *Christian Research Journal* 27, no. 2 (2004), http://www.equip.org/PDF/DA111.pdf (accessed April 12, 2011).

Maugh, Thomas H., II, "Biblical Pool Uncovered in Jerusalem," *Los Angeles Times*, August 9, 2005, A8.

Mayr, Ernst. "The Nature of the Darwinian Revolution," *Science*, June 2, 1972, 981.

McCann, J. C., Jr. "Seleucus," in Geoffrey W. Bromiley, ed., *The International Standard Bible Encyclopedia*, vol. 4. Grand Rapids: Eerdmans, 1988.

McGoodwin, Michael. "Epic of Gilgamesh: Summary." Prepared 2001, revised 2006, http://www.mcgoodwin.net/pages/otherbooks/gilgamesh.html (accessed August 19, 2010).

Meichtry, Stacy. "New Views of Judas Reflect New Views on Evil," Religion News Service, April 6, 2006, http://religionnews.com/ArticleofWeek040606.html (accessed December 18, 2006.)

Metzger, Bruce M. "The Jehovah's Witnesses and Jesus Christ," *Theology Today*, vol. 10, no. 1 (April 1953), 76, http://www.newreformationpress.com/freebies/Bruce%20 Metzger%20-%20The%20Jehovah's%20Witnesses%20and%20Jesus%20Christ.pdf (accessed February 22, 2011).

Meyers, Stephen C. "Harold Camping: 1994?" *Christian Research Journal* 16, no. 3 (1994) 45, http://www.equip.org/articles/harold-camping-1994 (accessed April 12, 2011).

Millard, R. "Persia," in *New Bible Dictionary*, ed. J. D. Douglas et al. 2nd ed. Wheaton, IL: Tyndale, 1962.

Miller, Glenn M. "Good Question . . . Does God condone slavery in the Bible?" March 18, 2004, http://christianthinktank.com/qnoslave.html (accessed March 2, 2011).

Miller, Kevin D. "Did the Exodus Never Happen?" *Christianity Today*, September 7, 1998, http://www.christianitytoday.com/ct/1998/september7/8ta044.html (accessed July 1, 2010).

Milns, R. D., "Alexander the Great," in *The Anchor Bible Dictionary*, vol. 1, David Noel Freedman, ed. New York: Doubleday, 1992.

Neumayr, George. "Obama's Campaign-Season Christianity," *American Spectator*, September 30, 2010, online at http://spectator.org/archives/2010/09/30/obamas -campaign-season-christi (accessed March 17, 2010).

New World Encyclopedia online. "Curse of Ham," http://www.newworldencyclopedia.org /entry/Curse_of_Ham (accessed March 21, 2011).

New World Encyclopedia online. "Gilgamesh, Epic of," http://www.newworldencyclopedia .org/entry/Epic_of_Gilgamesh (accessed March 23, 2011).

New World Encyclopedia online. "Great Flood." http://www.newworldencyclopedia.org /entry/Great_Flood (accessed August 18, 2011).

New World Encyclopedia online. "Wilhelmina, of the Netherlands," (http://www.new worldencyclopedia.org/entry/Wilhelmina_of_the_Netherlands (accessed March 21, 2011).

Obama, Barack. "News and Speeches: Call to Renewal Key Note Address" June 28, 2006, http://blog.beliefnet.com/stevenwaldman/2008/11/obamas-historic-call-to-renewa .html.

Olshansky, S., Jay Leonard Hayflick, and Bruce A. Carnes, "No Truth to the Fountain of Youth," *Scientific American*, December 29, 2008, http://www.scientificamerican .com/article.cfm?id=no-truth-to-the-fountain-of-youth (accessed March 24, 2011).

Osanai, Nozomi. *A Comparative Study of the Flood Accounts in the Gilgamesh Epic and Genesis*. Online at http://www.answersingenesis.org/home/area/flood/introduction .asp (accessed April 14, 2011).

Passantino, Gretchen. "Camping's New Book Continues His Rejection of the Church," *Christian Research Journal* 25, no. 3 [2003]: 57, http://www.equip.org/articles/the -end-of-the-church-age-and-after (accessed April 12, 2011).

Porphyry, Malchus. *Against the Christians*, from Attalus, "Porphyrius: Comments on Daniel," http://www.attalus.org/translate/daniel.html (accessed March 24, 2011).

Regan, Donald T. "For the Record," *Time*, May 16, 1988.

Russell, Rusty. Bible History Online. "Biblical Archaeology: Assyria," http://www.bible -history.com/subcat.php?id=36 (accessed July 22, 2010).

_____. Bible History Online. "Sennacherib's Hexagonal Prism," http://www.bible -history.com/empires/prism.html (accessed April 12, 2011).

Sarigianis, Steve. "Noah's Flood: A Bird's-Eye View." Reasons to Believe website, http:// www.reasons.org/astronomy/noahs-flood/noahs-flood-article-1 (accessed August 16, 2010).

Sarna, Nahum M., revised by Hershel Shanks. "Israel in Egypt: The Egyptian Sojourn and the Exodus," *Ancient Israel*, 1999, http://members.bib-arch.org/publication.asp?Pub ID=BSBKAI&Volume=0&Issue=0&ArticleID=2 (accessed June 21, 2010).

Shanks, Hershel. "Assyrian Palace Discovered in Ashdod." *Biblical Archaeology Review*,

Jan/Feb 2007, 56–60, http://members.bib-arch.org/publication.asp?PubID=BSBA& Volume=33&Issue=1&ArticleID=11 (accessed July 21, 2011).

_____. "The Siloam Pool: Where Jesus Cured the Blind Man," *Biblical Archeology Review* 31, no. 5, Sep/Oct (2005): 16–23.

_____. "Sound Proof." *Biblical Archaeology Review,* Sep/Oct 2008, 50–57, 78. http://members.bib-arch.org/publication.asp?PubID=BSBA&Volume=34&Issue=5&ArticleID=13 (accessed April 14, 2011).

Singer, Rabbi Tovia. "Why Didn't the Red Ribbon on the Head of the Scapegoat Turn White in 30 C.E.?" http://www.outreachjudaism.org/like-a-lion.html (accessed August 9, 2010).

Sproul, R. C., "The Word of God in the Hands of Man," *Tabletalk,* April 1, 2009, http://www.ligonier.org/learn/articles/word-god-hands-man (accessed April 7, 2011).

Strohmer, Charles. "Is There a Christian Zodiac, a Gospel in the Stars?" *Christian Research Journal* 22, no. 4, online at http://www.equip.org/PDF/DG240.pdf (accessed April 14, 2011).

Thomas, Deborah A. "Uncovering Nineveh." *Archaeology Odyssey,* Sep/Oct 2004, 24–31, 54. http://members.bib-arch.org/publication.asp?PubID=BSAO&Volume=7&Issue=5&ArticleID=6 (accessed April 14, 2011)

Thompson, Thomas L. "On Reading the Bible for History: A Response," *Journal of Biblical Studies* 1:3 (2001), http://journalofbiblicalstudies.org/Issue3/Short_Study/on _reading_the_bible_for_history.htm (accessed June 30, 2010).

Till, Farrell. "The Myth of Prophecy Fulfillment." Summer 1993. http://www.holysmoke .org/hs01/daniel.fal (accessed October 11, 2010).

University of Oxford, Bodleian Philosophy Faculty Library, "Manuscripts and Rare Books," http://www.bodleian.ox.ac.uk/philosophy/collections/manuscripts (accessed March 21, 2011).

Vergano, Dan, and Cathy Lynn Grossman, "Long-Lost Gospel of Judas Recasts 'Traitor,'" *USA Today,* April 6, 2006, http://www.usatoday.com/news/religion/2006-04-06 -judas_x.htm (accessed March 17, 2011).

Vermes, Geza. "Jesus in the Eyes of Josephus," *Standpoint,* Jan./Feb. 2010, http://www .standpointmag.co.uk/node/2507/full (accessed April 11, 2011).

Wallace, Daniel B. "The Gospel of John: Introduction, Argument, Outline," http://www .bible.org/page.asp?page_id=1328 (accessed July 7, 2006).

Walton, John H., "The Four Kingdoms of Daniel," *Journal of the Evangelical Theological Society,* 29.1 (1986): 25–36, http://www.biblicalstudies.org.uk/article_daniel _walton.html (accessed April 7, 2011).

"West Wing Skewers Laura Schlessinger," http://www.robertslevinson.com/gaylesissues/ features/collect/newsnotes/bl_tidbit0005.htm (accessed March 21, 2011), previously at www.gaylesissues.about.com.

White, James. "Dangerous Airwaves: Harold Camping's Call to Flee the Church," *Christian Research Journal* 25, no. 1 (2002): 20–25, 41–43, http://www.equip.org/articles /harold-camping (accessed April 12, 2011).

Whitehorne, John. "Seleucus," in David Noel Freedman, ed., *The Anchor Bible Dictionary,* vol. 5 New York: Doubleday, 1992.

Wilford, John Noble. "From Israeli Site, News of House of David," *New York Times,* August 6, 1993, http://www.nytimes.com/1993/08/06/world/from-israeli-site-news -of-house-of-david.html?scp=3&sq=Avraham%20Biran&st=cse (accessed June 30, 2010).

Woodlee, Yolanda, "D.C. Mayor Acted 'Hastily,' Will Rehire Aide, *Washington Post,*

February 4, 1999, A1, http://www.washingtonpost.com/wp-srv/local/longterm/williams/williams020499.htm (accessed February 22, 2011).

Woollcombe, K. J. "The Biblical Origins and Patristic Development of Typology," in G. W. H. Lampe and K. J. Woollcombe, *Essays on Typology*, part of the Studies in Biblical Theology series, Naperville, IL: Alec R. Allenson, Inc., 1957.

Young, T. Cuyler, Jr., "Cyrus," in *The Anchor Bible Dictionary*, vol. 1. David Noel Freedman, ed. New York: Doubleday, 1992.

Subject Index

Scripture Index

374

About the Author

HANK HANEGRAAFF is host of *Bible Answer Man*, heard daily throughout the United States and Canada. He is president of the Christian Research Institute (CRI) and author of runaway bestsellers such as *The Prayer of Jesus* and *The Complete Bible Answer Book—Collector's Edition*. Hank and his wife, Kathy, are parents to twelve children.

www.equip.org